Pelican Books

Organization Theory

D. S. Pugh is Professor and Head of Systems
at the Open University.

Edited by D. S. Pugh

Organization Theory
Selected Readings

Second Edition

Penguin Books

Penguin Books Ltd, Harmondsworth, Middlesex, England
Viking Penguin Inc., 40 West 23rd Street, New York, New York 10010, U.S.A.
Penguin Books Australia Ltd, Ringwood, Victoria, Australia
Penguin Books Canada Ltd, 2801 John Street, Markham, Ontario, Canada L3R 1B4
Penguin Books (N.Z.) Ltd, 182–190 Wairau Road, Auckland 10, New Zealand

First published 1971
Reprinted 1973, 1974, 1975, 1976, 1977, 1978, 1979, 1980, 1981, 1982, 1983
Second edition 1984
Reissued in Pelican Books 1985

Made and printed in Great Britain by
Cox & Wyman Ltd, Reading
Set in 9/11 pt Linotron Times Roman by
Rowland Phototypesetting Ltd, Bury St Edmunds, Suffolk

For my children, Helena, Jonathan and Rosalind,
who already spend most of their waking lives
in formal organizations

Contents

Part Three **Behaviour in Organizations** 277

Introduction

Organization theory is the body of thinking and writing which addresses itself to the problem of how to organize. The basis of selection for this wide-ranging volume has been to include those writers whose work has had a clear impact on thinking, practice and research in the subject. They have all stimulated work by others, some of it in support of their theories, some of it highly critical. Their views are the subject of much current debate. In every case (except one, which will be explained later) the readings are primary sources, so that the reader may be in a position to sample the direct impact of the writer and his work.

More specifically, organization theory can be defined as the study of the structure, functioning and performance of organizations and the behaviour of groups and individuals within them. The subject has a long history which can be traced back, for example, to the Old Testament, when decentralization through the appointment of judges was undertaken to relieve the load on the chief executive. The first English textbooks appeared in the thirteenth century.[1] It is, however, in the present century that the administrative, as distinct from the political, aspects have come to the fore. It is also in this century that the impact of social science thinking has built up until it has become a major force. It is still, though, a heterogeneous study, with the systematic analysis of sociologists, psychologists and economists mingling with distilled practical experience of managers, administrators and consultants.

These writers have attempted to draw together information and distil theories of how organizations function and how they should be managed. Their writings have been theoretical in the sense that they have tried to discover generalizations applicable to all organizations. Every act of a manager rests on assumptions about what has happened and conjectures about what will happen; that is to say it rests on theory. Theory and practice are inseparable. As a cynic once put it: when someone says he is a practical man, what he means is that he is using

1. e.g. Robert Grosseteste, *The Rules of Saint Robert*: cf. Keil (1965).

old-fashioned theories! All the writers on this subject, who include many busy chief executives, believe that there is a necessity continually to examine, criticize and up-date thinking about the organization and how it functions if it is to develop and not to decay.

The concept of organizational behaviour is basic to this field. From this point of view the task of management can be considered as the organization of individuals' behaviour in relation to the physical means and resources to achieve the desired goal. The basic problem in this subject to which all writing may be related is: '*How much* organization and control of behaviour is necessary for efficient functioning?' It is in the implied answer to this question on the control of organizational behaviour that two sides of a continuing debate may be usefully distinguished. On the one hand there are those who may be called the 'organizers' who maintain that more and better control is necessary for efficiency. They point to the advantage of specialization and clear job definitions, standard routines and clear lines of authority. On the other hand there are those who, in this context, may be called the 'behaviouralists' who maintain that the continuing attempt to increase control over behaviour is self-defeating; that the inevitable rigidity in functioning, apathy in performance, and counter-control through informal relationships, means that increased efficiency does not necessarily occur with increased control. Even when it does it is only in the short term and at the cost of internal conflict and greatly reducing the organization's ability to cope with the inevitable environmental changes which take place in the long term.

It is around this continuing dilemma that the study of organization theory takes place. It is a dilemma because, of course, both sides of the discussion are right. It is not possible to opt for one view *to the exclusion of* the other, and it is one of the basic tasks of management to determine the optimum degree of control necessary to operate efficiently. This must be affected by many factors, such as the size of the organization, the training and experience of its members and the techniques used in the manufacture of the product or the carrying out of the service. It is through a study of the constraints in relation to the objectives that the most efficient organizational control systems can be established.

This volume has been arranged, inevitably somewhat arbitrarily, in three separate but highly interrelated sections. In Part One the selection focuses on the structure of organizations, examining the workings of the authority, task allocation and communication systems. Part Two is concerned with management and decision making, the functions and the processes which they involve. Part Three on behaviour in organizations presents the work of those who have studied the effects of the form of organization and management on the behaviour of its members.

I am grateful to Iain Rangeley who compiled the Index and to Sue Taylor for secretarial assistance.

For the second edition of this selection – issued concurrently with the third edition of the companion introductory text *Writers on Organizations* by Pugh, Hickson and Hinings – a thorough revision has been carried out and about half the material represents new contributions to the subject.

I am grateful to Margaret Blunden and David Hickson for discussions about possible selections and to Helena Pugh for a revision of the index.

Reference

KEIL, I. (1965), 'Advice to the magnates: management education in the 13th century', *Bulletin of the Association of Teachers of Management*, no. 17, March. pp. 2–8.

Part One **The Structure of Organizations**

All organizations have to make provision for continuing activities directed toward the achievement of given aims. Regularities in activities such as task allocation, coordination and supervision are established which constitute the organization's structure. The contributors to this section examine in a systematic way, comparatively across numbers of organizations, the causes and the results of structural forms encountered.

Weber (Reading 1) analysed three general types of organization stemming from the bases of wielding authority, and drew attention to the fact that in modern society the bureaucratic type has become dominant because, he considered, of its greater technical efficiency. In doing so he formed the starting point of a series of sociological studies designed to examine the nature and functioning of bureaucracy, and particularly to draw attention to the dysfunctions of this structural form which were left out of the original analysis. The contribution of March and Simon (Reading 2) is the only one in this volume which is not a primary source, and it is included because it cogently and creatively summarizes many studies which have been undertaken with this 'bureaucratic dysfunction' approach. They show that the inadequacies of bureaucracy may, paradoxically, be just as great a cause for its perpetuation as its efficiencies. Burns (Reading 3) forms one culmination of this approach when he contrasts, on the basis of studies of firms in stable and changing environmental conditions, bureaucratic with organismic structures. In the latter, authority, task allocation and communication are extremely flexible, in contrast to the rigid rules and procedures of bureaucracy.

Woodward (Reading 4) presents results to suggest that the structure of manufacturing concerns is strongly related to the technology of production and thus opens a debate on whether it is possible to conceive of basic principles of structure which are appropriate to all organizations. Pugh (Reading 5) describes work carried out with his colleagues which measures the range of degrees of specialization, standardization and centralization of authority structures and investigates the effects of contextual factors such as size, technology, ownership, interdependence, etc., on the characteristic differences found. Lawrence and Lorsch (Reading 6) analyse the degree of structural differentiation necessary for a firm to function in a particular environment and the corresponding integration mechanisms required for it to be a high performer.

Crozier (Reading 7) focuses his analysis behind the structure to the recurring strategic and tactical 'games' which are played by individuals or groups in organizations which develop power through bargaining relationships, while Jaques (Reading 8) considers that the basic depth-structure of an organization is established by the manager–subordinate relationships which have different time-spans of work discretion.

1 M. Weber

Legitimate Authority and Bureaucracy

From M. Weber, *The Theory of Social and Economic Organisation*, Free Press, 1947, translated and edited by A. M. Henderson and T. Parsons, pp. 328–40. (Footnotes as in the original.)

The three pure types of legitimate authority

There are three pure types of legitimate authority. The validity of their claims to legitimacy may be based on:

1. Rational grounds – resting on a belief in the 'legality' of patterns of normative rules and the right of those elevated to authority under such rules to issue commands (legal authority).

2. Traditional grounds – resting on an established belief in the sanctity of immemorial traditions and the legitimacy of the status of those exercising authority under them (traditional authority); or finally,

3. Charismatic grounds – resting on devotion to the specific and exceptional sanctity, heroism or exemplary character of an individual person, and of the normative patterns or order revealed or ordained by him (charismatic authority).

In the case of legal authority, obedience is owed to the legally established impersonal order. It extends to the persons exercising the authority of office under it only by virtue of the formal legality of their commands and only within the scope of authority of the office. In the case of traditional authority, obedience is owed to the *person* of the chief who occupies the traditionally sanctioned position of authority and who is (within its sphere) bound by tradition. But here the obligation of obedience is not based on the impersonal order, but is a matter of personal loyalty within the area of accustomed obligations. In the case of charismatic authority, it is the charismatically qualified leader as such who is obeyed by virtue of personal trust in him and his revelation, his heroism or his exemplary qualities so far as they fall within the scope of the individual's belief in his charisma.

1. The usefulness of the above classification can only be judged by its results in promoting systematic analysis. The concept of 'charisma' ('the gift of grace') is taken from the vocabulary of early Christianity. For the

Christian religious organization Rudolf Sohm, in his *Kirchenrecht*, was the first to clarify the substance of the concept, even though he did not use the same terminology. Others (for instance, Hollin, *Enthusiasmus und Bussgewalt*) have clarified certain important consequences of it. It is thus nothing new.

2. The fact that none of these three ideal types, the elucidation of which will occupy the following pages, is usually to be found in historical cases in 'pure' form, is naturally not a valid objection to attempting their conceptual formulation in the sharpest possible form. In this respect the present case is no different from many others. Later on the transformation of pure charisma by the process of routinization will be discussed and thereby the relevance of the concept to the understanding of empirical systems of authority considerably increased. But even so it may be said of every empirically historical phenomenon of authority that it is not likely to be 'as an open book'. Analysis in terms of sociological types has, after all, as compared with purely empirical historical investigation, certain advantages which should not be minimized. That is, it can in the particular case of a concrete form of authority determine what conforms to or approximates such types as 'charisma', 'hereditary charisma', 'the charisma of office', 'patriarchy', 'bureaucracy', the authority of status groups,[1] and in doing so it can work with relatively unambiguous concepts. But the idea that the whole of concrete historical reality can be exhausted in the conceptual scheme about to be developed is as far from the author's thoughts as anything could be.

Legal authority with a bureaucratic administrative staff[2]

Legal authority: The pure type with employment of a bureaucratic administrative staff

The effectiveness of legal authority rests on the acceptance of the validity of the following mutually inter-dependent ideas.

1. That any given legal norm may be established by agreement or by imposition, on grounds of expediency or rational values or both, with a claim to obedience at least on the part of the members of the corporate group. This is, however, usually extended to include all persons within

1. *Ständische*. There is no really acceptable English rendering of this term – Ed.
2. The specifically modern type of administration has intentionally been taken as a point of departure in order to make it possible later to contrast the others with it.

the sphere of authority or of power in question – which in the case of territorial bodies is the territorial area – who stand in certain social relationships or carry out forms of social action which in the order governing the corporate group have been declared to be relevant.

2. That every body of law consists essentially in a consistent system of abstract rules which have normally been intentionally established. Furthermore, administration of law is held to consist in the application of these rules to particular cases; the administrative process in the rational pursuit of the interests which are specified in the order governing the corporate group within the limits laid down by legal precepts and following principles which are capable of generalized formulation and are approved in the order governing the group, or at least not disapproved in it.

3. That thus the typical person in authority occupies an 'office'. In the action associated with his status, including the commands he issues to others, he is subject to an impersonal order to which his actions are oriented. This is true not only for persons exercising legal authority who are in the usual sense 'officials', but, for instance, for the elected president of a state.

4. That the person who obeys authority does so, as it is usually stated, only in his capacity as a 'member' of the corporate group and what he obeys is only 'the law'. He may in this connection be the member of an association, of a territorial commune, of a church, or a citizen of a state.

5. In conformity with point 3, it is held that the members of the corporate group, in so far as they obey a person in authority, do not owe this obedience to him as an individual, but to the impersonal order. Hence, it follows that there is an obligation to obedience only within the sphere of the rationally delimited authority which, in terms of the order, has been conferred upon him.

The following may thus be said to be the fundamental categories of rational legal authority:

1. A continuous organization of official functions bound by rules.

2. A specified sphere of competence. This involves (a) a sphere of obligations to perform functions which has been marked off as part of a systematic division of labour. (b) The provision of the incumbent with the necessary authority to carry out these functions. (c) That the necessary means of compulsion are clearly defined and their use is

subject to definite conditions. A unit exercising authority which is organized in this way will be called an 'administrative organ'.[3]

There are administrative organs in this sense in large-scale private organizations, in parties and armies, as well as in the state and the church. An elected president, a cabinet of ministers, or a body of elected representatives also in this sense constitute administrative organs. This is not, however, the place to discuss these concepts. Not every administrative organ is provided with compulsory powers. But this distinction is not important for present purposes.

3. The organization of offices follows the principle of hierarchy; that is, each lower office is under the control and supervision of a higher one. There is a right of appeal and of statement of grievances from the lower to the higher. Hierarchies differ in respect to whether and in what cases complaints can lead to a ruling from an authority at various points higher in the scale, and as to whether changes are imposed from higher up or the responsibility for such changes is left to the lower office, the conduct of which was the subject of complaint.

4. The rules which regulate the conduct of an office may be technical rules or norms.[4] In both cases, if their application is to be fully rational, specialized training is necessary. It is thus normally true that only a person who has demonstrated an adequate technical training is qualified to be a member of the administrative staff of such an organized group, and hence only such persons are eligible for appointment to official positions. The administrative staff of a rational corporate group thus typically consists of 'officials', whether the organization be devoted to political, religious, economic – in particular, capitalistic – or other ends.

5. In the rational type it is a matter of principle that the members of the administrative staff should be completely separated from ownership of the means of production or administration. Officials, employees and workers attached to the administrative staff do not themselves own the non-human means of production and administration. These are rather provided for their use in kind or in money, and the official is obligated to render an accounting of their use. There exists, furthermore, in principle complete separation of the property belonging to the organization,

---

3. *Behörde.*

4. Weber does not explain this distinction. By a 'technical rule' he probably means a prescribed course of action which is dictated primarily on grounds touching efficiency of the performance of the immediate functions, while by 'norms' he probably means rules which limit conduct on grounds other than those of efficiency. Of course, in one sense all rules are norms in that they are prescriptions for conduct, conformity with which is problematic – Ed.

which is controlled within the sphere of office, and the personal property of the official, which is available for his own private uses. There is a corresponding separation of the place in which official functions are carried out, the 'office' in the sense of premises, from living quarters.

6. In the rational type case, there is also a complete absence of appropriation of his official position by the incumbent. Where 'rights' to an office exist, as in the case of judges, and recently of an increasing proportion of officials and even of workers, they do not normally serve the purpose of appropriation by the official, but of securing the purely objective and independent character of the conduct of the office so that it is oriented only to the relevant norms.

7. Administrative acts, decisions and rules are formulated and recorded in writing, even in cases where oral discussion is the rule or is even mandatory. This applies at least to preliminary discussions and proposals, to final decisions and to all sorts of orders and rules. The combination of written documents and a continuous organization of official functions constitutes the 'office'[5] which is the central focus of all types of modern corporate action.

8. Legal authority can be exercised in a wide variety of different forms which will be distinguished and discussed later. The following analysis will be deliberately confined for the most part to the aspect of imperative coordination in the structure of the administrative staff. It will consist in an analysis in terms of ideal types of officialdom or 'bureaucracy'.

In the above outline no mention has been made of the kind of supreme head appropriate to a system of legal authority. This is a consequence of certain considerations which can only be made entirely understandable at a later stage in the analysis. There are very important types of rational imperative coordination which, with respect to the ultimate source of authority, belong to other categories. This is true of the hereditary charismatic type, as illustrated by hereditary monarchy, and of the pure charismatic type of a president chosen by plebiscite. Other cases involve

5. *Bureau*. It has seemed necessary to use the English word 'office' in three different meanings, which are distinguished in Weber's discussion by at least two terms. The first is *Amt*, which means 'office' in the sense of the institutionally defined status of a person. The second is the 'work premises' as in the expression 'he spent the afternoon in his office'. For this Weber uses *Bureau*, as also for the third meaning which he has just defined, the 'organized work process of a group'. In this last sense an office is a particular type of 'organization', or *Betrieb* in Weber's sense. This use is established in English in such expressions as 'the District Attorney's Office has such and such functions.' Which of the three meanings is involved in a given case will generally be clear from the context – Ed.

rational elements at important points but are made up of a combination of bureaucratic and charismatic components, as is true of the cabinet form of government. Still others are subject to the authority of the chief of other corporate groups, whether their character be charismatic or bureaucratic; thus the formal head of a government department under a parliamentary regime may be a minister who occupies his position because of his authority in a party. The type of rational, legal administrative staff is capable of application in all kinds of situations and contexts. It is the most important mechanism for the administration of everyday profane affairs. For in that sphere, the exercise of authority and, more broadly, imperative coordination, consists precisely in administration.

The purest type of exercise of legal authority is that which employs a bureaucratic administrative staff. Only the supreme chief of the organization occupies his position of authority by virtue of appropriation, of election or of having been designated for the succession. But even *his* authority consists in a sphere of legal 'competence'. The whole administrative staff under the supreme authority then consists, in the purest type, of individual officials who are appointed and function according to the following criteria:[6]

1. They are personally free and subject to authority only with respect to their impersonal official obligations.

2. They are organized in a clearly defined hierarchy of offices.

3. Each office has a clearly defined sphere of competence in the legal sense.

4. The office is filled by a free contractual relationship. Thus, in principle, there is free selection.

5. Candidates are selected on the basis of technical qualifications. In the most rational case, this is tested by examination or guaranteed by diplomas certifying technical training, or both. They are *appointed*, not elected.

6. They are remunerated by fixed salaries in money, for the most part with a right to pensions. Only under certain circumstances does the employing authority, especially in private organizations, have a right to terminate the appointment, but the official is always free to resign. The salary scale is primarily graded according to rank in the hierarchy: but in

6. This characterization applies to the 'monocratic' as opposed to the 'collegial' type, which will be discussed below [not included].

addition to this criterion, the responsibility of the position and the requirements of the incumbent's social status may be taken into account.

7. The office is treated as the sole, or at least the primary, occupation of the incumbent.

8. It constitutes a career. There is a system of 'promotion' according to seniority or to achievement, or both. Promotion is dependent on the judgement of superiors.

9. The official works entirely separated from ownership of the means of administration and without appropriation of his position.

10. He is subject to strict and systematic discipline and control in the conduct of the office.

This type of organization is in principle applicable with equal facility to a wide variety of different fields. It may be applied in profit-making business or in charitable organizations, or in any number of other types of private enterprises serving ideal or material ends. It is equally applicable to political and to religious organizations. With varying degrees of approximation to a pure type, its historical existence can be demonstrated in all these fields.

1. For example, this type of bureaucracy is found in private clinics, as well as in endowed hospitals or the hospitals maintained by religious orders. Bureaucratic organization has played a major role in the Catholic Church. It is well illustrated by the administrative role of the priesthood[7] in the modern church, which has expropriated almost all of the old church benefices, which were in former days to a large extent subject to private appropriation. It is also illustrated by the conception of the universal Episcopate, which is thought of as formally constituting a universal legal competence in religious matters. Similarly, the doctrine of Papal infallibility is thought of as in fact involving a universal competence, but only one which functions *ex cathedra* in the sphere of the office, thus implying the typical distinction between the sphere of office and that of the private affairs of the incumbent. The same phenomena are found in the large-scale capitalistic enterprise; and the larger it is, the greater their role. And this is not less true of political parties, which will be discussed separately. Finally, the modern army is essentially a bureaucratic organization administered by that peculiar type of military functionary, the 'officer'.

7. *Kaplanokratie.*

2. Bureaucratic authority is carried out in its purest form where it is most clearly dominated by the principle of appointment. There is no such thing as a hierarchy of elected officials in the same sense as there is a hierarchical organization of appointed officials. In the first place, election makes it impossible to attain a stringency of discipline even approaching that in the appointed type. For it is open to a subordinate official to compete for elective honours on the same terms as his superiors, and his prospects are not dependent on the superior's judgment.[8]

3. Appointment by free contract, which makes free selection possible, is essential to modern bureaucracy. Where there is a hierarchical organization with impersonal spheres of competence, but occupied by unfree officials – like slaves or dependants, who, however, function in a formally bureaucratic manner – the term 'patrimonial bureaucracy' will be used.

4. The role of technical qualifications in bureaucratic organizations is continually increasing. Even an official in a party or a trade-union organization is in need of specialized knowledge, though it is usually of an empirical character, developed by experience, rather than by formal training. In the modern state, the only 'offices' for which no technical qualifications are required are those of ministers and presidents. This only goes to prove that they are 'officials' only in a formal sense, and not substantively, as is true of the managing director or president of a large business corporation. There is no question but that the 'position' of the capitalistic entrepreneur is as definitely appropriated as is that of a monarch. Thus at the top of a bureaucratic organization, there is necessarily an element which is at least not purely bureaucratic. The category of bureaucracy is one applying only to the exercise of control by means of a particular kind of administrative staff.

5. The bureaucratic official normally receives a fixed salary. By contrast, sources of income which are privately appropriated will be called 'benefices'.[9] Bureaucratic salaries are also normally paid in money. Though this is not essential to the concept of bureaucracy, it is the arrangement which best fits the pure type. Payments in kind are apt to have the character of benefices, and the receipt of a benefice normally implies the appropriation of opportunities for earnings and of positions. There are, however, gradual transitions in this field with many in-

8. On elective officials.
9. *Pfründen.*

termediate types. Appropriation by virtue of leasing or sale of offices or the pledge of income from office are phenomena foreign to the pure type of bureaucracy.

6. 'Offices' which do not constitute the incumbent's principal occupation, in particular 'honorary' offices, belong in other categories. The typical 'bureaucratic' official occupies the office as his principal occupation.

7. With respect to the separation of the official from ownership of the means of administration, the situation is essentially the same in the field of public administration and in private bureaucratic organizations, such as the large-scale capitalistic enterprise.

8. Collegial bodies will be discussed separately below [not included]. At the present time they are rapidly decreasing in importance in favour of types of organization which are in fact, and for the most part formally as well, subject to the authority of a single head. For instance, the collegial 'governments' in Prussia have long since given way to the monocratic 'district president'.[10] The decisive factor in this development has been the need for rapid, clear decisions, free of the necessity of compromise between different opinions and also free of shifting majorities.

9. The modern army officer is a type of appointed official who is clearly marked off by certain class distinctions. This will be discussed elsewhere [not included]. In this respect such officers differ radically from elected military leaders, from charismatic condottieri, from the type of officers who recruit and lead mercenary armies as a capitalistic enterprise, and, finally, from the incumbents of commissions which have been purchased. There may be gradual transitions between these types. The patrimonial 'retainer', who is separated from the means of carrying out his function, and the proprietor of a mercenary army for capitalistic purposes have, along with the private capitalistic entrepreneur, been pioneers in the organization of the modern type of bureaucracy. This will be discussed in detail below.[11]

---

10. *Regierungspräsident.*

11. The parts of Weber's work included in this translation contain only fragmentary discussions of military organization. It was a subject in which Weber was greatly interested and to which he attributed great importance for social phenomena generally. This factor is one on which, for the ancient world, he laid great stress in his important study, *Agrarverhält-nisse im Altertum*. Though at various points in the rest of *Wirtschaft und Gesellschaft* the subject comes up, it is probable that he intended to treat it systematically but that this was never done – Ed.

The monocratic type of bureaucratic administration

Experience tends universally to show that the purely bureaucratic type of administrative organization – that is, the monocratic variety of bureaucracy – is, from a purely technical point of view, capable of attaining the highest degree of efficiency and is in this sense formally the most rational known means of carrying out imperative control over human beings. It is superior to any other form in precision, in stability, in the stringency of its discipline, and in its reliability. It thus makes possible a particularly high degree of calculability of results for the heads of the organization and for those acting in relation to it. It is finally superior both in intensive efficiency and in the scope of its operations, and is formally capable of application to all kinds of administrative tasks.

The development of the modern form of the organization of corporate groups in all fields is nothing less than identical with the development and continual spread of bureaucratic administration. This is true of church and state, of armies, political parties, economic enterprises, organizations to promote all kinds of causes, private associations, clubs, and many others. Its development is, to take the most striking case, the most crucial phenomenon of the modern Western state. However many forms there may be which do not appear to fit this pattern, such as collegial representative bodies, parliamentary committees, soviets, honorary officers, lay judges, and what not, and however much people may complain about the 'evils of bureaucracy', it would be sheer illusion to think for a moment that continuous administrative work can be carried out in any field except by means of officials working in offices. The whole pattern of everyday life is cut to fit this framework. For bureaucratic administration is, other things being equal, always, from a formal, technical point of view, the most rational type. For the needs of mass administration today, it is completely indispensable. The choice is only that between bureaucracy and dilettantism in the field of administration.

The primary source of the superiority of bureaucratic administration lies in the role of technical knowledge which, through the development of modern technology and business methods in the production of goods, has become completely indispensable. In this respect, it makes no difference whether the economic system is organized on a capitalistic or a socialistic basis. Indeed, if in the latter case a comparable level of technical efficiency were to be achieved, it would mean a tremendous increase in the importance of specialized bureaucracy.

When those subject to bureaucratic control seek to escape the influence of the existing bureaucratic apparatus, this is normally possible only by creating an organization of their own which is equally subject to the process of bureaucratization. Similarly the existing bureaucratic apparatus is driven to continue functioning by the most powerful interests which are material and objective, but also ideal in character. Without it, a society like our own – with a separation of officials, employees, and workers from ownership of the means of administration, dependent on discipline and on technical training – could no longer function. The only exception would be those groups, such as the peasantry, who are still in possession of their own means of subsistence. Even in case of revolution by force or of occupation by an enemy, the bureaucratic machinery will normally continue to function just as it has for the previous legal government.

The question is always who controls the existing bureaucratic machinery. And such control is possible only in a very limited degree to persons who are not technical specialists. Generally speaking, the trained permanent official is more likely to get his way in the long run than his nominal superior, the Cabinet minister, who is not a specialist.

Though by no means alone, the capitalistic system has undeniably played a major role in the development of bureaucracy. Indeed, without it capitalistic production could not continue and any rational type of socialism would have simply to take it over and increase its importance. Its development, largely under capitalistic auspices, has created an urgent need for stable, strict, intensive, and calculable administration. It is this need which gives bureaucracy a crucial role in our society as the central element in any kind of large-scale administration. Only by reversion in every field – political, religious, economic, etc. – to small-scale organization would it be possible to any considerable extent to escape its influence. On the one hand, capitalism in its modern stages of development strongly tends to foster the development of bureaucracy, though both capitalism and bureaucracy have arisen from many different historical sources. Conversely, capitalism is the most rational economic basis for bureaucratic administration and enables it to develop in the most rational form, especially because, from a fiscal point of view, it supplies the necessary money resources.

Along with these fiscal conditions of efficient bureaucratic administration, there are certain extremely important conditions in the fields of communication and transportation. The precision of its functioning requires the services of the railway, the telegraph and the telephone, and becomes increasingly dependent on them. A socialistic form of organization would not alter this fact. It would be a question whether in a socialistic system it would be possible to provide conditions for carrying out as stringent bureaucratic organization as has been possible in a capitalistic order. For socialism would, in fact, require a still higher degree of formal bureaucratization than capitalism. If this should prove not to be possible, it would demonstrate the existence of another of those fundamental elements of irrationality in social systems – a conflict between formal and substantive rationality of the sort which sociology so often encounters.

Bureaucratic administration means fundamentally the exercise of control on the basis of knowledge. This is the feature of it which makes it specifically rational. This consists on the one hand in technical knowledge which, by itself, is sufficient to ensure it a position of extraordinary power. But in addition to this, bureaucratic organizations, or the holders of power who make use of them, have the tendency to increase their power still further by the knowledge growing out of experience in the service. For they acquire through the conduct of office a special knowledge of facts and have available a store of documentary material peculiar to themselves. While not peculiar to bureaucratic organizations, the concept of 'official secrets' is certainly typical of them. It stands in relation to technical knowledge in somewhat the same position as commercial secrets do to technological training. It is a product of the striving for power.

Bureaucracy is superior in knowledge, including both technical knowledge and knowledge of the concrete fact within its own sphere or interest, which is usually confined to the interests of a private business – a capitalistic enterprise. The capitalistic entrepreneur is, in our society, the only type who has been able to maintain at least relative immunity from subjection to the control of rational bureaucratic knowledge. All the rest of the population have tended to be organized in large-scale corporate groups which are inevitably subject to bureaucratic control. This is as inevitable as the dominance of precision machinery in the mass production of goods.

The following are the principal more general social consequences of bureaucratic control:

1. The tendency to 'levelling' in the interest of the broadest possible basis of recruitment in terms of technical competence.

2. The tendency to plutocracy growing out of the interest in the greatest possible length of technical training. Today this often lasts up to the age of thirty.

3. The dominance of a spirit of formalistic impersonality, *sine ira et studio*, without hatred or passion, and hence without affection or enthusiasm. The dominant norms are concepts of straightforward duty without regard to personal considerations. Everyone is subject to formal equality of treatment; that is, everyone in the same empirical situation. This is the spirit in which the ideal official conducts his office.

The development of bureaucracy greatly favours the levelling of social classes and this can be shown historically to be the normal tendency. Conversely, every process of social levelling creates a favourable situation for the development of bureaucracy; for it tends to eliminate class privileges, which include the appropriation of means of administration and the appropriation of authority as well as the occupation of offices on an honorary basis or as an avocation by virtue of wealth. This combination everywhere inevitably foreshadows the development of mass democracy, which will be discussed in another connection.

The 'spirit' of rational bureaucracy has normally the following general characteristics:

1. Formalism, which is promoted by all the interests which are concerned with the security of their own personal situation, whatever this may consist in. Otherwise the door would be open to arbitrariness and hence formalism is the line of least resistance.

2. There is another tendency, which is apparently in contradiction to the above, a contradiction which is in part genuine. It is the tendency of officials to treat their official function from what is substantively a utilitarian point of view in the interest of the welfare of those under their authority. But this utilitarian tendency is generally expressed in the enactment of corresponding regulatory measures which themselves have a formal character and tend to be treated in a formalistic spirit. This tendency to substantive rationality is supported by all those subject to authority who are not included in the class mentioned above as interested in the security of advantages already controlled. The problems which open up at this point belong in the theory of 'democracy'.

2   J. G. March and H. A. Simon

The Dysfunctions of Bureaucracy

From J. G. March and H. A. Simon, *Organizations*, Wiley, 1958, chapter 3, pp. 36–47.

Modern studies of 'bureaucracies' date from Weber (1946, 1947) as to both time and acknowledged intellectual debt. But, in a sense, Weber belongs more to the preceding chapter than he does to the present one. His major interests in the study of organizations appear to have been four: (1) to identify the characteristics of an entity he labelled 'bureaucracy'; (2) to describe its growth and the reasons for its growth; (3) to isolate the concomitant social changes; (4) to discover the consequences of bureaucratic organization for the achievement of bureaucratic goals (primarily the goals of a political authority). It is in the last-named interest that Weber most clearly differentiates himself from the other writers who will be considered here. Weber wishes to show to what extent bureaucratic organization is a rational solution to the complexities of modern problems. More specifically, he wishes to show in what ways bureaucratic organization overcomes the decision-making or 'computational' limits of individuals or alternative forms of organization (i.e. through specialization, division of labor, etc.).

Consequently, Weber appears to have more in common with Urwick, Gulick, and others than he does with those who regard themselves as his successors. To be sure, Weber goes beyond the 'machine' model in significant ways. In particular, he analyses in some detail the relation between an official and his office. But, in general, Weber perceives bureaucracy as an adaptive device for using specialized skills, and he is not exceptionally attentive to the character of the human organism.

When we turn from Weber to the more recent students of bureaucracy, however, we find them paying increasing attention to the 'unanticipated' responses of the organization members (Merton, 1936; Gouldner, 1957). Without denying Weber's essential proposition that bureaucracies are more efficient (with respect to the goals of the formal hierarchy) than are alternative forms of organization, the research and analysis of Merton (1940), Selznick (1949) and Gouldner (1954) have suggested important dysfunctional consequences of bureaucratic organization. In addition – explicitly in the case of Gouldner and implicitly in the other two authors – they have hypothesized that the unintended consequences of treating individuals as machines actually encourage a continued use of the 'machine' model.

The general structure of the theoretical systems of all three writers is remarkably similar. They use as the basic independent variable some form of organization or organizational procedure designed to control the activities of the organization members. These procedures are based primarily on what we have called the 'machine' model of human behavior. They are shown to have the consequences anticipated by the organizational leaders, but also to have other, unanticipated consequences. In turn, these consequences reinforce the tendency to use the control device. Thus, the systems may be depicted as in Figure 1.

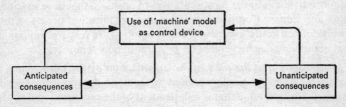

Figure 1   The general bureaucracy model

The several systems examined here posit different sets of variables and theoretical relations. However, their structures are sufficiently similar to suggest that these studies in 'bureaucracy' belong to a single class of theories.

The Merton model

Merton (1940) is concerned with dysfunctional organizational learning: organization members generalize a response from situations where the response is appropriate to similar situations where it results in consequences unanticipated and undesired by the organization. Merton asserts that changes in the personality of individual members of the organization stem from factors in the organizational structure. Here personality refers to any fairly reliable connection between certain stimuli and the characteristic responses to them. The label 'personality' is attached to such a response pattern when the pattern does not change easily or rapidly.

Merton's system of propositions begins with a *demand for control* made on the organization by the top hierarchy. This demand takes the form of an increased *emphasis on the reliability of behavior* within the organization. From the point of view of the top hierarchy, this represents a need for accountability and predictability of behavior. The techniques used to secure reliability draw upon what has been called here the 'machine' model of human behavior. Standard operating procedures are instituted, and control consists largely in checking to ensure that these procedures are, in fact, followed.

Three consequences follow from this emphasis on reliability in behavior and the techniques used to install it:

1. There is a reduction in the *amount of personalized relationships*. The bureaucracy is a set of relationships between offices, or roles. The official reacts to other members of the organization not as more or less unique individuals but as representatives of positions that have specified rights and duties. Competition within the organization occurs within closely defined limits; evaluation and promotion are relatively independent of individual achievement (e.g. promotion by seniority).

2. *Internalization of the rules of the organization* by the participants is increased. Rules originally devised to achieve organizational goals assume a positive value that is independent of the organizational goals. However, it is important to distinguish two phenomena, both of which have been called the 'displacement of goals'. In one case, a given stimulus evokes an activity perceived as leading to a preferred state of affairs. In a series of such situations, the repeated choice of the acceptable alternative causes a gradual transfer of the preference from the final state of affairs to the instrumental activity. In the other case, the choice of a desired alternative reveals additional desirable consequences not originally anticipated. The instrumental activity has, therefore, positively valued consequences even when it does not have the originally anticipated outcomes. It is this latter phenomenon (secondary reinforcement) that is operating in the present situation: the organizational setting brings about new personal or subunit consequences through participation in organizationally motivated actions.

3. There is increased *use of categorization as a decision-making technique*. To be sure, categorizing is a basic part of thinking in any situation. The special feature involved here is a tendency to restrict the categories used to a relatively small number and to enforce the first formally applicable category rather than search for the possible categories that might be applied and choose among them. An increase in the use of categorization for decision making decreases the *amount of search for alternatives*.

The reduction in personalized relationships, the increased internalization of rules, and the decreased search for alternatives combine to make the behavior of members of the organization highly predictable; i.e. they result in an increase in the *rigidity of behavior* of participants. At the same time, the reduction in personalized relationships (particularly with respect to internal competition) facilitates the development of an *esprit de corps*, i.e. increases the *extent to which goals are perceived as shared among members of the group*. Such a sense of commonness of purpose, interests and character increases the *propensity of organization members to defend each other against outside pressures*. This, in turn, solidifies the tendency toward rigid behavior.

The rigidity of behavior has three major consequences. First, it substantially satisfies the original demands for reliability. Thus, it meets an important maintenance need of the system. Further needs of this sort are met by strengthening in-group identification, as previously mentioned. Second, it increases the *defensibility of individual action*. Simple categories rigorously applied to individual cases without regard for personal features can only be challenged at a higher level of the hierarchy. Third, the rigidity of behaviour increases the *amount of difficulty with clients* of the organization and complicates the achievement of client satisfaction – a near-universal organizational goal. Difficulty with clients is further increased by an increase in the *extent of use of trappings of authority* by subordinates in the organization, a procedure that is encouraged by the in-group's defensiveness.

The maintenance of part of the system by the techniques previously outlined produces a continuing pressure to maintain these techniques, as would be anticipated. It is somewhat more difficult to explain why the organization would continue to apply the same techniques in the face of client dissatisfaction. Why do organizational members fail to behave in each case in a manner appropriate to the situation? For the answer one must extend Merton's explicit statements by providing at least one, and perhaps two, additional feedback loops in the system. (It is not enough to say that such behavior becomes a part of the 'personality'. One must offer some explanation of why this apparently maladaptive learning takes place.)

The second major consequence of rigidity in behavior mentioned above (increased defensibility of individual action) is a deterrent to discrimination that reinforces the emphasis on reliability of behavior. In addition, client dissatisfaction may in itself reinforce rigidity. On the one hand, client pressure at lower levels in the hierarchy tends to increase the *felt need for the defensibility of individual action*. On the other hand, remedial action demanded by clients from higher officials in the hierarchy may be misdirected. To the extent to which clients perceive themselves as being victims of discrimination (a perception that is facilitated in American culture by the importance attached to 'equal treatment'), the proposals of clients or of the officials to whom they complain will probably strengthen the emphasis on reliability of behavior. This conflict between 'service' and 'impartiality' as goals for public organizations seems to lie behind a good deal of the literature on public bureaucracies.

We see that Merton's model is a rather complex set of relations among a relatively large number of variables. A simplified version of the model, designed to illustrate its major features, is provided in Figure 2.

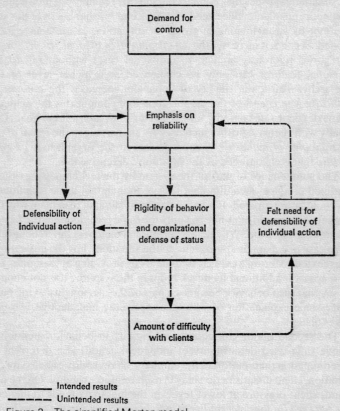

Figure 2   The simplified Merton model

The Selznick model

Where Merton emphasizes rules as a response to the demand for control, Selznick (1949) emphasizes the delegation of authority. Like Merton, however, Selznick wishes to show how the use of a control technique (i.e. delegation) brings about a series of unanticipated consequences. Also, like Merton, Selznick shows how these consequences stem from the problems of maintaining highly interrelated systems of interpersonal relations.

Selznick's model starts with the demand for control made by the top hierarchy. As a result of this demand, an increased *delegation of authority* is instituted.

Delegation, however, has several immediate consequences. As intended, it increases the *amount of training in specialized competences*. Restriction of attention to a relatively small number of problems increases experience within these limited areas and improves the employee's ability to deal with these problems. Operating through this mechanism, delegation tends to decrease the *difference between organizational goals and achievement*, and thus to stimulate more delegation. At the same time, however, delegation results in departmentalization and an increase in the *bifurcation of interests* among the subunits in the organization. The maintenance needs of the subunits dictate a commitment to the subunit goals over and above their contribution to the total organizational program. Many individual needs depend on the continued success and even expansion of the subunit. As in the previous example, the activities originally evaluated in terms of the organization goals are seen to have additional important ramifications for the subunits.

Bifurcation of interests is also stimulated by the specialized training that delegation (intendedly) produces. Training results in increased competence and, therefore, in increased *costs of changing personnel* and this results, in turn, in further differentiation of subunit goals.

The bifurcation within the organization leads to increased *conflict among organizational subunits*. As a consequence, the *content of decisions* made within the organization depends increasingly upon considerations of internal strategy, particularly if there is little *internalization of organizational goals by participants*. As a result there is an increase in the difference between organizational goals and achievement and this results in an increase in delegation.

This effect on daily decisions is accentuated by two other mechanisms in Selznick's system. The struggle for internal control not only affects directly the content of decisions, but also causes greater *elaboration of subunit ideologies*. Each subunit seeks success by fitting its policy into the official doctrine of the large organization to legitimize its demands. Such a tactic increases the *internalization of subgoals by participants* within subunits.

At the same time, the internalization of subgoals is reinforced by a feedback from the daily decisions it influences. The necessity for making daily decisions creates a system of precedents. Decisions depend primarily on the operational criteria provided by the organization, and, among these criteria, subunit goals are of considerable importance. Precedents tend to become habitual responses to the situations for which they are defined as relevant and thus to reinforce the internalization of subunit goals. Obviously, internalization of subgoals is partially dependent on the *operationality of organizational goals*. By operationality of goals, we mean the extent to which it is possible to observe and test how well goals are being achieved. Variations in the operationality of organizational goals affect the content of daily decisions and thus the extent of subunit goal internalization.

From this it is clear that delegation has both functional and dysfunctional consequences for the achievement of organizational goals. It contributes both to their realization and to their deflection. Surprisingly, the theory postulates that both increases and decreases in goal achievement cause an increase in delegation. Why does not normal learning occur here? The answer seems to be that when goals are not achieved, delegation is – within the framework of the 'machine' model – the correct response, and the model does not consider alternatives to simple delegation. On the other hand, the model offers explicitly at least two 'dampers' that limit the operation of the dysfunctional mechanisms. As is indicated in Figure 3, where the skeleton of the Selznick model is outlined, there are two (not entirely independent) variables treated as independent but potentially amenable to organizational control, each of which restrains the runaway features of daily decision making. By suitable changes in the extent to which organizational goals are operational or in the internalization of organizational goals by participants, some of the dysfunctional effects of delegation can be reduced. (To be sure, this ignores the possible effect of such procedures on the maintenance problems of the subunits and the consequent results for the larger organizations, but these are problems we are not prepared to attack at the moment.)

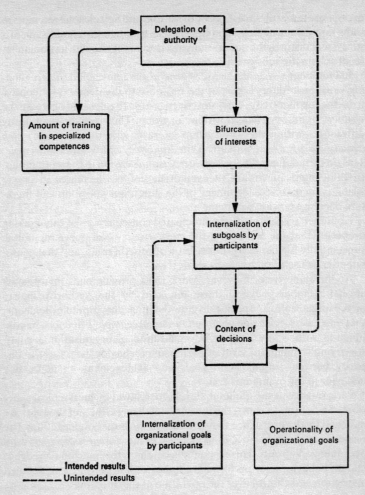

Figure 3   The simplified Selznick model

The Gouldner model

In terms of number of variables and relations, Gouldner's model (1954) is the simplest of the three presented here; but it exhibits the major features of the two previous systems. Like Merton, Gouldner is concerned with the consequences of bureaucratic rules for the maintenance of organization structure. Like both Merton and Selznick, he attempts to show how a control technique designed to maintain the equilibrium of a subsystem disturbs the equilibrium of a larger system, with a subsequent feedback on the subsystem.

In Gouldner's system, the *use of general and impersonal rules* regulating work procedures is part of the response to the demand for control from the top hierarchy. One consequence of such rules is to decrease the *visibility of power relations* within the group. The visibility of authority differences within the work group interacts with the *extent to which equality norms are held* to affect the *legitimacy of the supervisory role*. This, in turn, affects the *level of interpersonal tension* in the work group. In the American culture of egalitarian norms, decreases in power visibility increase the legitimacy of the supervisory position and therefore decrease tension within the group.

Gouldner argues that these anticipated consequences of rule-making do occur, that the survival of the work group as an operating unit is substantially furthered by the creation of general rules, and that consequently the use of such rules is reinforced.

At the same time, however, work rules provide cues for organizational members beyond those intended by the authority figures in the organization. Specifically, by defining unacceptable behavior, they increase *knowledge about minimum acceptable behavior*. In conjunction with a low level of internalization of organizational goals, specifying a minimum level of permissible behavior increases the disparity between organization goals and achievement by depressing behavior to the minimum level.

Performance at the minimum level is perceived by hierarchical superiors as a failure. In short, the internal stabilizing effects of the rules are matched by the unbalance they produce in the larger organization. The response to the unbalance is an increase in the *closeness of supervision* over the work group. This response is based on the 'machine' model of human behavior: low performance indicates a need for more detailed inspection and control over the operation of the 'machine'.

In turn, however, close supervision increases the visibility of power relations within the organization, raises the tension level in the work group, and thereby upsets the equilibrium originally based on the institution of rules. The broad outline of the model is shown in Figure 4.

Gouldner's model leaves some puzzles unexplained. In particular, why is increased supervision the supervisory response to low performance? It seems reasonable that the tendency to make such a response is affected both by role perceptions and by a third equilibrating pro-

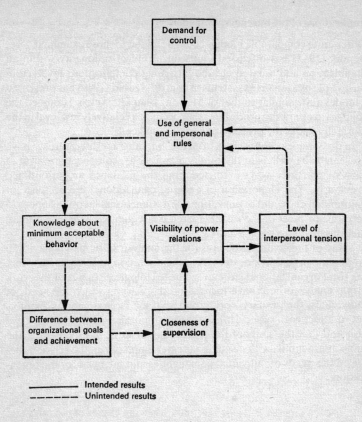

Figure 4   The simplified Gouldner model

cess in the system – the individual needs of the supervisors. Thus, the intensity of supervision is a function of the *authoritarianism* of supervisors and a function of the *punitivity of supervisory role perception*.

As in the Selznick model, the existence of 'dampers' on the system poses the question of their treatment as external variables. Appropriate manipulation of equality norms, perceived commonality of interest, and the needs of supervisors will restrict the operation of the dysfunctional features of the system. The failure of top management to use such techniques of control suggests that the system may be incompletely defined. [. . .]

J. G. March and H. A. Simon   37

Implications of the bureaucracy models

Other quite comparable models could be added to those examined here. Bendix (1947) has discussed limits on technical rationality within an organization and pointed out the intriguing complications involved in the use of spy systems as systems of control. Dubin (1949) has presented a model quite similar to that of Merton. Blau (1955) has examined the changes in operating procedures that occur at a relatively low level in the hierarchy under the pressure of work group needs.

In the sample of three cases from the 'bureaucracy' literature we have presented (as well as in the others mentioned), complications arise in each of the three ways predicted from the influence model outlined previously. The elaboration of evoking connections, the presence of unintended cues, and organizationally dysfunctional learning appear to account for most of the unanticipated consequences with which these theories deal.

Many of the central problems for the analysis of human behavior in large-scale organizations stem from the operation of subsystems within the total organizational structure. The sociological studies of the work group analyzed here have focused on the ways in which the needs of individuals, the primary work group, and the large organization interact to affect each other. [In] the study of morale and productivity, we also find that the study of the psychology of work has focused on the same interactions, with perhaps a greater emphasis on the relations between the needs of individual personalities and the needs of the organization.

References

BENDIX, R. (1947), 'Bureaucracy: the problem and its setting', *American Sociological Review*, no. 12, pp. 493–507.

BLAU, P. M. (1955), *The Dynamics of Bureaucracy*, Chicago University Press.

DUBIN, R. (1949), 'Decision-making by management in industrial relations', *American Journal of Sociology*, no. 54, pp. 292–7.

GOULDNER, A. W. (1954), *Patterns of Industrial Bureaucracy*, Free Press.

GOULDNER, A. W. (1957), 'Theoretical requirements of the applied social sciences', *American Sociological Review*, no. 22, pp. 91–102.

MERTON, R. K. (1936), 'The unanticipated consequences of purposive social action', *American Sociological Review*, no. 1, pp. 894–904.

MERTON, R. K. (1940), 'Bureaucratic structure and personality', *Social Forces*, no. 18, pp. 560–68.

SELZNICK, P. (1949), *TVA and the Grass Roots*, Berkeley.

WEBER, M. (1946), *From Max Weber: Essays in Sociology*, translated by H. H. Gerth and C. W. Mills, Oxford University Press.

WEBER, M. (1947), *The Theory of Social and Economic Organisation*, translated and edited by A. M. Henderson and T. Parsons, Free Press.

3 T. Burns

Mechanistic and Organismic Structures

T. Burns, 'Industry in a new age', *New Society*, 31 January 1963, pp. 17–20.

Industry has a long past. We are now near the end of the second century of industrialism in its recognizably modern form. To be conscious of the history of an institution like the industrial concern is to become alive in two essential considerations. First, that like any other institution – government, the church, the family, military forces, for example – industry has undergone substantial changes in its organizational form as well as in its activities, tasks and objectives. Secondly, and in consequence, unless we realize that industrial organization is still in the process of development, we are liable to be trapped into trying to use out-of-date organizational systems for coping with entirely new situations.

A sense of the past – and the very recent past – is essential to anyone who is trying to perceive the here-and-now of industrial organization. What is happening now is part of a continuing development. A study of this process will at least help firms avoid the traps they often fall into when they try to confront a situation of the newest kind with an organizational system appropriate to an earlier phase of industrial development. Adaptation to new challenge is not an automatic process: there are many factors against it.

What we recognize as industrialism is the product of two technologies, material and social. It has developed in spasmodic fashion from the rudimentary forms of the eighteenth century by alternate advances in first one technology and then the other.

The elementary form of industrialism is Adam Smith's conjunction of the division of labour traditional in advanced society with the extension of its advantages by 'those machines by which labour is so much facilitated and enlarged'.

The modern industrial system was founded at a time when the perception by early mechanical scientists that natural events 'obeyed' certain laws became widely diffused – in the eighteenth century. Samuel Smiles' legend that Arkwright was first struck by the feasibility of mechanical spinning 'by accidentally observing a hot piece of iron become elongated by passing between iron rollers' may be fiction, but it reflects truly the commonplace terms in which the new habits of scientific thought could be used by craftsmen-inventors, who saw not just an interesting analogy but one process obeying a law which might also apply to a different and entirely new process.

At the same time as Adam Smith was observing the archetypal form of the two technologies, a third step was being taken: the creation of the first successful factory by Strutt and Arkwright. By 1835 Ure could already discount the basic principles of division of labour as outdated and misleading. The industrial system was simply the factory system as developed by Arkwright: the term 'factory' meaning 'the combined operation of many work people, adult and young, in tending with assiduous skill a system of productive machines continuously impelled by a central power. It is the constant aim and tendency of every improvement in machinery to supersede human labour altogether.'

Factory organization stayed for three generations at the point at which Arkwright had left it. Marx's account contains the same essentials: a collection of machines in a building all driven by one prime mover, and, preferably, of the same type and engaged on the same process. Attending the machines were men and women who themselves were attended by 'feeders', most of them children, who fetched and carried away materials. There was also a 'superior, but numerically unimportant' class of maintenance and repair workers. All of these worked under a master, with perhaps a chief workman or foreman. The primitive social technology of the factory system still confined it, even by the 1850s, largely to the mass production of textiles.

Technical developments in transport and communications, the impact of the international exhibitions in London and Paris, free trade, the armaments revolutions supported by the development of machine tools and of steel, and chemical technology (in Germany first) all combined during the 1850s and 1860s to form the springboard, in material technology, of the next advance in the social techniques of industrial organization.

As yet, there is no account of how that advance took place. All that can be said is that with the extension of the factory system into engineering and chemicals, iron and steel processing, food manufacture and clothing, an organizational development took place which provided for the conduct and control of many complex series of production processes within the same plant. One overt sign of this development is the increase in the number of salaried officials employed in industry. The proportion of 'administrative employees' to 'production employees' in British manufacturing industry had risen to 8·6 per cent by 1907 and to 20 per cent by 1948. Similar increases took place in western Europe and the United States.

The growth in the numbers of industrial administrative officials, or managers, reflects the growth of organizational structures. Production department managers, sales managers, accountants, cashiers, inspectors, training officers, publicity managers, and the rest emerged as specialized parts of the general management function as industrial concerns increased in size. Their jobs were created, in fact, out of the eighteenth-century master's, either directly or at one or two removes. This gives them and the whole social structure which contains their newly created roles its hierarchical character. It is indeed a patrimonial structure. All rights and powers at every level derive from the boss; fealty, or 'responsibility', is owed to him; all benefits are 'as if' dispensed by him. The bond is more easily and more often broken than in pre-feudal polities, but loyalty to the concern, to employers, is still regarded not only as proper, but as essential to the preservation of the system.

Chester Barnard makes this point with unusual emphasis: 'The most important single contribution required of the executive, certainly the most universal qualification, is loyalty, domination by the organization personality.' More recently, A. W. Gouldner has pointed out 'much of W. H. Whyte's recent study of Organization Man is a discussion of the efforts by industry to attach managerial loyalty to the corporation.'

The development of the bureaucratic system made possible the increase in scale of undertakings characteristic of the first part of this century. It had other aspects. The divorce of ownership and management, although by no means absolute, went far enough to render survival of the enterprise (and the survival of the existing management) at least as important a consideration as making the best profit. Profit itself wears a different aspect in the large-scale corporation.

More important, the growth of bureaucracy – the social technology which made possible the second stage of industrialism – was only feasible because the development of material technology was held relatively steady. An industry based on major technological advances shows a high death-rate among enterprises in its early years; growth occurs when the rate of technical advance slows down. What happens is that consumer demand tends to be standardized through publicity and price reductions, and technical progress is consequently restrained. This enables companies to maintain relatively stable conditions, in which large-scale production is built up by converting manufacturing processes into routine cycles of activity for machines or semi-skilled assembly hands.

Under such conditions, not only could a given industrial company grow in size, not only could the actual manufacturing processes be routinized, mechanized and quickened, but the various management functions also could be broken down into specialisms and routines. Thus developed specialized management tasks: those of ensuring employee cooperation, of coordinating different departments, of planning and monitoring.

It is this second phase of industrialism which now dominates the institutional life of western societies. But while the greater part of the industrial system is in this second, bureaucratic phase of the historical development (and some older and smaller establishments remain in the first), it is now becoming clear that we have entered a third phase during the past two or three decades. J. K. Galbraith, in his *Affluent Society*, has described the new, more insecure relationship with the consumer which appears as production catches up and overtakes spontaneous domestic demand. The 'propensity to consume' has had to be stimulated by advertising, by styling, and by marketing promotions guided by research into the habits, motives, and potential 'needs' of consumers. At the same time, partly in an effort to maintain expansion, partly because of the stimulus of government spending on new military equipment, industry has admitted a sizeable influx of new technical developments.

There are signs that industry organized according to principles of bureaucracy – by now traditional – is no longer able to accommodate the new elements of industrial life in the affluent second half of the twentieth century. These new demands are made by large-scale research and development and by industry's new relationship with its markets. Both demand a much greater flexibility in internal organization, much higher levels of commitment to the commercial aims of the company from all its members, and an even higher proportion of administrators, controllers and monitors to operatives.

Recently, with G. M. Stalker, I made an attempt to elucidate the situation of concerns in the electronics industry which were confronted with rapidly changing commercial circumstances and a much faster rate of technical progress. I found it necessary to posit two 'ideal types' of working organization, the one mechanistic, adapted to relatively stable conditions, the other, 'organismic', adapted to conditions of change.

In mechanistic systems the problems and tasks which face the concern as a whole are, typically, broken down into specialisms. Each individual carries out his assigned task as something apart from the overall purpose of the company as a whole. 'Somebody at the top' is responsible for seeing that his work is relevant to that of others. The technical methods, duties, and powers attached to each post are precisely defined, and a high value is placed on precision and demarcation. Interaction within the working organization follows vertical lines – i.e. between superiors and subordinates. How a man operates and what he does is prescribed by his functional role and governed by instructions and decisions issued by superiors. This hierarchy of command is maintained by the assumption that the only man who knows – or should know – all about the company is the man at the top. He is the only one, therefore, who knows exactly how the human resources should be properly disposed. The management system, usually visualized as the complex hierarchy familiar in organization charts, operates as a simple control system, with information flowing upwards through a succession of filters, and decisions and instructions flowing downwards through a succession of amplifiers.

Mechanistic systems are, in fact, the 'rational bureaucracy' of an earlier generation of students of organization. For the individual, it provides an ordered world of work. His own decisions and actions occur within a stable constellation of jobs, skills, specialized knowledge, and sectional responsibilities. In a textile mill, or any factory which sees itself turning out any standardized product for a familiar and steady market, one finds decision making at all levels prescribed by the familiar.

As one descends through the levels of management, one finds more limited information and less understanding of the human capacities of other members of the firm. One also finds each person's task more and more clearly defined by his superior. Beyond a certain limit he has insufficient authority, insufficient information, and usually insufficient technical ability to be able to make decisions. He is informed quite clearly when this limit occurs; beyond it, he has one course open – to report to his superior.

Organismic systems are adapted to unstable conditions, when new and unfamiliar problems and requirements continually arise which cannot be broken down and distributed among specialist roles within a hierarchy. Jobs lose much of their formal definition. The definitive and enduring demarcation of functions becomes impossible. Responsibilities and functions, and even methods and powers, have to be constantly redefined through interaction with others participating in common tasks or in the solution of common problems. Each individual has to do his job with knowledge of overall purpose and situation of the company as a whole. Interaction runs laterally as much as vertically, and communication between people of different rank tends to resemble 'lateral' consultation rather than 'vertical' command. Omniscience can no longer be imputed to the boss at the top.

The head of one successful electronics concern, at the very beginning of the first interview of the whole study, attacked the idea of the organization chart as inapplicable in his concern and as a dangerous method of thinking. The first requirement of a management, according to him, was that it should make the fullest use of the capacities of its members; any individual's job should be as little defined as possible, so that it would 'shape itself' to his special abilities and initiative.

In this company, insistence on the least possible specification for managerial positions was much more in evidence than any devices for ensuring adequate interaction within the system. This did occur, but it was often due to physical conditions rather than to order by top management. A single-storeyed building housed the entire company, two thousand strong, from laboratories to canteen. Access to anyone was, therefore, physically simple and direct; it was easier to walk across to the laboratory door, the office door, or the factory door and look about for the person one wanted, than even to telephone. Written communication inside the factory was actively discouraged. More important than the physical set-up however was the need of each individual manager for interaction with others, in order to get his own functions defined, since these were not specified from above.

For the individual, the important part of the difference between the mechanistic and the organismic is in the degree of his commitment to the working organization. Mechanistic systems tell him what he has to attend to, and how, and also tell him what he does *not* have to bother with, what is *not* his affair, what is *not* expected of him – what he can post elsewhere as the responsibility of others. In organismic systems, such boundaries disappear. The individual is expected to regard himself as fully implicated in the discharge of any task appearing over his horizon. He has not merely to exercise a special competence, but to commit himself to the success of the concern's undertakings as a whole.

Mechanistic and organismic systems of management[1]

A mechanistic management system is appropriate to stable conditions. It is characterized by:

1. Source: Burns and Stalker (1966).

1. The *specialized differentiation* of functional tasks into which the problems and tasks facing the concern as a whole are broken down.

2. The *abstract nature* of each individual task, which is pursued with techniques and purposes more or less distinct from those of the concern as a whole.

3. The reconciliation, for each level in the hierarchy, of these distinct performances by the *immediate superiors*.

4. The *precise definition* of rights and obligations and technical methods attached to each functional role.

5. The *translation of rights* and obligations and methods into the responsibilities of a functional position.

6. *Hierarchic structure* of control, authority and communication.

7. A reinforcement of the hierarchic structure by the location of *knowledge* of actualities exclusively *at the top* of the hierarchy.

8. A tendency for *vertical interaction* between members of the concern, i.e. between superior and subordinate.

9. A tendency for operations and working behaviour to be *governed by superiors*.

10. *Insistence on loyalty* to the concern and obedience to superiors as a condition of membership.

11. A greater importance and prestige attaching to *internal* (local) than to general (cosmopolitan) knowledge, experience and skill.

The organismic form is appropriate to changing conditions, which give rise constantly to fresh problems and unforeseen requirements for action which cannot be broken down or distributed automatically arising from the functional roles defined within a hierarchic structure. It is characterized by:

1. The *contributive nature* of special knowledge and experience to the common task of the concern.

2. The *realistic* nature of the individual task, which is seen as set by the total situation of the concern.

3. The adjustment and *continual redefinition* of individual tasks through interaction with others.

4. The *shedding of responsibility* as a limited field of rights, obligations and methods. (Problems may not be posted upwards, downwards or sideways.)

5. The *spread of commitment* to the concern beyond any technical definition.

6. A *network structure* of control, authority, and communication.

7. Omniscience no longer imputed to the head of the concern; *knowledge* may be located anywhere in the network; this location becoming the centre of authority.

8. A *lateral* rather than a vertical direction of communication through the organization.

9. A content of communication which consists of *information and advice* rather than instructions and decisions.

10. *Commitment* to the concern's tasks and to the 'technological ethos' of material progress and expansion is more highly valued than loyalty.

11. Importance and prestige attach to *affiliations and expertise* valid in the industrial and technical and commercial milieux external to the firm.

In studying the electronics industry in Britain, we were occupied for the most part with companies which had been started a generation or more ago, well within the time period of the second phase of industrialization. They were equipped at the outset with working organizations designed by mechanistic principles. The ideology of formal bureaucracy seemed so deeply ingrained in industrial management that the common reaction to unfamiliar and novel conditions was to redefine, in more precise and rigorous terms, the roles and working relationships obtaining within management, along orthodox lines of organization charts and organization manuals. The formal structure was reinforced, not adapted. In these concerns the effort to make the orthodox bureaucratic system work produced what can best be described as pathological forms of the mechanistic system.

Three of these pathological systems are described below. All three were responses to the need for finding answers to new and unfamiliar problems and for making decisions in new circumstances of uncertainty.

First, there is the *ambiguous figure* system. In a mechanistic organization, the normal procedure for dealing with any matter lying outside the boundaries of one individual's functional responsibility is to refer it to the point in the system where such responsibility is known to reside, or, failing that, to lay it before one's superior. If conditions are changing rapidly such episodes occur frequently; in many instances, the immediate superior has to put such matters higher up still. A sizeable volume of matters for solution and decision can thus find their way to the head of the concern. There can, and frequently does, develop a system by which a large number of executives find – or claim – that they can only get matters settled by going to the top man.

So, in some places we studied, an ambiguous system developed of an official hierarchy, and a clandestine or open system of pair relationships between the head of the concern and some dozens of persons at different positions below him in the management. The head of the concern was overloaded with work, and senior managers whose standing depended on the mechanistic formal system felt aggrieved at being bypassed. The managing director told himself – or brought in consultants to tell him – to delegate responsibility and decision making. The organization chart would be redrawn. But inevitably, this strategy promoted its own counter measures from the beneficiaries of the old, latent system as the stream of novel and unfamiliar problems built up anew.

The conflict between managers who saw their standing and prospects depending on the ascendancy of the old system or the new deflected attention and effort into internal politics. All of this bore heavily on the time and effective effort the head of the company was free to apply to his proper function, the more so because political moves focused on controlling access to him.

Secondly, the *mechanistic jungle*. Some companies simply grew more branches of the bureaucratic hierarchy. Most of the problems which appeared in all these firms with pathological mechanisms manifested themselves as difficulties in communications. These were met, typically, by creating special intermediaries and interpreters: methods engineers, standardization groups, contract managers, post design engineers. Underlying this familiar strategy were two equally familiar clichés of managerial thinking. The first is to look for the solution of a problem, especially a problem of communication, in 'bringing somebody in' to deal with it. A new job, or possibly a whole new department, may then be created, which depends for its survival on the perpetuation of the difficulty. The second attitude probably comes from the traditions of productive management: a development engineer is not doing the job he is paid for unless he is at his drawing board, drawing, and so on. Higher management has the same instinctive reaction when it finds people moving about the works, when individuals it wants are not 'in their place'. There, managers cannot trust subordinates when they are not demonstrably and physically 'on the job'. Their response, therefore, when there was an admitted need for 'better communication' was to tether functionaries to their posts and to appoint persons who would specialize in 'liaison'.

The third kind of pathological response is the *super-personal* or committee system. It was encountered only rarely in the electronics firms we studied; it appeared sporadically in many of them, but it was feared as the characteristic disease of government administration. The committee is a traditional device whereby *temporary* commitments over and above those encapsulated in a single functional role may be contained within the system and discharged without enlarging the demands on individual functionaries, or upsetting the balance of power.

Committees are often set up where new kinds of work and/or unfamiliar problems seem to involve decisions, responsibilities and powers beyond the capabilities or deserts of any one man or department. Bureaucratic hierarchies are most prone to this defect. Here most considerations, most of the time, are subordinated to the career structure afforded by the concern (a situation by no means confined to the civil service or even to universities). The difficulty of filling a job calling for unfamiliar responsibility is overcome by creating a super-person – a committee.

Why do companies not adapt to new situations by changing their working organization from mechanistic to organismic? The answer seems to lie in the fact that the individual member of the concern is not only committed to the working organization as a whole. In addition, he is a member of a group or a department with sectional interests in conflict with those of other groups, and all of these individuals are deeply concerned with the position they occupy, relative to others, and their future security or betterment are matters of deep concern.

In regard to sectional commitments, he may be, and usually is, concerned to extend the control he has over his own situation, to increase the value of his personal contribution, and to have his resources possibly more thoroughly exploited and certainly more highly rewarded. He often tries to increase his personal power by attaching himself to parties of people who represent the same kind of ability and wish to enhance its exchange value, or to cabals who seek to control or influence the exercise of patronage in the firm. The interest groups so formed are quite often identical with a department, or the dominant groups in it, and their political leaders are heads of departments, or accepted activist leaders, or elected representatives (e.g. shop stewards). They become involved in issues of internal politics arising from the conflicting demands, such as those on allocation of capital, on direction of others, and on patronage.

Apart from this sectional loyalty, an individual usually considers his own career at least as important as the well-being of the firm, and while there may be little incompatibility in his serving the ends of both, occasions do arise when personal interests outweigh the firm's interests, or even a clear conflict arises.

If we accept the notion that a large number, if not all, of the members of a firm have commitments of this kind to themselves, then it is apparent that the resulting relationships and conduct are adjusted to other self-motivated relationships and conduct throughout the concern. We can therefore speak of the new career structure of the concern, as well as of its working organization and political system. Any concern will contain these three systems. All three will interact: particularly, the political system and career structure will influence the constitution and operation of the working organization.

(There are two qualifications to be made here. The tripartite system of commitments is not exhaustive, and is not necessarily self balancing. Besides commitments to the concern, to 'political' groups, and to his own career prospects, each member of a concern is involved in a multiplicity of relationships. Some arise out of social origin and culture. Others are generated by the encounters which are governed, or seem to be governed, by a desire for the comfort of friendship, or the satisfactions which come from popularity and personal esteem, or those other rewards of inspiring respect, apprehension or alarm. All relationships of this sociable kind, since they represent social values, involve the parties in commitments.)

Neither political nor career preoccupations operate overtly, or even, in some cases, consciously. They give rise to intricate manoeuvres and counter moves, all of them expressed through decisions, or in discussions about decisions, concerning the organization and the policies of the firm. Since sectional interests and preoccupations with advancement only display themselves in terms of the working organization, that organization becomes more or less adjusted to serving the ends of the political and career system rather than those of the concern. Interlocking systems of commitments – to sectional interests and to individual status – generate strong forces. These divert organizations from purposive adaptation. Out of date mechanistic organizations are perpetuated and pathological systems develop, usually because of one or the other of two things: internal politics and the career structure.

Reference

BURNS, T., and STALKER, G. M. (1966), *The Management of Innovation*, Tavistock.

4   J. Woodward

Management and Technology

From J. Woodward, *Management and Technology*, HMSO, 1958, pp. 4–21.

Introduction

The research described in this booklet was the first attempt in Britain to discover whether the principles of organization laid down by an expanding body of management theory correlate with business success when put into practice.

It was carried out between 1953 and 1957 by the Human Relations Research Unit of the South-East Essex Technical College. The original intention of the research workers was to look at the division of responsibilities between line supervision and the technical specialists who apply technology to the production process, and at the factors which determine the relationships between them. They soon found, however, that this line–staff relationship could not be studied in isolation, so they widened their investigations to include the whole structure of management and supervision. Their basic survey in 91 per cent of the manufacturing firms in south Essex with over 100 employees revealed considerable variations in the pattern of organization which could not be related to size of firm, type of industry or business success.

When, however, the firms were grouped according to similarity of objectives and techniques of production, and classified in order of the technical complexity of their production systems, each production system was found to be associated with a characteristic pattern of organization. It appeared that technical methods were the most important factor in determining organizational structure and in setting the tone of human relationships inside the firms. The widely accepted assumption that there are principles of management valid for all types of production systems seemed very doubtful – a conclusion with wide implications for the teaching of this subject.

After completing the survey the team studied more fully twenty firms selected along a scale of technical complexity, and made detailed case studies of three firms in which production systems were mixed or changing.

This summary covers all three stages of the research. It describes the background survey, giving enough of the information collected to show some of the main differences between the organizational patterns associated with each of the different systems of production. The more descriptive information obtained in the second stage of the research is used to provide explanations of these differences. Finally, the detailed case studies are briefly referred to and an attempt is made to show how the analysis of changes in technical demands due to innovation can help to solve in advance the problems of management organization likely to arise.

The survey

The area

The map shows the area covered by the survey [not included]. Industrial development came comparatively late to south Essex and newer industries such as oil refining, wireless, photography, pharmaceuticals, paperboard and vehicles predominate. Factory buildings are on the whole modern. So is management organization. Most factories here were built when the functions of ownership and management had already been separated and there are few long-established family businesses. A number of family firms did move here, but their history suggests that the move gave most of them an occasion for radical changes in management structure.

The firms

The investigation was confined to manufacturing firms in the area. Those concerned with mining and quarrying, building contracting and laundering were excluded, as were transport undertakings, public utilities and local authorities.

A long search produced a list of 203 manufacturing firms which was as comprehensive as humanly possible; it is unlikely that any firm employing 100 people or more was omitted.

The number employed ranged from a dozen to approximately 35,000 (see Table 1).

There are more large firms in south Essex than in the country generally, 9 per cent employing more than 1000 people as against 1·7 per cent overall. The 203 firms cover a wide range of industries. In most of them the number employed in the area represents between 1 and 2 per

Table 1
Size distribution of manufacturing firms in south Essex

Firms employing	Percentage of 203 firms	Percentage of labour force (119,400)
100 or less	46	3
101–250	24	7
251–500	12	8
501–1000	9	11
1001–2000	4	10
2001–4000	3	14
4001–8000	1	9
8000 and over	1	38
Totals	100	100

cent of the national total. In textiles and leather the percentage is particularly low, but in vehicles and chemicals it is as high as 7 per cent.

A 25 per cent sample survey of the ninety-five firms employing less than 100 people showed no clear-cut level of management between board and operators in most of them. The main survey was therefore confined to the 110 firms employing 100 people or more, of which 100, or 91 per cent, were willing and able to take part.

Of these 100 firms, sixty-eight had both their main establishment and their commercial headquarters inside the area; the rest had only branch factories.

Information obtained

A research worker visited each of the firms and obtained information under the following headings:

1. History, background and objectives.

2. Description of the manufacturing processes and methods.

3. Forms and procedures through which the firm was organized and operated.
(*a*) An organization chart.
(*b*) A simple analysis of costs into three main divisions: wages, materials and overheads.

(c) An analysis of the labour structure, including the size of the span of control at various levels and the following ratios:
  (i) Direct production workers to total personnel.
  (ii) Maintenance workers to direct production workers.
  (iii) Clerical and administrative to hourly paid personnel.
  (iv) Managers and supervisory staff to total personnel.
(d) The organization and operation of sales activities, research and development, personnel management, inspection, maintenance and purchasing.
(e) The procedures used in production control and planning.
(f) The procedures used in cost or budgetary control.
(g) The qualifications and training of managers and supervisory staff; management recruitment and training policy.

4. Information helpful in making an assessment of the firm's efficiency.

The assessment of efficiency

It is not easy to assess either the success of a firm or the effectiveness of a particular administrative expedient. The circular argument that an arrangement works because it exists is difficult to avoid. But an assessment was attempted. The firms were classified into three broad categories of success: average, below average and above average. The more obvious factors considered were profitability, market standing, rate of development and future plans. Questions were asked about the unit of measure commonly applied to the product, the volume of the industry's output, the proportion of that volume produced by the firm concerned and the nature of the market. More subjective factors considered included the reputation of the firm, both inside its industry and among local firms, the quality and attitudes of its management and supervisory staff, the rate of this staff's turnover and the opportunity provided for a complete and satisfying career in management.

Results

Organizational differences between firms

The 100 firms in the survey were organized and run in widely different ways. In only about half did the principles and concepts of management theory appear to have had much influence on organizational development.

In thirty-five firms there was an essentially 'line' or 'military' type of organization; two firms were organized functionally, almost exactly as recommended by Taylor fifty years ago (Taylor, 1910). The rest followed in varying degrees a line–staff pattern of organization; that is, they employed a number of functional specialists as 'staff' to advise those in the direct line of authority.

The number of distinct levels of management between board and operators varied from two to twelve; while the span of control of the chief executive[1] ranged from two to nineteen, and that of the first line supervisor[2] from seven to ninety. (An individual's span of control is the number of people directly responsible to him.)

Wages and salaries accounted for anything between 3 per cent and 50 per cent of total costs. Labour forces differed in character from firm to firm too; for example, the ratio of clerical and administrative staff to hourly paid workers ranged between 3:1 and 1:14; and that of direct to indirect labour between 1:3 and 15:1. Exactly half of the firms employed graduates or other professionally qualified staff. Thirty firms promoted their managers entirely from within, five from outside only and the remainder used both sources according to circumstances.

There was no obvious explanation of these differences in organizational structure; they did not appear to be related either to size or type of industry. Also, conformity with the 'rules' of management did not necessarily result in success or non-conformity in commercial failure. Of the twenty firms assessed as 'above average' in success only nine had a clearly defined organizational pattern of the orthodox kind.

New ideas about management

Did any common thread underlie these differences? One possible explanation was that they reflected the different personalities of the senior managers, another that they arose from the historical background of the firms. While such factors undoubtedly influenced the situation, they did not adequately explain it; they were not always associated with differences in organizational patterns or in the quality of human relations.

A new approach lay in recognizing that firms differed not only in size, kind of industry and organizational structure, but also in objectives. While the firms were all manufacturing goods for sale their detailed

1. The chief executive was in some cases the Chairman, in others the Managing Director and in others the General or Works Manager. In every case he presented the highest level of authority operating full-time on the spot.

2. i.e. the first level of authority that spent more than 50 per cent of the time on supervisory duties.

objectives depended on the nature of the product and the type of customer. Thus some firms were in more competitive industries than others, some were making perishable goods that could not be stored, some produced for stock and others to orders; in fact, marketing conditions were different in every firm. The underlying purpose varied too. For example, one firm had originally undertaken manufacture to demonstrate that the products of its mines could be effective substitutes for other more commonly used materials.

These differences in objectives controlled and limited the techniques of production that could be employed. A firm whose objective was to build prototypes of electronic equipment, for example, could not employ the technical methods of mass-production engineering. The criterion of the appropriateness of an organizational structure must be the extent to which it furthers the objectives of the firm, not, as management teaching sometimes suggests, the degree to which it conforms to a prescribed pattern. There can be no one best way of organizing a business.

This is perhaps not sufficiently recognized; management theorists have tried to develop a 'science' of administration relevant to all types of production. One result is that new techniques such as operational research and the various tools of automation have been regarded as aids to management and to industrial efficiency rather than as developments which may change the very nature of management.

Evidence is accumulating, particularly in the United States, that automation and other technological changes are often associated with considerable disturbance in the management systems of the firms concerned. New tools begin to change the task and the new task begins to change the organization and the qualities required to carry it out successfully. For example, work done in the United States has shown that the qualities required of the foreman on a motor-car assembly line appear to be very different from those required on transfer-line production (Walker and Guest, 1952). Expressions like 'leadership' or 'the art of foremanship', used so often in management literature, are losing much of their meaning. It is possible, for example, that leadership must be directive, participant, or *laissez-faire* according to circumstances. A good leader in one situation is not necessarily a good leader in another.

Two interesting questions have so far emerged. Are the management organization and supervisory qualities required in a firm in the process of radical technical change different from those required in a stable firm? Does the kind of organization required vary with the technical complexity of the manufacturing methods?

Differences in technical methods

The firms were grouped according to their technical methods. Ten different categories emerged (see Figure 1).

Firms in the same industry did not necessarily fall into the same group. For example, two tailoring firms of approximately equal size had very different production systems; one made bespoke suits, the other mass-produced men's clothing.

Measurement of technical complexity

The ten production groups listed in Figure 1 form a scale of technical complexity. (This term is used here to mean the extent to which the production process is controllable and its results predictable.) For example, targets can be set more easily in a chemical plant than in even the most up-to-date mass-production engineering shops, and the factors limiting production are known more definitely so that continual productivity drives are not needed.

Some of the firms studied used techniques of operational research to increase control over production limitation – but these could be effective only within limits set by technical methods, which were always the major factor determining the extent of control over production.

Production systems and technical progress

Grading firms according to their technical complexity implies no judgement of their progressiveness or backwardness, nor is it any indication of the attitude of their management towards technical innovation. Each production system has its particular applications and limitations. While there remains a demand for the gold-plated limousine or the bespoke suit, while large items of equipment have to be built, or while progress in industries like electronics proceeds too rapidly to permit standardization, there will be a place for unit production even though it is less advanced technically than other systems. Moreover, although continuous-flow production is applicable to the manufacture of single components, it is difficult as yet to foresee its use where many different component parts are assembled.

However, technical developments may from time to time enable a firm to achieve its objectives more effectively through a change in its production system, and a large proportion of manufacturing firms in the future are likely to be process firms. Indeed, although large-batch and

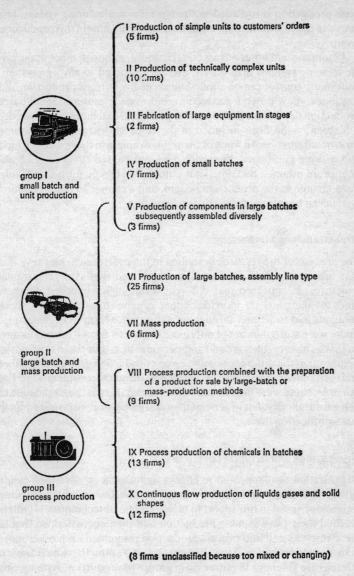

I Production of simple units to customers' orders
(5 firms)

II Production of technically complex units
(10 firms)

III Fabrication of large equipment in stages
(2 firms)

IV Production of small batches
(7 firms)

V Production of components in large batches
  subsequently assembled diversely
(3 firms)

group I
small batch and
unit production

VI Production of large batches, assembly line type
(25 firms)

VII Mass production
(6 firms)

group II
large batch and
mass production

VIII Process production combined with the preparation
  of a product for sale by large-batch or
  mass-production methods
(9 firms)

IX Process production of chemicals in batches
(13 firms)

X Continuous flow production of liquids gases and solid
  shapes
(12 firms)

group III
process production

(8 firms unclassified because too mixed or changing)

Figure 1

mass production is regarded as the typical manufacturing system, less than one third of the firms in south Essex are even now in this production group.

Automatic and other advanced techniques, although more appropriate to some systems than others, are not restricted to any one system. Automatic control can be applied most readily to mass production and continuous-flow process production, but even in unit and small-batch production devices for the control of individual machines can be used.

Sixteen of the firms included in the research had introduced some form of automation. In some of them, for example in those canning food and making mill-board, the production system had changed in consequence; in others it had not. Thus automation can be introduced without a change in the production system, and a change in the production system can be introduced without automation.

Organization and technology

The analysis of the research described in the previous chapter revealed that firms using similar technical methods had similar organizational structures. It appeared that different technologies imposed different kinds of demands on individuals and organizations, and that these demands had to be met through an appropriate form of organization. There were still a number of differences between firms – related to such factors as history, background and personalities – but these were not as significant as the differences between one production group and another and their influence seemed to be limited by technical considerations. For example, there were differences between managers in their readiness to delegate authority; but in general they delegated more in process than in mass-production firms.

Organization and technical complexity

Organization also appeared to change as technology advanced. Some figures showed a direct and progressive relationship with advancing technology (used in this report to mean 'system of techniques'). Others reached their peak in mass production and then decreased, so that in these respects unit and process production resembled each other more than the intermediate stage. Figures 2 and 3 show these two trends. (Details are given for the three main groups of production systems. See Figure 1.)

The number of levels of authority in the management hierarchy increased with technical complexity (see Figure 2).

The span of control of the first-line supervisor on the other hand reached its peak in mass production and then decreased (see Figure 3).

The ratio of managers and supervisory staff to total personnel in the different production systems is shown in some detail in Figure 4 as an indication of likely changes in the demand for managers as process production becomes more widespread. There were over three times as many managers for the same number of personnel in process firms as in unit-production firms. Mass-production firms lay between the two groups, with half as many managers as in process production for the same number of personnel.

The following characteristics followed the pattern shown in Figure 2 – a direct and progressive relationship with technical complexity.

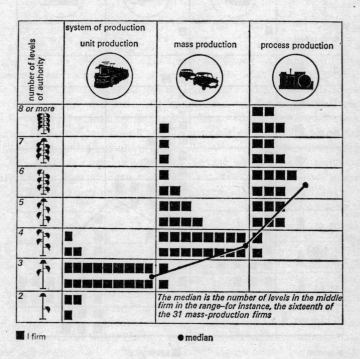

Figure 2

1. *Labour costs* decreased as technology advanced. Wages accounted for an average of 36 per cent of total costs in unit production, 34 per cent in mass production and 14 per cent in process production.

2. *The ratios of indirect labour* and of administrative and clerical staff to hourly paid workers increased with technical advances.

3. *The proportion of graduates* among the supervisory staff engaged on production increased too. Unit-production firms employed more professionally qualified staff altogether than other firms, but mainly on

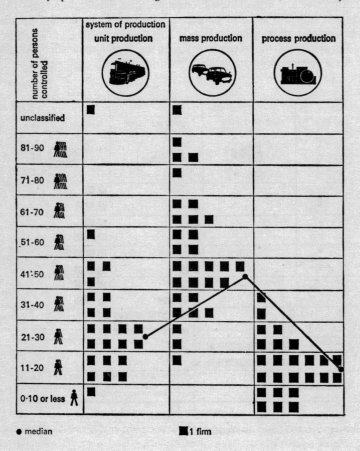

● median   ■ 1 firm

Figure 3

research or development activities. In unit-production and mass-production firms it was the complexity of the product that determined the proportion of professionally qualified staff, while in process industry it was the complexity of the process.

4. *The span of control of the chief executive* widened considerably with technical advance.

The following organizational characteristics formed the pattern shown in Figure 3. The production groups at the extremes of the technical scale resembled each other, but both differed considerably from the groups in the middle.

1. *Organization was more flexible* at both ends of the scale, duties and responsibilities being less clearly defined.

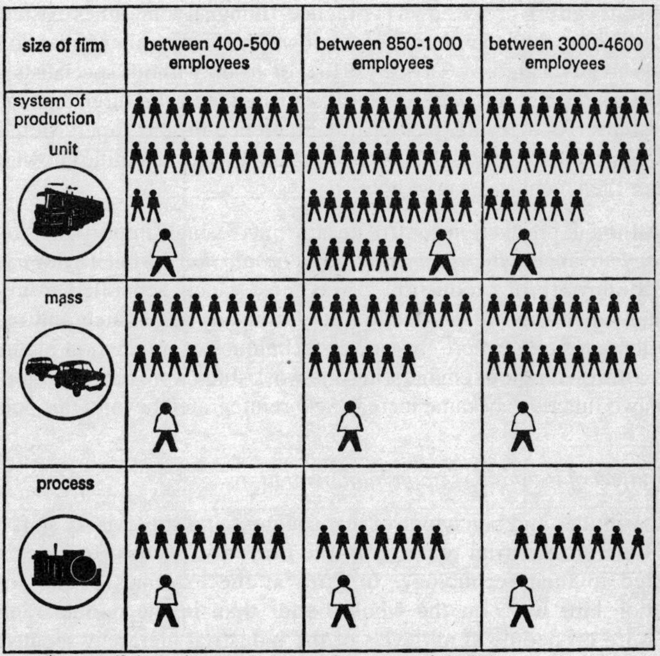

size of firm	between 400-500 employees	between 850-1000 employees	between 3000-4600 employees
system of production unit			
mass			
process			

supervisory staff shown in white jackets— other personnel shaded

Figure 4

2. The amount of *written, as opposed to verbal, communication* increased up to the stage of assembly-line production. In process-production firms, however, most of the communications were again verbal.

3. *Specialization between the functions of management* was found more frequently in large-batch and mass production than in unit or process production. In most unit-production firms there were few specialists; managers responsible for production were expected to have technical skills, although these were more often based on length of experience and on 'know-how' than on scientific knowledge. When unit production was based on mass-produced components more specialists were employed, however. Large-batch and mass-production firms generally conformed to the traditional line-and-staff pattern, the managerial and supervisory group breaking down into two sub-groups with separate, and sometimes conflicting, ideas and objectives. In process-production firms the line-and-staff pattern broke down in practice, though it sometimes existed on paper. Firms tended either to move towards functional organization of the kind advocated by Taylor (1910), or to do without specialists and incorporate scientific and technical knowledge in the direct executive hierarchy. As a result, technical competence in line supervision was again important, although now the demand was for scientific knowledge rather than technical 'know-how'.

4. Although production control became increasingly important as technology advanced, *the administration of production* – what Taylor called 'the brainwork of production' – was most widely separated from the actual supervision of production operations in large-batch and mass-production firms, where the newer techniques of production planning and control, methods engineering and work study were most developed. The two functions became increasingly reintegrated beyond this point.

The effect of technology upon human relations

The attitudes and behaviour of management and supervisory staff and the tone of industrial relations in the firms also seemed to be closely related to their technology. In firms at the extremes of the scale, relationships were on the whole better than in the middle ranges. Pressure on people at all levels of the industrial hierarchy seemed to build up as technology advanced, became heaviest in assembly-line production and then relaxed, so reducing personal conflicts. Some factors – the relaxation of pressure, the smaller working groups, the increasing ratio of supervisors to operators, and the reduced need for labour economy – were conducive to industrial peace in process production. Thus, although some management handled their labour problems more skilfully than others, these problems were much more difficult for firms in the middle ranges than for those in unit or process production. The production system seemed more important in determining the quality of human relations than did the numbers employed.

Size and technology

No significant relationship was revealed between the size of the firm and the system of production. There were small, medium and large firms in each of the main production groups.

Table 2 Production systems analysed by number employed

Production system	Number employed 101–250	251–1000	Over 1000	Total number of firms
Unit	7	13	4	24
Mass	14	12	5	31
Process	12	9	4	25
Totals	33	34	13	80

There were firms which employed relatively few people and yet had all the other characteristics of a large company, including a well-defined and developed management structure, considerable financial resources and a highly paid staff with considerable status in the local industrial community. This was particularly true of the smaller process-production firms. Some of these employed less than 500 people but had more of the characteristics of large-scale industry than unit- or mass-production firms with two or three times as many employees. As indicated already [p. 61] the ratio of management staff to the total number employed was found to increase as technology advanced. It appeared also that the size of the management group was a more reliable measure of the 'bigness' of a firm than its total personnel.

Moreover, although no relationship was found between organization and size in the general classification of firms, some evidence of such a relationship emerged when each of the production groups was considered separately. For example, in the large-batch and mass-production group the number of levels of authority and the span of control of both the chief executive and the first line supervisor both tended to increase with size.

Structure and success

Again, no relationship between conformity with the 'rules' of management and business success appeared in the preliminary analysis of the research data. The twenty firms graded as outstandingly successful seemed to have little in common.

When, however, firms were grouped on a basis of their production systems, the outstandingly successful ones had at least one feature in common. Many of their organizational characteristics approximated to the median of their production group. For example, in successful unit-production firms the span of control of the first line supervisor ranged from twenty-two to twenty-eight, the median for the group as a whole being twenty-three; in successful mass-production firms it ranged from forty-five to fifty, the median for the group being forty-nine; and in successful process-production firms it ranged from eleven to fifteen, the median for the group being thirteen (see Figure 3). Conversely the firms graded as below average in most cases diverged widely from the median.

The research workers also found that when the thirty-one large-batch and mass-production firms were examined separately there was a relationship between conformity with the 'rules' of management and business success. The medians approximated to the pattern of organization advocated by writers on management subjects. Within this limited range of production systems, therefore, observance of these 'rules' does appear to increase administrative efficiency. This is quite understandable because management theory is mainly based on the experience of practitioners in the field, much of which has been in large-batch and mass-production firms. Outside these systems, however, it appears that new 'rules' are needed and it should be recognized that an alternative kind of organizational structure might be more appropriate.

5   D. S. Pugh

The Measurement of Organization Structures:
Does Context Determine Form?

From *Organizational Dynamics*, spring 1973, pp. 19–34.

This article will give some answers, admittedly partial and preliminary, to the following questions. Are there any general principles of organization structure to which all organizations should adhere? Or does the context of the organization – its size, ownership, geographical location, technology of manufacture – determine what structure is appropriate? And how much latitude does the management of a company have in designing the organization initially and tampering with it later on? Obviously, the questions are interdependent. If the context of the organization is crucial to determining the suitable structure, then management operates within fairly rigid constraints: it can either recognize the structure predetermined by the context and make its decisions accordingly, or it can fail to recognize the structure indicated by the context, make the wrong decisions and impair the effectiveness and even the survival of the organization. This assumes, of course, that management retains the freedom to make the wrong decisions on structure.

Even more obviously, these questions are difficult to answer. Let us begin with the fact that systematic and reliable information on organizational structure is scarce. We have a plethora of formal organization charts that conceal as much as they reveal and a quantity of unsynthesized case material. What we need is a precise formulation of the characteristics of organization structure and the development of measuring scales with which to assess differences quantitatively.

We do know something about the decisions that top managers face on organizations. For example, should authority be centralized? Centralization may help maintain a consistent policy, but it may also inhibit initiative lower down the hierarchy. Again, should managerial tasks be highly specialized? The technical complexity of business life means that considerable advantages can accrue from allowing people to specialize in a limited field. On the other hand, these advantages may be achieved at the expense of their commitment to the overall objectives of the company.

Should a company lay down a large number of standard rules and procedures for employees to follow? These may ensure a certain uniformity of performance, but they may also produce frustration – and a tendency to hide behind the rules. Should the organization structure be 'tall' or 'flat'? Flat structures – with relatively few hierarchical levels – allow communications to pass easily up and down, but managers may become overloaded with too many direct subordinates. Tall structures allow managers to devote more time to subordinates, but may well overextend lines of command and distort communication.

All these choices involve benefits and costs. It also seems reasonable to suppose that the extent and importance of the costs and benefits will vary according to the situation of the company. All too often in the past these issues have been debated dogmatically in an 'either/or' fashion without reference to size, technology, product range, market conditions or corporate objectives. Operationally, the important question is: to what *degree* should organizational characteristics such as those above be present in different types of companies? To answer this question there must obviously be accurate comparative measures of centralization of authority, specialization of task, standardization of procedure, and so on, to set beside measurement of size, technology, ownership, business environment and level of performance. A programme of research aimed at identifying such measurements – of organization structure, operating context and performance – was inaugurated in the Industrial Administration Research Unit of the University of Aston a number of years ago, and continues in the Organizational Behaviour Research Group at the London Business School and elsewhere. The object of the research is threefold:

1. To discover in what ways an organization structures its activities.

2. To see whether or not it is possible to create statistically valid and reliable methods of measuring structural differences between organizations.

3. To examine what constraints the organization's context (i.e. its size, technology of manufacture, diffusion of ownership, etc.) imposes on the management structure.

Formal analysis of organization structure

Measurement must begin with ideas about which characteristics should be measured. In the field of organization structure the problem is not the absence of such ideas to distil from the range of academic discourse, but rather variables that can be clearly defined for scientific study.

From the literature available we have selected six primary variables or dimensions of organization structure:

Specialization: the degree to which an organization's activities are divided into specialized roles.

Standardization: the degree to which an organization lays down standard rules and procedures.

Standardization of employment practices: the degree to which an organization has standardized employment practices.

Formalization: the degree to which instructions, procedures, etc. are written down.

Centralization: the degree to which the authority to make certain decisions is located at the top of the management hierarchy.

Configuration: the 'shape' of the organization's role structure, e.g. whether the management chain of command is long or short, whether superiors have limited span of control – a relatively few subordinates – or broad span of control – a relatively large number of subordinates – and whether there is a large or small percentage of specialized or support personnel. Configuration is a blanket term used to cover all three variables.

We need to distinguish between the two forms of standardization because they are far from synonymous. High standardization of employment practices, for example, is a distinctive feature of personnel bureaucracies but not of work-flow bureaucracies.

In our surveys we have limited ourselves to work organizations employing more than 150 people – a work organization being analysed as one that employs (that is, pays) its members. We constructed scales from data on a first sample of fifty-two such organizations, including firms making motor-car bumpers and milk-chocolate buttons, municipal organizations that repaired roads or taught arithmetic, large department stores, small insurance companies, and so on. Several further samples duplicated the original investigation and increased the number of organizations to over two hundred.

Our problem was how to apply our six dimensions; how to go beyond individual experience and scholarship to the systematic study of existing organizations. We decided to use scales measuring the six dimensions of any organization, so that the positions of a particular organization on those scales form a profile of the organization.

Our approach to developing comparative scales was also guided by the need to demonstrate that the items forming a scale 'hang together', that is, that they are in some sense cumulative. We can represent an organization's comparative position on a characteristic by a numerical score, in the same way as an I.Q. score represents an individual's comparative intelligence. But just as an I.Q. is a sample of a person's intelligence taken for comparative purposes and does not detract from his uniqueness as a functioning individual, so our scales, being likewise comparative samples, do not detract from the uniqueness of each organization's functioning. They do, however, indicate limits within which the unique variations take place.

We began by interviewing at length the chief executive of the organization, who may be a works manager, an area superintendent or a chairman. There followed a series of interviews with department heads of varying status, as many as were necessary to obtain the information required. Interviews were conducted with standard schedules listing what had to be found out.

We were concerned to make sure that variables concerned both manufacturing and non-manufacturing organizations. We therefore asked each organization, for example, for which given list of potentially standard routines it had standardized procedure. (See Table 1 for sample questions in the six dimensions.)

Table 1   Sample questions in six dimensions

Specialization
1. Are the following activities performed by specialists, i.e. those exclusively engaged in the activities and not in the line chain of authority?
(*a*) Activities to develop, legitimize and symbolize the organizational purpose (e.g. public relations, advertising).
(*b*) Activities to dispose of, distribute and service the output (e.g. sales, service).
(*c*) Activities to obtain and control materials and equipment (e.g. buying, stock control).
(*d*) Activities to devise new outputs, equipment, processes (e.g. R. & D., development).
(*e*) Activities to develop and transform human resources (e.g. training, education).
(*f*) Activities to acquire information on the operational field (e.g. market research).
2. What professional qualifications do these specialists hold?

Table 1 – *cont.*

Standardization

1. How closely defined is a typical operative's task (e.g. custom, apprenticeship, rate fixing, work study)?
2. Are there specific procedures to ensure the perpetuation of the organization (e.g. R. & D. programmes, systematic market research)?
3. How detailed is the marketing policy (e.g. general aims only, specific policy worked out and adhered to)?
4. How detailed are the costing and stock-control systems (e.g. stock taking: yearly, monthly, etc.; costing: historical job costing, budgeting, standard cost system)?

Standardization of employment practices

1. Is there a central recruiting and interviewing procedure?
2. Is there a standard selection procedure for foremen and managers?
3. Is there a standard discipline procedure with set offences and penalties?

Formalization

1. Is there an employee handbook or rulebook?
2. Is there an organization chart?
3. Are there any written terms of reference or job descriptions? For which grades of employees?
4. Are there agenda and minutes for workflow (e.g. production) meetings?

Centralization

Which level in the hierarchy has the authority to
(*a*) decide which supplies of materials are to be used?
(*b*) decide the price of the output?
(*c*) alter the responsibilities or areas of work of departments?
(*d*) decide marketing territories to be covered?

Configuration

1. What is the chief executive's span of control?
2. What is the average number of direct workers per first-line supervisor?
3. What is the percentage of indirect personnel (i.e. employees with no direct or supervisory responsibility for work on the output)?
4. What is the percentage of employees in each functional specialism (e.g. sales and service, design and development, market research)?

On the other hand, because this was descriptive data about structure and was not personal to the respondent, we made no attempt to standardize the interview procedures themselves. At the same time, we tried to obtain documentary evidence to substantiate the verbal descriptions.

Analysis of six structural profiles

For purposes of discussion we have selected six organizations and have constructed the structural profiles for each one. Two are governmental organizations. The other four are in the private sector of the economy but the nature of the ownership varies drastically: one is family owned; another is owned jointly by a family and its employees; the third is a subsidiary of a large publicly owned company; the fourth is a medium-size publicly held company. The number of employees also varies widely from 16,500 in the municipal organization to only 1,200 in the manufacturing organization owned by the central government. We selected these six from the many available in order to demonstrate the sort of distinctive profiles we obtain for particular organizations and to underscore the way in which we can make useful comparisons about organizations on this basis.

With all this diversity, it is not too surprising that no two profiles look alike. What is surprising, and deserves further comment, are the similarities in some of the six dimensions between several of the six organizations (see Figure 1).

Organization A is a municipal department responsible for a public service. But it is far from being the classic form of bureaucracy described by Weber. By definition, such a bureaucracy would have an extremely high-score pattern on all our scales. That is, it would be highly specialized with many narrowly defined specialist 'officers', highly standardized in its procedures and highly formalized, with documents prescribing all activities and recording them in the files as precedents. If everything has to be referred upwards for decision, then it would also score as highly centralized. In configuration it would have a high proportion of 'supportive', administrative or 'non-workflow' personnel. But clearly this example does not fit the pattern completely; it is below standard in both specialization and configuration, which demonstrates the effectiveness of this method of determining empirically what profile actually exists, in overcoming stereotyped thinking.

Organization B represents a relatively unstructured family firm, relying more on traditional ways of doing things. Although it has the specialities usual in manufacturing industry (and hence a comparatively high specialization score) it has minimized standardized procedure and formalized paperwork.

Organization C represents 'big business'. It is the subsidiary of a very large company, and its profile shows the effects of size: generally, very high scores on specialization, standardization and formalization, but

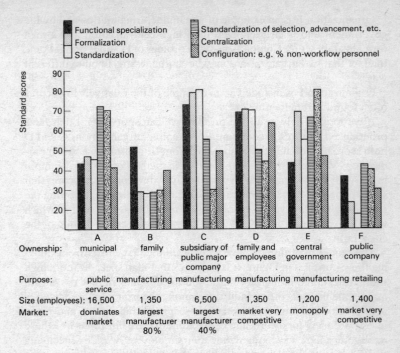

	Functional specialization		Standardization of selection, advancement, etc.
	Formalization		Centralization
	Standardization		Configuration: e.g. % non-workflow personnel

	A	B	C	D	E	F
Ownership:	municipal	family	subsidiary of public major company	family and employees	central government	public company
Purpose:	public service	manufacturing	manufacturing	manufacturing	manufacturing	retailing
Size (employees):	16,500	1,350	6,500	1,350	1,200	1,400
Market:	dominates market	largest manufacturer 80%	largest manufacturer 40%	market very competitive	monopoly	market very competitive

Figure 1   Structural profiles of six organizations

decentralized. The distinctively different relationship of centralization is typical. Centralization correlates *negatively* with almost all other structural scales. The more specialized, standardized and formalized the organization, the *less* it is centralized; or, to put it the other way round, the more it is decentralized. Therefore these scales do not confirm the common assumption that large organizations and the routines that go with them 'pass the buck' upwards for decision with elaborate staff offices; in fact, such an organization is relatively decentralized.

But it is not only a question of size, as the profile of organization D shows. It has the same number of employees as organization B, yet its structure is in striking contrast and is closer to that of a much larger firm. Clearly the policies and attitudes of the management of an organization may have a considerable effect on its structure, even though factors like size, technology and form of ownership set the framework within which the management must function.

Organization E is an example of a manufacturing unit owned by the government and is characterized by a high centralization and a high formalization score. Comparison of the profiles of D and E brings home the fact that two organizations may be 'bureaucratic' in quite different ways.

Organization F is included as an example of the relatively low scores often found in retailing.

If we look closely at all the profiles, we can spot several that have pronounced features in common. For example, organizations C and D both score high on functional specialization, formalization and standardization. Moreover, by using the statistical method of principal components analysis, we emerge with comparatively few composite scores that sum up the structural characteristics of each organization. Plotting the composite scores reveals several closely related clusters, four of which we will discuss in detail. (See Figure 2 for a visual representation of the clusters.)

The reader may already have recognized the first cluster from studying the six profiles in Figure 1. It indicates that high specialization, high standardization and high formalization form a pattern that prevails in large-scale manufacturing industry. Among the examples are factories in the vehicle-assembly industry, those processing metals and those mass-producing foodstuffs and confectionery. Organizations like these have gone a long way in regulating their employees' work by specifying their specialized roles, the procedures they are to follow in carrying out these roles and the documentation involved in what they have to do. In short, the pattern of scores among specialization, standardization and formalization denotes the range and pattern of structuring. Manufacturing industry therefore tends to have highly structured work activities: production schedules, quality-inspection procedures, returns of output per worker and per machine, firms recording maintenance jobs, etc. We can call this the *workflow bureaucracy* kind of organization. In Figure 1, organizations C and D follow this pattern. This kind of organization (placed in the lower right front box in Figure 2) usually has a high percentage of 'non-workflow' personnel (employees not directly engaged in production). Many of these are in the large specialized sections such as production planning and scheduling, quality inspection and testing, work study, and research and development, which generate standardization and formalization.

To some it may be surprising that the workflow-structured organization is relatively decentralized. The explanation appears to be that when the responsibilities of specialized roles are laid down, and activities are

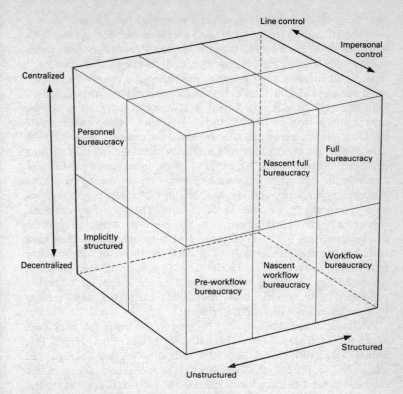

Figure 2 Relationships between the clusters

regulated by standardized procedures records, top management can afford to decentralize because the organizational machine will run as it has been set to run, and decisions will be made in the way they were intended with less need to refer them to the top.

Grouped in the upper left back box are organizations with a high centralization of authority and low structuring of activities. The authority of these organizations is centralized, usually concentrated in a controlling committee outside and above the unit itself, and in most cases such organizations do not structure daily work activities very much. However, their scores on a scale of procedures for standardization of selection, advancement, and so on, indicate that they do standardize or structure the employment activity. They have central recruitment, selection, disciplining and dismissal procedures and the like. Such an organization is called a *personnel bureaucracy*, since it bureaucratizes everything relating to employment, but not the daily work activity to anything like the same degree. Personnel bureaucracies are typically local or central government departments (for example, a municipal education department or the regional division of a government ministry) and the smaller branch factories of large corporations.

In general, there is less formal structuring of activities in service organizations than in manufacturing industries. Also, when service organizations are geographically dispersed over many sites or are publicly owned, the concentration of authority increases and they become personnel bureaucracies. An example of the influence of public ownership is the difference between one bus company owned by a local government authority and another, one of the largest remaining 'private' transport organizations in the country. The central government, through a holding corporation, owns fifty per cent of the equity of the private company, but takes no direct part in its operations. They have identical technologies (scores of 6 each on the scale of workflow integration) and are in the same size range (8,618 and 6,300 employees); therefore they are very close in structural profile, except for the higher concentration of authority in the municipal undertaking, which reflects its high dependence on local government.

A cluster of organizations can be seen in the lower left back box, which at first glance are low on both structuring and centralization. This minimal- structuring and dispersed authority suggests unregulated chaos. Not so; instead, this indicates that such organizations score low on the structural characteristics because the scales reflect overt regulation. We call such an organization an *implicitly structured organization*. These organizations are run not by explicit regulation but by implicitly transmitted custom, a common condition in small organizations where management and ownership overlap. On investigation, this hypothesis was supported. These implicitly structured organizations are comparatively small factories (within the size range of the sample); they tend to be independent of external links and their scores on concentration of ownership indicate that the operating control of the organization has remained with the directors who own them.

The upper right front box of Figure 2 includes those organizations that are high on both structuring and centralization and which therefore show the characteristics of a workflow bureaucracy (for example, standardization of task-control procedures), as in large manufacturing corporations, together with the characteristics of personnel bureaucracy (for example, centralized authority for decision making), as in government departments. This was in fact found to be the case. A central government branch factory, government-owned public services and nationalized industries fit this pattern. Thus, we may regard them as examples of *full bureaucracy*.

Analysis of organizational context

Once we have measured organization structure, the question arises: 'Do organizations of different size have different kinds of structure?' Similarly, organizations can range from being technologically very advanced to being very simple, or from being owned and controlled by one man to being owned by many people and controlled (i.e. actually run) by none of them. Clearly we must employ as much vigour in measuring the non-structural or contextual aspects of organizations as we did in measuring the structural factors. To guide the measuring, we have identified the principal dimensions of context as follows:

Origin and history: whether an organization was privately founded and the kinds of changes in ownership, locations, etc. it has experienced.

Ownership and control: the kind of ownership (e.g. private or public) and its concentration in a few hands or dispersion into many.

Size: the number of employees, net assets, market position, etc.

Charter: the number and range of goods and services.

Technology: the degree of integration achieved in an organization's work process.

Location: the number of geographically dispersed operating sites.

Interdependence: the extent to which an organization depends on customers, suppliers, trade unions, any owning groups, etc. Table 2 lists some examples of the information that was obtained.

Exploring structure and context

It has now become possible to explore the relationship between structural and contextual characteristics in a wide range of work organizations. How far, for example, is specialization a function of size? Note that the question is not 'Is specialization a result of large size or is it not?' We are now in a position to rephrase the question: *To what extent* is size associated with specialization? The correlation between size and overall

Table 2 Some contextual scales

Workflow integration
A highly workflow-integrated technology is signified by:
1. Automatic repeat-cycle equipment, self adjusting.
2. Single-purpose equipment.
3. Fixed 'line' or sequence of operations.
4. Single input point at commencement of 'line'.
5. No waiting time between operations.
6. No 'buffer stocks' between operations.
7. Breakdown anywhere stops workflow immediately.
8. Outputs of workflow (production) segments/departments become inputs of others, i.e. flow from department to department throughout.
9. Operations evaluated by measurement techniques against precise specifications.
A technology low in workflow integration is at the opposite extreme on these items.

Vertical integration (component scale of dependence)
1. Integration with suppliers: ownership and tied supply/long contracts/single orders.
2. Sensitivity of outputs volume to consumer influence: outputs for schedule and call off/orders/stock.
3. Integration with customers: ownership and tied market/long term contracts/regular contracts/single orders.
4. Dependence of organization on its largest customer: sole/major/medium/minor outlet.
5. Dependence of largest customer on organization: sole/major/medium/minor supplier.

Dependence
1. Status of organizational unit: branch/head branch/legal subsidiary/principal unit.
2. Unit size as a percentage of parent-group size.
3. Representation on policy-making boards.
4. Number of specialist services contracted out.
5. Vertical integration.

---

role-specialization in the first sample was 0·75 – size is thus the most important single element. But what part do other factors play? The correlation of 'workflow integration' – a scale that has been developed for measuring comparative technology (see Table 2) – and overall specialization was 0·38. This is not very large in itself, but since there is no relationship between size and technology (correlation of 0·08), we should expect an analysis using both dimensions to produce a higher relationship than size alone. This is in fact what happens, and the multiple correlation of size to technology and specialization is 0·81. Thus, knowing an organization's score on our scales of size *and* technology, we can predict to within relatively close limits what its specialization score will be. Likewise, knowing an organization's dependence on other organizations and its geographical dispersion over sites tells us a great deal about the likely centralization of authority in its structure (multiple correlation of 0·75).

These relationships between context and structure we have found to be reasonably stable in surveys of different samples. Where differences in the relationships have been found they have been easily related to the varying characteristics of the samples studied. In general, the framework has been adequate for thinking about the degree of constraint that contextual factors place on the design of organizational structures. The degree of constraint appears to be substantial (about 50 per cent of the variability between structures may be directly related to contextual features such as size, technology, interdependence, etc.) but it allows considerable opportunities for choice and variation in particular organizations based on the attitudes and views of top management.

In other words, context is a determining factor – perhaps overall the determining factor – which designs, shapes and modifies the structure of any organization. But within these contextual limits top management has plenty of leeway left to make its influence felt – 50 per cent is a major margin of freedom. With this approach we can discuss a number of basic issues of organizational design, such as those indicated at the beginning of this article. And we can conduct the discussion on the basis of a number of comparative empirical findings, which inevitably underline the range of variation possible, rather than merely on individual views and experiences, which inevitably tend towards dogmatic over-generalization. The two issues we will focus on are the relationship between size and formalization (paperwork procedures) and the effects of technology on organization structure.

Formalization of procedures

Using the measures that we have developed we can explore systematically the relationship between a structural feature of organization, such as the degree of formalization of paperwork procedures, and a contextual one, such as the size of operation (indicated by the number of personnel employed).

Formalization indicates the extent to which rules, procedures, instructions and communications are written down. How does the weight of documentation vary from organization to organization? Definitions of thirty-eight documents have been assembled, each of which can be used by any known work organization. They range from, for example, organization charts, memo forms, agendas and minutes to written terms of reference, job descriptions, records of maintenance performed, statements of tasks done or to be done on the output, handbooks and manuals of procedures. Scores range from 4 in a single-product foodstuffs factory where there are few such documents to 49 in a metals-processing plant where each routine procedure is documented in detail.

A wide range of differences in paperwork usage is found in all our surveys. What relation does this have to the size of organization? The correlations found range from 0·55 to 0·83 in different samples, demonstrating a strong tendency for the two to be mutually implicit while still allowing for many exceptions. Figure 3 gives examples of three typical organizations and also of two organizations that have considerably less paperwork, ar 1 two that have considerably more, than would be expected from their size alone.

The four unusual organizations emphasize the range of variation possible and lead us to look for factors other than size in explanation. Ownership patterns may play a part, the government-owned plant having more formalization than would be expected, the family retail firm having less. But the family manufacturing firm has considerably more, so the attitudes of its top management and their belief in the necessity for formal procedures becomes relevant. Similarly, the presence of professional staff in the municipal service is accompanied by the belief that they do not require such a high degree of control over their jobs because of their professional training.

One further important factor relating to formalization is clear: in our comparative surveys of international samples we have found that formalization is the one aspect of structure that clearly distinguishes U.S. and Canadian organizations from British ones. Size for size, North American organizations have a formalization score that is on average 50 per cent greater than their British counterparts. Since the relationship with size holds up in both cultures, and since in general American organizations are bigger than British ones, the average American manager is subjected to considerably more control through paperwork procedures than his British opposite number. The reason for this cultural difference we can only speculate on. It may be that in the more homogeneous British culture more can be taken for granted, whereas in the more

Three typical organizations

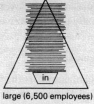

Size:	large (6,500 employees)	medium (2,900)	small (300)
Ownership:	limited company	municipal	subsidiary of a limited company
Purpose:	manufacturing	public service	food manufacturing
Formalization score:	49	27	4

Four unusual organizations

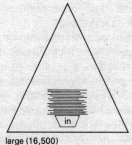

Size:	large (16,500)	small (300)
Ownership:	municipal	government
Purpose:	professional service	manufacturing
Formalization score:	25	37

Size:	medium (1,400)	medium (1,400)
Ownership:	family	family
Purpose:	retailing	manufacturing
Formalization score:	7	45

Figure 3 Formalization: examples from seven organizations

heterogeneous American culture controls, even in smaller organizations, must be spelled out formally to be effective.

The effects of technology on organizations

Does technology determine organization? Is the form of organization in a chemical plant, for instance, dictated by the fact that it is a chemical plant: that is, by its highly automated equipment and continuous-flow procedures? And is the organization of a batch production engineering factory shaped by the way its work is done: that is, by its rows of machine tools and its varying batches?

These are contentious questions. They also ask how far the number of levels of management, the centralization of major decisions, the proliferation of standard procedures, the development of specialist 'service' sections and the many other features of the structure of an organization depend on its technology.

In a study that has had considerable impact on both management- and behavioural-science writers, Joan Woodward in *Management and Technology* maintains that 'It was possible to trace a cause-and-effect relationship between a system of production and its associated organizational pattern and, as a result, to predict what the organizational requirements of a firm were likely to be, given its production system.'

Woodward took this view as a result of comparing as many as eighty firms on a unit and small batch, large batch and mass, and flow process classification. She found, for example, that the line of command from the chief executive of each firm was shortest in unit and small batch firms, lengthened in large batch and mass, and was longest in process firms. Another example of this relationship was the ratio of managers to total personnel, which also increased from unit to process technology.

In contrast, it appeared that the spans of control of the first-line production supervisors were widest in large batch and mass production (an average of 46), but dropped away in unit and small batch to an average of 22 and in process industries to an average of 14. Other suggested examples of this pattern were clear definition of duties and amount of paperwork, which were also greatest in large batch and mass technology.

Woodward's study immediately raised the question as to whether it was possible to develop general management principles of organization, as advocated by such writers as Fayol, Urwick, Gulick and Brown. Woodward maintained that this was now no longer possible. The principles that they had advocated, such as the necessity of clear lines of authority and responsibility (one man, one boss, etc.) and limited spans of control for effective supervision, might well apply in large batch and mass production forms, since they rested primarily on the experience of managers and consultants in this range of technology. But outside this range, in unit and jobbing and process technologies, different principles would probably be required.

The studies that we have carried out include replications of the Woodward work, since technology is one of a range of contextual factors that we examined. Equipped with a much more comprehensive analysis of organization structure than Woodward we can explore more systematically what are the *relative* effects of technology on organization structure.

In addition to using Woodward's categories, the present research programme also developed a measure of technology based on the items in Table 2 and labelled *Workflow integration*. This discriminates between organizations on the basis of the rigidity or flexibility of the sequence of operations carried out by the equipment on the work. This has affinities with the Woodward classification but is not equivalent to it. Thus it was possible to examine the relationships of these two measures with the dimensions of organization structure.

Did the organizations with the most process-oriented technologies have the largest scores on specialization of management roles, standardization of procedures, etc.? In the first study, taking manufacturing organizations only, a correlation of 0·52 was found between Woodward technology and standardization. This would suggest considerable support for the proposition that the technology of manufacture has considerable bearing on the management structure. But the advantage of a survey that takes a range of factors into account becomes immediately apparent when we consider their relationship. The correlation of size to specialization is 0·83 and to standardization 0·65, both of which are considerably higher than technology relationships. When we recall that size and technology are correlated among manufacturing organizations, and the effects of size are discounted by the technique known as partial correlation, then the remaining relationships between technology and structure are slight indeed (0·26 with specialization, 0·07 with standardization). In general, our studies have confirmed that the relationships of technology to the main structural dimensions in manufacturing organizations are always very small and play a secondary role relative to other contextual features such as size and interdependence with other organizations (such as owning group, customers, suppliers, etc.). Technology is shown to be related to manufacturing organization structures in a number of highly specific job ratios that we consider under *Configuration* in Table 1.

The ratio of subordinates to first-line supervisors is the only point at which the Woodward results and the present results agree exactly. Supervisors have most subordinates in large batch and mass production. This is where each foreman often has forty or fifty workers turning out large quantities of standard items, whereas in jobbing or in process plants he has a smaller group. Hence the proportion of employees in inspection work and maintenance work is also greatest at the large batch stage and lowest in both unit production and processing. The proportion in production control is highest from unit or jobbing to the mass stage, dropping away in process technologies where production control is built into the processes themselves and does not require the clerical and progress-chasing effort imposed by complex assemblies.

The detailed examination of these features is interesting, but it is of much less consequence than their implications taken as a whole. What is distinctive about them, as against the range of organizational characteristics not related to technology?

The first-mentioned characteristic of the ratio of subordinates to first-line supervisors is an element of organization at the level of the operative and his immediate boss. Obviously, the number of men a supervisor requires to run a row of lathes differs from the number he requires to run the more continuous integrated workflow of an automatic transfer machine. Thus the subordinate/supervisor ratio is an aspect of organization that reflects activities directly bound up with the technology itself. Also, it is the variety of equipment and products in batch production that demands larger numbers of inspectors and of maintenance personnel; unit and process technologies are less demanding in this respect. It is the complexity of technology both in variety of equipment and in sequences of operations that requires relatively larger numbers of production-control personnel than the more automated types of process technology.

The point is made more clearly by the contrast with activities such as accounting or market research, which are not directly implicated in the work technology itself: here, research results show no connection with technological factors.

As a result, it may be suggested that the connections between the workflow-integration measure of technology and the numbers engaged in employment and in purchasing and warehousing may be due to the intermediate position of these activities. They are closer to the production work itself than, for example, accounting, but not as close as inspection.

Among the extensive range of organizational features studied, therefore, only those directly centred on the production workflow itself show any connection with technology; these are all 'job counts' of employees on production-linked activities. Away from the shop floor, technology appears to have little influence on organization structure.

Further developments

Our continuing research programme is exploring new areas. For example, what changes in organization structure take place over time? In one small study we have already undertaken, 14 organizations were restudied after a period of four to five years. The organizations were all manufacturing firms and workflow bureaucracies in terms of Figure 2. There was an overall decrease in size from 5 to 10 per cent, as measured by number of employees, but the other contextual features remained constant. In spite of this stability there was a clear tendency for structuring scores to increase (more specialization, standardization, formalization), but for centralization to decrease. If within certain limits imposed by the organization's context top management is able to accentuate one of two broad strategies of control, *either* retaining most decision making at the top and tolerating wider spans of control *or* delegating decisions to lower-level specialists and relying on procedures and forms to maintain control, then on this evidence they are consistently choosing the second alternative, at least in manufacturing.

Clearly, more evidence is required before the significance of this trend can be evaluated. And evidence is also required on the *processes* by which organization structures are changed. What are the interdepartmental power struggles, the interpersonal conflicts, the pressures for and resistance to proposed changes that make up the evolving structure as it responds to changes in the organization's context? Studies have already been carried out that show a clear relationship of structure to organizational climate and morale. One study, for example, has shown that greater structuring of activities is accompanied by more formal interpersonal relationships and that greater centralization of authority leads to a greater degree of 'social distance' between the levels in an organization: social distance being the degree to which a manager regards his supervisor as a superior and not as a colleague as well. These important structural constraints need to be more fully investigated.

D. S. Pugh   85

Implications of the research

It has long been realized that an organization's context is important in the development of its structure. What is surprising is the magnitude of the relationships outlined above. People often speak as if the personalities of the founder and directors of a business had been the most important influence in creating the present organization. Other people point to historical crises or the vagaries of government policy as being the stimuli that caused the business to develop in a particular way. Though we would certainly expect personality, events and policies to play their part, the fact that information relating solely to an organization's context enables us to make such accurate predictions indicates that context is more important than is generally realized.

The manager of the future will have available to him ever-increasing amounts of information, and will be anxious to know what signals he should primarily attend to. If he knows what is crucial to organization functioning he can manage by exception. What types and amounts of environmental change can occur before internal adjustments must be made to maintain performance?

The fact that there is now available a reliable system of comparative measures of organization context and structure enables the many managers who have collaborated in these surveys to place their organizations in relation to others more easily and to work towards evaluating the costs and benefits of the forms of management structure that could help them to meet the challenges of the future.

Bibliography

The full details of the research described in this paper are given in:

D. S. PUGH and D. J. HICKSON (1976), *Organizational Structure in its Context: The Aston Programme I*, Gower Publishing.

D. S. PUGH and C. R. HININGS (1976), *Organizational Structure Extensions and Replications: The Aston Programme II*, Gower Publishing.

D. S. PUGH and R. L. PAYNE (1977), *Organizational Behaviour in its Context: The Aston Programme III*, Gower Publishing.

D. J. HICKSON and C. J. MCMILLAN (1981), *Organization and Nation: The Aston Programme IV*, Gower Publishing.

6 P. R. Lawrence and J. W. Lorsch

High-performing Organizations in Three Environments

From P. R. Lawrence and J. W. Lorsch, *Organization and Environment*,
Harvard University Press, 1967, chapter 6.

In this chapter we shall summarize and amplify the answers we have
found to the major question of this study: What types of organization are
most effective under different environmental conditions? By comparing
three high-performing organizations we can arrive at a more concise
understanding of how their internal differences were related to their
ability to deal effectively with different sets of environmental condition.
This comparison also provides a more complete picture of each organization, to allow the reader to move beyond the numerical measures and
gain a fuller appreciation of the distinct characters of these three
effective organizations. While our focus will be on the high performers,
we shall draw occasionally on our findings about the other organizations
for help in clarifying our conclusions.

It may seem, in this summary, that we are describing 'ideal types' of
organizations, which can cope effectively with different environmental
conditions. This inference is not valid for two reasons. First, we believe
that the major contribution of this study is not the identification of any
'type' of organization that seems to be effective under a particular set of
conditions. Rather, it is the increased understanding of a complex set of
interrelationships among internal organizational states and processes
and external environmental demands. It is these relationships that we
shall explain further in this chapter. Second, although all three high-
performing organizations were effective in dealing with their particular
environments, it would be naive to assume that they were ideal. Each
one had problems. One characteristic that the top managers in these
organizations seemed to have in common was a constant search for ways
to improve their organization's functioning.

Organizational states and environmental demands

In each industry, as we have seen, the high-performing organization
came nearer to meeting the demands of its environment than its less
effective competitors. The most successful organizations tended to

maintain states of differentiation and integration consistent with the diversity of the parts of the environment and the required interdependence of these parts. The differences in the demands of these three environments meant that the high-performing plastics organization was more highly differentiated than the high-performing food organization, which in turn was more differentiated than the high-performing container organization. Simultaneously, all three high-performing organizations were achieving approximately the same degree of integration.

To illustrate the varying states of differentiation among these three organizations, we can use hypothetical encounters among managers in both the plastics and the container high-performing organizations. In the plastics organization we might find a sales manager discussing a potential new product with a fundamental research scientist and an integrator. In this discussion the sales manager is concerned with the needs of the customer. What performance characteristics must a new product have to perform in the customer's machinery? How much can the customer afford to pay? How long can the material be stored without deteriorating? Further, our sales manager, while talking about these matters, may be thinking about more pressing current problems. Should he lower the price on an existing product? Did the material shipped to another customer meet his specifications? Is he going to meet this quarter's sales targets?

By contrast, our fundamental scientist is concerned about a different order of problems. Will this new product provide a scientific challenge? To get the desired result, could he change the molecular structure of a known material without affecting its stability? What difficulties will he encounter in solving these problems? Will this be a more interesting project to work on than another he heard about last week? Will he receive some professional recognition if he is successful in solving the problem? Thus our sales manager and our fundamental scientist not only have quite different goal orientations, but they are thinking about different time dimensions – the sales manager about what is going on today and in the next few months; the scientist, how he will spend the next few years.

But these are not the only ways in which these two specialists are different. The sales manager may be outgoing and concerned with maintaining a warm, friendly relationship with the scientist. He may be put off because the scientist seems withdrawn and disinclined to talk about anything other than the problems in which he is interested. He may also be annoyed that the scientist seems to have such freedom in choosing what he will work on. Furthermore, the scientist is probably often late for appointments, which, from the salesman's point of view, is no way to run a business. Our scientist, for his part, may feel uncomfortable because the salesman seems to be pressing for immediate answers to technical questions that will take a long time to investigate. All these discomforts are concrete manifestations of the relatively wide differences between these two men in respect to their working and thinking styles and the departmental structures to which each is accustomed.

Between these different points of view stands our integrator. If he is effective, he will understand and to some extent share the viewpoints of both specialists and will be working to help them communicate with each other. We do not want to dwell on his role at this point, but the mere fact that he is present is a result of the great differences among specialists in his organization.

In the high-performing container organization we might find a research scientist meeting with a plant manager to determine how to solve a quality problem. The plant manager talks about getting the problem solved as quickly as possible, in order to reduce the spoilage rate. He is probably thinking about how this problem will affect his ability to meet the current production schedule and to operate within cost constraints. The researcher is also seeking an immediate answer to the problem. He is concerned not with its theoretical niceties, but with how he can find an immediate applied solution. What adjustments in materials or machine procedures can he suggest to get the desired effect? In fact, these specialists may share a concern with finding the most feasible solution. They also operate in a similar, short-term time dimension. The differences in their interpersonal style are also not too large. Both are primarily concerned with getting the job done, and neither finds the other's style of behavior strange. They are also accustomed to quite similar organizational practices. Both see that they are rewarded for quite specific short-run accomplishments, and both might be feeling similar pressures from their superiors to get the job done. In essence, these two specialists, while somewhat different in their thinking and behavior patterns, would not find it uncomfortable or difficult to work together in seeking a joint solution to a problem. Thus they would need no integrator.

These two hypothetical examples show clearly that the differentiation in the plastics organization is much greater than in the equally effective container concern. The high-performing food organization fell between the extremes of differentiation represented by the other two organizations. These examples illustrate another important point stressed earlier: that the states of differentiation and integration within any organization are antagonistic. Other things (such as the determinants of conflict resolution) being equal, the more highly differentiated the units of an organization are, the more difficult it will be to achieve integration among them. The implications of this finding for our comparison of these three high-performing organizations should be clear. Achieving integration becomes more problematic as we move from the relatively undifferentiated container organization, past the moderately differentiated food organization, to the highly differentiated plastics organization. The organizational problems of achieving the required states of both differentiation and integration are more difficult for a firm in the plastics industry than for one in the container industry. The next issue on which we shall compare these three organizations, then, is the devices they use to resolve conflict and achieve effective integration in the face of these varying degrees of differentiation.

Integrative devices

Each of these high-performing organizations used a different combination of devices for achieving integration. As the reader will recall, the plastics organization had established a special department, one of whose primary activities was the integration of effort among the basic functional units (Table 1). In addition, this organization had an elaborate set of permanent integrating teams, each made up of members from the various functional units and the integrating department. The purpose of these teams was to provide a formal setting in which interdepartmental conflicts could be resolved and decisions reached. Finally, this organization also placed a great deal of reliance on direct contact among managers at all levels, whether or not they were on a formal team, as a further means of reaching joint decisions. As Table 1 suggests, this organization, the most highly differentiated of the three high performers, had the most elaborate set of formal mechanisms for achieving integration and in addition also relied heavily on direct contact between managers.

The food organization had somewhat less complex formal integrative devices. Managers within the various functional departments were assigned integrating roles. Occasionally, when the need for collaboration became especially urgent around a particular issue, temporary teams, made up of specialists from the various units involved, were formed. Managers in this organization also relied heavily on direct contact with their colleagues in other units. In this organization the managerial manpower devoted to integration was less than that in the

Table 1 Comparison of integrative devices
in three high-performing organizations

	Plastics	Food	Container
Degree of differentiation*	10·7	8·0	5·7
Major integrative devices	1. Integrative department	1. Individual integrators	1. Direct managerial contact
	2. Permanent cross-functional teams at three levels of management	2. Temporary cross-functional teams	2. Managerial hierarchy
	3. Direct managerial contact	3. Direct managerial contact	3. Paper system
	4. Managerial hierarchy	4. Managerial hierarchy	
	5. Paper system	5. Paper system	

* High score means greater actual differentiation.

plastics organization. Yet, compared with the container firm, the food organization was devoting a large amount of managerial time and effort to this activity.

Integration in the container organization was achieved primarily through the managerial hierarchy, with some reliance on direct contact among functional managers and on paperwork systems that helped to resolve the more routine scheduling question. Having little differentiation, this organization was able to achieve integration by relying largely on the formal chain of command. We are not implying that the other two organizations did not use this method at all. As Table 1 suggests, some integration did occur through the hierarchy as well as through paper systems in both of these organizations. But the great differences among functional managers seemed to necessitate the use of additional integrating devices in these two organizations.

From this discussion we can see another partial determinant of effective conflict resolution. This is the appropriateness of the choice that management makes about formal integrating devices. The comparison of these devices in these three high-performing organizations indicates that, if they are going to facilitate the process of conflict resolution, they should be fairly elaborate when the organization is highly differentiated and integration is thus more difficult. But when the units in the organization are not highly differentiated, simpler devices seem to work quite effectively. As we have already seen, however, the appropriate choice of an integrating device is not in itself sufficient to assure effective settlement of differences. All the plastics and food organizations, regardless of performance level, had some type of integrating device besides the managerial hierarchy. These devices were not equally helpful in interdepartmental decision making because, as we have pointed out, some of the organizations did not meet many of the other partial determinants of effective conflict resolution. However, there was evidence in all organizations that these devices did serve some useful purpose. To at least a minimal extent they helped to bridge the gap between highly differentiated functional departments. By contrast, in the low-performing container organization there was no evidence that the integrating unit was serving a useful purpose. Given the low differentiation within the organization, there seemed to be no necessity for an integrating department.

This comparison of the integrating devices in the three high-performing organizations points up the relationship between the types of integrating mechanisms and the other partial determinants of effective conflict resolution. We have stressed earlier that these determinants are interdependent. Even though we have not been able to trace the relationship systematically, this statement seems to include the final partial determinant, the choice of integrative devices. In all these organizations the choice of integrative devices clearly affected the level at which decisions were made as well as the relative influence of the various basic units.

We should also remember that any one of these determinants is only partial and that they should be seen as immediate determinants only. We have not explored the causes underlying them.

Comparison of effective conflict-resolving practices

Because of differences in the demands of each environment and the related differences in integrative devices, each of these high-performing organizations had developed some different procedures and practices for resolving interdepartmental conflict. However, certain important determinants of effective conflict resolution prevailed in all three organizations. We shall first examine the differences, then explore the similarities.

Differences in conflict resolution

The three effective companies differed in the relative influence of the various departments in reaching interdepartmental decisions. In the plastics organization it was the integrating department that had the highest influence. This was consistent with the conditions in that organization's environment. The high degree of differentiation and the complexity of problems made it necessary for the members of the integrating unit to have a strong voice in interdepartmental decisions. Their great influence meant that they could work effectively among the specialist managers in resolving interdepartmental issues.

In the food organization the research and marketing units had the highest influence. This too was in line with environmental demands and with the type of integrating device employed. Since there was no integrating unit, the two departments dealing with the important market and scientific sectors of the environment needed high influence if they were effectively to resolve conflicts around issues of innovation. However, as we also indicated earlier, there was ample evidence that within these two units the individuals who were formally designated as integrators did have much influence on decisions.

The pattern of departmental influence in the container organization contributed to the effective resolution of conflict for similar reasons. Here the members of the sales and production departments had the highest influence. This was appropriate, since the top managers in these two departments had to settle differences over scheduling and customer service problems. If these managers or their subordinates had felt that the views of their departments were not being given adequate consideration, they would have been less effective in solving problems and implementing decisions.

Here again we have been restating comparatively the findings reported in earlier chapters. Such reiteration helps us to understand how this factor of relative departmental influence contributes to performance in different environments. Each high-performing organization had its own pattern, but each of these was consistent with the demands of the most critical competitive issue.

A second important difference among these three organizations in respect to conflict resolution lay in the pattern of total and hierarchical influence. The food and plastics organizations had higher total influence than their less effective competitors, and, related to this, the influence on decisions was distributed fairly evenly through several levels (Figure 1). The lower-level and middle-level managers who had the necessary detailed knowledge also had the influence necessary to make relevant decisions. In fact, they seemed to have as much influence on decisions as their top-level superiors. In the container industry, on the other hand, total influence in the high performer was lower than in the low performer, and the decision-making influence was significantly more concentrated at the upper management levels. This was consistent with the conditions in this environment. Since the information required to make decisions (especially the crucial scheduling decisions) was available at the top of the organization, it made sense for many decisions to be reached at this level, where the positional authority also resided.

The importance of the differences in these influence lines can be better understood if we let some of the managers in each organization speak for themselves. In the plastics organization lower and middle managers described their involvement in decisions in this way:

> When we have a disagreement, ninety-nine times out of a hundred we argue it out and decide ourselves. We never go up above except in extreme cases.

> We have disagreements, but they don't block progress, and they do get resolved by us. I would say on our team we have never had a problem which had to be taken up with somebody above us.

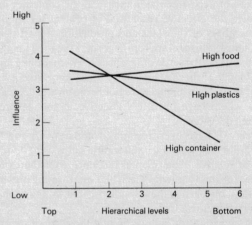

Figure 1   Distribution of influence in three high-performing organizations*

* Lines fitted by least-square method. The difference in the slope of the lines between the high-performing food and the high-performing container organization was significant at 0·001. This difference between the high-performing plastics and the high-performing container organization was significant at 0·005. There was no significant difference between the food and plastics organizations.

We could use these teams to buck it up to the higher management, but I think this would be a weak committee and a weak individual, and I am not willing to give my freedom up. They give you all the rope you need. If you need their help, they are there; if you don't need them, don't bother them.

The last manager quoted went on to substantiate a point made by many of his colleagues: While lower and middle managers made most decisions at their own level, they also recognized that major issues, which might have implications for products other than their own, should be discussed with higher management. But this discussion always took place *after* they had agreed on the best course of action for their own products.

Over and over, these lower and middle managers indicated their own responsibility for decisions and their feeling that to ask their superiors to resolve conflicts would be to acknowledge their own inadequacy. A higher-level manager stressed that this was also the view at his level:

Top management has told these fellows, 'We want you to decide what is best for your business, and we want you to run it. We don't want to tell you how to run it.' We assume that nobody in the company knows as much about a business as the men on that team.

This same flavor was evident in remarks gathered in the food organization. Here, too, middle and lower managers stressed their own involvement in decisions.

Given these facts, the reader may be wondering about the activities of the upper echelons of management in the plastics and food organizations. If they were not involved in these decisions, what were they doing? While we made no detailed study of their activity, the data collected in interviews indicated clearly that they had plenty to keep them busy. First, they had the problems of administering their respective functional units. Second, they reviewed decisions made by their subordinates to make certain that the specialists working on one part of the product line were not doing anything that would adversely affect another part. In addition, in their dynamic environments they are constantly concerned with the search for new and longer-range opportunities, which would fall outside the purview of any of their subordinates. In this regard we found that in all the effective organizations the managers' time horizons became longer-ranged as one moved up the hierarchy. This tendency was particularly marked in the plastics and food organizations. This, too, suggested that top executives in the food and plastics organizations were heavily involved in longer-range issues and problems.

The tone of comments by managers in the container organization about who made decisions was dramatically different from that in the other two organizations. The middle and lower managers in the container organization emphasized the chief executive's and the other officers' roles in decision making:

My primary contact is with [sales vice-president and the chief executive]. This contact is around who we are going to give the containers to, because of our oversold position. They will determine which ones we are going to take care of . . . Actually, what you really need though is [the chief executive's] decision. I usually start out these kinds of conflicts with [the production scheduling manager], but when somebody has to get heard, it ends up with [the chief executive]. Usually I am in contact with him three or four times a day.

When there is a problem I try to tell [production vice-president] the facts and make some recommendations. He makes the decisions or takes it up to [the chief executive]. He doesn't get reversed very often. Sometimes he may say to me, 'I agree with you, go ahead and do it,' and then [the chief executive] will change it.

The sales vice-president explained his own involvement, emphasizing application of the available facts:

[The chief executive] holds a weekly scheduling meeting on Monday, which includes him, myself, the scheduling manager, and a couple of the sales managers, depending upon what the crucial problems are. The scheduling manager has prepared the schedule on Friday. On Monday we tear it apart. This business is like playing an organ. You've got to hit the right keys, or it just doesn't sound right. The keys we play with are on the production schedule. In these meetings, though, the final decision rests with [the chief executive]. He gets the facts from us, and we influence the decision, but if there is any doubt, he decides.

All these comments serve to underline the differences in the distribution of influence between plastics and foods on the one hand and containers on the other. These differences directly reflect differences in their respective environments.

Similarities in conflict resolution

So far, we have accentuated the important differences in these organizations in terms of the determinants of conflict resolution. Let us now look at some similarities. First, however, we should stress again that the differences actually stemmed from a fundamental similarity: each of these organizations had developed conflict-resolving practices consistent with its environment.

The first major similarity among these organizations is in the basis of influence of the managers most centrally involved in achieving integration and resolving conflict. In all three organizations these managers, whatever their level, had reputations in the company for being highly competent and knowledgeable. Their large voice in interdepartmental decisions was seen as legitimate by other managers because of this competence. To return to the point made earlier, the positional influence of the managers assigned the task of helping to resolve interdepartmental conflict was consistent with their influence based on competence. Unlike the situation in some of the low-performing organizations, these two important sources of influence coincided in all these effective organizations. This point is illustrated by comments about the competence of the managers centrally concerned with conflict resolution in each organization.

In the container company, as we indicated earlier, the chief executive was regarded as extremely knowledgeable about the various facets of the business. As one manager expressed it:

> The fact is, as I understand it, that he is almost a legend in the industry. He knows every function in this company better than any of the people who are supposed to be handling that function.

But the chief executive was not the only one who had this respect. Managers in this organization also emphasized the knowledge and ability of the other top executives. A research engineer described the competence of the research director:

> I think another thing related to the close supervision I receive is the nature of the [research director]. He is an exceptional kind of guy, and he seems to know all the details and everything going on in the plant, and in the lab. He is continually amazing people in this regard.

A similar point was made about the production vice-president by one of his plant managers:

> Oh yes, I hear from [the production vice-president], but if he wants you, you are in trouble. You hear from him for sure, if your figures are too far off. He is pretty understanding. If you can explain, he understands. He also can really help you out on a serious production problem. He can tell you what to do. He knows just how far a job should be run before it should be pulled off.

In this organization, as these comments suggest, the knowledge and expertise of the top managers gained them respect from their subordinates and legitimated their strong influence over decisions. In the foods and plastics organizations the knowledge-based influence worked in a similar manner to justify the high influence of the middle managers centrally involved in helping to resolve interdepartmental conflict. Comments similar to those cited in earlier chapters may help to highlight this point. An integrator in the food organization explained the importance of expertise in his job:

> Generally, the way I solve these problems is through man-to-man contact. I think face-to-face contact is the very best thing. Also, what we [the integrators] find is that most people develop a heavy respect for expertise, and this is what we turn to when we need to work out an issue with the fellows in other departments.

Similarly, a fundamental research scientist in the plastics organization indicated (as did many others in this organization) that he believed the members of the integrating unit to be competent, which helped them to achieve collaboration:

> I believe we have a good setup in [the integrating unit]. They do an excellent job of bringing the industry problems back to somebody who can do something about them. They do an excellent job of taking the projects out and finding uses for them. In recent years I think it has been staffed with competent men.

In all three high-performing organizations, then, our data suggest a consistency in three factors that helped those primarily responsible for achieving integration to settle interdepartmental disputes. The managers who were assigned the responsibility for resolving conflict were at a level in the organization where they had the knowledge and information required to reach interdepartmental decisions and they were regarded as competent by their associates. Thus (1) *positional influence*, (2) *influence based on competence*, and (3) *the actual knowledge and information required to make decisions* all coincided. While there was this similarity, as we pointed out above, the level at which influence and knowledge were concentrated varied among the organizations because of differences in the certainty of their respective environments.

A second important similarity in these three organizations lay in the mode of behavior employed to resolve conflict. All three, as we have seen, relied heavily on open confrontation. The managers involved in settling conflicts were accustomed to open discussion of all related issues and to working through differences until they found what appeared to be an optimal solution. This was so regardless of the level at which the conflicts were handled. Typical comments from managers in each of the three organizations illustrate this point more vividly than the numerical data reported earlier. A researcher in the plastics organization described how he and his colleagues resolved conflicts:

I haven't gotten into any disagreements yet where we let emotions stand in the way. We just go to the data and prove out which is right. If there is still some question about it, somebody can do the work to re-examine it. Emotions come up now and then. However, we usually have group decisions, so if I am not getting anywhere, I have to work it out with the others.

A production engineer in the food organization expressed a similar viewpoint:

We often will disagree as to basic equipment. When we can't agree on what equipment to use, we will collaborate on some tests [with research], and sometimes we will run it both ways to find out what is the best way. Actually, the way this works out, one of their fellows and I will be at each other's desk doing a lot of scratching with a pencil trying to figure out the best answer and to support our point of view. We will finally agree on what is the best way to go. It is a decision we reach together.

The director of research in the container organization discussed his role in the resolution of conflict with the chief executive:

I am sure a lot of people would say this is a one-man company. Sure, [the chief executive] keeps close tabs on the dollars, and I must keep good score for him in regard to everything we spend. He is pretty gentle with me, and I have no run-ins with him. He talked to me this morning about a problem, and I knew that regardless of whether I said yes or disagreed with him he would have gone along and taken my advice. He likes to complain a lot, and holler and bellow and be like a wild bull, but he gives up when he sees a good case. He'll ask for a real good story, and we have to give it to him, but if it *is* a good story, he will go along with us.

We should emphasize several important points about this comment. It and similar remarks from the major executives in the container organization indicated that while the chief executive was strong and dominant, he expected to have all points of view and pertinent information discussed before making a decision. These responses likewise indicated that there was give and take in these discussions and that the other major executives often influence the outcome, if the facts supported their point of view. It is also worth noting, as a comment from a plant manager in this organization suggests, that lower managers used the same method to resolve conflicts:

I'm an easy-going sort of fellow, but I get mad sometimes. When we get something to fight about, we just say it, face the problem, and it is over. We get the issue out on the table and solve it. It has to be done that way. [The production vice-president] does it that way. We all follow his lead.

While these statements all deal with technical issues, we could cite similar comments concerning marketing problems. The important fact to emphasize is that these three organizations relied on confrontation as a mode for resolving interdepartmental conflict to a greater extent than all but one of the other organizations (the low-performing food organization). This fact does not seem unrelated to the importance of competence and knowledge as a basis of influence for the managers primarily responsible for resolving conflicts. High value was traditionally placed on knowledge and expertise in all three organizations. Consequently, managers were very willing to see disagreements settled on this basis.

This reliance on confrontation suggests another important characteristic of all three organizations: managers must have had sufficient trust in their colleagues and, particularly in the case of the container organization, in their superiors to discuss openly their own points of view as they related to the issues at hand. They seemed to feel no great concern that expressing disagreement with someone else's position (even a superior's) would be damaging to their careers. This feeling of trust apparently fostered effective problem solving and decision making.

Summary comparison of the high-performing organizations

The plastics organization, which functioned in the most dynamic and diverse of the three environments, was consequently most highly differentiated of the three high-performing organizations. Since this condition could create major problems in maintaining the required state of integration, this organization, as we have seen, had developed an elaborate set of formal devices (both an integrating unit and cross-functional teams) to facilitate the resolution of conflict and the achievement of integration. Because market and scientific factors were uncertain and complex, the lower and middle echelons of management had to be involved in reaching joint departmental decisions; these managers were centrally involved in the resolution of conflict. This organization also met all the determinants of effective conflict resolution. The integrators had balanced orientations and felt that they were being rewarded for the total performance of their product group. Relative to the functional managers they had high influence, which was based on their competence and knowledge. In resolving conflict all the managers relied heavily on open confrontation.

In contrast to the plastics organization, the container organization was in a relatively stable and homogeneous environment. Thus its functional units were not highly differentiated, which meant that the only formal integrating device required was the managerial hierarchy. But in using this device this organization also met the determinants of effective conflict resolution. The sales and production units, which were centrally involved in the crucial decisions related to scheduling and delivery, both felt that they had much influence over decisions. Around these issues influence was concentrated at the top of the organization, where top managers could centrally collect the relevant information to reach decisions. Middle managers, particularly those dealing with technical matters, did have some influence. The great influence of the top managers stemmed not only from their position, but also from their competence and knowledge. Finally, conflicts between departments were resolved and decisions reached through problem-solving behavior.

In these two paragraphs we have described two quite different organizations, each of which is well equipped to deal with its own external environment. Another way to understand the contrasts between them is to examine the major sources of satisfaction and of stress for the executives in each. While we made no systematic effort to collect such data in the plastics organization, the contrast between the two organizations can be clearly seen from interview comments of the managers in each organization. Managers in both organizations were generally quite well satisfied with their situations, but they were finding satisfaction for some quite different reasons. In the plastics organization an important source of satisfaction was the active involvement in decisions. Middle managers often expressed the feeling that they were running their own firms. One product manager in the sales department put it this way:

> Our present organization allows us as individuals to more formally play a role in decision making, which we didn't do before. Now, with the teams, we can make a decision which will affect the profit. We can see the results of our efforts more realistically than we could before. Now that it has management approval, it has a nice flavor. It's nice to be doing something they approve of. The product manager has no formal authority. But putting him on the team gives him some sort of authority. I'm not sure what kind of authority it is, but it makes my job more meaningful . . . Of course, we all recognize that the other guys on the team are depending upon our effort, so we make an effort to produce.

Managers in the container organization, however, indicated that they liked their jobs for quite a different reason – because they knew where to get a decision made. One manager expressed it in this manner:

He [the chief executive] does all the scheduling himself, and in essence what you have is a large organization run by one man. This is a refreshing switch from the organization where I had previously worked. I find this very beneficial. If I want something decided, I can go right to him and get a direct decision. You tell him what you want to do, and he will tell you right then and there whether he will let you do it or whether he won't.

The sources of dissatisfaction and stress in the two organizations were also different. A manager in the plastics organization described some of the points of concern to him:

I worked for another company which was different, where there were fairly definite lines of authority. This place was quite a revelation to me. In my old company we always knew whose jobs things were. Occasionally here we run into situations where we don't know whose jobs things are . . . All of these meetings take a lot of time. I used to spend eight hours by myself, and I thought I could get more things done. I feel now that I spend time on committees instead of making autocratic decisions, but this isn't really a disadvantage, as we do get better solutions . . . Also, there can be conflict between your position as a functional manager and as a team member. The more empathy with others you have, the worse it gets.

What disturbed this manager and a few others was the ambiguity of responsibility and relationships in this organization. Many managers often had dual loyalties – to their functional superiors and to their team colleagues. They had to decide themselves what needed to be done. The involvement of many managers in interdepartmental decision making made these difficulties unavoidable, and it also meant that managers who had a low tolerance for ambiguity and uncertainty did not always enjoy their work.

By contrast, the few managers in the container organization who expressed dissatisfaction were most concerned because upper managers seemed to be so involved in their activities. As one man said:

Your boss is telling you to check something, and then he jumps down your throat five minutes later. They should know what you are doing and try to give you some answers, or else they should let you do it . . . I know this job involves a lot of pressure, particularly because at first you are just getting ignored around here and then they are jumping on you, and the pressure is really acute. Somebody has to be the whipping boy around here, and that is just part of this job.

These data suggest two things. The first is quite obvious – that these two organizations were quite different places in which to work. The second inference is more speculative. There is some suggestion, from the tone of the interviews, that the managers in the two organizations had somewhat different personality needs. Those in the plastics organization seemed to prefer more independence and had a greater tolerance for ambiguity, while those in the container company were perhaps better satisfied with greater dependence upon authority and were more bothered by ambiguity. While there may have been these differences in personality needs, each organization (as well as the food organization) seemed to provide a setting in which many members could gain a sense of competence in their job. This provided them with important sources of satisfaction. The fact that so few managers in either organization did express any dissatisfaction with such different organizational climates would suggest that this is so. While we have no way to confirm this speculation, it does raise again the importance of the point made earlier, that the organization must fit not only the demands of the environment, but also the needs of its members.

In any case, the contrast between the plastics and the container organizations is very sharp. In a sense, they represent opposite ends on a continuum, one dealing with a very dynamic and diverse environment, where innovation is the dominant issue, while the other is dealing with a very stable and homogeneous environment, where regularity and consistency of operations were important. The food organization, as our discussion has suggested, was in many ways like the plastics organization. The differences between them seemed to be more of degree than of kind. While the food environment was not so dynamic and diverse as that of plastics, it seemed to be towards that end of the continuum. The integrating devices, although not so elaborate as those in the plastics organization, were of the same nature, designed to provide linkage at the middle- and lower-managerial levels. The two organizations met most of the same determinants of effective conflict resolution. The major difference between them was that the plastics organization appeared to be devoting more of its managerial manpower to devices that facilitated the resolution of conflict. The important point, however, is that the food organization, like the other effective organizations, had developed a set of internal states and characteristics consistent with the demands of its particular environment.

We should, however, recognize one limit to this conclusion. Each of these organizations had developed characteristics that were in tune with the demands of its *present* environment. Whether these same characteristics will provide long-run viability depends, of course, on whether the environmental demands change in the future. Given the widely observed tendency toward greater scientific, technological, and market change, the plastics and food organizations would seem to be in a more favorable position to maintain their high performance. Major technological or market changes in the container industry would almost certainly create serious problems for the high-performing container organization. This suggests that the managements in stable industries must develop within their organizations some capabilities for watching for environmental changes and preparing to adapt to them. It also suggests that in the future more and more organizations may resemble the high-performing plastics and food organizations.

A contingency theory of organizations

From this comparison we have seen that it is possible to understand the differences in the internal states and processes of these three effective organizations on the basis of the differences in their external environments. This, along with the comparison between the high performers and the other organizations in each environment, has provided us with some important leads as to what characteristics organizations must have in order to cope effectively with different environmental demands. These findings suggest a contingency theory of organization which recognizes their systemic nature. The basic assumption underlying such a theory, which the findings of this study strongly support, is that organizational variables are in a complex interrelationship with one another and with conditions in the environment.

In this study we have found an important relationship among external variables (the certainty and diversity of the environment, and the strategic environmental issue), internal states of differentiation and integration, and the process of conflict resolution. If an organization's internal states and processes are consistent with external demands, the findings of this study suggest that it will be effective in dealing with its environment.

More specifically, we have found that the state of differentiation in the effective organization was consistent with the diversity of the parts of the environment, while the state of integration achieved was consistent with the environmental demand for interdependence. But our findings have also indicated that the states of differentiation and integration are inversely related. The more differentiated an organization, the more difficult it is to achieve integration. To overcome this problem, the effective organization has integrating devices consistent with the diversity of the environment. The more diverse the environment, and the more differentiated the organization, the more elaborate the integrating devices.

The process of conflict resolution in the effective organization is also related to these organizational and environmental variables. The locus of influence to resolve conflict is at a level where the required knowledge about the environment is available. The more unpredictable and uncertain the parts of the environment, the lower in the organizational hierarchy this tends to be. Similarly, the relative influence of the various functional departments varies, depending on which of them is vitally involved in the dominant issues posed by the environment. These are the ways in which the determinants of effective conflict resolution are contingent on variations in the environment. Four other determinants, however, seem to be interrelated only with other organizational variables and are present in effective organizations in all environments. Two of these are the confrontation of conflict and influence based on competence and expertise. The other two factors are only present in those effective organizations that have established special integrating roles outside the managerial hierarchy – a balanced orientation for the integrators and a feeling on their part that they are rewarded for achieving an effectively unified effort. Our findings indicate that when an organization meets most of these determinants of effective conflict resolution, both the general ones and those specific to its environment, it will be able to maintain the required states of differentiation and integration.

This contingency theory of organizations suggests the major relationships that managers should think about as they design and plan organizations to deal with specific environmental conditions. It clearly indicates that managers can no longer be concerned about the one best way to organize. Rather, this contingency theory, as supported and supplemented by the findings of other recent research studies, provides at least the beginning of a conceptual framework with which to design organizations according to the tasks they are trying to perform.

7 M. Crozier

Comparing Structures and Comparing Games

From G. Hofstede and S. Kassem (eds.), *European Contributions to Organization Theory*, Van Gorcum, 1976, pp. 193–207.

The choice of a paradigm for studying organizations

Few fields of study have attracted people from as many different disciplines, with as many different methods and goals, as the field of organizations. Economists and social psychologists have their own way of reasoning about organizations; political scientists and sociologists have several ways amongst themselves, while students of new disciplines, such as decision and communications theorists, tend to cut across these approaches. Moreover, specific methodological problems tend to oppose those who still cling to the descriptive case-studies approach to those who try out comparative measurement of samples of organizations, and both the case-study and the measurement people to those who work from an axiomatic and normative point of view.

This confusion should not be summarily dismissed. Half-baked analogies and adventurous loans from one discipline to another can lead to creative effervescence; misunderstanding may be stimulating. A new assessment of the state of the art and, more specifically, a new debate on research strategy seems nevertheless long overdue.

It is our feeling, however, that such clarification should not be done from a logical perspective with priority given to theory or to method, but that one should focus first of all on the research paradigm authors are using and ask from that angle new questions about theory and about method.

Studying cases and sampling structures

Among the numerous debates which have polarized the field during the past twenty years, such as those opposing the decision-making approach to anthropological field study, the axiomatic–rationalistic approach to the empirical kind of theory building, the action-oriented, normative kind of research to the positivistic, value-free one, the most fateful one has been the rather simple methodological debate about case studies versus sampling techniques. The issue can be summarized very roughly by stating that the kind of methodology prevailing in the fifties, which was the case-studies analysis, implied a certain kind of paradigm and that the new methodology that became fashionable in the middle and late sixties implied a radical, although not very conscious, change of paradigm.

Concretely, the case studies[1] method had three basic characteristics: it was a global approach in which the main kind of reasoning was that of description and understanding and not measurement; it could not be sharply distinguished from a social, psychological, and anthropological approach, from which disciplines it was freely borrowing methods and concepts; it was focusing on the informal, on what people experience, much more than on goals and results. These characteristics were closely associated with the dominant paradigm, which could be summarized briefly as follows: formal goals and formal rules do not bring the expected results because of the existence of organizations as autonomous social systems the basic elements of which are the phenomena of social interaction and of leadership; the central questions to be asked are questions about the processes of interaction and the processes of leadership.

The basic weakness of this paradigm was threefold: first, its basic questions were not focusing on organizations as units but on processes within organizations; second, its methods for generalizing its hypotheses were to go from one case to theory and back to another case, which meant great difficulty in using scientific evidence to test any kind of theory; third, it was easily associated with a kind of functionalist philosophy, based on the superiority of consensus and harmony, which gradually appeared to be too soft-headed.

The sixties have seen the emergence and progressive predominance of a hard-headed, supposedly more scientific approach; intended to produce evidence by measuring hard facts bearing specifically on the organizational phenomenon, i.e. on organizations as units. For this purpose, the main effort has been toward producing data on samples of organizations and on using statistical analyses of these data for proving or disproving hypotheses. This has meant a sharp break with social psychology and anthropology and the development of new questions that were compatible with the new evidence; what kind of variables do affect organizations' characteristics and what kind of impact do those

1. Classical studies of the period have been those of Selznick (1949), Gouldner (1954) and Blau (1955).

characteristics have on an organization's results? Behind these questions a new paradigm emerged, which I see developing around the problem of structure: some environmental variables or problems determine the structure of an organization, and the structure of an organization or the fit between the structure and the problem determine its effectiveness.

This paradigm has led to innumerable demonstrations of the influence of diverse sets of variables on organizational performance, but most of the time this has been mediated by the basic problem of structures, and very often with a normative orientation: which structure is the best?[2] While very promising at first, with a welcome new and much clearer view on the importance of the environment of organizations and especially technology, this paradigm has led to more and more formalistic studies with less and less meaningful results.

It was suffering three very strong biases. First, it was very deterministic in an old-fashioned, simplistic way which was not adequate for a phenomenon of high order complexity such as organizations; second, it was incapable of dealing with the cultural variable and tended to overemphasize a universalistic single best way; third, it never questioned the implicit assumption it made in equating structure (and practically formal structure) with all other organizational characteristics, since it made structure the only mediating link between the environment of an organization and its output. True enough, the theoretical view was much more complex, but the necessity of measurement forced most authors to this reductionist position at the operational, that is at the crucial level.

Comparing games: a hospital example

It is the validity of this latter paradigm which I would like to question here. I will now use two successive examples to show that a new paradigm, more fruitful heuristically, although less apparently scientific in the simple sense, could be developed. To progress in this direction, we should focus the comparison upon *games* and not upon *structures* and we should re-examine our theoretical assumptions about the basic problem of power.

Instead of conceiving of organizational behaviour as the answer of a set of individuals with their own personal and collective motivations to the demands of a constraining structure, and their adjustment to its

2. See among others Pugh, in Hofstede and Kassem (1976), and Blau and Schoenherr (1971).

prescribed roles and routines, one could visualize it as the result of the strategy each one of them has adopted in the one or several games in which he participates. An organization can thus be considered as a set of games, more or less explicitly defined, between groups of partners who have to play with each other. These games are played according to some informal rules which cannot be easily predicted from the prescribed roles of the formal structure. One can discover these rules, however, as well as the pay-offs and the possible rational strategies of the participants, by analyzing the players' recurrent behaviour. This could eventually be formalized according to rough game-theory models.[3] But what people deal with in these games can also be expressed in terms of power relationships, which means that it has direct affective connotations and consequences. Games can therefore be understood also as depending on the individual and collective capacities (partly cultural, partly organizational) for dealing with the tensions created by such relationships (see Peaucelle, 1969; Crozier, 1973).

I would like to take as a first example recent research done by Kuty (1973) on power relationships between physicians, nurses, and patients in four hemodialysis units in two Belgian and two French hospitals. This research is a mixture of the case-study method and of the comparative approach. It focuses, however, on organizational units within hospitals and not on hospitals as organizations. But these units have a high degree of organizational autonomy and by analysing their functioning one can test some of the most fundamental aspects of the dominant paradigm.

Here we have four very similar units in four different hospital settings using the same complex and very constraining technology: hemodialysis kidney machines. This would be a good case for showing the way in which technology commands structure and behaviour; yet not only is it impossible to predict the kind of working arrangements by considering technology only, but Kuty finds two widely different, even opposite, patterns of working arrangements and human and social relations. Two of the units are characterized by clear-cut role distinctions; a hierarchical pattern of power relationships; a strong priority given by the physicians to their technical function; a very poor communications system built on secrecy; and the complete passivity of the patients accompanied by strong secondary psychosomatic reactions. The two other units show a relative blurring of the professional roles; complex interpersonal relationships cutting across these roles, in which patients themselves

3. This has been done for the Industrial Monopoly case in Crozier (1964), *The Bureaucratic Phenomenon*. Such formalization can be done *ex post* – i.e. when one knows the outcomes. The strategies and the pay-offs can be interesting only for comparative purposes.

participate, some of them enjoying very strong bargaining positions; a relatively open and active communication system, and a much lesser degree of psychosomatic reactions on the part of the patients.

According to the dominant paradigm, one should focus on the structure to find out what kind of variables outside technology could have influenced it. But the formal structure does not vary very much, and inasmuch as it does so, i.e. between the French and the Belgian settings, this is not relevant since one of the hierarchical units is in France and the other in Belgium.[4]

The subject matter of the comparison should not therefore be the structure, but the system, which can be aptly formalized with the model of the game. And the question becomes: why do the various partners play a formalistic game of isolation and non-communication in two of the units, with the physicians concentrating on their technical expertise and the patients on the expression of psychosomatic symptoms, while in the two other units they play a game of open communication, the patients invading the field of technical expertise and the physicians entering the field of interpersonal relations?

Explaining the difference in games in the hospital example

To answer the above-mentioned question, one should first try to understand what kind of problem these people have to solve and what kind of solution corresponds to the game they play. The problem, of course, is to fight a most dramatic fight against death with the help of a new technology which is very effective within certain limits, but only to maintain life, not to cure the disease.[5] The source of uncertainty in this process is less and less its technical dimension, since the use of the machine has been quickly routinized, but more and more the patient's capacity to handle the problem physically and psychologically and the capacity of the physician to help him. Another element which structures the problem is the possibility of restoring the patient's health and independence by a grafting operation. This surgical intervention, however, is still highly risky, and for it to succeed the psychological as well as the physical state of the patient is very important.

4. This also shows that two different national cultures can be compatible with two very opposite kinds of working arrangements. I do not want to overemphasize this argument, however, inasmuch as the differences, although not negligible, are not as strong as the usual differences between developed societies.
5. This problem seems in many respects quite similar to the one analyzed by Miller and Gwynne (1972) and described by Miller in Hofstede and Kassem (1976).

Now two opposite solutions can be given to the problem. One is the technical one: physicians concentrate on their technical and medical expertise; they take all decisions concerning the patient and use their expertise as a charisma to soothe him. This solution is clearly unrealistic, since it does not take into account the large part of uncertainty that the patient controls. But it has the merit of simplifying the problem and making it possible to apply the technology to all cases. With the second solution, the physicians recognize the patient's contribution and by recognizing it, they can strengthen the patient's capacity to handle the situation. This completely changes the bargaining power of the partners: the patient can bargain both directly and by using his influence over other patients. The whole game changes, forcing the physicians and the nurses to be involved. This strains their capacities as well as those of the patients. And the problem becomes that of under what conditions and through what processes this is feasible.

In the four cases studied by Kuty, the key decisions in this respect seem to have been decisions concerning the boundaries of the units.[6] The hierarchical units had chosen early to practise an open admission policy, that is to admit all patients whatever their condition and to concentrate on the use of the machine without taking into account the feasibility of grafting. The open communication units had chosen to be very selective and to admit only those patients who seemed to be good risks for this kind of intervention. They were conversely closely associated with the surgical units that would perform it. In the first case, it is quite clear that an open communications policy would have been extremely difficult to use, since many of the patients would not have tolerated discussing their cases, in view of the widely different risks they represented. In the second, on the other hand, patients were homogeneous and strong enough to support each other. Furthermore, the involvement of the physicians with grafting meant the predominance of a common goal.

One could still try, of course, to fit this analysis into the dominant paradigm by combining the influence of technology with the characteristics of the market and showing what kind of organizational structure fits with such a combination. But when entering that kind of argument, one is already changing the mode of reasoning. And one has to go further, since the evidence shows, first, the wide margin of choice that may exist for combining the factors; second, that the reason for a choice may be an

6. Compare the problem described by Hjelholt in Hofstede and Kassem (1976) with regard to the Hammerfest fisherman.

ideological reason: the charismatic leader of one of the open communications units wanted to promote new kinds of human relations in the hospital; third, that the success of these new arrangements did not depend on this 'structural choice' only, but on the building up of a collective capacity to cooperate and cope with the tensions and fears associated with the risk of death. This means that there are other inputs in the system than 'objective' inputs such as the technological variables, but also that what is considered as an output – individual and group behaviour – has to be considered also as an input, and, finally, that there is nothing central one can pinpoint as a structure to be detached from the games people play.

The longitudinal analysis made by Kuty of the development of the open communications units is extremely interesting, inasmuch as it shows very concretely the long interplay between the situation and the problem on the one side and the capacity of the partners and the characteristics of their games on the other side. The units move from a charismatic concentration of the communication, prestige and power-relationships r.?twork to a more open, multipolar system with the progressive involvement of nurses and patients. But they do it through crises in a sort of trial-and-error process. One should remark finally that they have not reached a stable 'best way', but have tended to regress frequently according to interpersonal configurations.

One last remark: one may have noticed that the inside game of free communication, tolerance, and lack of intergroup barriers has been made possible only because of the existence of strong barriers at a higher level, whose existence and use supposes another very different game played by the physicians, and especially by the head of the service, with other units and with the environment.

Such a contrast between two opposite solutions within the same structures, solutions drawn according to some early choices and the development of human capacities to manage the game these choices implied, may appear to be a sort of limit case; but we have several instances of similar oppositions, and in any case they do exemplify the existence of a wider range of solutions for organizational problems and the importance of the key variable for their use: the *collective capacity of the people concerned to handle the tensions these games create.*

An example from French public administration

I would like now to take as a second example a very different kind of case, the case of the complex politico-administrative system at the 'departmental'[7] level in France. I have just completed with Jean-Claude Thoenig a research program on this problem which concentrated on three departmental units (out of 100) where all the influential people were interviewed (about 200 per unit) (Crozier and Thoenig, 1975). The analysis of this case, supported by an extensive background of organizational studies carried out in a number of French public agencies, may be helpful for reconsidering all the implications of this comparison of games and for showing the method, the mode of reasoning and the emerging new paradigm which is involved in such an approach.

The first issue we were investigating concerned the existence of a joint system incorporating the different participants in the decision-making process, that is, a relationship of interdependence with some regulating mechanisms. We had shown earlier the importance of the interdependence of two roles such as the role of prefect[8] and the role of mayor (Worms, 1966). Here we wanted to prove that these relationships and many similar ones were part of a broader, more complex system.

Empirically, what we could show was, first, the existence of complex but very stable games between the different participants and the organizations they represented; second, the interlocking of these games; and third, the existence of some common characteristics which supposed some basic regulations.

To begin with, there emerged from our data and observations the recurrence at the operational level of a very strong model of a prevailing game which can be summarized as follows:

1. Contrary to what one would expect, the very centralized public agencies do not have a close control over their field officers with regard to departmental decision making. Communications are difficult. Higher-ups do not know and do not want to know field officers as long as there are no problems. This is management by exception but without policy.

2. There is also no communication between peers. Mayors do not talk openly of their problems and their deals to other mayors. They always try to settle their problems individually. Field officers conversely never

7. A 'department' in France is what elsewhere would be called a 'province'. The entire country is divided into 100 departments.

8. The prefect is a civil servant who is appointed by the national government to be in charge of one department, that is (1) to direct a staff of civil servants in charge of general administration, (2) to coordinate the work of all field officers of the different specialized ministries, (3) to be the executive officer of the autonomous departmental unit under the theoretically deliberative responsibility of an elected general council, (4) to audit the activities of the mayors.

put up a common front among themselves, not even within the same corps. They may defend their status and conditions with a jealous fervour, but they keep aloof for their job and decisions.

3. The kind of bargaining taking place between these very individualistic decision makers is basically a divide-and-rule game where one partner has the leading hand because he stands alone in dealing with a collection of individuals. The field officer for Equipment, in charge of Public Works, deals individually with two dozen mayors in a district and is therefore in a position to determine the nature of his relationships with them as he feels best. He is supposed to serve them, but tells them what they should ask him if they want to get help.

4. People accept their inferiority in one game inasmuch as they are always part of other games where they may be in a superior position.

5. These games are interlocked according to a recurrent cross-control pattern. For example, the field officer for Equipment may impose his views on 'his' mayors, but when one tries to understand what kind of 'policies' he may pursue, one discovers that he is very much influenced indirectly by the local political climate. More precisely, he seems to be very sensitive to the cues he receives from the local influentials, for example, the member of the General Council of the area he serves. The departmental director of Equipment, his superior in the bureaucracy, does not want to and usually cannot direct him. He can, of course, impose the general standards and the numerous rules; he does not, however, intervene in local policies, except when dealing with the political influentials who in their turn intervene with the field officer.

This criss-crossing is a very cumbersome game where the converging bargaining relationships do not allow for easy and clear understanding. Regulation is not achieved by command, evaluation and control, but indirectly by the results of games where each partner fights for his own interests without regard for his peers and superiors and must cater to the wishes of a stronger partner over whom his superiors and the whole milieu has an influence.

We have moved from the game to some elements of regulation. But if we consider the system as a whole, we discover that the field is not uniform and that, although the model we have described is highly dominant, we also find one recurrent exception to the model. This recurrent exception develops around the elected official who holds a plurality of offices. Such a person has indeed a strategic advantage in a system where communication is slow and difficult and where misunderstanding is general. He who can bargain at two or three different levels where his opposite partners cannot communicate enjoys a superior bargaining position at each of them and is thus sure to win everywhere if he knows how far he can go. Moreover, since every inside player knows where the advantage lies and why, the 'notable' holding a plurality of offices will be the man to watch – from which fact he will derive a lot of influence and therefore a capacity to get things done. The system will be structured around such situations of dominance. He will be a sort of gatekeeper whose favourable position comes from the mere fact that he can reward his friends without having to punish his enemies and that everyone thinks he is powerful.

Finally, one can suggest that to the game of divide and rule, which is in this case the operational game, there had to be added a game of exception and access, which is the second-level game.

There are many other angles in such an extremely complex system, where a lot of similar but also opposite games are interlocked with each other. But if one tries to form a simple view by looking at these first elements, one can see very definite common characteristics. First, this is a system where decisions are made in secrecy and which is allergic to public debate. Second, this is a very restrictive system where the problem of access becomes consequently a basic problem. Third, this is a system which hides from any kind of interference; the cross-control game is the best protective device against outside pressure and change. Fourth, this is a system whose small number of influential figures protected from outside publicity can monopolize access and therefore will become indispensable and enjoy very long tenure. This is by consequence a very conservative system. And its conservatism justifies and legitimizes the intervention of the central government and public administration to which it is the necessary counterweight.

Such a reasoning may help understand the extraordinary stability of such a system, however poor its performances, and the extraordinary errors made by people who use the management kind of counseling to impose changes by rationalizing the structure according to some 'one best way' formula of centralizing and decentralizing.

Here again, it is evident that the basic games are more meaningful for explaining action and performances than the formal structure of roles, authority, and decision-making powers, and that such basic games are a human invention to answer the problem of cooperation. Its development is conditioned by the nature of the problem, but also by the capacity of the people concerned and their experience and traditions.

The study of games as a general approach to organization research

Can we now generalize? It can be argued that both our examples should be dismissed, since the former does not deal with a formal organization as a unit but with sub-units of an organization, while the latter deals with a loose system encompassing several very different kinds of organizations. But former experience teaches that, on the contrary, these examples do exemplify basic problems of all organized systems, of which the classic bureaucratic kind of Weberian organizations are but a special case and to some extent quite a limited one. It is my feeling that we tend to overemphasize the hierarchical model as an explanatory framework, even, and maybe all the more, if we are intent on fighting it; we tend, therefore, to miss the triangular cross-control relationships, the recurrent conflicts over goals and boundaries through which the most important regulations and the most decisive orientations are achieved. We also misunderstand the models of government by exception and the real nature of the game at the top of the organization. In such a perspective, the present dominant paradigm has become counterproductive. Because of the kind of framework within which most sociologists are reasoning, they are incapable of asking these new questions seriously.

A reversal of the trend should begin with a reversal of method, which would be at the same time the advent of a new kind of research strategy. Instead of focusing on the structure and the allocation of power, formal or informal, one should focus on the games around which meaningful relationships develop and without which the different partners' strategies do not make sense. Focusing on games, however, has the disadvantage of making formalizing much more difficult and preventing for quite some time any kind of measurement, at least at the organizational level. We have, I think, to accept this and to try to move first from literary description to some kind of qualitative assessment, instead of requiring immediately some irrelevant statistical sophistication.

To achieve a real understanding, two main orientations will have to be developed jointly. First of all we ought to know about the most common recurrent games at the operational level and to develop methods to formalize their characteristics. This would lead to an interplay with game theory. From this angle formal structural characteristics can be understood as some of the determinants of the rules of the game in interplay with the socio-psychological capacities of the players.

Second, we ought to focus on the regulations of the games taking place in an organization and on the game of regulation one can discover behind the power play among the decision makers. Drawing boundaries, defining the problem to be solved, will influence the relationship between the players, but it will also have basic consequences for the regulation of the whole and because of the consequences will be deeply structured by the anticipations of the necessary feedbacks. What seems to be clear from our examples already is that the vague assumption of homology between the relationships at the top and the relationships at the bottom of the pyramid is radically false. An organization or a broader system such as the one described are not regulated according to the same principles that are operating at the primary group level. One interesting hypothesis seems to concern the importance of government by exception and the importance of an organization's or system's weaknesses for the building of the regulation game.

A new reading of my observations on French public administration could be done along these lines. The stratification system, which may be one recurrent structural feature, can be analyzed as a choice of boundaries isolating subsystems and structuring the problems to be solved.[9] Centralization is a first kind of regulatory game which develops around the problems that cannot be solved within the sub-systems. But this is a very formalistic game which can handle only part of the exceptions. The real regulation game is the power game around the loopholes of the whole apparatus, and this game is of a completely different nature.

Although differences at first glance seem to be striking, we have found some similarities with this model in the government of large scale private enterprises, where the gap between general management and operational executives seems to be a basic characteristic of the regulation game of the organization.

Cross-cultural comparisons will be decisive in such a perspective. I feel that they will help us understand much better the area of autonomy for human choice for social learning and institutional investment, inasmuch as they will show the differences between the possible solutions to the same problem or the different ways to structure the problem. Up to now these possibilities were stifled by the paralyzing influence of the dominant paradigm, which did not allow for a real search for the autonomy of the human construct as a basic input in the organizational set-up.[10]

9. See a new formulation of this problem in Crozier (1972), 'The French Bureaucratic Style', *The Stalled Society*, ch. 5.
10. See also Luhmann's paper in Hofstede and Kassem (1976).

Outlines for a new paradigm

This kind of research strategy implies two kinds of theoretical orientations, out of which one can see a new paradigm emerging. First of all, there is a new kind of reasoning about power. Power problems were beginning to re-emerge in the early sixties at the end of the functionalist period. But they were quickly discarded because of the elusiveness of the concept and the impossibility of operationalizing and measuring it. March's otherwise very brilliant article on 'the power of power' was most unfortunate in this respect (March, 1963). When power now re-emerges because of the gradual realization of the weakness of the central scheme of research, this is still within the framework of the old paradigm, that is, as if it were a commodity whose allocation could be studied from a normative and from a structural point of view (see Perrow, 1972; Hinings *et al.*, 1974).

To go one step forward, one should forget about power as a commodity whose amount could be measured and focus instead on power as a bargaining relationship over time within a framework of constraints which the actors cannot easily change. As a bargaining relationship, the power game centers around the predictability of behaviour. As a bargaining relationship over time, it implies a consideration of strategy which can be viewed as the utilization of the objective and artificial uncertainties which derive from the interplay between the goals chosen by the organization and the technical means available to it. At a second level, it raises the technical problem of the sources of uncertainty existing objectively, of the way these are dealt with according to the structuring of the problems one is handling, and of the structuring of the information about them.

There is, then, a second kind of theoretical orientation, which is the consideration of an organization as a system of games for solving the problems raised by the contextual constraints, and not only as a social system whose activities are finalized. We have already discussed such an assumption. It can be added that it raises a whole new set of questions.

The dominant paradigm revolved around the basic question concerning the structure: how contextual variables determine the basic structural features of an organization and how these features command the behaviour of the members and the performances of the organization. The new paradigm emerges first around the idea that the contextual features of the organization should not be considered as variables determining the structure of the organization, but as problems to be solved, and, second, around the idea that structure is not the necessary nodal point of the organization, but that the games with their rational mathematical features as well as their human parameters will be a much more concrete and rich focal point.

Research questions then become: what are the different systems of games that can solve the same problems – i.e. the meeting of the same contextual constraints? What kind of capacities do they require from the members concerned? How do such capacities develop and how do new games and new systems of games become possible?

References

BLAU, P. M. (1955), *The Dynamics of Bureaucracy*, University of Chicago Press.

BLAU, P. M., and SCHOENHERR, R. A. (1971), *The Structure of Organizations*, Basic Books.

CROZIER, M. (1964), *The Bureaucratic Phenomenon*, University of Chicago Press and Tavistock Publications.

CROZIER, M. (1973), *The Stalled Society*, The Viking Press.

CROZIER, M., and THOENIG, J. C. (1975), 'La régulation des systèmes organisés complexes', *Revue Française de Sociologie*, 16, July.

GOULDNER, A. (1954), *Patterns of Industrial Bureaucracy*, Free Press.

HININGS, C. R., HICKSON, D. J., PENNINGS, J. M., and SCHNECK, R. E. (1974), 'Structural Conditions of Intraorganizational Power', *Administrative Science Quarterly*, 19, pp. 22–44.

HOFSTEDE, G., and KASSEM, M. S. (1976), *European Contributions to Organization Theory*, Van Gorcum.

KUTY, O. (1973), 'Le pouvoir du malade: analyse sociologique des unités de rein artificiel', doctorate thesis, Université René Descartes, Paris.

MARCH, J. G. (1963), 'The Power of Power', *American Political Science Review*, 57.

MILLER, E. J., and GWYNNE, G. V. (1972), *A Life Apart: a Pilot Study of Residential Institutions for the Physically Handicapped and the Young Chronic Sick*, Tavistock Publications.

PEAUCELLE, J. L. (1969), 'Théorie des jeux et sociologie des organisations: application aux résultats du phénomène bureaucratique', *Sociologie du Travail*, 2, pp. 22–43.

PERROW, C. (1972), *Complex Organizations: a Critical Essay*, Scott, Foresman & Co.

SELZNICK, P. (1949), *TVA and the Grass Roots*, University of California Press.

WORMS, J. P. (1966), 'Le préfet et ses notables', *Sociologie du Travail*, 8, pp. 249–75.

8 E. Jaques

The Stratified Depth-structure of Bureaucracy

From E. Jaques, *A General Theory of Bureaucracy*, Heinemann, 1976, chapter 8.

We have now considered the associations which establish bureaucratic hierarchies, the manager–subordinate molecules out of which they are made, and the nature of the work which they are established to accomplish. That gives enough material to make it possible to approach one of the central questions about the bureaucratic hierarchy, the question upon which our theory will hinge: namely, why is it that this structure is the only type of human organization so far discovered for bringing large numbers of people to work together in one united enterprise?

For bureaucratic systems are divided into a hierarchy of horizontal strata and tend to be pyramid-shaped. These hierarchical strata do not at first sight appear to be established in any uniform way, there being variations in the number of manifest strata in different organizations and in different parts of the same organization. Work with time-span measurement, however, has revealed that underlying this conglomeration of manifest strata there is a consistent and definable depth-structure from which neither the manifest nor the extant structure can depart too far without collapsing. This underlying system of organizational strata appears to be universal and constitutes one of the fundamental properties of bureaucratic hierarchies.

Once the fixed pattern of these strata is grasped, a general view of bureaucratic organizational structure can be obtained which is like looking into the symmetrical and regular structure of a crystal. The time-span structure of these strata is a fundamental quantitative characteristic of bureaucracy.

Consequences of 'too many' levels of organization

It is an almost universal disease of bureaucratic systems that they have too many levels of organization. This disease manifests itself in a number of commonly known symptoms. Among these familiar symptoms are: the occurrence of much bypassing because of excessively long lines of command; uncertainty as to whether a person's manager is really the next one up on the organization chart, or the one above him, or even the one above him; uncertainty as to whether a manager's subordinates are really just the ones immediately below him on the organization chart, or perhaps the ones below them as well; too much passing of paper up and down too many levels (the red tape phenomenon); a feeling on the part of subordinates of being too close to their managers as shown on the chart; a feeling of organizational clutter, of managers 'breathing down their subordinates' necks', of too many levels involved in any problem, of too many cooks, of too much interference, of not being allowed to get on with the work in hand.

Consideration of these symptoms raises the question of just how many levels there ought to be in a bureaucratic hierarchy. Another way of asking the same question is to consider what ought to be the length of the vertical line joining two roles in manager–subordinate relationship. Scrutiny of the literature makes it apparent that no general rules have been formulated. Controversy has been framed in terms of the advantage of 'flat' organization as against 'steep' organization, but in none of these arguments has the question even been asked, much less resolved, of how many levels there ought to be.

Three or four levels may be realistic, or even five or six or seven. But most people would consider a hundred levels or even fifty, or perhaps even twenty, to be too many. Why? What is it that determines how many levels there ought to be in any given hierarchy? In considering this question of number of levels it is essential to state what kinds of level or stratum. The usual meaning is that of so-called grades. Grades are strata used for ascribing status to individuals, for stating payment brackets, and for advancing individuals in pay and status. These grading systems commonly become used also for describing the organization of work and management. This second use occurs uncritically and by default. It is a source of enormous confusion. In discussing bureaucratic levels, therefore, we shall confine our attention to work-strata – the strata concerned with work organization and managerial levels.

True managers, quasi-managers, and bureaucratic levels

This problem of how many working levels there ought to be can be illustrated by reference to a number of different types of bureaucratic hierarchy. Here, for example, are descriptions of four lines of command (examination will show them to be based upon gradings) as set out in the manifest organization charts in a factory, in a civil service department, in

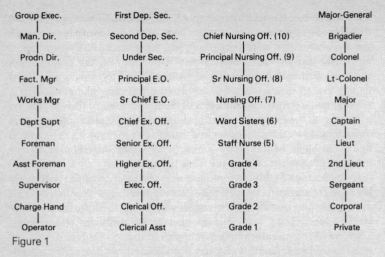

Group Exec.	First Dep. Sec.		Major-General
Man. Dir.	Second Dep. Sec.	Chief Nursing Off. (10)	Brigadier
Prodn Dir.	Under Sec.	Principal Nursing Off. (9)	Colonel
Fact. Mgr	Principal E.O.	Sr Nursing Off. (8)	Lt -Colonel
Works Mgr	Sr Chief E.O.	Nursing Off. (7)	Major
Dept Supt	Chief Ex. Off.	Ward Sisters (6)	Captain
Foreman	Senior Ex. Off.	Staff Nurse (5)	Lieut
Asst Foreman	Higher Ex. Off.	Grade 4	2nd Lieut
Supervisor	Exec. Off.	Grade 3	Sergeant
Charge Hand	Clerical Off.	Grade 2	Corporal
Operator	Clerical Asst	Grade 1	Private

Figure 1

a hospital nursing organization, and in the infantry. Let us examine each in turn in terms of one factor: namely, who is experienced as manager of whom.

In the factory, if you ask the operator who is manager, he will probably ask if what you mean by his manager is his 'boss'. He will then want to know whether you mean his 'boss' or his 'real boss'. The distinction here is between what the operator would call 'my real boss' – the one from whom he feels he stands a chance of getting a decision about himself – and the 'middlemen' or 'straw bosses' who are pushed in between him and his real boss, and through whom he must go if he wants to see his boss. The operator would then probably pick the assistant foreman or foreman as his real boss, with the charge hand and supervisor (and possibly the assistant foreman) as middlemen or straw bosses.

The same phenomenon occurs higher up as well. For example, the invoice department manager might well refer to the accounts-office manager as his manager for 'administrative purposes', but the chief accountant as his direct manager where 'real accounts work' is concerned. Or the vice-presidents of a corporation might work with the deputy president as being their 'coordinative' manager, the president being the real immediate manager who meets directly with them all in the planning and control of corporate activities. Nowhere in the line of command is it possible to predict whether or not a subordinate will experience the next up on the organization chart (the manifest situation) as his real manager (the extant situation).

From the manager's point of view a mirror image is obtained. He may wish to appear well organized, and emphasize that his immediate subordinates are those shown immediately below him on the chart. But he too will admit that it does not necessarily always work quite that way, and that he must often make direct contact with subordinates two and three levels down 'in order to get work done'. This bypassing is seen as necessary even though it might not make good management theory!

In a department in the Civil Service the same answers can be obtained, perhaps couched in slightly different terms. A Senior Executive Officer (SEO) says, 'The CEO is my manager, and I am the manager of the HEOs. But what you probably cannot understand is that in the Civil Service we work in teams. It's not like in industry. The CEO, the HEOs and myself all pitch in together and work as a team.' The meaning of this statement becomes clear when further analysis reveals that the extant situation is that the SEO is really a staff assistant to the CEO and helps him to control and coordinate his (the CEO's) HEO subordinates; that is to say, what is manifestly

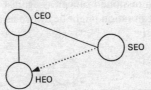

Figure 2

is extantly

Figure 3

Again, as in the industrial example, the same kind of obscurity can be found at any or all levels in the system.

In a nursing organization, a Chief Nursing Officer (CNO) of a hospital group describes her relationship with her manifestly subordinate Principal Nursing Officers (PNOs) as one in which 'I am really the coordinator of a group of colleagues and not really their manager. You can't work in nursing with these strong managerial relationships. You all have to work together in the interests of the patients.' The extant situation is that of the CNO's being a coordinative colleague, in contrast to the manifest manager–subordinate relationship.

And again, in a military organization – in this case the infantry – it is easy to draw the organization chart as shown.

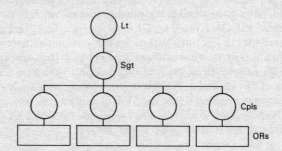

Figure 4

But what does it mean? A corporal – whatever the manifest organization – is not extantly accountable for the performance of the soldiers in his section; he is really an assistant, like a leading hand or a charge hand – someone who helps the real commander to control the platoon. Similarly, the platoon sergeant is not the platoon commander, however the organization chart is drawn. He is an assistant to the platoon commander. It is the platoon commander who is directly accountable for the performance of everyone in his platoon, including the sergeant and the corporals. This accountability is indicated in the distinction between being a commissioned officer as against a non-commissioned officer. The manifest situation might be drawn as above, but the extant situation is more nearly

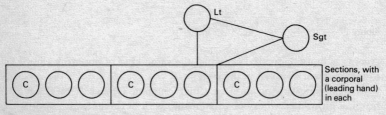

Figure 5

Equally, higher in the line of command it will never be found that a lieutenant-colonel battalion commander has majors as direct fighting subordinates, who in turn have captains, who in turn have lieutenants, who in turn have second lieutenants, and so on down into the NCO levels. They would all be killed while trying to sort out who was giving orders to whom. It is only in managerial text books (and, unfortunately, increasingly in military training now that it is incorporating managerial theory) that military organization takes on this manifest form.

The conclusion from these and other experiences of bureaucratic organization in some twenty different countries, including Eastern Europe, is that it is never possible to tell from an organization chart just who is manager of whom: in effect, it is a wise manager (or subordinate) who knows his own subordinate (or manager).

Just how confusing it can all become can readily be seen the moment the concepts of deputy and assistant are introduced. Is a deputy president, or deputy secretary, or deputy works manager, or deputy catering officer, or deputy engineer, or deputy accountant, and so on ('assistant' for 'deputy' can be substituted in each case) a genuine managerial level,

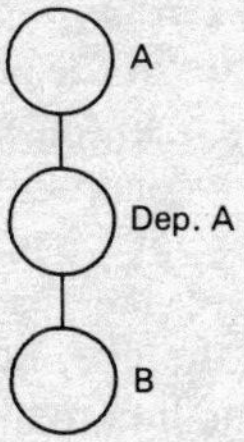

Figure 6

or is he a managerial assistant,

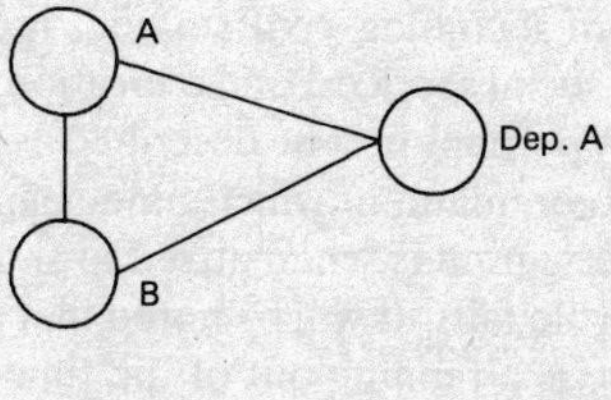

Figure 7

or is he merely someone who acts for the manager when he is away?

E. Jaques   125

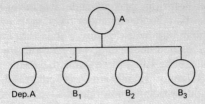

Figure 8   Dep.A   B₁   B₂   B₃

It is usually difficult to know just what is the extant situation – the occupants of the roles being confused. Organizational confusion of this kind is tailor-made for buck-passing, everyone willing to be manager in accord with the manifest organization chart when everything is going well, but retreating to the extant situation when things are going badly.

Time-span boundaries and managerial strata

The manifest picture of bureaucratic organization is a confusing one. There appears to be no rhyme or reason for the structures that are developed, in number of levels, in titling, or even in the meaning to be

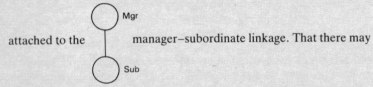

attached to the   manager–subordinate linkage. That there may

be more reasons than meets the eye, however, in the underlying or depth-structure of bureaucratic hierarchies became apparent from an accidental series of observations, hit upon quite separately and independently in Holland and in England during 1957 and 1958.[1] The findings were accidental in the sense that they were discovered in the course of studies being carried out for other purposes. The same findings have since been obtained in many other countries and in all types of bureaucratic system including civil service, industry and commerce, local government, social services, and education.

The findings may perhaps best be described as follows. Figure 9 shows a series of lines of command in which time-spans have been measured for each role. The diagram is schematized to show the time-span bands within which each role falls. It will be noted that as one moves higher up the hierarchy there is a fanning out of the time-spans, a phenomenon

1. In Holland by F. C. Hazekamp and his co-workers at the Dutch General Employers Confederation, and in England at the Glacier Metal Company.

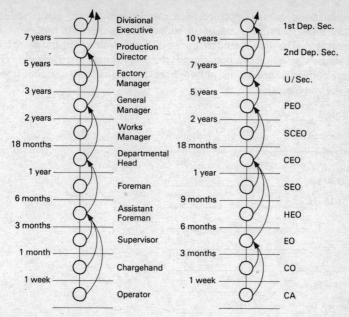

7 years	Divisional Executive		10 years	1st Dep. Sec.
5 years	Production Director		7 years	2nd Dep. Sec.
3 years	Factory Manager		5 years	U/Sec.
2 years	General Manager		2 years	PEO
18 months	Works Manager		18 months	SCEO
1 year	Departmental Head		1 year	CEO
6 months	Foreman		9 months	SEO
3 months	Assistant Foreman		6 months	HEO
1 month	Supervisor		3 months	EO
1 week	Chargehand		1 week	CO
	Operator			CA

Figure 9

which occurs universally. The arrows from each role denote the occupant's feeling of where his real manager is situated as against his manifest manager.

What might at first sight appear to be a rather messy diagram reveals on closer examination the following interesting regularities: everyone in a role below 3-month time-span feels the occupant of the first role above 3-month time-span to be his real manager; between 3-month and 1-year time-span the occupant of the first role above 1-year time-span is felt to be the real manager; between 1- and 2-year time-span, the occupant of the first role above the 2-year time-span is felt to be the real manager; between 2- and 5-year time-span, the occupant of the first role above the 5-year time-span is felt to be the real manager; between 5- and 10-year time-span, the occupant of the first role above the 10-year time-span is felt to be the real manager. Sufficient data have not been obtained to show where the cut-off points are above 10-year time-span, but preliminary findings suggest a boundary at the 20-year level.

This regularity – and it has so far appeared constantly in over 100 studies – points to the existence of a structure underlying bureaucratic organization, a sub-structure or a structure in depth, composed of managerial strata with consistent boundaries measured in time-span as illustrated. The data extend to the over-15-year time-span, and there has been the suggestion of a boundary at the 20-year time-span in some very large employment systems, although this finding has not been confirmed by measurement.

Table 1

Time-span	Stratum
	Str-7
(?) 20 yrs	
10 yrs	Str-6
5 yrs	Str-5
2 yrs	Str-4
1 yr	Str-3
3 mths	Str-2
	Str-1

The data suggest that this apparently general depth-structure of bureaucratic stratification is universally applicable, and that it gives a formula for the design of bureaucratic organization. The formula is easily applied. Measure the level of work in time-span of any role, managerial or not, and that time-span will give the stratum in which that role should be placed. For example, if the time-span is 18 months, that makes it a Str-3 role; or 9 months, a Str-2 role.

If the role is a managerial role, not only can the stratum of the role be ascertained, but also how many strata of organization there should requisitely be, including shop- or office-floor Str-1 roles if any. Measure the level of work in time-span of the top role of the bureaucratic hierarchy – say, chief executive of the hierarchy, or departmental head of a department within the hierarchy – and that time-span will give the stratum in which that role will fall, and therefore the number of organizational strata required below that role. For example, if the role time-spans at 3 years, it makes the bureaucracy a Str-4 institution, and calls for four levels of work organization including the top role and the shop- or office-floor if the work roles go down to that level. If the bottom work role, however, is above the 3-month time-span – say, for example,

6 months, as may be the case in some types of professional institution – then the institution will require only three levels of work organization, namely, Str-4, an intermediate Str-3, and the bottom professional Str-2.[2]

One-stratum distance and optimum manager–subordinate relationships

The occurrence of too many levels in bureaucratic systems creates difficulties, both for the staff members personally and for the effectiveness of the institution. These difficulties can be illustrated by reference to the self-explanatory conception of roles being within the same stratum, or at one-stratum distance (in contiguous strata), or at more-than-one-stratum distance.

Optimum manager–subordinate relationships require that the time-spans of the two roles be such as to place them in contiguous strata – the *one-stratum distance hypothesis*. When the actual differences in level of work between manager and subordinate posts deviate from this pattern of one-stratum distance, certain effects can be observed. Thus, for example, if B is set up as the manager in charge of C, and they both fall within the same stratum rather than within contiguous strata (there is less than one-stratum distance between them), then a full-scale manager–subordinate relationship will not occur. The subordinate will be found to have a great deal of contact with his manager-once-removed. Regular by-passing of the manifest immediate manager occurs. At salary review time it is the manager-once-removed rather than the immediate manager who reviews the subordinate's performance and decides the assessment, taking recommendations from the manifest manager. Similarly, when it is a matter of appointing somebody to the

2. The progression of the time-span boundaries of strata has an interesting geometric–logarithmic quality; above the 3-month time-span they occur at 1 year, 2 years, 5 years, 10 years, 20 years; that is, at approximately equal logarithmic intervals. This progression suggests the operation of a fundamental psychological process in line with the Weber–Fechner law (to produce the psychological experience of arithmetically equal increase in sensation the stimulus must increase geometrically).

If we treat each executive stratum as one arithmetic unit of responsibility, the equitable work-payment scale can then be plotted against those units (see Figure 10). A possible interpretation of the straight-line geometric progression from the 3-month time-span is that logarithmic increases in responsibility input as represented by the logarithmically increasing felt-fair pay are necessary to produce the experience of arithmetic increases in responsibility as represented by each work-stratum. If this interpretation could be validated it would help to explain the shape of the equitable work-payment scale and would strengthen the notion that all work-strata are arithmetic unitary equivalents from the psychological point of view.

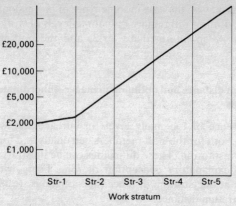

Figure 10

subordinate role, the manager-once-removed tends to involve himself not only in setting policy for the selection but also in the selection itself.

In such circumstances the manifest manager is in the difficult 'middle-man' or 'straw boss' situation. He may try to make up for his muddied authority by throwing his weight around in order to gain a semblance of authority, or else he may just retire into doing the minimum necessary and staying out of trouble. The manager-once-removed (who is the extant manager) is also in trouble in that he cannot have the untrammel-led contact he requires with his extant subordinates. He does have a natural scapegoat in the apparent manager, should anything go wrong. As for the subordinate, his manifest immediate manager is not his real manager. He will be in an uncomfortable relationship with that manager if he attempts to bypass him, and tied up with red tape if he does not. He will not be able to have much confidence in his manifest manager's assessment of his performance.

Some of the worst features not only of red tape in bureaucracy but of autocratic dominance and rigidity, or of laissez-faire withdrawal, are created by the widespread occurrence of this less-than-one-stratum distance situation. If this analysis is correct, then many of the social psychological studies of managerial or supervisory behaviour and styles[3]

3. There are countless such studies; for example, to mention only a few, J. R. P. French, Jr, and R. Snyder (1959), *Leadership and Interpersonal Power*; R. Lippitt *et al.* (1952), *The Dynamics of Power*; P. Lawrence (1958), *The Changing of Organizational Behaviour Patterns*; R. L. Kahn and D. Katz (1953), *Leadership Practices in Relation to Productivity and Morale*.

may need to be looked at again in terms of whether the managers and supervisors were extantly in a manager–subordinate relationship with their so-called subordinates, or only manifestly so. The latter is the most likely, unless proved otherwise.

In short, something less than a full-scale manager–subordinate relationship will be found extantly to exist between the apparent manager and subordinate. But because the manifest situation calls for the apparent manager to act as though he were manager, it can only encourage irresponsible management. Fortunately, most people are sufficiently constructive in their orientation to their work to get on in spite of these organization-stimulated difficulties.

If, on the other hand, as in Figure 11, the manager and his subordinate Sub_1 are in non-contiguous strata (and therefore, at more-than-one-stratum distance), Sub_1 is not experienced as being in the same category as the manager's other subordinates, Sub_2 and Sub_3, who are in the contiguous stratum. Typical of the situation of more-than-one-stratum distance between manager and subordinate roles is the relationship between a manager and his secretary or his personal assistant, the level of work in whose role may be two or more strata lower than that of the manager and one or more strata lower than that of the team of immediate subordinates. Secretaries and personal assistants are not conceived of as part of the immediate command. They are not considered to be full-scale colleagues of the manager's other subordinates. They are assistants to that manager in helping him to do detailed parts of his own tasks such as typing, gathering information, conveying his instructions, etc., which he would have to spend a lot of time doing himself if he did not have such assistance.

But it can happen that a manager's extant operational subordinates are at more-than-one-stratum distance. If they are, they will feel too far away from him; he will have to get down to too much detail in order to

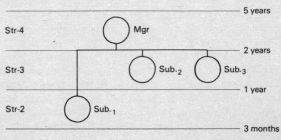

Figure 11

manage them; he will wish that he had an interposed manager between himself and them – and that is in fact the requisite solution to the problem. On the subordinate's side, the manager appears too distant also; he seems impatient, and expects too much and too quick understanding; the subordinate feels it difficult to cope.

In summary, then, what is postulated is the existence of a universal bureaucratic depth-structure, composed of organizational strata with boundaries at levels of work represented by time-spans of 3 months, 1 year, 2 years, 5 years, 10 years, and possibly 20 years and higher. These strata are real strata in the geological sense, with observable boundaries and discontinuity. They are not mere shadings and gradations. Requisite organization of bureaucracy must be designed in such a way that manager–subordinate role relationships will be established at one-stratum distance (except for personal assistants of various kinds).

Part Two **Management and Decision Making**

All organizations have to be managed, and the tasks and the processes which this involves have been the subject of much thought. In particular, attempts have been made to generalize the analyses so that they may be of use to managers in a large variety of organizations in their attempts to manage better. The contributors to this section have tried to present overall principles distilled from their experience, all of which have attracted much support and much criticism.

Fayol (Reading 9) was the first of the modern management writers to propound a theoretical analysis of what managers have to do and by what principles they have to do it; an analysis which has withstood half a century of critical discussion. His principles of authority and responsibility, unity of command, good order, *esprit de corps*, etc. are the common currency of management parlance. Taylor (Reading 10) set out to challenge management with his 'scientific management' approach, which promised increased efficiency through extreme specialization and tight control of tasks (including those of managers as well as workers). His ideas made him a controversial figure in his own day, and he has remained so since, but from him has come the approach to management through time study, work study and industrial engineering, which are important parts of the control procedures of many organizations.

Sloan (Reading 11), from his years of experience as head of the largest industrial corporation in the world – General Motors of America – advocates a basic managerial process of 'coordinated decentralization' which is practised in his organization and has had considerable influence on many others.

Sir Geoffrey Vickers (Reading 12), from his equally long years of experience of management in Britain, presents his analysis of what he considers the most basic managerial skill: the art of judgement.

H. A. Simon (Reading 13) is the founding father of the Carnegie approach to management which focuses on the processes and procedures of decision making. In this tradition is the work of March (Reading 14), on decisions and rational choice, and Lindblom (Reading

15), who demonstrates the inevitably limited rationality of managerial decisions. Vroom (Reading 16) presents a procedure for designing a rational decision-making process to take account of the situation in which the manager is operating.

9 H. Fayol

General Principles of Management

From H. Fayol, *General Industrial Management*, Pitman, 1949, chapter 4, pp. 19–42.

The managerial function finds its only outlet through the members of the organization (body corporate). Whilst the other functions bring into play material and machines the managerial function operates only on the personnel. The soundness and good working order of the body corporate depend on a certain number of conditions termed indiscriminately principles, laws, rules. For preference I shall adopt the term principles whilst dissociating it from any suggestion of rigidity, for there is nothing rigid or absolute in management affairs, it is all a question of proportion. Seldom do we have to apply the same principle twice in identical conditions; allowance must be made for different changing circumstances, for men just as different and changing and for many other variable elements.

Therefore principles are flexible and capable of adaptation to every need; it is a matter of knowing how to make use of them, which is a difficult art requiring intelligence, experience, decision and proportion. Compounded of tact and experience, proportion is one of the foremost attributes of the manager. There is no limit to the number of principles of management, every rule or managerial procedure which strengthens the body corporate or facilitates its functioning has a place among the principles so long, at least, as experience confirms its worthiness. A change in the state of affairs can be responsible for change of rules which had been engendered by that state.

I am going to review some of the principles of management which I have most frequently had to apply, viz.

1. Division of work.
2. Authority.
3. Discipline.
4. Unity of command.
5. Unity of direction.
6. Subordination of individual interests to the general interest.
7. Remuneration.

8. Centralization.
9. Scalar chain (line of authority).
10. Order.
11. Equity.
12. Stability of tenure of personnel.
13. Initiative.
14. *Esprit de corps*.

Division of work

Specialization belongs to the natural order; it is observable in the animal world, where the more highly developed the creature the more highly differentiated its organs; it is observable in human societies where the more important the body corporate[1] the closer is the relationship between structure and function. As society grows, so new organs develop destined to replace the single one performing all functions in the primitive state.

The object of division of work is to produce more and better work with the same effort. The worker always on the same part, the manager concerned always with the same matters, acquire an ability, sureness and accuracy which increase their output. Each change of work brings in its train an adaptation which reduces output. Division of work permits of reduction in the number of objects to which attention and effort must be directed and has been recognized as the best means of making use of individuals and of groups of people. It is not merely applicable to technical work, but without exception to all work involving a more or less considerable number of people and demanding abilities of various types, and it results in specialization of functions and separation of powers. Although its advantages are universally recognized and although possibility of progress is inconceivable without the specialized work of learned men and artists, yet division of work has its limits which experience and a sense of proportion teach us may not be exceeded.

1. '*Body corporate*'. Fayol's term '*corps social*', meaning all those engaged in a given corporate activity in any sphere, is best rendered by this somewhat unusual term becase (*a*) it retains his implied biological metaphor; (*b*) it represents the structure as distinct from the process of organization.

The term will be retained in all contexts where these two requirements have to be met (Translator's note).

Authority and responsibility

Authority is the right to give orders and the power to exact obedience. Distinction must be made between a manager's official authority deriving from office and personal authority, compounded of intelligence, experience, moral worth, ability to lead, past services, etc. In the make-up of a good head personal authority is the indispensable complement of official authority. Authority is not to be conceived of apart from responsibility, that is apart from sanction – reward or penalty – which goes with the exercise of power. Responsibility is a corollary of authority, it is its natural consequence and essential counterpart, and wheresoever authority is exercised responsibility arises.

The need for sanction, which has its origin in a sense of justice, is strengthened and increased by this consideration, that in the general interest useful actions have to be encouraged and their opposite discouraged. Application of sanction to acts of authority forms part of the conditions essential for good management, but it is generally difficult to effect, especially in large concerns. First, the degree of responsibility must be established and then the weight of the sanction. Now, it is relatively easy to establish a workman's responsibility for his acts and a scale of corresponding sanctions; in the case of a foreman it is somewhat difficult, and proportionately as one goes up the scalar chain of business, as work grows more complex, as the number of workers involved increases, as the final result is more remote, it is increasingly difficult to isolate the share of the initial act of authority in the ultimate result and to establish the degree of responsibility of the manager. The measurement of this responsibility and its equivalent in material terms elude all calculation.

Sanction, then, is a question of kind, custom, convention, and judging it one must take into account the action itself, the attendant circumstances and potential repercussions. Judgment demands high moral character, impartiality and firmness. If all these conditions are not fulfilled there is a danger that the sense of responsibility may disappear from the concern.

Responsibility valiantly undertaken and borne merits some consideration; it is a kind of courage everywhere much appreciated. Tangible proof of this exists in the salary level of some industrial leaders, which is much higher than that of civil servants of comparable rank but carrying no responsibility. Nevertheless, generally speaking, responsibility is feared as much as authority is sought after, and fear of responsibility paralyses much initiative and destroys many good qualities. A good leader should possess and infuse into those around him courage to accept responsibility.

The best safeguard against abuse of authority and against weakness on the part of a higher manager is personal integrity and particularly high moral character of such a manager, and this integrity, it is well known, is conferred neither by election nor ownership.

Discipline

Discipline is in essence obedience, application, energy, behaviour and outward marks of respect observed in accordance with the standing agreements between the firm and its employees, whether these agreements have been freely debated or accepted without prior discussion, whether they be written or implicit, whether they derive from the wish of the parties to them or from rules and customs, it is these agreements which determine the formalities of discipline.

Discipline, being the outcome of different varying agreements, naturally appears under the most diverse forms; obligations of obedience, application, energy, behaviour, vary, in effect, from one firm to another, from one group of employees to another, from one time to another. Nevertheless, general opinion is deeply convinced that discipline is absolutely essential for the smooth running of business and that without discipline no enterprise could prosper.

This sentiment is very forcibly expressed in military handbooks, where it runs that 'Discipline constitutes the chief strength of armies.' I would approve unreservedly of this aphorism were it followed by this other, 'Discipline is what leaders make it.' The first one inspires respect for discipline, which is a good thing, but it tends to eclipse from view the responsibility of leaders, which is undesirable, for the state of discipline of any group of people depends essentially on the worthiness of its leaders.

When a defect in discipline is apparent or when relations between superiors and subordinates leave much to be desired, responsibility for this must not be cast heedlessly, and without going further afield, on the poor state of the team, because the ill mostly results from the ineptitude of the leaders. That, at all events, is what I have noted in various parts of France, for I have always found French workmen obedient and loyal provided they are ably led.

In the matter of influence upon discipline, agreements must be set side by side with command. It is important that they be clear and, as far as is possible, afford satisfaction to both sides. This is not easy. Proof of that exists in the great strikes of miners, railwaymen and civil servants which, in these latter years, have jeopardized national life at home and elsewhere and which arose out of agreements in dispute or inadequate legislation.

For half a century a considerable change has been effected in the mode of agreements between a concern and its employees. The agreements of former days fixed by the employer alone are being replaced, in ever increasing measure, by understandings arrived at by discussion between an owner or group of owners and workers' associations. Thus each individual owner's responsibility has been reduced and is further diminished by increasingly frequent State intervention in labour problems. Nevertheless, the setting up of agreements binding a firm and its employees from which disciplinary formalities emanate, should remain one of the chief preoccupations of industrial heads.

The well-being of the concern does not permit, in cases of offence against discipline, of the neglect of certain sanctions capable of preventing or minimizing their recurrence. Experience and tact on the part of a manager are put to the proof in the choice and degree of sanctions to be used, such as remonstrances, warnings, fines, suspensions, demotion, dismissal. Individual people and attendant circumstances must be taken into account. In fine, discipline is respect for agreements which are directed at achieving obedience, application, energy, and the outward marks of respect. It is incumbent upon managers at high levels as much as upon humble employees, and the best means of establishing and maintaining it are:

1. Good superiors at all levels.
2. Agreements as clear and fair as possible.
3. Sanctions (penalties) judiciously applied.

Unity of command

For any action whatsoever, an employee should receive orders from one superior only. Such is the rule of unity of command, arising from general and ever-present necessity and wielding an influence on the conduct of affairs, which to my way of thinking, is at least equal to any other principle whatsoever. Should it be violated, authority is undermined, discipline is in jeopardy, order disturbed and stability threatened. This rule seems fundamental to me and so I have given it the rank of principle. As soon as two superiors wield their authority over the same person or department, uneasiness makes itself felt and should the cause persist, the disorder increases, the malady takes on the appearance of an animal organism troubled by a foreign body, and the following consequences are to be observed: either the dual command ends in disappearance or elimination of one of the superiors and organic well-being is restored, or else the organism continues to wither away. In no case is there adaptation of the social organism to dual command.

Now dual command is extremely common and wreaks havoc in all concerns, large or small, in home and in State. The evil is all the more to be feared in that it worms its way into the social organism on the most plausible pretexts. For instance:

1. In the hope of being better understood or gaining time or to put a stop forthwith to an undesirable practice, a superior S^2 may give orders directly to an employee E without going via the superior S^1. If this mistake is repeated there is dual command with its consequences, viz., hesitation on the part of the subordinate, irritation and dissatisfaction on the part of the superior set aside, and disorder in the work. It will be seen later that it is possible to by-pass the scalar chain when necessary, whilst avoiding the drawbacks of dual command.

2. The desire to get away from the immediate necessity of dividing up authority as between two colleagues, two friends, two members of one family, results at times in dual command reigning at the top of a concern right from the outset. Exercising the same powers and having the same authority over the same men, the two colleagues end up inevitably with dual command and its consequences. Despite harsh lessons, instances of this sort are still numerous. New colleagues count on their mutual regard, common interest and good sense to save them from every conflict, every serious disagreement and, save for rare exceptions, the illusion is short-lived. First an awkwardness makes itself felt, then a certain irritation and, in time, if dual command exists, even hatred. Men cannot bear dual command. A judicious assignment of duties would have reduced the danger without entirely banishing it, for between two superiors on the same footing there must always be some question ill-defined. But it is riding for a fall to set up a business organization with two superiors on equal footing without assigning duties and demarcating authority.

3. Imperfect demarcation of departments also leads to dual command: two superiors issuing orders in a sphere which each thinks his own, constitutes dual command.

4. Constant linking up as between different departments, natural intermeshing of functions, duties often badly defined, create an everpresent danger of dual command. If a knowledgeable superior does not put it in order, footholds are established which later upset and compromise the conduct of affairs.

In all human associations, in industry, commerce, army, home, State, dual command is a perpetual source of conflicts, very grave sometimes, which have special claim on the attention of superiors of all ranks.

Unity of direction

This principle is expressed as: one head and one plan for a group of activities having the same objective. It is the condition essential to unity of action, coordination of strength and focusing of effort. A body with two heads is in the social as in the animal sphere a monster, and has difficulty in surviving. Unity of direction (one head one plan) must not be confused with unity of command (one employee to have orders from one superior only). Unity of direction is provided for by sound organization of the body corporate, unity of command turns on the functioning of the personnel. Unity of command cannot exist without unity of direction, but does not flow from it.

Subordination of individual interest to general interest

This principle calls to mind the fact that in a business the interest of one employee or group of employees should not prevail over that of the concern, that the interest of the home should come before that of its members and that the interest of the State should have pride of place over that of one citizen or group of citizens.

It seems that such an admonition should not need calling to mind. But ignorance, ambition, selfishness, laziness, weakness, and all human passions tend to cause the general interest to be lost sight of in favour of individual interest and a perpetual struggle has to be waged against them. Two interests of a different order, but claiming equal respect, confront each other and means must be found to reconcile them. That represents one of the great difficulties of management. Means of effecting it are:

1. Firmness and good example on the part of superiors.
2. Agreements as fair as is possible.
3. Constant supervision.

Remuneration of personnel

Remuneration of personnel is the price of services rendered. It should be fair and, as far as is possible, afford satisfaction both to personnel and firm (employee and employer). The rate of remuneration depends, firstly, on circumstances independent of the employer's will and employee's worth, viz. cost of living, abundance or shortage of personnel, general business conditions, the economic position of the business, and after that it depends on the value of the employee and mode of payment adopted. Appreciation of the factors dependent on the employer's will and on the value of employees, demands a fairly good knowledge of business, judgment, and impartiality. Later on in connection with selecting personnel we shall deal with assessing the value of employees; here only the mode of payment is under consideration as a factor operating on remuneration. The method of payment can exercise considerable influence on business progress, so the choice of this method is an important problem. It is also a thorny problem which in practice has been solved in widely different ways, of which so far none has proved satisfactory. What is generally looked for in the methods of payment is that:

1. It shall assure fair remuneration.
2. It shall encourage keenness by rewarding well-directed effort.
3. It shall not lead to over-payment going beyond reasonable limits.

I am going to examine briefly the modes of payment in use for workers, junior managers, and higher managers.

Workers

The various modes of payment in use for workers are:

1. Time rates.
2. Job rates.
3. Piece rates.

These three modes of payment may be combined and give rise to important variations by the introduction of bonuses, profit-sharing schemes, payment in kind, and non-financial incentives.

1. *Time rates*. Under this system the workman sells the employer, in return for a pre-determined sum, a day's work under definite conditions. This system has the disadvantage of conducing to negligence and of

demanding constant supervision. It is inevitable where the work done is not susceptible to measurement and in effect it is very common.

2. *Job rates*. Here payment made turns upon the execution of a definite job set in advance and may be independent of the length of the job. When payment is due only on condition that the job be completed during the normal work spell, this method merges into time rate. Payment by daily job does not require as close a supervision as payment by the day, but it has the drawback of levelling the output of good workers down to that of mediocre ones. The good ones are not satisfied, because they feel that they could earn more; the mediocre ones find the task set too heavy.

3. *Piece rates*. Here payment is related to work done and there is no limit. This system is often used in workshops where a large number of similar articles have to be made, and is found where the product can be measured by weight, length or cubic capacity, and in general is used wherever possible. It is criticized on the grounds of emphasizing quantity at the expense of quality and of provoking disagreements when rates have to be revised in the light of manufacturing improvements. Piecework becomes contract work when applied to an important unit of work. To reduce the contractor's risk, sometimes there is added to the contract price a payment for each day's work done.

Generally, piece rates give rise to increased earnings which act for some time as a stimulus, then finally a system prevails in which this mode of payment gradually approximates to time rates for a pre-arranged sum.

The above three modes of payment are found in all large concerns; sometimes time rates prevail, sometimes one of the other two. In a workshop the same workman may be seen working now on piece rates, now on time rates. Each one of these methods has its advantages and drawbacks, and their effectiveness depends on circumstances and the ability of superiors. Neither method nor rate of payment absolves management from competence and tact, and keenness of workers and peaceful atmosphere of the workshop depend largely upon it.

Bonuses

To arouse the worker's interest in the smooth running of the business, sometimes an increment in the nature of a bonus is added to the time, job or piece rate: for good time keeping, hard work, freedom from machine breakdown, output, cleanliness, etc. The relative importance, nature and qualifying conditions of these bonuses are very varied. There are to be found the small daily supplement, the monthly sum, the annual award, shares or portions of shares distributed to the most meritorious, and also even profit-sharing schemes such as, for example, certain monetary allocations distributed annually among workers in some large firms. Several French collieries started some years back the granting of a bonus proportional to profits distributed or to extra profits. No contract is required from the workers save that the earning of the bonus is subject to certain conditions, for instance, that there shall have been no strike during the year, or that absenteeism shall not have exceeded a given number of days. This type of bonus introduced an element of profit-sharing into miners' wages without any prior discussion as between workers and employer. The workman did not refuse a gift, largely gratuitous, on the part of the employer, that is, the contract was a unilateral one. Thanks to a successful trading period the yearly wages have been appreciably increased by the operation of the bonus. But what is to happen in lean times? This interesting procedure is as yet too new to be judged, but obviously it is no general solution of the problem.

In the mining industry there is another type of bonus, dependent upon the selling price of coal. The sliding scale of wages depending on a basic rate plus a bonus proportionate to the local selling price, which had long flourished in Wales, but was discontinued when minimum wages legislation came into force, is today the principle regulating the payment of miners in the Nord and Pas de Calais *départements*, and has also been adopted in the Loire region. This system established a certain fixed relationship between the prosperity of the colliery and the miner's wage. It is criticized on the grounds that it conduces to limitation of production in order to raise selling price. So we see that it is necessary to have recourse to a variety of methods in order to settle wages questions. The problem is far from being settled to everyone's satisfaction and all solutions are hazardous.

Profit-sharing

Workers. The idea of making workers share in profits is a very attractive one and it would seem that it is from there that harmony as between Capital and Labour should come. But the practical formula for such sharing has not yet been found. Workers' profit-sharing has hitherto come up against insurmountable difficulties of application in the case of large concerns. Firstly, let us note that it cannot exist in enterprises having no monetary objective (State services, religions, philanthropic, scientific societies) and also that it is not possible in the case of businesses running at a loss. Thus profit-sharing is excluded from a great number of concerns. There remain the prosperous business concerns and of these latter the desire to reconcile and harmonize workers' and employers' interests is nowhere so great as in French mining and metallurgical industries. Now, in these industries I know of no clear application of workers' profit-sharing, whence it may be concluded forthwith that the matter is difficult, if not impossible. It is very difficult indeed. Whether a business is making a profit or not the worker must have an immediate wage assured him, and a system which would make workers' payment depend entirely on eventual future profit is unworkable. But perhaps a part of wages might come from business profits. Let us see. Viewing all contingent factors, the worker's greater or lesser share of activity or ability in the final outcome of a large concern is impossible to assess and is, moreover, quite insignificant. The portion accruing to him of distributed dividend would at the most be a few centimes on a wage of five francs for instance, that is to say the smallest extra effort, the stroke of a pick or of a file operating directly on his wage, would prove of greater advantage to him. Hence the worker has no interest in being rewarded by a share in profits proportionate to the effect he has upon profits. It is worthy of note that, in most large concerns, wage increases, operative now for some twenty years, represent a total sum greater than the amount of capital shared out. In effect, unmodified real profit-sharing by workers of large concerns has not yet entered the sphere of practical business politics.

Junior managers. Profit-sharing for foremen, superintendents, engineers, is scarcely more advanced than for workers. Nevertheless, the influence of these employees on the results of a business is quite considerable, and if they are not consistently interested in profits the only reason is that the basis for participation is difficult to establish. Doubtless managers have no need of monetary incentive to carry out their duties, but they are not indifferent to material satisfactions and it must be acknowledged that the hope of extra profit is capable of arousing their enthusiasm. So employees at middle levels should, where possible, be induced to have an interest in profits. It is relatively easy in businesses which are starting out or on trial, where exceptional effort can yield outstanding results. Sharing may then be applied to overall business profits or merely to the running of the particular department of the employee in question. When the business is of long standing and well run the zeal of a junior manager is scarcely apparent in the general outcome, and it is very hard to establish a useful basis on which he may participate. In fact, profit-sharing among junior managers in France is very rare in large concerns. Production or workshop output bonuses – not to be confused with profit-sharing – are much more common.

Higher managers. It is necessary to go right up to top management to find a class of employee with frequent interest in the profits of large-scale French concerns. The head of the business, in view of his knowledge, ideas and actions, exerts considerable influence on general results, so it is quite natural to try and provide him with an interest in them. Sometimes it is possible to establish a close connection between his personal activity and its effects. Nevertheless, generally speaking, there exist other influences quite independent of the personal capability of the manager which can influence results to a greater extent than can his personal activity. If the manager's salary were exclusively dependent upon profits, it might at times be reduced to nothing. There are, besides, businesses being built up, wound up or merely passing through temporary crisis, wherein management depends no less on talent than in the case of prosperous ones, and wherein profit-sharing cannot be a basis for remuneration for the manager. In fine, senior civil servants cannot be paid on a profit-sharing basis. Profit-sharing, then, for either higher managers or workers, is not a general rule of remuneration. To sum up, then: profit-sharing is a mode of payment capable of giving excellent results in certain cases, but is not a general rule. It does not seem to me possible, at least for the present, to count on this mode of payment for appeasing conflict between Capital and Labour. Fortunately, there are other means which hitherto have been sufficient to maintain relative social quiet. Such methods have not lost their power and it is up to managers to study them, apply them, and make them work well.

Payment in kind, welfare work, non-financial incentives

Whether wages are made up of money only or whether they include various additions such as heating, light, housing, food, is of little consequence provided that the employee be satisfied.

From another point of view, there is no doubt that a business will be better served in proportion as its employees are more energetic, better educated, more conscientious and more permanent. The employer should have regard, if merely in the interests of the business, for the health, strength, education, morale, and stability of his personnel.

These elements of smooth running are not acquired in the workshop alone, they are formed and developed as well, and particularly, outside it, in the home and school, in civil and religious life. Therefore, the employer comes to be concerned with his employees outside the works and here the question of proportion comes up again. Opinion is greatly divided on this point. Certain unfortunate experiments have resulted in some employers stopping short their interest at the works gate and at the regulation of wages. The majority consider that the employer's activity may be used to good purpose outside the factory confines provided that there be discretion and prudence, that it be sought after rather than imposed, be in keeping with the general level of education and taste of those concerned and that it have absolute respect for their liberty. It must be benevolent collaboration, not tyrannical stewardship, and therein lies an indispensable condition of success.

The employer's welfare activities may be of various kinds. In the works they bear on matters of hygiene and comfort: ventilation, lighting, cleanliness, canteen facilities. Outside the works they bear on housing accommodation, feeding, education, and training. Provident schemes come under this head.

Non-financial incentives only come in in the case of large scale concerns and may be said to be almost exclusively in the realm of government work. Every mode of payment likely to make the personnel more valuable and improve its lot in life, and also to inspire keenness on the part of employees at all levels, should be a matter for managers' constant attention.

Centralization

Like division of work, centralization belongs to the natural order; this turns on the fact that in every organism, animal or social, sensations converge towards the brain or directive part, and from the brain or directive part orders are sent out which set all parts of the organism in movement. Centralization is not a system of management good or bad of itself, capable of being adopted or discarded at the whim of managers or of circumstances; it is always present to a greater or less extent. The question of centralization or decentralization, is a simple question of proportion, it is a matter of finding the optimum degree for the particular concern. In small firms, where the manager's orders go directly to subordinates, there is absolute centralization; in large concerns, where a long scalar chain is interposed between manager and lower grades, orders and counter-information, too, have to go through a series of intermediaries. Each employee, intentionally or unintentionally, puts something of himself into the transmission and execution of orders and of information received too. He does not operate merely as a cog in a machine. What appropriate share of initiative may be left to intermediaries depends on the personal character of the manager, on his moral worth, on the reliability of his subordinates, and also on the condition of the business. The degree of centralization must vary according to different cases. The objective to pursue is the optimum utilization of all faculties of the personnel.

If the moral worth of the manager, his strength, intelligence, experience and swiftness of thought allow him to have a wide span of activities he will be able to carry centralization quite far and reduce his seconds in command to mere executive agents. If, conversely, he prefers to have greater recourse to the experience, opinions, and counsel of his colleagues whilst reserving to himself the privilege of giving general directives, he can effect considerable decentralization.

Seeing that both absolute and relative values of manager and employees are constantly changing, it is understandable that the degree of centralization or decentralization may itself vary constantly. It is a problem to be solved according to circumstances, to the best satisfaction of the interests involved. It arises, not only in the case of higher authority, but for superiors at all levels and not one but can extend or confine, to some extent, his subordinates' initiative.

The finding of the measure which shall give the best overall yield: that is the problem of centralization or decentralization. Everything which goes to increase the importance of the subordinate's role is decentralization, everything which goes to reduce it is centralization.

Scalar chain

The scalar chain is the chain of superiors ranging from the ultimate authority to the lowest ranks. The line of authority is the route followed – via every link in the chain – by all communications which start from or go to the ultimate authority. This path is dictated both by the need for some transmission and by the principle of unity of command, but it is not always the swiftest. It is even at times disastrously lengthy in large concerns, notably in governmental ones. Now, there are many activities whose success turns on speedy execution, hence respect for the line of authority must be reconciled with the need for swift action.

Let us imagine that section F has to be put into contact with section P in a business whose scalar chain is represented by the double ladder G-A-Q thus

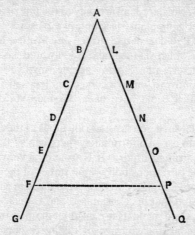

By following the line of authority the ladder must be climbed from F to A and then descended from A to P, stopping at each rung, then ascended again from P to A, and descended once more from A to F, in order to get back to the starting point. Evidently it is much simpler and quicker to go directly from F to P by making use of FP as a 'gang plank' and that is what is most often done. The scalar principle will be safeguarded if managers E and O have authorized their respective subordinates F and P to treat directly, and the position will be fully regularized if F and P inform their respective superiors forthwith of what they have agreed upon. So long as F and P remain in agreement, and so long as their actions are approved by their immediate superiors, direct contact may be maintained, but from the instant that agreement ceases or there is no approval from the superiors direct contact comes to an end, and the scalar chain is straightway resumed. Such is the actual procedure to be observed in the great majority of businesses. It provides for the usual exercise of some measure of initiative at all levels of authority. In the small concern, the general interest, viz. that of the concern proper, is easy to grasp, and the employer is present to recall this interest to those tempted to lose sight of it. In government enterprise the general interest is such a complex, vast, remote thing, that it is not easy to get a clear idea of it, and for the majority of civil servants the employer is somewhat mythical and unless the sentiment of general interest be constantly revived by higher authority, it becomes blurred and weakened and each section tends to regard itself as its own aim and end and forgets that it is only a cog in a big machine, all of whose parts must work in concert. It becomes isolated, cloistered, aware only of the line of authority.

The use of the 'gang plank' is simple, swift, sure. It allows the two employees F and P to deal at one sitting, and in a few hours, with some question or other which via the scalar chain would pass through twenty transmissions, inconvenience many people, involve masses of paper, lose weeks or months to get to a conclusion less satisfactory generally than the one which could have been obtained via direct contact as between F and P.

Is it possible that such practices, as ridiculous as they are devastating, could be in current use? Unfortunately there can be little doubt of it in government department affairs. It is usually acknowledged that the chief cause is fear of responsibility. I am rather of the opinion that it is insufficient executive capacity on the part of those in charge. If supreme authority A insisted that his assistants B and L made use of the 'gang plank' themselves and made its use incumbent upon their subordinates C and M, the habit and courage of taking responsibility would be established and at the same time the custom of using the shortest path.

It is an error to depart needlessly from the line of authority, but it is an even greater one to keep to it when detriment to the business ensues. The latter may attain extreme gravity in certain conditions. When an employee is obliged to choose between the two practices, and it is impossible for him to take advice from his superior, he should be courageous enough and feel free enough to adopt the line dicated by the general interest. But for him to be in this frame of mind there must have been previous precedent, and his superiors must have set him the example – for example must always come from above.

Order

The formula is known in the case of material things 'A place for everything and everything in its place'. The formula is the same for human order 'A place for everyone and everyone in his place'.

Material order

In accordance with the preceding definition, so that material order shall prevail, there must be a place appointed for each thing and each thing must be in its appointed place. Is that enough? Is it not also necessary that the place shall have been well chosen? The object of order must be avoidance of loss of material, and for this object to be completely realized not only must things be in their place suitably arranged but also the place must have been chosen so as to facilitate all activities as much as possible. If this last condition be unfulfilled, there is merely the appearance of order. Appearance of order may cover over real disorder. I have seen a works yard used as a store for steel ingots in which the material was well stacked, evenly arranged and clean and which gave a pleasing impression of orderliness. On close inspection it could be noted that the same heap included five or six types of steel intended for different manufacture all mixed up together. Whence useless handling, lost time, risk of mistakes because each thing was not in its place. It happens, on the other hand, that the appearance of disorder may actually be true order. Such is the case with papers scattered about at a master's whim which a well-meaning but incompetent servant re-arranges and stacks in neat piles. The master can no longer find his way about them. Perfect order presupposes a judiciously chosen place and the appearance of order is merely a false or imperfect image of real order. Cleanliness is a corollary of orderliness, there is no appointed place for dirt. A diagram representing the entire premises divided up into as many sections as there are employees responsible facilitates considerably the establishing and control of order.

Social order

For social order to prevail in a concern there must, in accordance with the definition, be an appointed place for every employee and every employee be in his appointed place. Perfect order requires, further, that the place be suitable for the employee and the employee for the place – in English idom, 'The right man in the right place'.

Thus understood, social order presupposes the successful execution of the two most difficult managerial activities: good organization and good selection. Once the posts essential to the smooth running of the business have been decided upon and those to fill such posts have been selected, each employee occupies that post wherein he can render most service. Such is perfect social order 'A place for each one and each one in his place'. That appears simple, and naturally we are so anxious for it to be so that when we hear for the twentieth time a government departmental head assert this principle, we conjure up straightway a concept of perfect administration. This is a mirage.

Social order demands precise knowledge of the human requirements and resources of the concern and a constant balance between these requirements and resources. Now this balance is most difficult to establish and maintain and all the more difficult the bigger the business, and when it has been upset and individual interests resulted in neglect or sacrifice of the general interest, when ambition, nepotism, favouritism, or merely ignorance, has multiplied positions without good reason or filled them with incompetent employees, much talent and strength of will and more persistence than current instability of ministerial appointments presupposes, are required in order to sweep away abuses and restore order.

As applied to government enterprise the principle of order 'A place for each one and each one in his place' takes on an astounding breadth. It means national responsibility towards each and all, everyone's destiny mapped out, national solidarity, the whole problem of society. I will stay no longer over this disturbing extension of the principle of order. In private business and especially in those of restricted scope it is easier to maintain proportion as between selection and requirements. As in the case of orderly material arrangement, a chart or plan makes the establishment and control of human arrangement much more easy. This represents the personnel in entirety, and all sections of the concern together with the people occupying them. This chart will come up again in the chapter on Organization [not included].

Equity

Why equity and not justice? Justice is putting into execution established conventions, but conventions cannot foresee everything, they need to be interpreted or their inadequacy supplemented. For the personnel to be encouraged to carry out its duties with all the devotion and loyalty of which it is capable it must be treated with kindliness, and equity results from the combination of kindliness and justice. Equity excludes neither forcefulness nor sternness and the application of it requires much good sense, experience and good nature.

Desire for equity and equality of treatment are aspirations to be taken into account in dealing with employees. In order to satisfy these requirements as much as possible without neglecting any principle or losing sight of the general interest, the head of the business must frequently summon up his highest faculties. He should strive to instil sense of equity throughout all levels of the scalar chain.

Stability of tenure of personnel

Time is required for an employee to get used to new work and succeed in doing it well, always assuming that he possesses the requisite abilities. If when he has got used to it, or before then, he is removed, he will not have had time to render worthwhile service. If this be repeated indefinitely the work will never be properly done. The undesirable consequences of such insecurity of tenure are especially to be feared in large concerns, where the settling in of managers is generally a lengthy matter. Much time is needed indeed to get to know men and things in a large concern in order to be in a position to decide on a plan of action, to gain confidence in oneself and inspire it in others. Hence it has often been recorded that a mediocre manager who stays is infinitely preferable to outstanding managers who merely come and go.

Generally the managerial personnel of prosperous concerns is stable, that of unsuccessful ones is unstable. Instability of tenure is at one and the same time cause and effect of bad running. The apprenticeship of a higher manager is generally a costly matter. Nevertheless, changes of personnel are inevitable; age, illness, retirement, death, disturb the human make-up of the firm; certain employees are no longer capable of carrying out their duties, whilst others become fit to assume greater responsibilities. In common with all the other principles, therefore, stability of tenure of personnel is also a question of proportion.

Initiative

Thinking out a plan and ensuring its success is one of the keenest satisfactions for an intelligent man to experience. It is also one of the most powerful stimulants of human endeavour. This power of thinking out and executing is what is called initiative, and freedom to propose and to execute belongs, too, each in its way, to initiative. At all levels of the organizational ladder zeal and energy on the part of employees are augmented by initiative. The initiative of all, added to that of the manager, and supplementing it if need be, represents a great source for strength for business. This is particularly apparent at difficult times; hence it is essential to encourage and develop this capacity to the full.

Much tact and some integrity are required to inspire and maintain everyone's initiative, within the limits imposed, by respect for authority and for discipline. The manager must be able to sacrifice some personal vanity in order to grant this sort of satisfaction to subordinates. Other things being equal, moreover, a manager able to permit the exercise of initiative on the part of subordinates is infinitely superior to one who cannot do so.

Esprit de corps

'Union is strength.' Business heads would do well to ponder on this proverb. Harmony, union among the personnel of a concern, is great strength in that concern. Effort, then, should be made to establish it. Among the countless methods in use I will single out specially one principle to be observed and two pitfalls to be avoided. The principle to be observed is unity of command; the dangers to be avoided are (1) a misguided interpretation of the motto 'divide and rule', (2) the abuse of written communications.

1 Personnel must not be split up

Dividing enemy forces to weaken them is clever, but dividing one's own team is a grave sin against the business. Whether this error results from inadequate managerial capacity or imperfect grasp of things, or from egoism which sacrifices general interest to personal interest, it is always reprehensible because harmful to the business. There is no merit in sowing dissension among subordinates; any beginner can do it. On the contrary, real talent is needed to coordinate effort, encourage keenness, use each man's abilities, and reward each one's merit without arousing possible jealousies and disturbing harmonious relations.

2 Abuse of written communications

In dealing with a business matter or giving an order which requires explanation to complete it, usually it is simpler and quicker to do so verbally than in writing. Besides, it is well known that differences and misunderstandings which a conversation could clear up, grow more bitter in writing. Thence it follows that, wherever possible, contacts should be verbal; there is a gain in speed, clarity and harmony. Nevertheless, it happens in some firms that employees of neighbouring departments with numerous points of contact, or even employees within a department, who could quite easily meet, only communicate with each other in writing. Hence arise increased work and complications and delays harmful to the business. At the same time, there is to be observed a certain animosity prevailing between different departments or different employees within a department. The system of written communications usually brings this result. There is a way of putting an end to this deplorable system and that is to forbid all communications in writing which could easily and advantageously be replaced by verbal ones. There again, we come up against a question of proportion.

It is not merely by the satisfactory results of harmony obtaining as between employees of the same department that the power of unity is shown: commercial agreements, unions, associations of every kind, play an important part in business management.

The part played by association has increased remarkably in half a century. I remember, in 1860, workers of primary industries without cohesion, without common bond, a veritable cloud of individual dust particles; and out of that the union has produced collective associations, meeting employers on equal terms. At that same time, bitter rivalry prevailed between large firms, closely similar, which has given place gradually to friendly relations, permitting of the settlement of most common interests by joint agreement. It is the beginning of a new era which already has profoundly modified both habits and ideas, and industrial heads should take this development into account.

There I bring to an end this review of principles, not because the list is exhausted – this list has no precise limits – but because to me it seems at the moment especially useful to endow management theory with a dozen or so well-established principles, on which it is appropriate to concentrate general discussion. The foregoing principles are those to which I have most often had recourse. I have simply expressed my personal opinion in connection with them. Are they to have a place in the management code which is to be built up? General discussion will show.

This code is indispensable. Be it a case of commerce, industry, politics, religion, war or philanthropy, in every concern there is a management function to be performed, and for its performance there must be principles, that is to say acknowledged truths regarded as proven on which to rely. And it is the code which represents the sum total of these truths at any given moment.

Surprise might be expressed at the outset that the eternal moral principles, the laws of the Decalogue and Commandments of the Church are not sufficient guide for the manager, and that a special code is needed. The explanation is this: the higher laws of religious or moral order envisage the individual only, or else interests which are not of this world, whereas management principles aim at the success of associations of individuals and at the satisfying of economic interests. Given that the aim is different, it is not surprising that the means are not the same. There is no identity, so there is no contradiction. Without principles one is in darkness and chaos; interest, experience and proportion are still very handicapped, even with the best principles. The principle is the lighthouse fixing the bearings but it can only serve those who already know the way into port.

10 F. W. Taylor

Scientific Management[1]

From F. Taylor, *Scientific Management*, Harper & Row, 1947, pp. 39–73.

What I want to try to prove to you and make clear to you is that the principles of scientific management when properly applied, and when a sufficient amount of time has been given to make them really effective, must in all cases produce far larger and better results, both for the employer and the employees, than can possibly be obtained under even this very rare type of management which I have been outlining, namely, the management of 'initiative and incentive', in which those on the management's side deliberately give a very large incentive to their workmen, and in return the workmen respond by working to the very best of their ability at all times in the interest of their employers.

I want to show you that scientific management is even far better than this rare type of management.

The first great advantage which scientific management has over the management of initiative and incentive is that under scientific management the initiative of the workmen – that is, their hard work, their good will, their ingenuity – is obtained practically with absolute regularity, while under even the best of the older type of management this initiative is only obtained spasmodically and somewhat irregularly. This obtaining, however, of the initiative of the workmen is the lesser of the two great causes which make scientific management better for both sides than the older type of management. By far the greater gain under scientific management comes from the new, the very great and the extraordinary burdens and duties which are voluntarily assumed by those on the management's side.

These new burdens and new duties are so unusual and so great that they are to the men used to managing under the old school almost inconceivable. These duties and burdens voluntarily assumed under scientific management, by those on the management's side, have been divided and classified into four different groups and these four types of new duties assumed by the management have (rightly or wrongly) been called the 'principles of scientific management'.

1. Testimony to the House of Representatives Committee, 1912.

The first of these four groups of duties taken over by the management is the deliberate gathering in on the part of those on the management's side of all of the great mass of traditional knowledge, which in the past has been in the heads of the workmen, and in the physical skill and knack of the workmen, which they have acquired through years of experience. The duty of gathering in of all this great mass of traditional knowledge and then recording it, tabulating it and, in many cases, finally reducing it to laws, rules and even to mathematical formulae, is voluntarily assumed by the scientific managers. And later, when these laws, rules and formulae are applied to the everyday work of all the workmen of the establishment, through the intimate and hearty cooperation of those on the management's side, they invariably result, first, in producing a very much larger output per man, as well as an output of a better and higher quality; and, second, in enabling the company to pay much higher wages to their workmen; and, third, in giving to the company a larger profit. The first of these principles, then, may be called the development of a science to replace the old rule-of-thumb knowledge of the workmen; that is, the knowledge which the workmen had, and which was, in many cases, quite as exact as that which is finally obtained by the management, but which the workmen nevertheless in nine hundred and ninety-nine cases out of a thousand kept in their heads, and of which there was no permanent or complete record.

A very serious objection has been made to the use of the word 'science' in this connection. I am much amused to find that this objection comes chiefly from the professors of this country. They resent the use of the word science for anything quite so trivial as the ordinary, every-day affairs of life. I think the proper answer to this criticism is to quote the definition recently given by a professor who is, perhaps, as generally recognized as a thorough scientist as any man in the country – President McLaurin, of the Institute of Technology, of Boston. He recently defined the word science as 'classified or organized knowledge of any kind'. And surely the gathering in of knowledge which, as previously stated, has existed, but which was in an unclassified condition in the minds of workmen, and then the reducing of this knowledge to laws and rules and formulae, certainly represents the organization and classification of knowledge, even though it may not meet with the approval of some people to have it called science.

The second group of duties which are voluntarily assumed by those on the management's side, under scientific management, is the scientific selection and then the progressive development of the workmen. It becomes the duty of those on the management's side to deliberately study the character, the nature, and the performance of each workman with a view to finding out his limitations on the one hand, but even more important, his possibilities for development on the other hand; and then, as deliberately and as systematically to train and help and teach this workman, giving him, wherever it is possible, those opportunities for advancement which will finally enable him to do the highest and most interesting and most profitable class of work for which his natural abilities fit him, and which are open to him in the particular company in which he is employed. This scientific selection of the workman and his development is not a single act; it goes on from year to year and is the subject of continual study on the part of the management.

The third of the principles of scientific management is the bringing of the science and the scientifically selected and trained workmen together. I say 'bringing together' advisedly, because you may develop all the science that you please, and you may scientifically select and train workmen just as much as you please, but unless some man or some men bring the science and the workman together all your labor will be lost. We are all of us so constituted that about three-quarters of the time we will work according to whatever method suits us best; that is, we will practice the science or we will not practice it; we will do our work in accordance with the laws of the science or in our own old way, just as we see fit unless someone is there to see that we do it in accordance with the principles of the science. Therefore I use advisedly the words 'bringing the science and the workman together'. It is unfortunate, however, that this word 'bringing' has rather a disagreeable sound, a rather forceful sound; and, in a way, when it is first heard it puts one out of touch with what we have come to look upon as the modern tendency. The time for using the word 'bringing', with a sense of forcing, in relation to most matters, has gone by; but I think that I may soften this word down in its use in this particular case by saying that nine-tenths of the trouble with those of us who have been engaged in helping people to change from the older type of management to the new management – that is, to scientific management – that nine-tenths of our trouble has been to 'bring' those on the management's side to do their fair share of the work and only one-tenth of our trouble has come on the workman's side. Invariably we find very great opposition on the part of those on the management's side to do their new duties and comparatively little opposition on the part of the workmen to cooperate in doing their new duties. So that the word 'bringing' applies much more forcefully to those on the management's side than to those on the workman's side.

The fourth of the principles of scientific management is perhaps the most difficult of all of the four principles of scientific management for the average man to understand. It consists of an almost equal division of the actual work of the establishment between the workmen, on the one hand, and the management, on the other hand. That is, the work which under the old type of management practically all was done by the workman, under the new is divided into two great divisions, and one of these divisions is deliberately handed over to those on the management's side. This new division of work, this new share of the work assumed by those on the management's side, is so great that you will, I think, be able to understand it better in a numerical way when I tell you that in a machine shop, which, for instance, is doing an intricate business – I do not refer to a manufacturing company, but, rather, to an engineering company; that is, a machine shop which builds a variety of machines and is not engaged in manufacturing them, but, rather, in constructing them – will have one man on the management's side to every three workmen; that is, this immense share of the work – one-third – has been deliberately taken out of the workman's hands and handed over to those on the management's side. And it is due to this actual sharing of the work between the two sides more than to any other one element that there has never (until this last summer) been a single strike under scientific management. In a machine shop, again, under this new type of management there is hardly a single act or piece of work done by any workman in the shop which is not preceded and followed by some act on the part of one of the men in management. All day long every workman's acts are dovetailed in between corresponding acts of the management. First, the workman does something, and then a man on the management's side does something, and then the workman does something; and under this intimate, close, personal cooperation between the two sides it becomes practically impossible to have a serious quarrel.

Of course I do not wish to be understood that there are never any quarrels under scientific management. There are some, but they are the very great exception, not the rule. And it is perfectly evident that while the workmen are learning to work under this new system, and while the management is learning to work under this new system, while they are both learning, each side to cooperate in this intimate way with the other, there is plenty of chance for disagreement and for quarrels and misunderstandings, but after both sides realize that it is utterly impossible to turn out the work of the establishment at the proper rate of speed and have it correct without this intimate, personal cooperation, when both sides realize that it is utterly impossible for either one to be successful without the intimate, brotherly cooperation of the other, the friction, the disagreements, and quarrels are reduced to a minimum. So I think that scientific management can be justly and truthfully characterized as management in which harmony is the rule rather than discord.

There is one illustration of the application of the principles of scientific management with which all of us are familiar and with which most of us have been familiar since we were small boys, and I think this instance represents one of the best illustrations of the application of the principles of scientific management. I refer to the management of a first-class American baseball team. In such a team you will find almost all of the elements of scientific management.

You will see that the science of doing every little act that is done by every player on the baseball field has been developed. Every single element of the game of baseball has been the subject of the most intimate, the closest study of many men, and finally, the best way of doing each act that takes place on the baseball field has been fairly well agreed upon and established as a standard throughout the country. The players have not only been told the best way of making each important motion or play, but they have been taught, coached and trained to it through months of drilling. And I think that every man who has watched first-class play, or who knows anything of the management of the modern baseball team, realizes fully the utter impossibility of winning with the best team of individual players that was ever gotten together unless every man on the team obeys the signals or orders of the coach and obeys them at once when the coach gives those orders; that is, without the intimate cooperation between all members of the team and the management, which is characteristic of scientific management.

Now, I have so far merely made assertions; I have merely stated facts in a dogmatic way. The most important assertion I have made is that when a company, when the men of a company and the management of a company have undergone the mental revolution that I have referred to earlier in my testimony, and that when the principles of scientific management have been applied in a correct way in any particular occupation or industry that the results must, inevitably, in all cases, be far greater and better than they could possibly be under the best of the older types of management, even under the especially fine management of 'initiative and incentive', which I have tried to outline.

I want to try and prove the above-stated fact to you gentlemen. I want to try now and make good in this assertion. My only hope of doing so lies in showing you that whenever these four principles are correctly applied to work, either large or small, to work which is either of the most elementary or the most intricate character, that inevitably results follow which are not only greater, but enormously greater, than it is possible to accomplish under the old type of management. Now, in order to make this clear I want to show the application of the four principles first to the most elementary, the simplest kind of work that I know of, and then to give a series of further illustrations of one class of work after another, each a little more difficult and a little more intricate than the work which preceded it, until I shall finally come to an illustration of the application of these same principles to about the most intricate type of mechanical work that I know of. And in all of these illustrations I hope that you will look for and see the application of the four principles I have described. Other elements of the stories may interest you, but the thing that I hope you will see and have before you in all cases is the effect of the four following elements in each particular case: First, the development of the science, i.e. the gathering in on the part of those on the management's side of all the knowledge which in the past has been kept in the heads of the workmen; second, the scientific selection and the progressive development of the workmen; third, the bringing of the science and the scientifically selected and trained men together; and, fourth, the constant and intimate cooperation which always occurs between the men on the management's side and the workmen.

I ordinarily begin with a description of the pig-iron handler. For some reason, I don't know exactly why, this illustration has been talked about a great deal, so much, in fact, that some people seem to think that the whole of scientific management consists in handling pig-iron. The only reason that I ever gave this illustration, however, was that pig-iron handling is the simplest kind of human effort; I know of nothing that is quite so simple as handling pig-iron. A man simply stoops down and with his hands picks up a piece of iron, and then walks a short distance and drops it on the ground. Now, it doesn't look as if there was very much room for the development of a science; it doesn't seem as if there was much room here for the scientific selection of the man nor for his progressive training, nor for cooperation between the two sides; but, I can say, without the slightest hesitation, that the science of handling pig-iron is so great that the man who is fit to handle pig-iron as his daily work cannot possibly understand that science; the man who is physically able to handle pig-iron and is sufficiently phlegmatic and stupid to choose this for his occupation is rarely able to comprehend the science of handling pig-iron; and this inability of the man who is fit to do the work to understand the science of doing his work becomes more and more evident as the work becomes more complicated, all the way up the scale.

I assert, without the slightest hesitation, that the high-class mechanic has a far smaller chance of ever thoroughly understanding the science of his work than the pig-iron handler has of understanding the science of his work, and I am going to try and prove to your satisfaction, gentlemen, that the law is almost universal – not entirely so, but nearly so – that the man who is fit to work at any particular trade is unable to understand the science of that trade without the kindly help and cooperation of men of a totally different type of education, men whose education is not necessarily higher but a different type from his own.

I dare say most of you gentlemen are familiar with pig-iron handling and with the illustration I have used in connection with it, so I won't take up any of your time with that. But I want to show you how these principles may be applied to some one of the lower classes of work. You may think I am a little highfalutin when I speak about what may be called the atmosphere of scientific management, the relations that ought to exist between both sides, the intimate and friendly relations that should exist between employee and employer. I want, however, to emphasize this as one of the most important features of scientific management, and I can hardly do so without going into detail, without explaining minutely the duties of both sides, and for this reason I want to take some of your time in explaining the application of these four principles of scientific management to one of the cheaper kinds of work, for instance, to shoveling. This is one of the simplest kinds of work, and I want to give you an illustration of the application of these principles to it.

Now, gentlemen, shoveling is a great science compared with pig-iron handling. I dare say that most of you gentlemen know that a good many pig-iron handlers can never learn to shovel right; the ordinary pig-iron handler is not the type of man well suited to shoveling. He is too stupid; there is too much mental strain, too much knack required of a shoveler for the pig-iron handler to take kindly to shoveling.

You gentlemen may laugh, but that is true, all right; it sounds ridiculous, I know, but it is a fact. Now, if the problem were put up to any of you men to develop the science of shoveling as it was put up to us, that is, to a group of men who had deliberately set out to develop the science of doing all kinds of laboring work, where do you think you would begin? When you started to study the science of shoveling I make the assertion that you would be within two days – just as we were within two days – well on the way toward development of the science of shoveling. At least you would have outlined in your minds those elements which required careful, scientific study in order to understand the science of shoveling. I do not want to go into all of the details of shoveling, but I will give you some of the elements, one or two of the most important elements of the science of shoveling; that is, the elements that reach further and have more serious consequences than any other. Probably the most important element in the science of shoveling is this: There must be some shovel load at which a first-class shoveler will do his biggest day's work. What is that load? To illustrate: When we went to the Bethlehem Steel Works and observed the shovelers in the yard of that company, we found that each of the good shovelers in that yard owned his own shovel; they preferred to buy their own shovels rather than to have the company furnish them. There was a larger tonnage of ore shoveled in that works than of any other material and rice coal came next in tonnage. We would see a first-class shoveler go from shoveling rice coal with a load of 3½ pounds to the shovel to handling ore from the Massaba Range, with 38 pounds to the shovel. Now, is 3½ pounds the proper shovel load or is 38 pounds the proper shovel load? They cannot both be right. Under scientific management the answer to this question is not a matter of anyone's opinion; it is a question for accurate, careful, scientific investigation.

Under the old system you would call in a first-rate shoveler and say, 'See here, Pat, how much ought you to take on at one shovel load?' And if a couple of fellows agreed, you would say that's about the right load and let it go at that. But under scientific management absolutely every element in the work of every man in your establishment, sooner or later, becomes the subject of exact, precise, scientific investigation and knowledge to replace the old, 'I believe so', and 'I guess so'. Every motion, every small fact becomes the subject of careful, scientific investigation.

What we did was to call in a number of men to pick from, and from these we selected two first-class shovelers. Gentlemen, the words I used were 'first-class shovelers'. I want to emphasize that. Not poor shovelers. Not men unsuited to their work, but first-class shovelers. These men were then talked to in about this way, 'See here, Pat and Mike, you fellows understand your job all right; both of you fellows are first-class men; you know what we think of you; you are all right now; but we want to pay you fellows double wages. We are going to ask you to do a lot of damn fool things, and when you are doing them there is going to be someone out alongside of you all the time, a young chap with a piece of paper and a stop watch and pencil, and all day long he will tell you to do these fool things, and he will be writing down what you are doing and snapping the watch on you and all that sort of business. Now, we just want to know whether you fellows want to go into that bargain or not? If you want double wages while that is going on all right, we will pay you double; if you don't, all right, you needn't take the job unless you want to; we just called you in to see whether you want to work this way or not.

'Let me tell you fellows just one thing: If you go into this bargain, if you go at it, just remember that on your side we want no monkey business of any kind; you fellows will have to play square; you fellows will have to do just what you are supposed to be doing; not a damn bit of soldiering on your part; you must do a fair day's work; we don't want any rushing, only a fair day's work and you know what that is as well as we do. Now, don't take this job unless you agree to these conditions, because if you start to try to fool this same young chap with the pencil and paper he will be onto you in fifteen minutes from the time you try to fool him, and just as surely as he reports you fellows as soldiering you will go out of this works and you will never get in again. Now, don't take this job unless you want to accept these conditions; you need not do it unless you want to; but if you do, play fair.'

Well, these fellows agreed to it, and, as I have found almost universally to be the case, they kept their word absolutely and faithfully. My experience with workmen has been that their word is just as good as the word of any other set of men that I know of, and all you have to do is to have a clear, straight, square understanding with them and you will get just as straight and fair a deal from them as from any other set of men. In this way the shoveling experiment was started. My remembrance is that we first started them on work that was very heavy, work requiring a very heavy shovel load. What we did was to give them a certain kind of heavy material ore, I think, to handle with a certain size of shovel. We sent these two men into different parts of the yards, with two different men to time and study them, both sets of men being engaged on the same class of work. We made all the conditions the same for both pairs of men, so as to be sure that there was no error in judgement on the part of either of the observers and that they were normal, first-class men.

The number of shovel loads which each man handled in the course of the day was counted and written down. At the end of the day the total tonnage of the material handled by each man was weighed and this weight was divided by the number of shovel loads handled, and in that way, my remembrance is, our first experiment showed that the average shovel load handled was 38 pounds, and that with this load on the shovel the man handled, say, about 25 tons per day. We then cut the shovel off, making it somewhat shorter, so that instead of shoveling a load of 38 pounds it held a load of approximately 34 pounds. The average, then, with the 34 pound load, of each man went up, and instead of handling 25 he had handled thirty tons per day. These figures are merely relative, used to illustrate the general principles, and I do not mean that they were the exact figures. The shovel was again cut off, and the load made approximately 30 pounds, and again the tonnage ran up, and again the shovel load was reduced, and the tonnage handled per day increased, until at about 21 or 22 pounds per shovel we found that these men were doing their largest day's work. If you cut the shovel load off still more, say until it averages 18 pounds instead of 21½, the tonnage handled per day will begin to fall off, and at 16 pounds it will be still lower, and so on right down. Very well; we now have developed the scientific fact that a workman well suited to his job, what we call a first-class shoveler, will do his largest day's work when he has a shovel load of 21½ pounds.

Now, what does that fact amount to? At first it may not look to be a fact of much importance, but let us see what it amounted to right there in the yard of the Bethlehem Steel Co. Under the old system, as I said before, the workmen owned their shovels, and the shovel was the same size whatever the kind of work. Now, as a matter of common sense, we saw at once that it was necessary to furnish each workman each day with a shovel which would hold just 21½ pounds of the particular material which he was called upon to shovel. A small shovel for the heavy material, such as ore, and a large scoop for light material, such as ashes. That meant, also, the building of a large shovel room, where all kinds of laborers' implements were stored. It meant having an ample supply of each type of shovel, so that all the men who might be called upon to use a certain type in any one day could be supplied with a shovel of the size desired that would hold just 21½ pounds. It meant, further, that each day each laborer should be given a particular kind of work to which he was suited, and that he must be provided with a particular shovel suited to that kind of work, whereas in the past all the laborers in the yard of the Bethlehem Steel Co. had been handled in masses, or in great groups of men, by the old-fashioned foreman, who had from twenty-five to one hundred men under him and walked them from one part of the yard to another. You must realize that the yard of the Bethlehem Steel Co. at that time was a very large yard. I should say that it was at least 1½ or 2 miles long and, we will say, a quarter to a half mile wide, so it was a good large yard; and in that yard at all times an immense variety of shoveling was going on.

There was comparatively little standard shoveling which went on uniformly from day to day. Each man was likely to be moved from place to place about the yard several times in the course of the day. All of this involved keeping in the shovel room ten or fifteen kinds of shovels, ranging from a very small flat shovel for handling ore up to immense scoops for handling rice coal, and forks with which to handle the coke, which, as you know, is very light. It meant the study and development of the implement best suited to each type of material to be shoveled, and assigning, with the minimum of trouble, the proper shovel to each one of the four to six hundred laborers at work in that yard. Now, that meant mechanism, human mechanism. It meant organizing and planning work at least a day in advance. And, gentlemen, here is an important fact, that the greatest difficulty which we met with in this planning did not come from the workmen. It came from the management's side. Our greatest difficulty was to get the heads of the various departments each day to inform the men in the labor office what kind of work and how much of it was to be done on the following day.

This planning the work one day ahead involved the building of a labor office where before there was no such thing. It also involved the equipping of that office with large maps showing the layout of the yards so that the movements of the men from one part of the yard to another could be laid out in advance, so that we could assign to this little spot in the yard a certain number of men and to another part of the yard another set of men, each group to do a certain kind of work. It was practically like playing a game of chess in which four to six hundred men were moved about so as to be in the right place at the right time. And all this, gentlemen, follows from the one idea of developing the science of shoveling; the idea that you must give each workman each day a job to which he is well suited and provide him with just that implement which will enable him to do his biggest day's work. All this, as I have tried to make clear to you, is the result that followed from the one act of developing the science of shoveling.

In order that our workmen should get their share of the good that came from the development of the science of shoveling and that we should do what we set out to do with our laborers – namely, pay them 60 per cent higher wages than were paid to any similar workmen around that whole district. Before we could pay them these extra high wages it was necessary for us to be sure that we had first-class men and that each laborer was well suited to his job, because the only way in which you can pay wages 60 per cent higher than other people pay and not overwork your men is by having each man properly suited and well trained to his job. Therefore, it became necessary to carefully select these yard laborers; and in order that the men should join with us heartily and help us in their selection it became necessary for us to make it possible for each man to know each morning as he came in to work that on the previous day he had earned his 60 per cent premium, or that he had failed to do so. So here again comes in a lot of work to be done by the management that had not been done before. The first thing each workman did when he came into the yard in the morning – and I may say that a good many of them could not read and write – was to take two pieces of paper out of his pigeonhole; if they were both white slips of paper, the workman knew he was all right. One of those slips of paper informed the man in charge of the tool room what implement the workman was to use on his first job and also in what part of the yard he was to work. It was in this way that each one of the 600 men in that yard received his orders for the kind of work he was to do and the implement with which he was to do it, and he was also sent right to the part of the yard where he was to work, without any delay whatever. The old-fashioned way was for the workmen to wait until the foreman got good and ready and had found out by asking some of the heads of departments what work he was to do, and then he would lead the gang off to some part of the yard and go to work. Under the new method each man gets his orders almost automatically; he goes right to the tool room, gets the proper implement for the work he is to do, and goes right to the spot where he is to work without any delay.

The second piece of paper, if it was a white piece of paper, showed this man that he had earned his 60 per cent higher wages; if it was a yellow piece of paper the workman knew that he had not earned enough to be a first-class man, and that within two or three days something would happen, and he was absolutely certain what this something would be. Every one of them knew that after he had received three or four yellow slips a teacher would be sent down to him from the labor office. Now, gentlemen, this teacher was no college professor. He was a teacher of shoveling; he understood the science of shoveling; he was a good shoveler himself, and he knew how to teach other men to be good shovelers. This is the sort of man who was sent out of the labor office. I want to emphasize the following point, gentlemen: The workman, instead of hating the teacher who came to him – instead of looking askance at him and saying to himself, 'Here comes one of those damn nigger drivers to drive me to work' – looked upon him as one of the best friends he had around there. He knew that he came out there to help him, not to nigger drive him. Now, let me show you what happens. The teacher comes, in every case, not to bulldoze the man, not to drive him to harder work than he can do, but to try in a friendly, brotherly way to help him, so he says, 'Now, Pat, something has gone wrong with you. You know no workman who is not a high-priced workman can stay on this gang, and you will have to get off of it if we can't find out what is the matter with you. I believe you have forgotten how to shovel right. I think that's all there is the matter with you. Go ahead and let me watch you awhile. I want to see if you know how to do the damn thing, anyway.'

Now, gentlemen, I know you will laugh when I talk again about the science of shoveling. I dare say some of you have done some shoveling. Whether you have or not, I am going to try to show you something about the science of shoveling, and if any of you have done much shoveling, you will understand that there is a good deal of science about it.

There is a good deal of refractory stuff to shovel around a steel works; take ore, or ordinary bituminous coal, for instance. It takes a good deal of effort to force the shovel down into either of these materials from the top of the pile, as you have to when you are unloading a car. There is one right way of forcing the shovel into materials of this sort, and many wrong ways. Now, the way to shovel refractory stuff is to press the forearm hard against the upper part of the right leg just below the thigh, like this (indicating), take the end of the shovel in your right hand and when you push the shovel into the pile, instead of using the muscular effort of your arms, which is tiresome, throw the weight of your body on the shovel like this (indicating); that pushes your shovel in the pile with hardly any exertion and without tiring the arms in the least. Nine out of ten workmen who try to push a shovel in a pile of that sort will use the strength of their arms, which involves more than twice the necessary exertion. Any of you men who don't know this fact just try it. This is one illustration of what I mean when I speak of the science of shoveling, and there are many similar elements of this science. Now, this teacher would find, time and time again, that the shoveler had simply forgotten how to shovel; that he had drifted back to his old wrong and inefficient way of shoveling, which prevented him from earning his 60 per cent higher wages. So he would say to him, 'I see all that is the matter with you is that you have forgotten how to shovel; you have forgotten what I showed you about shoveling some time ago. Now, watch me,' he says, 'this is the way to do the thing.' And the teacher would stay by him, two, three, four or five days, if necessary, until he got the man back again into the habit of shoveling right.

Now, gentlemen, I want you to see clearly that, because that is one of the characteristic features of scientific management; this is not nigger driving; this is kindness; this is teaching; this is doing what I would like mighty well to have done to me if I were a boy trying to learn how to do something. This is not a case of cracking a whip over a man and saying, 'Damn you, get there.' The old way of treating with workmen, on the other hand, even with a good foreman, would have been something like this: 'See here, Pat, I have sent for you to come up here to the office to see me; four or five times now you have not earned your 60 per cent increase in wages; you know that every workman in this place has got to earn 60 per cent more wages than they pay in any other place around here, but you're no good and that's all there is to it; now, get out of this.' That's the old way. 'You are no good; we have given you a fair chance; get out of this', and the workman is pretty lucky if it isn't 'get to hell out of this', instead of 'get out of this'.

The new way is to teach and help your men as you would a brother; to try to teach him the best way and show him the easiest way to do his work. This is the new mental attitude of the management toward the men, and that is the reason I have taken so much of your time in describing this cheap work of shoveling. It may seem to you a matter of very little consequence, but I want you to see, if I can, that this new mental attitude is the very essence of scientific management; that the mechanism is nothing if you have not got the right sentiment, the right attitude in the minds of the men, both on the management's side and on the workman's side. Because this helps to explain the fact that until this summer there has never been a strike under scientific management.

The men who developed the science of shoveling spent, I should say, four or five months studying the subject and during that time they investigated not only the best and most efficient movements that the men should make when they are shoveling right, but they also studied the proper time for doing each of the elements of the science of shoveling. There are many other elements which go to make up this science, but I will not take up your time describing them.

Now, all of this costs money. To pay the salaries of men who are studying the science of shoveling is an expensive thing. As I remember it there were two college men who studied this science of shoveling and also the science of doing many other kinds of laboring work during a period of about three years; then there were a lot of men in the labor office whose wages had to be paid, men who were planning the work which each laborer was to do at least a day in advance; clerks who worked all night so that each workman might know the next morning when he went to work just what he had accomplished and what he had earned the day before; men who wrote out the proper instructions for the day's work for each workman. All of this costs money; it costs money to measure or weigh up the materials handled by each man each day. Under the old method the work of fifty or sixty men was weighed up together; the work done by a whole gang was measured together. But under scientific management we are dealing with individual men and not with gangs of men. And in order to study and develop each man you must measure accurately each man's work. At first we were told that this would be impossible. The former managers of this work told me 'You cannot possibly measure up the work of each individual laborer in this yard; you might be able to do it in a small yard, but our work is of such an intricate nature that it is impossible to do it here.'

I want to say that we had almost no trouble in finding some cheap way of measuring up each man's work, not only in that yard but throughout the entire plant.

But all of that costs money, and it is a very proper question to ask whether it pays or whether it doesn't pay, because, let me tell you, gentlemen, at once, and I want to be emphatic about it, scientific management has nothing in it that is philanthropic; I am not objecting to philanthropy, but any scheme of management which has philanthropy as one of its elements ought to fail; philanthropy has no part in any scheme of management. No self-respecting workman wants to be given things, every man wants to earn things, and scientific management is no scheme for giving people something they do not earn. So, if the principles of scientific management do not pay, then this is a miserable system. The final test of any system is, does it pay?

At the end of some three and a half years we had the opportunity of proving whether or not scientific management did pay in its application to yard labor. When we went to the Bethlehem Steel Co. we found from 400 to 600 men at work in that yard, and when we got through 140 men were doing the work of the 400 to 600, and these men handled several million tons of material a year.

We were very fortunate to be able to get accurate statistics as to the cost of handling a ton of materials in that yard under the old system and under the new. Under the old system the cost of handling a ton of materials had been running between seven and eight cents, and all you gentlemen familiar with railroad work know that this is a low figure for handling materials. Now, after paying for all the clerical work which was necessary under the new system for the time study and the teachers, for building and running the labor office and the implement room, for constructing a telephone system for moving men about the yard, for a great variety of duties not performed under the old system, after paying for all these things incident to the development of the science of shoveling and managing the men the new way, and including the wages of the workmen, the cost of handling a ton of material was brought down from between seven and eight cents to between three and four cents, and the actual saving, during the last six months of the three and one-half years I was there, was at the rate of $78,000 a year. That is what the company got out of it; while the men who were on the labor gang received an average of sixty per cent more wages than their brothers got or could get anywhere around that part of the country. And none of them were overworked, for it is no part of scientific management ever to overwork any man; certainly overworking these men could not have been done with the knowledge of anyone connected with scientific management, because one of the first requirements of scientific management is that no man shall ever be given a job which he cannot do and thrive under through a long term of years. It is no part of scientific management to drive anyone. At the end of three years we had men talk to and investigate all of these yard laborers and we found that they were almost universally satisfied with their jobs.

Of course certain men are permanent grouches and when we run across that kind we all know what to expect. But, in the main, they were the most satisfied and contented set of laborers I have ever seen anywhere; they lived better than they did before, and most of them were saving a little money; their families lived better, and as to having any grouch against their employers, those fellows, every one, looked upon them as the best friends they ever had, because they taught them how to earn 60 per cent more wages than they had ever earned before. This is the round-up of both sides of this question. If the use of the system does not make both sides happier, then it is no good.

To give you one illustration of the application of scientific management to a rather high class of work, gentlemen, bricklaying, so far as I know, is one of the oldest of the trades, and it is a truly extraordinary fact that bricks are now laid just about as they were two thousand years before Christ. In England they are laid almost exactly as they were then; in England the scaffold is still built with timbers lashed together – in many cases with the bark still on it – just as we see that the scaffolds were made in old stone-cut pictures of bricklaying before the Christian era. In this country we have gone beyond the lashed scaffold, and yet in most respects it is almost literally true that bricks are still laid as they were four thousand years ago. Virtually the same trowel, virtually the same brick, virtually the same mortar, and, from the way in which they were laid, according to one of my friends, who is a brick work contractor and a student of the subject, who took the trouble to take down some bricks laid four thousand years ago to study the way in which the mortar was spread, etc., it appears that they even spread the mortar in the same way then as we do now. If, then, there is any trade in which one would say that the principles of scientific management would produce but small results, that the development of the science would do little good, it would be in a trade which thousands and thousands of men through successive generations had worked and had apparently reached, as far as methods and principles were concerned, the highest limit of efficiency four thousand years ago. In bricklaying this would seem to be true since practically no progress has been made in this art since that time. Therefore, viewed broadly, one would say that there was a smaller probability that the principles of scientific management could accomplish notable results in this trade than in almost any other.

Mr Frank Gilbreth is a man who in his youth worked as a bricklayer; he was an educated man and is now a very successful contractor. He said to me, some years ago, 'Now, Taylor, I am a contractor, putting up all sorts of buildings, and if there is one thing I know it is bricklaying; I can go out right now, and I am not afraid to back myself, to beat any man I know of laying bricks for ten minutes, both as to speed and accuracy; you may think I am blowing, but that is one way I got up in the world. I cannot stand it now for more than ten minutes; I'm soft; my hands are tender, I haven't been handling bricks for years, but for ten minutes I will back myself against anyone. I want to ask you about this scientific management; do you think it can be applied to bricklaying? Do you believe that these things you have been shouting about (at that time it was called the 'task system'), do you believe these principles can be applied to bricklaying?' 'Certainly,' I said, 'some day some fellow will make the same kind of study about bricklaying that we have made of other things, and he will get the same results.' 'Well,' he said, 'if you really think so, I will just tell you who is going to do it, his name is Frank Gilbreth.'

I think it was about three years later that he came to me and said: 'Now, I'm going to show you something about bricklaying. I have spent three years making a motion and time study of bricklaying, and not I alone did it; my wife has also spent almost the same amount of her time studying the problems of bricklaying, and I think she has made her full share of the progress which has been made in the science of bricklaying.' Then he said, 'I will show you just how we went to work at it. Let us assume that I am now standing on the scaffold in the position that the bricklayer occupies when he is ready to begin work. The wall is here on my left, the bricks are there in a pile on the scaffold to my right, and the mortar is here on the mortar-board alongside of the bricks. Now, I take my stand as a bricklayer and am ready to start to lay bricks, and I said to myself, "What is the first movement that I make when I start to lay bricks?" I take a step to the right with the right foot. Well, is that movement necessary? It took me a year and a half to cut out that motion – that step to the right – and I will tell you later how I cut it out. Now, what motion do I make next? I stoop down to the floor to the pile of bricks and disentangle a brick from the pile and pick it up off the pile. "My God," I said, "that is nothing short of barbarous." Think of it! Here I am a man weighing over 250 pounds, and every time I stoop down to pick up a brick I lower 250 pounds of weight down two feet so as to pick up a brick weighing 4 pounds, and then raise my 250 pounds of weight up again, and all of this to lift up a brick weighing 4 pounds. Think of this waste of effort. It is monstrous. It took me – it may seem to you a pretty long while – but it took a year and a half of thought and work to cut out that motion; when I finally cut it out, however, it was done in such a simple way that anyone in looking at the method which I adopted would say, "There is no invention in that, any fool could do that; why did you take a year and a half to do a little thing like that?" Well, all I did was to put a table on the scaffold right alongside of me here on my right side and put the bricks and mortar on it, so as to keep them at all times at the right height, thus making it unnecessary to stoop down in picking them up. This table was placed in the middle of the scaffold with the bricklayer on one side of it, and with a walkway on the other side along which the bricks were brought by wheelbarrow or by hod to be placed on the table without interfering with the bricklayer or even getting in his way.' Then Mr Gilbreth made his whole scaffold adjustable, and a laborer was detailed to keep all of the scaffolds at all times at such a height that as the wall goes up the bricks, the mortar, and the men will occupy that position in which the work can be done with the least effort.

Mr Gilbreth has studied out the best position for each of the bricklayer's feet and for every type of bricklaying the exact position for the feet is fixed so that the man can do his work without unnecessary movements. As a result of further study both on the part of Mr and Mrs Gilbreth, after the bricks are unloaded from the cars and before bringing them to the bricklayer they are carefully sorted by a laborer and placed with their best edges up on a simple wooden frame, constructed so as to enable him to take hold of each brick in the quickest time and in the most advantageous position. In this way the bricklayer avoids either having to turn the brick over or end for end to examine it before laying it, and he saves also the time taken in deciding which is the best edge and end to place on the outside of the wall. In most cases, also, he saves the time taken in disentangling the brick from a disorderly pile on the scaffold. This 'pack of bricks', as Mr Gilbreth calls his loaded wooden frames, is placed by the helper in its proper position on the adjustable scaffold close to the mortar box.

We have all been used to seeing bricklayers tap each brick after it is placed on its bed of mortar several times with the end of the handle of the trowel so as to secure the right thickness for the joint. Mr Gilbreth found that by tempering the mortar just right the bricks could be readily bedded to the proper depth by a downward pressure of the hand which lays them. He insisted that the mortar mixers should give special attention to tempering the mortar and so save the time consumed in tapping the brick.

In addition to this he taught his bricklayers to make simple motions with both hands at the same time, where before they completed a motion with the right hand before they followed it later with one made by the left hand. For example, Mr Gilbreth taught his bricklayers to pick up a brick in the left hand at the same time that he takes a trowel of mortar with the right hand. This work with two hands at the same time is, of course, made possible by substituting a deep mortar box for the old mortar-board, on which the mortar used to spread out so thin that a step or two had to be taken to reach it, and then placing the mortar box and the brick pile close together and at the proper height on his new scaffold.

Now, what was the practical outcome of all this study? To sum it up he finally succeeded in teaching his bricklayers, when working under the new method, to lay bricks with five motions per brick, while with the old method they used eighteen motions per brick. And, in fact, in one exceedingly simple type of bricklaying he reduced the motions of his bricklayers from eighteen to two motions per brick. But in the ordinary bricklaying he reduced the motions from eighteen to five. When he first came to me, after he had made this long and elaborate study of the motions of bricklayers, he had accomplished nothing in a practical way through this study, and he said, 'You know, Fred, I have been showing all my friends these new methods of laying bricks and they say to me, "Well, Frank, this is a beautiful thing to talk about, but what in the devil do you think it amounts to? You know perfectly well the unions have forbidden their members to lay more than so many bricks per day; you know they won't allow this thing to be carried out." ' But Gilbreth said, 'Now, my dear boy, that doesn't make an iota of difference to me. I'm just going to see that the bricklayers do the right thing. I belong to the bricklayers' union in Boston, and the next job that I get in Boston this thing goes through. I'm not going to do it in any underhanded way. Everyone knows that I have always paid higher wages than the union scale in Boston. I've got a lot of friends at the head of the unions in Boston, and I'm not afraid of having any trouble.'

He got his job near Boston, and he went to the leaders of the union and told them just what you can tell any set of sensible men. He said to them, 'I want to tell you fellows some things that you ought to know. Most of my contracts around here used to be brick jobs; now, most of my work is in reinforced concrete or some other type of construction, but I am first and last a bricklayer; that is what I am interested in, and if you have any sense you will just keep your hands off and let me show you bricklayers how to compete with the reinforced concrete men. I will handle the bricklayers myself. All I want of you leaders is to keep your hands off and I will show you how bricklayers can compete with reinforced concrete or any other type of construction that comes along.'

Well, the leaders of the union thought that sounded all right, and then he went to the workmen and said to them, 'No fellow can work for me for less than $6·50 a day – the union rate was $5 a day – but every man who gets on this job has got to lay bricks my way; I will put a teacher on the job to show you all my way of laying bricks and I will give every man plenty of time to learn, but after a bricklayer has had a sufficient trial at this thing, if he won't do my way or cannot do my way, he must get off the job.' Any number of bricklayers were found to be only too glad to try the job, and I think he said that before the first story of the building was up he had the whole gang trained to work in the new way, and all getting their $6·50 a day when before they only received $5 per day; I believe those are the correct figures; I am not absolutely sure about that, but at least he paid them a very liberal premium above the average bricklayer's pay.

It is one of the principles of scientific management to ask men to do things in the right way, to learn something new, to change their ways in accordance with the science, and in return to receive an increase of from 30 to 100 per cent in pay, which varies according to the nature of the business in which they are engaged.

11   A. P. Sloan, Jr

The Management of General Motors

From A. P. Sloan, Jr, 'The management: how it works',
My Years with General Motors, Doubleday, 1964, chapter 23.

It is not easy to say why one management is successful and another is
not. The causes of success or failure are deep and complex, and chance
plays a part. Experience has convinced me, however, that for those who
are responsible for a business, two important factors are motivation and
opportunity. The former is supplied in good part by incentive compensation, the latter by decentralization.

But the matter does not end there. It has been a thesis of this book that
good management rests on a reconciliation of centralization and decentralization, or 'decentralization with coordinated control'.

Each of the conflicting elements brought together in this concept has
its unique results in the operation of a business. From decentralization
we get initiative, responsibility, development of personnel, decisions
close to the facts, flexibility – in short, all the qualities necessary for an
organization to adapt to new conditions. From coordination we get
efficiencies and economies. It must be apparent that coordinated decentralization is not an easy concept to apply. There is no hard and fast rule
for sorting out the various responsibilities and the best way to assign
them. The balance which is struck between corporate and divisional
responsibility varies according to what is being decided, the circumstances of the time, past experience, and the temperaments and skills of
the executives involved.

The concept of coordinated decentralization evolved gradually at
General Motors as we responded to tangible problems of management.
As I have shown, at the time its development began, some four decades
ago, it was clearly advisable to give each division a strong management
which would be primarily responsible for the conduct of its business. But
our experience in 1920–21 also demonstrated the need for a greater
measure of control over the divisions than we had attained. Without
adequate control from the central office, the divisions got out of hand,
and failed to follow the policies set by corporation management, to the
great detriment of the corporation. Meanwhile, the corporation management was in no position to set the best policies, since it was without

appropriate and timely data from the divisions. A steady flow of operating data, for which procedures were later set up, finally made real coordination possible.

That still left us with the problem of finding the right combination of freedom for the divisions and control over them. The combination could not be set once and for all, of course. It varies with changing circumstances, and the responsibility for determining administrative organization is a continuing one. Thus, at one time, responsibility for the styling of the cars and other products was vested in the divisions. Since then it has been found desirable to place the responsibility for developing the general style characteristics of all our major products in the Styling Staff. This was suggested partly by the physical economies to be gained by coordinated styling. In addition, we learned from experience that work of higher quality could be obtained by utilizing, corporation-wide, the highly developed talents of the specialists. The adoption of any particular style is now a joint responsibility of the division concerned, the Styling Staff, and the central management.

Such continuing adjustments in the relative responsibility assumed by the division management and central management are permitted by the decentralized organization of General Motors whenever experience or changed circumstances present opportunities for improved or more economical performance. In my time as chief executive officer only a modest degree of supervision was actually exercised by general officers over division managers. I believe that basically the same is the case today, although changed circumstances and new and more complex problems have resulted in a somewhat closer degree of coordination than existed in my time.

In General Motors we do not follow the textbook definition of line and staff. Our distinction is between the central office (which includes staff) and the divisions. Broadly speaking, the staff officers – being primarily specialists – do not have line authority, yet in certain matters of established policy, they may communicate the application of such policy directly to a division.

The responsibility of the central management is to determine which decisions can be made more effectively and efficiently by the central office and which by the divisions. In order that such determinations be informed and knowledgeable, the central management depends heavily on the staff officers. Indeed, many of the important decisions of central management are first formulated in collaboration with the staff in the policy groups, and then adopted, after discussion, by the governing committees. Consequently, the staff is the real source of many decisions that are formally adopted by the committees. For example, the basic decision to participate in the manufacture of diesel locomotives was largely based on product research by the staff.

Some of the general staff activities, such as legal work, have no counterparts in the divisions. Other general staff activities correspond to activities in each of the divisions, among them engineering, manufacturing, and distribution activities. But there are some important distinctions between these staff and divisional activities: the general staffs are concerned with longer-range problems, and with problems of broader application, than their opposite numbers in the divisions. The corresponding divisional staffs are engaged largely in the applications of policies and programs already developed. There have been exceptions to this, however, as when a project has been approved for development in a division. An example is the development of the Corvair.

The economies that flow from central-office activities are considerable and the cost comes on the average to less than 1 per cent of the corporation's net sales. Through the general staff the divisions get their services cheaper than if they provided them or bought them on the outside, and they get better services. The latter feature is, in my opinion, by far the more important. The staff contributions in the fields of styling, finance, technical research, advanced engineering, personnel and labor relations, legal affairs, manufacturing and distribution are outstanding and certainly worth a large multiple of their cost.

Several kinds of economies are made possible by centralized staff operations. Among the most important are the economies that derive from the coordination of the divisions. These arise through the sharing of ideas and developments among general officers and divisional personnel. The divisions contribute ideas and techniques both to each other and to central management. Much of our managerial and engineering talent, and many of our general officers, have come out of the divisions. The development of high-compression engines and automatic transmissions, for example, was the work of both staff and divisions. Our progress in aviation engines and in diesel engines came out of the development work of both.

Under the decentralized operation of the divisions, problems of like kind are met in different ways by different division managers, subject to the advice of the central office of the corporation. Out of this process comes a winnowing of techniques and ideas, and a development of judgments and skills. The quality of General Motors' management as a whole derives in part from this shared experience with common goals and from divisional rivalry within the framework of these common goals.

There are also the economies of specialization possible under our decentralized system. It is an axiom of economics that costs are reduced and trade created by specialization and the division of labor. Applied to General Motors, this has meant that our internal supplying divisions which specialize in the production of components must be fully competitive in price, quality, and service; if they are not, the purchasing divisions are free to buy from outside sources. Even when we have decided to make an item rather than buy it, and have established production of the item, it is by no means a closed decision that we will stay in that line of production. We try, wherever possible, to test our internal supplying divisions against external competitors and to make a continuing judgment on whether it is better to make or to buy.

The popular misconception that it always pays to make an item yourself rather than to buy it is based on the assumption of a cost saving. The argument runs that by making instead of buying, you can save the extra cost of your supplier's profit. But the fact is that if the suppliers' profit is a normal, competitive one, you must expect to make it on your own investment, or else there is no net saving. General Motors does not engage in the production of raw materials, as do some of its competitors, and we purchase a large proportion of the items that go into our end products, because there is no reason to believe that by producing them we could obtain better products or service, or a lower price.

Of the total cost of sales of our products, purchases of parts, materials, and services from outside sources account for 55 to 60 per cent.

The role of the division managers is an important one in our continuing efforts to maintain both efficiency and adaptability. These managers make almost all of the divisional operating decisions, subject, however, to some important qualifications. Their decisions must be consistent with the corporation's general policies; the results of the division's operations must be reported to the central management; and the division officers must 'sell' central management on any substantial changes in operating policies and be open to suggestions from the general officers.

The practice of selling major proposals is an important feature of General Motors' management. Any proposal must be sold to central management and if it affects other divisions it must be sold to them as well. Sound management also requires that the central office should in most cases sell its proposals to the divisions, which it does through the policy groups and group executives. The selling approach provides an important extra safeguard in General Motors against ill-considered decisions, over and above the safeguards normally implied in the responsibility of corporate officers to shareholders. It assures that any basic decision is made only after thorough consideration by all parties concerned.

Our decentralized organization and our tradition of selling ideas, rather than simply giving orders, impose the need upon all levels of management to make a good case for what they propose. The manager who would like to operate on a hunch will usually find it hard to sell his ideas to others on this basis. But, in general, whatever sacrifice might be entailed in ruling out a possibly brilliant hunch is compensated for by the better-than-average results which can be expected from a policy that can be strongly defended against well-informed and sympathetic criticism. In short, General Motors is not the appropriate organization for purely intuitive executives, but it provides a favorable environment for capable and rational men. In some organizations, in order to tap the potentialities of a genius, it is necessary to build around him and tailor the organization to his temperament. General Motors on the whole is not such an organization although Mr Kettering was an obvious exception.

Our management policy decisions are arrived at by discussions in the governing committees and policy groups. These were not the creation of a single inspired moment, but the result of a long process of development in dealing with a fundamental problem of management, that of placing responsibility for policy in the hands of those best able both to make the decisions and to assume the responsibility. To a certain extent this involves a contradiction. On the one hand, those best able to assume responsibility must have broad business perspective oriented toward the interest of the shareholder. On the other hand, those best qualified to make specific decisions must be close to the actual operation of the business. We have attempted to resolve this contradiction principally by dividing the policy-making responsibilities within central management between the Finance Committee and the Executive Committee, as I have shown.

Another source of policy recommendation is the Administration Committee, which is charged with the responsibility of making recommendations to the president with respect to the manufacturing and selling activities of the corporation, and on any other matters affecting the business and affairs of the corporation that may be referred to it by the president or the Executive Committee. The president is the chairman of the committee and, at the present time, its membership includes the members of the Executive Committee, two group executives who are not members of the Executive Committee, the general managers of the car and truck divisions, the general manager of Fisher Body Division, and the general manager of the Overseas Operations Division.

Under this separation of responsibility, policy development and recommendation are mainly the duty of the groups in central management made up of the men closest to operations. They work very closely, of course, with men from the divisions, and divisional men are on some policy groups. The Executive Committee, which views the corporation as a whole and at the same time is closely familiar with operating problems, has a somewhat judicial function. It makes the fundamental decisions on the basis of the work of the policy groups and the Administration Committee, plus the committee members' close knowledge of operating conditions. The Finance Committee, which includes non-employee directors in its membership, exercises its responsibility and authority in the area of broader corporate policy.

Much of my life in General Motors was devoted to the development, organization and periodic reorganization of these governing groups in central management. This was required because of the paramount importance, in an organization like General Motors, of providing the right framework for decisions. There is a natural tendency to erode that framework unless it is consciously maintained. Group decisions do not always come easily. There is a strong temptation for the leading officers to make decisions themselves without the sometimes onerous process of discussion, which involves selling your ideas to others. The group will not always make a better decision than any particular member would make; there is even the possibility of some averaging down. But in General Motors I think the record shows that we have averaged up. Essentially this means that, through our form of organization, we have been able to adapt to the great changes that have taken place in the automobile market in each of the decades since 1920.

12 Sir Geoffrey Vickers

The Art of Judgement

From G. Vickers, 'Judgement', The Sixth Elbourne Memorial Lecture, *The Manager*, January 1961, pp. 31–9.

I am honoured to have been asked to give the sixth in this series of lectures, founded to perpetuate the memory of Edward Tregaskiss Elbourne, to whom, as founder of the Institute of Industrial Administration, the British Institute of Management owes a special, as well as a general, debt of gratitude. My five predecessors have painted comprehensive pictures, worthy of the wide-ranging interests and unifying concepts of the man we are here to honour. My approach is more selective. I ask you to consider one only of the qualities which are needed for management: the quality of good judgement. But my short title will invite us to a longer journey than we shall compass in the period of the lecture.

I choose this subject because it fascinates me, but I have more respectable reasons for my choice. Judgement is an important quality in a manager; perhaps more eagerly sought and more highly paid than any. It is also an elusive quality, easier to recognize than to define, easier to define than to teach. To some it has an aura of mystery, suggesting unidentified, intuitive powers behind the inexplicably accurate hunch. Others believe that its deepest secrets are already familiar to those who programme computers. Our language and our thought on the subject are alike imprecise. If I can contribute to their better ordering, I feel that I shall be doing something worthy, at least in intention, of an Elbourne lecturer.

We use the word judgement in many contexts. Applying it to business executives, we have in mind, I think, the power of reaching 'right' decisons (whatever that may mean) when the apparent criteria are so complex, inadequate, doubtful or conflicting as to defeat the ordinary man. Even in this sense judgement is, of course, not confined to business executives, for it is required equally by statesmen, generals and princes of the Church; and even in this sense we may be unsure where it begins and ends. When our government in 1940 shipped tanks to Egypt, through precarious seas, away from a country still in danger, to take part in operations still unplanned, Sir Winston Churchill took responsibility for a decision, apparently rash, which was justified by results. Shall we call this 'good judgement'? What of the decision of Bolivar, when, in the swampy delta of the Orinoco, he announced to a few ragged followers that he had that day founded the Republic of Gran Columbia and had fixed its capital at Bogota, a thousand miles away across the Andes? He too was justified by results. Are these exercises of the same faculty which led Mr Henry Ford to create Model T40?

Judges of the Supreme Court exercise judgement; yet politicians and civil servants, who take what they call administrative decisions, have generally maintained, in a controversy now thirty years old, that the rightness of their judgements is not a matter which courts of law can competently review. The opposite view is now gaining ground. What is the difference between the judgement of judges and the judgement of administrators?

What of the scientists? Vesalius rejected the view, accepted in his day, that the dividing wall of the heart is pierced by invisible passages. He proved to be right, and he is rightly remembered as a hero of scientific scepticism. Harvey assumed the existence of invisible passages connecting the arteries with the veins, an assumption then new and commended only by the fact that it was required by his theory of the circulation of the blood. He proved to be right too; and he is rightly remembered as a hero of – scientific intuition. Did these two men show 'good judgement' in the same sense?

What of the doctor making a diagnosis? What of the artist painting out a tone or a form which, in his judgement, disturbs the balance of his picture? What of the connoisseur who chooses the artist's work from among a hundred others, because he judges it to be of higher and more enduring merit? What of the man in a moral dilemma who judges one personal claim on him to be more weighty than another; and of his neighbours, who judge his decision as right or wrong? All these are exercising judgement; and though their fields are remote from that of the business executive, their activities are not. For the business executive also has occasion to act judicially, to make diagnoses, to weigh moral issues, to judge as connoisseur, even, perhaps, to compose in his own medium as an artist. It seems that we shall have to decide whether the word 'judgement' in all these contexts stands for one mental activity or many.

Three types of judgement

I shall distinguish three broad types of judgement. Harvey and Vesalius made judgements about the state of affairs 'out there'. They revised the currently accepted view of external reality. I will call such judgements 'reality judgements'.

Churchill, Bolivar and Ford also made reality judgements; but they went further. They made judgements of what to do about it; and they committed themselves to action on the basis of these judgements. I will call such judgements 'action judgements'. In my examples, what strikes us most about their action judgement is that it 'came off'. In each case it achieved the desired result.

There is, however, a third element in these judgements – the judgement of what result was most to be desired. This I will call a value judgement. Churchill, Bolivar and Ford would not be remembered in these contexts unless they had been convinced of the value of victory in the Middle East, of creating independent republics of the Spanish-American colonies, of building a popular car; and these were not the only judgements of value which underlay their decisions.

In each case the value judgement is separate from the action judgement; it can be separately criticized. That the action succeeded does not prove that it was well conceived. Some strategists criticized the British emphasis on the Middle Eastern theatre of war. San Martin thought that the new states of South America should have been set up as constitutional monarchies. Even Henry Ford's 'tin Lizzie' was criticized – on aesthetic grounds. Hindsight often leads us to wish that our well-laid plans had failed.

I shall return in a moment to consider the part played by these three kinds of judgement – value judgement, reality judgement, action judgement – in the making of business decisions. First, I want to inquire how we recognize these judgements as good. The answer is curious and somewhat disturbing.

The credentials of judgement

The capillaries which were invisible to Harvey can now be demonstrated by improved microscopy. His judgement has been confirmed by observation. Yet even the so-called facts of observation need judgement to give them meaning, a judgement often difficult and hazardous. Moreover, few reality judgements can be confirmed by observation, even after the event; for many relevant facts of a situation – the state of someone's mind, for example – are not observable and change constantly and unpredictably, not least through the effects of judgements made about them. In the ultimate analysis, all reality judgements are matters of inference and can be confirmed or challenged only by new reality judgements, based on further inferences.

With action judgements we feel on firmer ground; we can check them against their results. Yet this is at best a rough and ready test, especially at the level of my examples. Who can say whether the courses which were not tried would not have worked out better than the one which was chosen? Moreover, every choice involves weighing probabilities. The course rightly chosen as of least risk may none the less prove lethal; the course of most risk may still come off. Results no doubt confirm judgements with some assurance when similar choices are repeated in controlled conditions often enough for the laws of probability to speak with authority; but it is hard to see how such an objective test can be applied to the judgements of the statesman or the top executive. It would seem that the validation of action judgements also is a matter of judgement.

When we consider value judgements we find the same situation in a much more extreme form. The validation of a value judgement is necessarily a value judgement. Churchill, Bolivar and Ford told themselves what they meant by success. Those who disagreed with them could do so only by appealing to different standards, representing value judgements of their own. There would seem to be no means whereby the adjudicating mind can escape responsibility for the standards of value to which it commits itself.

I have distinguished three kinds of judgement, often present together – value judgement, reality judgement and action judgement – and I have reached the conclusion that the higher the level of judgement involved, the less possible it is to find an objective test by which to prove that the judgement is good. The appraisal of judgement is itself an act of judgement. In particular, value judgements are logically incapable of being validated by an objective test. They cannot be proved true or false. They can only be approved as right or condemned as wrong by the exercise of another value judgement.

Does this condemn us to pure subjectivism? In my view definitely not. The status of judgements which are neither objective nor subjective has been analysed on a grand scale, with special regard to scientific judgements, by Professor Michael Polanyi,[1] himself an outstanding physical

1. M. Polanyi (1958). *Personal Knowledge*, Routledge & Kegan Paul.

scientist – and I find myself broadly in agreement with his views, as far as I understand them – but to pursue the philosophic issue involved would take me far beyond the limits of this lecture. Nor need I do so, for the concept of responsible choice – that is, of decision which is personal yet made with a sense of obligation to discover the 'rules of rightness'[2] applicable to the particular situation – is a familiar concept in business, which we trust and use many times a day, even though neither philosophers nor psychologists can explain it.

Judgement and decision

We sometimes use the word 'judgement' as if it meant the same as 'decision', but this is too narrow an interpretation. A good judge of men, for example, *reveals* his good judgement by the appointments and changes he makes, but the judgement which guides those decisions is something which he exercises continually as he observes and appraises the people around him. I will ask you to consider an example of this sort in some detail.

One morning, Mr Redletter, the managing director of The Weathercock Company (all the characters in my illustrations are imaginary), reached the conclusion that the company's chief supplies officer, Mr A, was not up to his job; that somehow he must be removed from his post and replaced by Mr B. What precipitated this decision I will inquire later. For the moment I ask you to accept it as a fact and to follow it backwards and forwards in time.

To reach this conclusion Mr Redletter must have had in his head an idea of where the Weathercock Company was going and of where he wanted it to go; of the part which the supplies department was playing in the company's effectiveness and the part which it should be playing; of Mr A's performance as its head and of what its head's performance should be; and of the probable performance of Mr B. All these ideas were the cumulative result of several years' experience of the company and its staff. They were not mere observations, they were judgements. These judgements go in pairs; a judgement of the situation as it is compared with a judgement of the situation as it might be. It is the disparity between the two which has moved Mr Redletter to his decision. These are the two types of judgement which I have already distinguished as reality judgement and value judgement. They are closely connected.

2. The expression is Polanyi's.

Mr Redletter's idea of Mr A is not a mere catalogue of Mr A's past performances. It is an hypothesis sufficiently comprehensive to explain all he knows about Mr A, and from which he can assess Mr A's probable performance in various roles; his potentialities and power of learning; his current trend of development or deterioration; his probable response to promotion or transfer. Even so, it is not complete. It is selective and the selection reflects the nature of his interest in Mr A, which is that of a manager in a functional subordinate. Mr A's doctor or wife or colleague on the local borough council would each have a different picture of Mr A – different not merely because of their differing gifts and opportunities for forming a judgement, but also because of their differing interests in Mr A. Someone who had no interest at all in Mr A could have no picture of him.

Thus the nature of Mr Redletter's interest in Mr A defines what aspects of Mr A he shall select for attention and valuation. The same is true of his interest in the supplies department. So when Mr Redletter asked himself, 'Can we wear Mr A any longer as Chief Supplies Officer?' he found the materials for an answer already in his head. Nor were these merely 'raw' materials. They were an accumulation of judgements, leading to ever more complete hypotheses about Mr A and the supplies department. On the other hand, what he found in his head was not *the* answer. This question redefined his interest and called for a revaluation of the problem, leaving his ideas of Mr A and the supplies department, however, slightly changed.

The result we know. For the first time, on this particular morning, Mr Redletter, comparing his value judgement with his reality judgement, reached the answer 'no'.

Let us now follow that silent decision forwards. What is to be done? This I have called the action judgement. It takes the form of a dialogue between Mr Redletter, the man of judgement, and an invaluable but irritating boffin in his head who makes uncritical but sometimes brilliant suggestions.

'Move him to another job?'
'He'd be worse elsewhere.'

'Retire him early under the pension scheme?'
'We can't – he's below the minimum age.'

'Give him his notice and let him go?'
'We couldn't do that with old A in all the circumstances, it wouldn't be fair.'

'Make him an ex gratia *allowance?'*
'Anything big enough to mitigate hardship would be a most awkward precedent.'

'Must you really do it now?'
'YES.'

Silence: then –

'Well, you could divide the department, leave A in charge of the bit he knows, put B in charge of the rest, let them both report to C for the time being; then, in two years when C retires . . .'

'M'yes. We *might . . .'*

You will notice that all these tentative action judgements except the last one are rejected because they are either impracticable or inconsistent with Mr Redletter's idea of the sort of employer the company wished to be: in other words, by a reality judgement or a value judgement.

I have now squeezed all I want from this example. The results can be summarized as follows:

1. Judgement is a fundamental, continuous process, integral with our thinking.

2. It has three aspects – for simplicity, three kinds of judgement: value judgement, reality judgement, action judgement. The first two are the more fundamental and important. Action judgement is only called for by the interaction of value judgement and reality judgement, and is only selected by further use of the same criteria.

3. The aspects of the situation which are appreciated (reality judgement) and evaluated (value judgement) are determined by the interest of the judging mind.

All these forms of judgement are mental skills. It remains to ask of what they consist; and how they may be trained. Before I turn to these questions I will take up one which I have left unanswered. Why did Mr Redletter reach his conclusion just then? This inquiry will lead me to explore the meaning of initiative and the relation between initiative and judgement.

Judgement and initiative

What precipitated Mr Redletter's action judgement? Had Mr A just dropped an enormous 'clanger', costing the company most of a year's profit? Or had Mr Redletter so radically revised his ideas of what a supplies department should be that Mr A's interpretation of his role, though unchanged and accepted for many years, suddenly became intolerable?

These are remote points on a continuous scale. The disparity between reality judgement and value judgement may widen because of a change either in the situation as we see it (our reality judgement) or in the standards of value which we apply to it (our value judgment). This scale is important and I will illustrate it by two other episodes in the earlier history of the Weathercock Company. The decision involved in both is collective. What I have said applies equally, as I believe, to collective and to individual decisions. In collective decisions, however, varying views on reality, value and action are expressed by different voices and are more easily distinguished than when their clashes and accommodations take place within a single head.

In the first episode we find the directors of the Weathercock Company in an emergency meeting one Thursday. The bank has refused to extend the overdraft sufficiently to provide the pay packets on the following day except upon unwelcome and onerous terms. After long debate, the directors accept the bank's terms, telling each other that they have no choice. Strictly speaking they had a choice; they might have said 'no' or failed to say 'yes', which would have been the same thing. To choose this alternative, however, would be to choose the immediate and irreversible dissolution of the undertaking and of their own authority, and that in the most untidy fashion. The bank's terms raised no objections which could make such a course preferable.

I will now introduce you to the board of the Weathercock Company some years later. The situation has been transformed. Output is maximal, orders and cash are alike embarrassing in their abundance. The only troubles are troubles of growth, and the worst of these is that the company has no longer any physical room to grow.

They are agreed that something must be done but embarrassed by the variety of possible courses and divided on the merits of the few which are seriously considered. Mr Redletter wants to build a new factory and a new site in a new town twenty miles away; and in it he wants an impressive slice of space to develop a new business in moulded plastics, which, with the reluctant consent of his board, he had set up in some precious floor space of the present works a year or two before.

None of his colleagues supports the managing director; the arguments against his plan are impressive. The firm will lose most of its present employees and face others with hard choices. It will break its connections with its home town and its home site. The economies claimed for the move are offset by an x representing the unknown variables which will be set loose by so radical a change. And why moulded plastics, when the traditional business is doing so well?

The final decision was in no one's mind when the debate began but was unanimously adopted in the end and pleased everyone. The undertaking would stay where it was, make better use of existing space, and would swallow the coveted area begrudged to plastics. It would also buy a large site in the place favoured by Mr Redletter and build there a small factory – for the moulded plastic business only. Mr Redletter was well content; his pet venture could expand all the better in this relative isolation; the rest could still move out, maybe, one day later on. The others were content also. They got what they wanted, escaped all threats – and kept the managing director happy. You will note that the managing director, though in a minority of one, got his way in what most mattered to him because all his colleagues felt it was essential to any settlement that they should keep him, and keep him happy. These two situations illustrate what I will call the gradient of initiative.

The gradient of initiative

The first is an extreme case. The company is on the verge of insolvency. An instability – the imbalance between money in and money out – which has been progressively affecting its performance for some time, is about to cross a critical threshold, beyond which its effects will overflow in all directions and bring the system to disorganization and dissolution.

The effect of instability on a system is usually of this form. The most clear-cut example is physical death. A living organism is an organization, maintained by the delicately balanced intake and outflow of air, food and water, and equipped with admirable devices for keeping these balances – and many others – within critical limits. The maintenance of this system is a necessary, though not of course a sufficient, condition for the highest achievement of human intellect and feeling; and among the humble but necessary skills of living we recognize the skill of keeping alive and healthy – normally as a condition of all we want to do with life, occasionally, as when we are escaping from a fire or a furious bull, as an end in itself.

Similarly, for business, solvency is not an end, but it is a precondition of successful existence and when threatened it may become an end in itself.

Political organizations such as nation states are similarly liable to changes of this step-function form. There is, however, a difference in the degree of irreversible change illustrated by these examples. The dead organism dissolves; all its constituents rearrange themselves in new and less improbable configurations. The bankrupt business, after liquidation, may reappear more or less changed. Someone will probably carry on much the same business in the same building with some of the old plant. Some of the former employees may be re-engaged. Only the accounts will show a complete break. Alternatively, if technical liquidation is avoided the only continuity may be the old losses, carefully preserved for the benefit of the newcomer's future income tax.

Wars and political revolutions raise even more difficult questions as to the identity of the future system with that of the past. These difficulties are due largely to our habits of language and thought, which invest their objects with an unreal degree of wholeness and independence. I refer to them only to establish two ideas which are important to my argument.

I wish to distinguish first between the conditions which establish a given measure of freedom and the reasons which explain how that freedom is actually used. In my case-history, the establishment of the company's liquidity was one of the conditions which enabled it to grow and ultimately to go in for moulding plastics; but it throws no light at all on why the company chose to go in for moulding plastics. For this we must explore the past history of the managing director.

This may seem obvious; but it is often by no means easy to be sure whether a given explanation explains why something happened or merely explains how its happening was possible. The theory of evolution has been supposed for the last century to explain why life on this planet has developed as it has; but serious and respected thinkers today contend that the theory merely explains how that development, among others, became possible.[3]

Arising out of this distinction, I wish to establish the idea that an organization, like an organism, can conveniently be regarded as a hierarchy of systems, each dependent on, but not explained by, those below. The variables which determine the solvency of a business could be described and discussed without any reference to the nature of the undertaking's product, the interests of its staff, the ambitions of its directors or a host of other things which fill the agenda at its meetings. In the first situation, solvency was in such peril that the field of choice was minimal. As with the man escaping from the bull, the preservation of

3. See, for example, M. Greene (1958), *British Journal for Philosophy of Science*, 9, nos. 34 and 35.

basic conditions had become itself a dominating goal of policy. In the second situation, the basic conditions of existence were sufficiently secure to enable the directors to realize a variety of possible values, even some which they had not contemplated before. The future depended not on the adroitness of their actions but on the quality of their dreams. The gradient of initiative leads from the familiar track, where events are in control, to the uncharted spaces where dreams, whether 'right' dreams or 'wrong' dreams, can and must take charge and where that man is lost who cannot dream at all.

Thus skill in value judgement is increasingly demanded as human initiative widens. It is to be expected that some leaders who show the greatest resource in conditions of extreme difficulty will be less successful when they must seek guidance, not from without, but from within themselves.

The action judgement

I will now revert to the question left unanswered at the end of an earlier section. What are the mental processes underlying the three aspects of judgement?

The judgement which has been most carefully studied is what I have called the 'pure' action judgement. This is typified in Köhler's classic learning experiments with apes. The motivation (value judgement) is standardized; the animal wants a bunch of bananas which is out of reach. The situation is standardized; the materials for a solution are all in sight. Only one solution is possible, so no choice between solutions is involved. The means to be used – a hooked stick, a few boxes – are not, as far as can be avoided, charged with an affective meaning of their own. The issue is simply whether the creature can see how to use these neutral objects as means to an end.

The process by which one ape does, while another ape does not, succeed – suddenly, but after prolonged incubation – in 'seeing' the boxes as a potential increase in height, the stick as a potential increase in reach, remains a fascinating psychological puzzle.

Now consider a human example. As a very inexperienced subaltern in the old war, my company commander once said to me, 'Vickers, the company will bathe this afternoon. Arrange.' In the Flemish hamlet where we were billeted the only bath of any kind was in the local nunnery. The nuns were charity itself but I could not ask them to bathe a hundred men. I reviewed other fluid-containing objects – cattle drinking troughs, empty beer barrels – and found practical or ethical objections to them all; and at that point I had the misfortune to meet my company commander again and was forced to admit that I had not yet found the answer. He was annoyed. 'Whatever have you been doing all this time?' he said, and then, turning his own mind to the problem, as it seemed for the first time, he added, 'Take the company limbers off their wheels, put the tilts inside, four baths each four feet square, four men to a bath, do the job in an hour, why don't you use your brains?'

Simple indeed; but his solution involved two steps which my mind had not taken – the apprehension that a vehicle is a collection of bits and pieces, of which, for some purposes, the wheels may be irrelevant; and the apprehension that a tilt tailored to cover a protruding load and keep rainwater out, would fit and serve equally well, pushed into the empty waggon, to keep bathwater in.

My company commander – unlike myself – showed a mental ability like that of Köhler's more successful apes, though higher in degree; a facility for uncoupling the elements of a familiar idea and recombining them in a new way – for seeing a limber as two potential baths on irrelevant wheels, without forgetting that it is primarily and must again become a vehicle. This is a faculty useful in the research and development department and equally in the board room. Let us call it ingenuity.

The meaning of ingenuity

Yet it must involve more than we usually associate with ingenuity. The mere multiplication of alternative means to an end might only make the choice harder, unless it were accompanied by some gift which guides the problem-solver in the general direction of the still undiscovered solution. The literature of problem-solving, no less than common experience, attests our capacity for searching with a lively sense of 'warm . . . warmer . . . *warmer* . . .' when we do not know what we are looking for.

It would seem, then, that even the pure action judgement involves mental faculties which are still highly obscure. Yet the pure action judgement is too simple a process to be seen outside the laboratory. Even my efforts to improvise bathing facilities were hedged about with reality judgements and value judgements of great complexity; reality judgements about what our Flemish hosts would stand with equanimity from their British billetees, and value judgements defining the kind of solution which would be acceptable to me, having regard to its impact on the troops, the inhabitants, my company commander and myself.

The action judgement is involved in answering any question of the form, 'What shall I do about it?' when 'it' has been defined by judgements of reality and value. In implementing a decision, this question may have to be asked several times. 'What shall we do about the supplies department?' 'We will change the head.' 'What shall we do about changing the head?' 'We will divide the department and . . .' 'What shall we do about this decision to divide . . .?' 'First we will tell A and then B and then . . .'

Thus each decision sets a more precise problem for the next exercise of action judgement; and at each stage there is assumed a set of criteria for determining between different solutions. These criteria are supplied by further judgements of reality and value. 'That would not be legal.' 'That would not be fair.' 'That would not be possible.' And so on.

This process has many interesting aspects which I have no time to pursue. I will refer to two only. First, what solutions are considered and in what order? Professor Simon[4] has pointed out that the solutions which are weighed are usually far fewer than the totality of possible solutions which exist. Often the totality is too large to be reviewed, however briefly, in the time available. Random selection seldom if ever occurs. Some mental process narrows the field rapidly to a short list of alternatives, which alone are carefully compared.

Some elements of this selective process are apparent. A man seeking a solution to a problem will usually review first the solutions which are approved by custom or his own experience for dealing with problems which seem similar; or he may try first the responses which are most accessible to him or which he most enjoys. Occasionally, however, explanations fail us and we have to credit the problem-solver with an intuitive feeling for the approach which is likely to prove fruitful, though we can see no clue by which it is recognized. This is the heuristic element in ingenuity, to which I have already referred.

Professor Simon assumes that the fully rational course is to examine every possible solution and to choose the 'best'. It seems clear to me that this is not the way the brain works. The criterion, I suggest, is not the best but the 'good enough'. The human brain scans possible solutions in an order which is itself determined by the complex and obscure factors to which I have referred; and it stops as soon as a solution is not rejected by criteria of reality or value.

If all solutions are rejected and no new ones can be devised, the standard of the acceptable has to be lowered and the process is then repeated. The unsuccessful series of rehearsals is not wasted, for it prepares the mind for the change of standard.

4. H. A. Simon (1959), *Administrative Behaviour*, 2nd edn, Macmillan.

The reality judgement

I turn now to the reality judgement. This, too, involves analysis and synthesis, often repeated. It requires the ready handling, dissociating, reassociating of the elements in our thought which I have called ideas or concepts. It, too, has scope for ingenuity. Yet it seems to me to require somewhat different qualities of mind.

The problem-solver has his problem to guide him. The reality judgement, on the other hand, leads us as far afield as we let it; for the aspect of the situation with which it is concerned is as wide as our interest, and we can follow it in time until imagination fails us. One of the gifts needed by those who make reality judgments is to know where to stop: to sense the point beyond which the best estimate of trends is not worth making.

The maker of reality judgements is for the time being an observer; not like the maker of action judgements, an agent. He needs detachment, objectivity, balance, a clear head to follow the complex permutations of the possible and the practicable; a stout heart, to give as much reality to the unwelcome as to the welcome. Where the maker of action judgements must above all be ingenious, persistent and bold, the maker of reality judgements must be honest, clear-sighted and brave. Above all, perhaps, he needs a ready sense for those aspects of the situation which are most relevant. And here, too, the man of outstanding judgement shows such an unerring sense for those facts which will be found to matter most that it is safer to give his unexplained facility a special name and call it also an heuristic gift.

The value judgement

The value judgement raises problems far more obscure. Clearly it is fundamental; if we were not concerned with values which we wanted to realize and preserve we should have no interest in the situation and no incentive to action. The basic difficulty in all complex decisions is to reconcile the conflicting values involved – in my first example, the supply needs of the undertaking, the deserts of Mr A, the board's reputation as an employer, the preservation of tacit rules governing promotion and discharge and so on.

All these values are standards of what the undertaking should seek and expect of itself and others. I will call them norms. They are not settled in the abstract terms but they are implicit in every major decision. Executives absorb them from these decisions and still more from the experience of participating in the making of decisions, and by the same process they contribute to the setting of these standards and to their constant revision. Thus the maker of value judgements is not an observer but an agent. He needs not so much detachment as commitment, for his judgement commits him to implications far wider than he can know.

In approaching their decisions, executives usually find the appropriate standards of value ready to hand. They cannot depart abruptly either from their own past standard or from those current in their industry. In deciding how to treat Mr A, for example, the possible range of decision was closely limited. Thus executives, in making value judgements, are seldom conscious of doing more than apply a rule.

Yet, viewed over time, it is obvious that these standards are constantly changed by the very process of applying them, just as the common law is developed and even changed by accumulating precedents. The ghost of the economic man should not persuade us to ignore the fact that business undertakings today are governed by most complex value systems. Those who direct them must somehow provide themselves with standards of what the undertaking expects of itself – standards sufficiently coherent to be usable, yet sufficiently comprehensive to define its divergent responsibilities to employees, shareholders, consumers, suppliers, locality, industry, government and community. In every one of these fields the standards of industry today are markedly different from what they were a few decades ago; and the standards of individual undertakings differ from one to another and also change with time.

Thus in every value judgement there is latent a creative process; a resetting of the norms which are being applied.

We can as yet give no satisfactory account of the process by which we resolve problems of conflicting value. We only beg the question when we talk of maximizing satisfactions, for the satisfactions we maximize are set by ourselves; and there is no evidence that we reduce those disparate imponderables to a common measure, so that they can be added and weighed. There is indeed much evidence that we do not.

I have already expressed the belief that in the ultimate analysis, the validity of our norm-setting cannot be validated or falsified by results. It can be approved or condemned only by reference to a sense of rightness for which the adjudicating mind must take responsibility. This is obviously true of the artist and the connoisseur of art and conduct. That it is equally true of the scientist is the theme of Professor Polanyi's book. I believe it to be equally true of the business executive.

This survey of the processes involved in judgement may well leave us in doubt how far the mechanical and mathematical models of decision making – now so popular – as distinct from mechanical and mathematical aids to decision making are of any relevance. On this important and controversial question I have time for only one comment. In so far as these models are concerned only with what I have called pure action judgement they would seem to have no bearing on any of the main issues which I have raised; for the pure action judgement is unknown in real life. In so far as they assert or suggest that the pure action judgement is the typical decision-making situation, they do a vast disservice both to the inquiry and to the undoubtedly great contribution which, with a more modest approach, they could make to it.

Innate capacities for judgement

The extent to which we can develop judgement in ourselves and others is limited by our, and their, inherent capacity for the many mental activities involved. In these it seems clear that human beings differ widely. Minds differ greatly in their capacity for handling, arranging and combining the symbols with which we think. They differ in their ability to recognize causal and other relationships within actual or imagined sequences of events. We can say with confidence of some problems that they are too difficult for A to solve: of some situations that they are too complex for B to comprehend.

It may even be that men differ in the faculties they use. Dr Grey Walter[5] has suggested that those who are unusually gifted with visual imagination reach some decisions in ways quite different from the ways used by others, not less intelligent, who are unusually devoid of this gift. He claims further that the electro-encephalogram distinguishes the two types, each of which contains, he suggests, about a tenth of the population.

Men differ further in the moral qualities involved in judgement. C could comprehend the situation, he could solve the problem: but has he the guts to go on trying until he succeeds? Will the mere stress of having to try impair his capacity for success? (Examinations rightly test this moral quality, no less than the intellectual ones which they are designed to explore.) This difference is so important that we rate executives for decisiveness, as well as for good judgement, reserving the highest rewards for those who excel in both, but recognizing that the ability to decide at all is a prior requisite, and in some cases a major one. Lord Wavell, in some famous lectures on generalship, said that stupidity in

5. D. W. Grey Walter (1953), *The Living Brain*, Duckworth, p. 152.

generals should never excite surprise. For generals are chosen from that small, preselected class of men who are tough enough to be generals at all. From such heavy-duty animals, refinements of intellect and sensibility should not be expected.

Lord Wavell's dictum, to which he was so notable an exception, is of general application. No one can exercise good judgement unless he can support both the stress of the office in which the judgement is to be exercised, and the stress of the judgement itself. Not all high offices are in themselves as stressful as that of a general in the field; but the stress inherent in judgement itself is inescapable. Between value judgement and reality judgement there is tension, characteristic of all human life. It may lead to the kind of breakdown which psychiatrists meet in patients who have lost touch with reality, or who torment themselves with an impossible level of aspiration. Distortions of judgement due to the same cause are common enough in boardrooms, as for instance when a board is faced with a problem of redundancy too large to be handled within the rules of what it has come to regard as fair. The opposite error of those who protect themselves by failing to aspire enough is more common, and much more wasteful, but more easily overlooked.

Again, the sheer difficulty of keeping the judgement of value and reality from running away into irresolvable complexity is itself a source of stress, and accounts for the familiar distinction between men of action and men of thought. The simplicity which characterizes the thought processes of men of action has often seemed to me excessive; but it is nevertheless essential to individual good judgement that a man's capacity for judgements of value and reality shall be related to his own capacity for action judgement. One of the merits of business organization is that these different human capacities can be combined.

Finally, clear judgement of value and reality only makes more frustrating the common human state of helplessness, when no effective action can be taken; and this is as common in business life as in life at large.

Courage and endurance are not the only moral qualities associated with good judgement. D has guts in plenty but he is conceited, full of personal prejudice, takes offence easily; in brief, is not sufficiently selfless or sufficiently disciplined to achieve that combination of detachment and commitment which good judgement demands.

Finally, apart from these moral qualities, I have expressed the belief that judgement needs that sensitivity to form, which, in various guises, distinguishes the connoisseur of art or conduct, the scientist and the judge, and which is equally required in the business executive.

The training of management

Have I given the impression that good judgement is to be expected only from those who combine the qualities of philosopher, hero and saint to a degree rarely found even among top people? I hope not. In so far as it involves peculiarly human qualities of intellect, sensibility, character and will, it does indeed give scope for every kind of excellence, yet equally, just because it is so human a quality, it is not likely to be lacking in anyone we recognize as fully human.

It is indeed ubiquitous; for it is involved in some degree in every exercise of discretion. Among the debts of gratitude which business people owe to Dr Elliott Jaques, I give a high place to his finding[6] that, among all the jobs, from highest to lowest, in the undertaking which he has studied so carefully, not one fails to involve some elements of discretion, some duty, essential to its performance, which is not and cannot be specified in the instructions given to the holder. We are not paid, says Dr Elliott Jacques, for doing what we are told to do, but for doing rightly that part of our job which is left to our discretion; and we rate our own and our fellows' jobs on our estimate of the weight of this discretionary element.

If Dr Jaques is right, judgement is the most universal requirement not only of managerial work but of all work. The distribution of roles on an organization chart may thus be seen, not merely as an allocation of duties but as an allocation of discretions, increasing up the hierarchy in the quality of the judgement they demand.

This picture helps us to answer the question, 'How is judgement developed?' The whole structure of industry is or should be a school of judgement, in the course of which individuals may develop, by practice and example, both the general qualities of mind, heart and will, which all judgement demands, and their own particular aptitudes which determine the kind of judgement in which they can become most proficient.

In such a school everyone is both learner and teacher. The teaching function is both positive and negative. It is positive in that it requires every member of the organization in his daily work to set an example in the exercise of judgement and to supervise its exercise by those for whom he is responsible. It is negative in that it requires everyone to respect the field of discretion of his subordinates, as he expects his superiors to respect his own – especially when he himself is more expert than they in the very same field.

6. Elliott Jaques (1956), *Measurement of Responsibility*, Tavistock Publications.

Conclusion

As I feared, my short title, like a conjuror's hat, has produced more curious objects than I have had time to examine to your satisfaction or my own. The material is far from tidy; the hat is far from empty; and my time is overspent. Apart from displaying what I believe to be the main dimensions of the problem and setting question marks in appropriate places, I have tried to do no more than on the one hand to couple the higher executive – in the exercise of this, his most precious and highly-paid endowment – with those excellent minds in other fields, whose function he must so often copy unawares; on the other hand, to link him with the humblest servants in his own undertaking, on whose judgement he must rely, as they on his, and from among whom it should be his delight, as it is his duty, to develop minds capable of better judgement than his own.

13   H. A. Simon

Decision Making and Organizational Design

From H. A. Simon, 'The executive as decision maker' and 'Organizational design: man-machine systems for decision making', *The New Science of Management Decision*, Harper & Row, 1960, chapter I, pp. 1–8, and chapter 5, pp. 35–50.

The executive as decision maker

What part does decision making play in managing? I shall find it convenient to take mild liberties with the English language by using 'decision making' as though it were synonymous with 'managing'.

What is our mental image of a decision maker? Is he a brooding man on horseback who suddenly rouses himself from thought and issues an order to a subordinate? Is he a happy-go-lucky fellow, a coin poised on his thumbnail, ready to risk his action on the toss? Is he an alert, gray-haired businessman, sitting at the board of directors' table with his associates, caught at the moment of saying 'aye' or 'nay'? Is he a bespectacled gentleman, bent over a docket of papers, his pen hovering over the line marked (X)?

All of these images have a significant point in common. In them, the decision maker is a man at the moment of choice, ready to plant his foot on one or another of the routes that lead from the crossroads. All the images falsify decision by focusing on its final moment. All of them ignore the whole lengthy, complex process of alerting, exploring and analysing that precede that final moment.

Intelligence, design and choice in decision making

In treating decision making as synonymous with managing, I shall be referring not merely to the final act of choice among alternatives but rather to the whole process of decision. Decision making comprises three principal phases: finding occasions for making a decision; finding possible courses of action; and choosing among courses of action. These three activities account for quite different fractions of the time budgets of executives. The fractions vary greatly from one organization level to another and from one executive to another, but we can make some generalizations about them even from casual observation. Executives spend a large fraction of their time surveying the economic, technical, political and social environment to identify new conditions that call for new actions. They probably spend an even larger fraction of their time, individually or with their associates, seeking to invent, design and develop possible courses of action for handling situations where a decision is needed. They spend a small fraction of their time in choosing among alternative actions already developed to meet an identified problem and already analysed for their consequences. The three fractions, added together, account for most of what executives do.[1]

The first phase of the decision-making process – searching the environment for conditions calling for decision – I shall call *intelligence* activity (borrowing the military meaning of intelligence). The second phase – inventing, developing and analysing possible courses of action – I shall call *design* activity. The third phase – selecting a particular course of action from those available – I shall call *choice* activity.

Let me illustrate these three phases of decision. In the past five years, many companies have reorganized their accounting and other data-processing activities in order to make use of large electronic computers. How has this come about? Computers first became available commercially in the early 1950s. Although, in some vague and general sense, company managements were aware that computers existed, few managements had investigated their possible applications with any thoroughness before about 1955. For most companies, the use of computers required no decision before that time because it hadn't been placed on the agenda. (Cyert, Simon and Trow, 1956.)

The intelligence activity preceding the introduction of computers tended to come about in one of two ways. Some companies – for example, in the aircraft and atomic energy industries – were burdened with enormously complex computations for engineering design. Because efficiency in computation was a constant problem, and because the design departments were staffed with engineers who could understand, at least in general, the technology of computers, awareness of computers and their potentialities came early to these companies. After computers were already in extensive use for design calculations, businesses with a large number-processing load – insurance companies, accounting departments in large firms, banks – discovered these new devices and began to consider seriously their introduction.

Once it was recognized that computers might have a place in modern

1. The way in which these activities take shape within an organization is described in some detail in March and Simon (1958), chapters 6 and 7.

business, a major design task had to be carried out in each company before they could be introduced. It is now a commonplace that payrolls can be prepared by computers. Programs in both the general and computer senses for doing this are relatively easy to design in any given situation.[2] To develop the first computer programs for preparing payroll, however, was a major research and development project. Few companies having carried their investigations of computers to the point where they had definite plans for their use, failed to install them. Commitment to the new course of action took place gradually as the intelligence and design phases of the decision were going on. The final choice was, in many instances, almost *pro forma*.

Generally speaking, intelligence activity precedes design, and design activity precedes choice. The cycle of phases is, however, far more complex than this sequence suggests. Each phase in making a particular decision is itself a complex decision-making process. The design phase, for example, may call for new intelligence activities; problems at any given level generate subproblems that, in turn, have their intelligence, design, and choice phases, and so on. There are wheels within wheels within wheels. Nevertheless, the three large phases are often clearly discernible as the organizational decision process unfolds. They are closely related to the stages in problem solving first described by John Dewey (1910):

What is the problem?
What are the alternatives?
Which alternative is best?

It may be objected that I have ignored the task of carrying out decisions. I shall merely observe by the way that seeing that decisions are executed is again decision-making activity. A broad policy decision creates a new condition for the organization's executives that calls for the design and choice of a course of action for executing the policy. Executing policy, then, is indistinguishable from making more detailed policy. For this reason, I shall feel justified in taking my pattern for decision making as a paradigm for most executive activity.

Developing decision-making skills

It is an obvious step from the premise that managing is decision making to the conclusion that the important skills for an executive are decision-

2. For a good discussion on the use of the computer for such purposes, see Gregory and Van Horn (1960).

making skills. It is generally believed that good decision makers, like good athletes, are born, not made. The belief is about as true in the one case as it is in the other.

That human beings come into the world endowed unequally with biological potential for athletic prowess is undeniable. They also come endowed unequally with intelligence, cheerfulness and many other characteristics and potentialities. To a limited extent, we can measure some aspects of that endowment – height, weight, perhaps intelligence. Whenever we make such measurements and compare them with adult performance, we obtain significant, but low, correlations. A man who is not a natural athlete is unlikely to run the four-minute mile; but many men who are natural athletes have never come close to that goal. A man who is not 'naturally' intelligent is unlikely to star in science; but many intelligent scientists are not stars.

A good athlete is born when a man with some natural endowment, by dint of practice, learning and experience develops that natural endowment into a mature skill. A good executive is born when a man with some natural endowment (intelligence and some capacity for interacting with his fellow men) by dint of practice, learning and experience develops his endowment into a mature skill. The skills involved in intelligence, design and choosing activities are as learnable and trainable as the skills involved in driving, recovering and putting a golf ball. I hope to indicate some of the things a modern executive needs to learn about decision making.

Executive responsibility for organizational decision making

The executive's job involves not only making decisions himself, but also seeing that the organization, or part of an organization, that he directs makes decisions effectively. The vast bulk of the decision-making activity for which he is responsible is not his personal activity, but the activity of his subordinates.

Nowadays, with the advent of computers, we can think of information as something almost tangible; strings of symbols which, like strips of steel or plastic ribbons, can be processed – changed from one form to another. We can think of white-collar organizations as factories for processing information. The executive is the factory manager, with all the usual responsibilities for maintaining the factory operation, getting it back into operation when it breaks down, and proposing and carrying through improvements in its design.

There is no reason to expect that a man who has acquired a fairly high level of personal skill in decision-making activity will have a correspondingly high skill in designing efficient decision-making systems. To imagine that there is such a connection is like supposing that a man who is a good weight lifter can therefore design cranes. The skills of designing and maintaining the modern decision-making systems we call organizations are less intuitive skills. Hence, they are even more susceptible to training than the skills of personal decision making.

Programmed and nonprogrammed decisions

In discussing how executives now make decisions, and how they will make them in the future, let us distinguish two polar types of decisions. I shall call them *programmed decisions* and *nonprogrammed decisions*, respectively. Having christened them, I hasten to add that they are not really distinct types, but a whole continuum, with highly programmed decisions at one end of that continuum and highly unprogrammed decisions at the other end. We can find decisions of all shades of gray along the continuum, and I use the terms programmed and nonprogrammed simply as labels for the black and the white of the range.[3]

Decisions are programmed to the extent that they are repetitive and routine, to the extent that a definite procedure has been worked out for handling them so that they don't have to be treated *de novo* each time they occur. The obvious reason why programmed decisions tend to be repetitive, and vice versa, is that if a particular problem recurs often enough, a routine procedure will usually be worked out for solving it. Numerous examples of programmed decisions in organizations will occur to you: pricing ordinary customers' orders; determining salary payments to employees who have been ill; reordering office supplies.

Decisions are nonprogrammed to the extent that they are novel, unstructured and consequential. There is no cut-and-dried method for handling the problem because it hasn't arisen before, or because its precise nature and structure are elusive or complex, or because it is so important that it deserves a custom-tailored treatment. General Eisenhower's D-Day decision is a good example of a nonprogrammed decision. Remember, we are considering not merely the final act of ordering the attack, but the whole complex of intelligence and design activities that preceded it. Many of the components of the decisions were programmed – by standard techniques for military planning – but

3. See March and Simon (1958), pp. 139–42 and 177–80, for further discussion of these types of decisions. The labels used there are slightly different.

before these components could be designed they had to be provided with a broader framework of military and political policy.

I have borrowed the term program from the computer trade, and intend it in the sense in which it is used there. A *program* is a detailed prescription or strategy that governs the sequence of responses of a system to a complex task environment. Most of the programs that govern organizational response are not as detailed or as precise as computer programs. However, they all have the same intent: to permit an adaptive response of the system to the situation.

In what sense, then, can we say that the response of a system to a situation is nonprogrammed? Surely something determines the response. That something, that collection of rules of procedure, is by definition a program. By nonprogrammed I mean a response where the system has no specific procedures to deal with situations like the one at hand, but must fall back on whatever *general* capacity it has for intelligent, adaptive, problem-oriented action. In addition to his specific skills and specific knowledge, man has some general problem-solving capacities. Given almost any kind of situation, no matter how novel or perplexing, he can begin to reason about it in terms of ends and means.

This general problem-solving equipment is not always effective. Men often fail to solve problems, or they reach unsatisfactory solutions. But man is seldom completely helpless in a new situation. He possesses general problem-solving equipment which, however inefficient, fills some of the gaps in his special problem-solving skills. And organizations, as collections of men, have some of this same general adaptive capacity.

The cost of using general-purpose programs to solve problems is usually high. It is advantageous to reserve these programs for situations that are truly novel, where no alternative programs are available. If any particular class of situations recurs often enough, a special-purpose program can be developed which gives better solutions and gives them more cheaply than the general problem-solving apparatus.

My reason for distinguishing between programmed and nonprogrammed decisions is that different techniques are used for handling the programmed and the nonprogrammed aspects of our decision making. The distinction, then, will be a convenient one for classifying these techniques. I shall use it for that purpose, hoping that the reader will remind himself from time to time that the world is mostly gray with only a few spots of pure black or white.

The four-fold Table 1 will provide a map of the territory I propose to cover. In the northern half of the map are some techniques related to

Table 1 Traditional and modern techniques of decision making

Types of decisions	Decision-making techniques traditional	modern
Programmed: Routine, repetitive decisions Organization develops specific processes for handling them	1. Habit 2. Clerical routine: Standard operating procedures 3. Organization structure: Common expectations A system of subgoals Well-defined informational channels	1. Operations Research: Mathematical analysis Models Computer simulation 2. Electronic data processing
Nonprogrammed: One-shot, ill-structured novel policy decisions Handled by general problem-solving processes	1. Judgement, intuition, and creativity 2. Rules of thumb 3. Selection and training of executives	Heuristic problem-solving techniques applied to: (a) training human decision makers (b) constructing heuristic computer programs

programmed decision making, in the southern half, some techniques related to nonprogrammed decision making. In the western half of the map I placed the classical techniques used in decision making – the kit of tools that has been used by executives and organizations from the time of the earliest recorded history up to the present generation. In the eastern half of the map I placed the new techniques of decision making – tools that have been forged largely since the Second World War, and that are only now coming into extensive use in management in this country. I shall proceed across the map from west to east, and from north to south, taking up, in order, the north-west and the south-west quadrants, the north-east quadrant, and the south-east quadrant.

I can warn you now to what conclusion this journey is going to lead. We are in the midst of a major revolution in the art or science – whichever you prefer to call it – of management and organization. I shall try to describe the nature of this revolution and, in my final chapter, to discuss its implications.

Organizational design: man–machine systems for decision making

With operations research and electronic data processing we have acquired the technical capacity to automate programmed decision making and to bring into the programmed area some important classes of decisions that were formerly unprogrammed. Important innovations in decision-making processes in business are already resulting from these discoveries.

With heuristic programming, we are acquiring the technical capacity to automate nonprogrammed decision making. The next two decades will see changes in business decision making and business organization that will stem from this second phase in the revolution of our information technology. I should like now to explore, briefly, what the world of business will look like as these changes occur. (See Leavitt and Whisler, 1958, and Simon, 1960.)

Not all or, perhaps, most of the changes we may anticipate have to do with automation. As I pointed out earlier, the advance we may expect in the effectiveness of human decision-making processes is equally significant. Nevertheless, there has been so much public discussion about the automation and mechanization of data processing that I feel obliged to make some preliminary comments on this topic.

Some comments on automation

Although we always acknowledge our debt to machinery for the high productivity of Western industrial society, we almost always accompany that acknowledgment with warnings and head shakings about the unfortunate side effects that industrialization brings. Our concern about mechanization focuses on two points in particular: the hazard it creates of large-scale unemployment, and its supposed tendency to routinize work, draining it of the intrinsic satisfactions it might have possessed. Even management people, long accustomed to reassuring their blue-collar and clerical workers on these points, reveal exactly the same anxieties when the talk turns to the automation of decision making.

Automation and unemployment. In public discussion the danger of worker displacement through automation has been emphasized all out of proportion to its probable importance. The level of employment in a society is not related in any direct or necessary way to the level of automation in that society. There is absolutely no evidence that a society cannot and will not consume all the goods, services and leisure that the society can produce, provided that the social and economic institutions are even moderately well adapted to their functions of regulating production and distribution. If productivity increases especially rapidly in some sector of the economy (as, for example, productivity in agriculture has in the American economy), it may lead to significant temporary dislocation and technological unemployment of existing skills. There is no reason why the many should benefit from increases in productivity at the expense of the few who are displaced. Any society can and should devise means for eliminating most of the inequity associated with the displacement of skills.

I am aware that few societies in the past have done a good job of handling the undesirable transient effects of automation. This does not mean that it cannot be done, that we should blame our woes on automation, or that we should eschew the significant benefits resulting from productivity increases to avoid dealing with these transition problems. Fortunately, as past history shows, we will not, in fact, take the last-named course.

The pace of automation. How difficult it will be to take care of the transient effects of automation depends on the speed with which the automation occurs. A principal factor in regulating the rate of automation is the supply of capital for investment in the new equipment that is required. We can make a very rough estimate of what would be required for the complete automation of data processing and decision making.

Taking the respective income shares of capital and labor in total national income as the basis for our estimate, we may say that at the present time about four-fifths of the productive capacity of the American economy resides in its labor force, one-fifth in physical capital. Investment occurs at an annual rate of roughly ten per cent of the capital stock. Hence, it would take perhaps forty years – several generations – to accumulate capital equivalent in value to the capitalized value of the labor force.

If automated data-processing and decision-making devices just reached the break-even point where they were competitive with non-mechanized human data processing and decision making, it would still take several generations to bring about enough investment in the new automated systems to double the per capita productivity of the economy. Moreover, a 25 per cent increase in the technological efficiency of the *human* data processors and decision makers would produce as large an increase in productivity as this total investment in automated procedures.

I don't want to put more weight on these sorts of 'iffy' estimates than they will bear. Consideration of the quantities involved may have a useful sobering influence, however, on our prophecies of Utopia or of doom.

The composition of the labor force. We shall assume, then, that automation may affect the complexion of the labor force, but will not affect the employment level – except that general high incomes may lead to an increase in voluntary leisure. The division of labor between man and automatic devices will be determined by the doctrine of comparative advantage: those tasks in which machines have *relatively* the greatest advantage in productivity over men will be automated; those tasks in which machines have relatively the least advantage will remain manual.

I have done some armchair analysis of what this proposition means for predictions of the occupational profile twenty years hence. I do not have time to report this analysis in detail here, but I can summarize my conclusions briefly. Technologically, as I have argued earlier, machines will be capable, within twenty years, of doing any work that a man can do. Economically, men will retain their greatest comparative advantage in jobs that require flexible manipulation of those parts of the environment that are relatively rough – some forms of manual work, control of some kinds of machinery (e.g. operating earth-moving equipment), some kinds of nonprogrammed problem solving, and some kinds of service activities where face-to-face human interaction is of the essence. Man will be somewhat less involved in performing the day-to-day work of the organization, and somewhat more involved in maintaining the system that performs the work.[4]

The routinization of work. We do not need to debate whether work was more creative and more enjoyable before the Industrial Revolution or after. A more fruitful question is whether the kinds of automation that are going on now in factories and in offices tend to increase or decrease work satisfactions, tend to enrich or impoverish the lives of the people who are employed there.

There are now in print some half-dozen studies that cast some light on the question.[5] The conclusion I have reached upon examining these is

4. What little evidence we have on recent factory automation suggests that it does not greatly change the distribution of skill levels. My own estimate is that the same will prove true of the automation of clerical and managerial work. This is so basically because humans will retain their comparative advantage in tasks that match their skills and abilities. Man will be, as always, the measure of what man can do relatively well. See H. A. Simon (1960) and H. A. Simon (1957), chapter 12, 'Productivity and Urban Rural Population Balance'.

5. Two good references are James R. Bright (1958) and S. Lilley (1957).

that there is no uniform tendency of mechanization or automation to make factory and office work either more routine or less routine. The introduction of the assembly line was generally an influence in the direction of routinization. But as the level of factory automation has risen – especially the automation of repetitive manipulative tasks – automation has probably tended to make work less, rather than more, routine, and has loosened the linkage between the pace of the man and the pace of the machine.

How do these generalizations, based largely on observations of factory automation, apply to the automation of data-processing tasks? I have already essayed an answer in the previous section: Men will retain their greatest comparative advantage in jobs that require flexible manipulation of those parts of the environment that are relatively rough. Applied to the present issue, this means, I think, that automation will result in somewhat less routine or at least less repetitiveness in the work of the inhabitants of clerical offices and executive suites.

Implicit in virtually all discussions of routine is the assumption that any increase in the routinization of work decreases work satisfaction and impairs the growth and self-realization of the worker. Not only is this assumption unbuttressed by empirical evidence, but casual observation of the world about us suggests that it is false. I mentioned earlier Gresham's Law of Planning – that routine drives out nonprogrammed activity. A completely unstructured situation, to which one can apply only the most general problem-solving skills, without specific rules or direction, is, if prolonged, painful for most people. Routine is a welcome refuge from the trackless forests of unfamiliar problem spaces (March and Simon, 1958, p. 185).

The work on curiosity of Berlyne (1954) and others suggests that some kind of principle of moderation applies. People (and rats) find the most interest in situations that are neither completely strange nor entirely known – where there is novelty to be explored, but where similarities and programs remembered from past experience help guide the exploration. Nor does creativity flourish in completely unstructured situations. The almost unanimous testimony of creative artists and scientists is that the first task is to impose limits on the situation if the limits are not already given. The pleasure that the good professional experiences in his work is not simply a pleasure in handling difficult matters; it is a pleasure in using skillfully a well-stocked kit of well-designed tools to handle problems that are comprehensible in their deep structure but unfamiliar in their detail.

We must be cautious, then, in inferring, because managerial work will be more highly programmed in the future than it has been in the past – as it almost certainly will – that it will thereby be less satisfying or less creative.

Some fundamentals of organizational design

An organization can be pictured as a three-layered cake. In the bottom layer, we have the basic work processes – in the case of a manufacturing organization, the processes that procure raw materials, manufacture the physical product, warehouse it and ship it. In the middle layer, we have the programmed decision-making processes, the processes that govern the day-to-day operation of the manufacturing and distribution system. In the top layer, we have the nonprogrammed decision-making processes, the processes that are required to design and redesign the entire system, to provide it with its basic goals and objectives, and to monitor its performance.

Automation of data processing and decision making will not change this fundamental three-part structure. It may, by bringing about a more explicit description of the entire system, make the relations among the parts clear and more explicit.

The hierarchical structure of organizations.[6] Large organizations are almost universally hierarchical in structure. That is to say, they are divided into units which are subdivided into smaller units, which are, in turn, subdivided, and so on. They are also generally hierarchical in imposing on this system of successive partitionings a pyramidal authority structure. However, for the moment, I should like to consider the departmentalization rather than the authority structure.

Hierarchical subdivision is not a characteristic that is peculiar to human organizations. It is common to virtually all complex systems of which we have knowledge.

Complex biological organisms are made up of subsystems – digestive, circulatory and so on. These subsystems are composed of organs, organs of tissues, tissues of cells. The cell is, in turn, a hierarchically organized unit, with nucleus, cell wall, cytoplasm and other subparts.

The complex systems of chemistry and physics reveal the same picture of wheels within wheels within wheels. A protein molecule – one of the organismic building blocks – is constructed out of simpler structures, the amino acids. The simplest molecules are composed of atoms, the atoms

6. The speculations of the following paragraphs are products of my joint work over recent years with Allen Newell.

of so-called elementary particles. Even in cosmological structures, we find the same hierarchical pattern: galaxies, planetary systems, stars and planets.

The near universality of hierarchy in the composition of complex systems suggests that there is something fundamental in this structural principle that goes beyond the peculiarities of human organization. I can suggest at least two reasons why complex systems should generally be hierarchical:

1. *Among possible systems of a given size and complexity, hierarchical systems, composed of subsystems, are the most likely to appear through evolutionary processes.* A metaphor will show why this is so. Suppose we have two watchmakers, each of whom is assembling watches of ten thousand parts. The watchmakers are interrupted from time to time by the telephone, and have to put down their work. Now watchmaker A finds that whenever he lays down a partially completed watch, it falls apart again, and when he returns to it, he has to start reassembling it from the beginning. Watchmaker B, however, has designed his watches in such a way that each watch is composed of ten subassemblies of one thousand parts each, the subassemblies being themselves stable components. The major subassemblies are composed, in turn, of ten stable subassemblies of one hundred parts each, and so on. Clearly, if interruptions are at all frequent, watchmaker B will assemble a great many watches before watchmaker A is able to complete a single one.

2. *Among systems of a given size and complexity, hierarchical systems require much less information transmission among their parts than do other types of systems.* As was pointed out many years ago, as the number of members of an organization grows, the number of *pairs* of members grows with the square (and the number of possible subsets of members even more rapidly). If each member, in order to act effectively, has to know in detail what each other member is doing, the total amount of information that has to be transmitted in the organization will grow at least proportionately with the square of its size. If the organization is subdivided into units, it may be possible to arrange matters so that an individual needs detailed information only about the behavior of individuals in his own unit, and aggregative summary information about average behavior in other units. If this is so, and if the organization continues to subdivide into suborganizations by cell division as it grows in size, keeping the size of the lowest level subdivisions constant, the total amount of information that has to be transmitted will grow only slightly more than proportionately with size.

These two statements are, of course, only the grossest sorts of generalization. They would have to be modified in detail before they could be applied to specific organizational situations. They do provide, however, strong reasons for believing that almost any system of sufficient complexity would have to have the rooms-within-rooms structure that we observe in actual human organizations. The reasons for hierarchy go far beyond the need for unity of command or other considerations relating to authority.

The conclusion I draw from this analysis is that the automation of decision making, irrespective of how far it goes and in what directions it proceeds, is unlikely to obliterate the basically hierarchical structure of organizations. The decision-making process will still call for departmentalization and sub-departmentalization of responsibilities. There is some support for this prediction in the last decade's experience with computer programming. Whenever highly complex programs have been written – whether for scientific computing, business data processing or heuristic problem solving – they have always turned out to have a clear-cut hierarchical structure. The over-all program is always subdivided into subprograms. In programs of any great complexity, the subprograms are further subdivided, and so on. Moreover, in some general sense, the higher-level programs control or govern the behavior of the lower-level programs, so that we find among these programs relations of authority among routines that are not dissimilar to those we are familiar with in human organizations.[7]

Since organizations are systems of behavior designed to enable humans and their machines to accomplish goals, organizational form must be a joint function of human characteristics and the nature of the task environment. It must reflect the capabilities and limitations of the people and tools that are to carry out the tasks. It must reflect the resistance and ductility of the materials to which the people and tools apply themselves. What I have been asserting, then, in the preceding paragraphs is that one of the near universal aspects of organizational form, hierarchy, reflects no very specific properties of man, but a very general one. An organization will tend to assume hierarchical form whenever the task environment is complex relative to the problem-solving and communicating powers of the organization members and their tools. Hierarchy is the adaptive form for finite intelligence to assume in the face of complexity.

7. The exercise of authority by computer programs over others is not usually accompanied by affect. Routines do not resent or resist accepting orders from other routines.

The organizations of the future, then, will be hierarchies, no matter what the exact division of labor between men and computers. This is not to say that there will be no important differences between present and future organizations. Two points, in particular, will have to be re-examined at each stage of automation:

1. What are the optimal sizes of the building blocks in the hierarchy? Will they become larger or smaller? This is the question of centralization and decentralization.

2. What will be the relations among the building blocks? In particular, how far will traditional authority and accountability relations persist, and how far will they be modified? What will be the effect of automation upon subgoal formation and subgoal identification?

Size of the building blocks: centralization and decentralization. One of the major contemporary issues in organization design is the question of how centralized or decentralized the decision-making process will be – how much of the decision making should be done by the executives of the larger units, and how much should be delegated to lower levels. But centralizing and decentralizing are not genuine alternatives for organizing. The question is not whether we shall decentralize, but how far we shall decentralize. What we seek, again, is a golden mean: we want to find the proper level in the organization hierarchy – neither too high nor too low – for each important class of decisions.

Over the past twenty or more years there has been a movement toward decentralization in large American business organizations. This movement has probably been a sound development, but it does *not* signify that more decentralization is at all times and under all circumstances a good thing. It signifies that at a particular time in history, many American firms, which had experienced almost continuous long-term growth and diversification, discovered that they could operate more effectively if they brought together all the activities relating to individual products or groups of similar products and decentralized a great deal of decision making to the departments handling these products or product groups. At the very time this process was taking place there were many cross-currents of centralization in the same companies – centralization, for example, of industrial relations activities. There is no contradiction here. Different decisions need to be made in different organizational locations, and the best location for a class of decisions may change as circumstances change.

There are usually two pressures toward greater decentralization in a business organization. First, it may help bring the profit motive to bear on a larger group of executives by allowing profit goals to be established for individual subdivisions of the company. Second, it may simplify the decision-making process by separating out groups of related activities – production, engineering, marketing and finance for particular products – and allowing decisions to be taken on these matters within the relevant organizational subdivisions. Advantages can be realized in either of these ways only if the units to which decision is delegated are natural subdivisions – if, in fact, the actions taken in one of them do not affect in too much detail or too strongly what happens in the others. Hierarchy always implies intrinsically some measure of decentralization. It always involves a balancing of the cost savings through direct local action against the losses through ignoring indirect consequences for the whole organization.

Organizational form, I said earlier, must be a joint function of the characteristics of humans and their tools and the nature of the task environment. When one or the other of these changes significantly, we may expect concurrent modifications to be required in organizational structure – for example, in the amount of centralization or decentralization that is desirable.

When the cable and the wireless were added to the world's techniques of communication, the organization of every nation's foreign office changed. The ambassador and minister who had exercised broad, discretionary decision-making functions in the previous decentralized system, were now brought under much closer central control. The balance between the costs in time and money of communication with the center, and the advantages of coordination by the center had been radically altered.

The automation of important parts of business data-processing and decision-making activity, and the trend toward a much higher degree of structure and programming of even the nonautomated part will radically alter the balance of advantage between centralization and decentralization. The main issue is not the economics of scale – not the question of whether a given data-processing job can better be done by one large computer at a central location or a number of smaller ones, geographically or departmentally decentralized. Rather, the main issue is how we shall take advantage of the greater analytic capacity, the larger ability to take into account the interrelations of things, that the new developments in decision making give us. A second issue is how we shall deal with the technological fact that the processing of information within a coordinated computing system is orders of magnitude faster than the input-output rates at which we can communicate from one such system to another, particularly where human links are involved.

Let us consider the first issue: the capacity of the decision-making system to handle intricate interrelations in a complex system. In many factories today, the extent to which the schedules of one department are coordinated in detail with the schedules of a second department, consuming, say, part of the output of the first, is limited by the computational complexity of the scheduling problem. Often the best we can do is to set up a reasonable scheduling scheme for each department and put a sizeable buffer inventory of semi-finished product between them to prevent fluctuations in the operation of the first from interfering with the operation of the second. We accept the cost of holding the inventory to avoid the cost of taking account of detailed scheduling interactions.

We pay large inventory costs, also, to permit factory and sales management to make decisions in semi-independence of each other. The factory often stocks finished products so that it can deliver on demand to sales warehouses; the warehouses stock the same product so that the factory will have time to manufacture a new batch after an order is placed. Often, too, manufacturing and sales departments make their decisions on the basis of independent forecasts of orders.

With the development of operations research techniques for determining optimal production rates and inventory levels, and with the development of the technical means to maintain and adjust the data that are required, large savings are attainable through inventory reductions and the smoothing of production operations, but at the cost of centralizing to a greater extent than in the past the factory scheduling and warehouse ordering decisions. Since the source of the savings is in the coordination of the decisions, centralization is unavoidable if the savings are to be secured.

The mismatch – unlikely to be removed in the near future – between the kinds of records that humans produce readily and read readily and the kinds that automatic devices produce and read readily is a second technological factor pushing in the direction of centralization. Since processing steps in an automated data-processing system are executed in a thousandth or even millionth of a second, the whole system must be organized on a flow basis with infrequent intervention from outside. Intervention will take more and more the form of designing the system itself – programming – and less and less the form of participating in its minute-by-minute operation. Moreover, the parts of the system must mesh. Hence, the design of decision-making and data-processing systems will tend to be a relatively centralized function. It will be a little like ship design. There is no use in one group of experts producing the design for the hull, another the design for the power plant, a third the plans for the passenger quarters, and so on, unless great pains are taken at each step to see that all these parts will fit into a sea-worthy ship.

It may be objected that the question of motivation has been overlooked in this whole discussion. If decision making is centralized how can the middle-level executive be induced to work hard and effectively? First, we should observe that the principle of decentralized profit-and-loss accounting has never been carried much below the level of product-group departments and cannot, in fact, be applied successfully to fragmented segments of highly interdependent activities. Second, we may question whether the conditions under which middle-management has in the past exercised its decision-making prerogatives were actually good conditions from a motivational standpoint.

Most existing decentralized organization structures have at least three weaknesses in motivating middle-management executives effectively. First, they encourage the formation of and loyalty to subgoals that are only partly parallel with the goals of the organization. Second, they require so much nonprogrammed problem solving in a setting of confusion that they do not provide the satisfactions which, we argued earlier, are valued by the true professional. Third, they realize none of the advantages, which by hindsight we find we have often gained in factory automation, of substituting machine-paced (or better, system-paced) for man-paced operation of the system.[8]

The question of motivation we have just raised has a broader relevance than the issue of decentralization and I will discuss it later, in the section on authority and responsibility relations. Meanwhile, we can summarize the present discussion by saying that the new developments in decision making will tend to induce more centralization in decision-making activities at middle-management levels.

Authority and responsibility. Let me draw a sketch of the factory manager's job today. How far it is a caricature, and how far a reasonably accurate portrait, I shall let you decide. What is the factory manager's authority? He can hire and fire. He can determine what shall be

---

8. The general decline in the use of piece-rates is associated with the gradual spread of machine-paced operations through the factory with the advance of automation. In evaluating the human consequences of this development, we should not accept uncritically the common stereotypes that were incorporated so effectively in Charlie Chaplin's *Modern Times*. Frederick Taylor's sophisticated understanding of the relations between incentives and pace, expressed, for example, in his story of the pig-iron handler, is worth pondering.

produced in his factory and how much. He can make minor improvements in equipment and recommend major ones. In doing all of these things, he is subject to all kinds of constraints and evaluations imposed by the rest of the organization. Moreover, the connection between what he decides and what actually happens in the factory is often highly tenuous. He proposes, and a complex administrative system disposes.

For what is the factory manager held accountable? He must keep his costs within the standards of the budget. He must not run out of items that are ordered. If he does, he must produce them in great haste. He must keep his inventory down. His men must not have accidents. And so on.

Subject to this whole range of conflicting pressures, controlling a complex system whose response to instruction is often erratic and unpredictable, the environment of the typical middle-management executive – of which the factory manager is just one example – is not the kind of environment a psychologist would design to produce high motivation. The manager responds in understandable ways. He transmits to his subordinates the pressures imposed by his superiors – he becomes a work pusher, seeking to motivate by creating for his subordinates the same environment of pressure and constraint that he experiences. He and his subordinates become expediters, dealing with the pressure that is felt at the moment by getting out a particular order, fixing a particular disabled machine, following up a particular tardy supplier.

I do not want to elaborate the picture further. The important point is that the task of middle managers today is very much taken up with pace setting, with work pushing and with expediting. As the automation and rationalization of the decision-making process progress, these aspects of the managerial job are likely to recede in importance.

If a couple of terms are desired to characterize the direction of change we may expect in the manager's job, I would propose rationalization and impersonalization. In terms of subjective feel the manager will find himself dealing more than in the past with a well-structured system whose problems have to be diagnosed and corrected objectively and analytically, and less with unpredictable and sometimes recalcitrant people who have to be persuaded, prodded, rewarded, and cajoled. For some managers, important satisfactions derived in the past from interpersonal relations with others will be lost. For other managers, important satisfactions from a feeling of the adequacy of professional skills will be gained.

My guess, and it is only a guess, is that the gains in satisfaction from the change will overbalance the losses. I have two reasons for making this guess: first, because this seems to be the general experience in factory automation as it affects supervisors and managers; second, because the kinds of interpersonal relations called for in the new environment seem to me generally less frustrating and more wholesome than many of those we encounter in present-day supervisory relations. Man does not generally work well with his fellow man in relations saturated with authority and dependence, with control and subordination, even though these have been the predominant human relations in the past. He works much better when he is teamed with his fellow man in coping with an objective, understandable, external environment. That will be more and more his situation as the new techniques of decision making come into wide use.

A final sketch of the new organization

Perhaps in the preceding paragraphs I have yielded to the temptation to paint a Utopian picture of the organization that the new decision-making techniques will create. If so, I have done so from an urge to calm the anxieties that are so often and so unnecessarily aroused by the stereotype of the robot. These anxieties are unnecessary because the existence in the world today of machines that think, and of theories that explain the processes of human thinking, subtracts not an inch, not a hair, from the stature of man. Man is always vulnerable when he rests his case for his worth and dignity on how he differs from the rest of the world, or on the special place he has in God's scheme or nature's. Man must rest his case on what he is. This is in no way changed when electronic systems can duplicate some of his functions or when some of the mystery of his processes of thought is taken away.

The changes I am predicting for the decision-making processes in organizations do not mean that workers and executives will find the organizations they will work in strange and unfamiliar. In concluding, I should like to emphasize the aspects in which the new organization will much resemble those we know now.

1. Organizations will still be constructed in three layers: an underlying system of physical production and distribution processes, a layer of programmed (and probably largely automated) decision processes for governing the routine day-to-day operation of the physical system and a layer of nonprogrammed decision processes (carried out in a man–machine system) for monitoring the first-level processes, redesigning them and changing parameter values.

2. Organizations will still be hierarchical in form. The organization will be divided into major subparts, each of these into parts, and so on, in familiar forms of departmentalization. The exact bases for drawing departmental lines may change somewhat. Product divisions may become even more important than they are today, while the sharp lines of demarcation among purchasing, manufacturing, engineering and sales are likely to fade.

But there is a more fundamental way in which the organizations of the future will appear to those in them very much like the organizations of today. Man is a problem-solving, skill-using, social animal. Once he has satisfied his hunger, two main kinds of experiences are significant to him. One of his deepest needs is to apply his skills, whatever they be, to challenging tasks – to feel the exhilaration of the well-struck ball or the well-solved problem. The other need is to find meaningful and warm relations with a few other human beings – to love and be loved, to share experience, to respect and be respected, to work in common tasks.

Particular characteristics of the physical environment and the task environment are significant to man only as they affect these needs. The scientist satisfies them in one environment, the artist in another; but they are the same needs. A good business novel or business biography is not about business. It is about love, hate, pride, craftsmanship, jealousy, comradeship, ambition, pleasure. These have been, and will continue to be man's central concerns.

The automation and rationalization of decision making will, to be sure, alter the climate of organizations in ways important to these human concerns. I have indicated what some of the changes may be. On balance, they seem to me changes that will make it easier rather than harder for the executive's daily work to be a significant and satisfying part of his life.

References

BERLYNE, D. E. (1954), 'A theory of human curiosity', *British Journal of Psychology*, vol. 45, pp. 180–91.

BRIGHT, J. R. (1958), *Automation and Management*, Graduate School of Business Administration, Harvard University.

CYERT, R. M., SIMON, H. A., and TROW, D. B. (1956), 'Observation of a business decision', *Journal of Business*, vol. 29, pp. 237–48.

DEWEY, J. (1910), *How We Think*, Heath, chapter 8.

GREGORY, R. H., and VAN HORN, R. L. (1960), *Automatic Data-Processing Systems*, Wadsworth.

LEAVITT, H. J., and WHISLER, T. L. (1958), 'Management in the 1980s', *Harvard Business Review*, vol. 36, no. 6, November–December, pp. 41–8.

LILLEY, S. (1957), *Automation and Social Progress*, International Publishers.

MARCH, J. G., and SIMON, H. A. (1958), *Organizations*, Wiley.

SIMON, H. A. (1957), *Models of Man*, Wiley.

SIMON, H. A. (1960), 'The corporation: will it be managed by machines?', in M. Anshen and G. L. Bach (eds.), *Management and Corporations, 1985*, McGraw-Hill, pp. 17–55.

14   J. G. March

The Technology of Foolishness

From J. G. March and J. P. Olsen, *Ambiguity and Choice in Organizations,*
Universitetsforlaget, 1976, chapter 5, pp. 69–81.

Choice and rationality

The concept of choice as a focus for interpreting and guiding human
behavior has rarely had an easy time in the realm of ideas. It is beset by
theological disputations over free will, by the dilemmas of absurdism, by
the doubts of psychological behaviorism, by the claims of historical,
economic, social, and demographic determinism. Nevertheless, the idea
that humans make choices has proven robust enough to become a major
matter of faith in important segments of contemporary western civilization. It is a faith that is professed by virtually all theories of social
policy making.

The major tenets of this faith run something like this. Human beings
make choices. If done properly, choices are made by evaluating alternatives in terms of goals on the basis of information currently available.
The alternative that is most attractive in terms of the goals is chosen. The
process of making choices can be improved by using the technology of
choice. Through the paraphernalia of modern techniques, we can
improve the quality of the search for alternatives, the quality of information, and the quality of the analysis used to evaluate alternatives.
Although actual choice may fall short of this ideal in various ways, it is an
attractive model of how choices should be made by individuals, organizations, and social systems.

These articles of faith have been built upon, and have stimulated,
some scripture. It is the scripture of theories of decision making. The
scripture is partly a codification of received doctrine and partly a source
for that doctrine. As a result, our cultural ideas of intelligence and our
theories of choice bear some substantial resemblance. In particular,
they share three conspicuous interrelated ideas.

The first idea is the *pre-existence of purpose*. We find it natural to base
an interpretation of human choice behavior on a presumption of human
purpose. We have, in fact, invented one of the most elaborate termin-
ologies in the professional literature: 'values', 'needs', 'wants', 'goods',

'tastes', 'preferences', 'utility', 'objectives', 'goals', 'aspirations', 'drives'. All of these reflect a strong tendency to believe that a useful interpretation of human behavior involves defining a set of objectives that (a) are prior attributes of the system, and (b) make the observed behavior in some sense intelligent vis-à-vis those objectives.

Whether we are talking about individuals or about organizations, purpose is an obvious presumption of the discussion. An organization is often defined in terms of its purpose. It is seen by some as the largest collectivity directed by a purpose. Action within an organization is justified (or criticized) in terms of the purpose. Individuals explain their own behavior, as well as the behavior of others, in terms of a set of value premises that are presumed to be antecedent to the behavior. Normative theories of choice begin with an assumption of a pre-existent preference-ordering defined over the possible outcomes of a choice.

The second idea is the *necessity of consistency*. We have come to recognize consistency both as an important property of human behavior and as a prerequisite for normative models of choice. Dissonancy theory, balance theory, theories of congruency in attitudes, statuses, and performances have all served to remind us of the possibilities for interpreting human behavior in terms of the consistency requirements of a limited-capacity information-processing system.

At the same time, consistency is a cultural and theoretical virtue. Action should be made consistent with belief. Actions taken by different parts of an organization should be consistent with each other. Individual and organizational activities are seen as connected with each other in terms of their consequences for some consistent set of purposes. In an organization, the structural manifestation of the dictum of consistency is the hierarchy with its obligations of coordination and control. In the individual, the structural manifestation is a set of values that generates a consistent preference-ordering.

The third idea is the *primacy of rationality*. By rationality I mean a procedure for deciding what is correct behavior by relating consequences systematically to objectives. By placing primary emphasis on rational techniques, we implicitly have rejected – or seriously impaired – two other procedures for choice: (a) the processes of intuition, by means of which people may do things without fully understanding why and (b) the processes of tradition and faith, through which people do things because that is the way they are done.

Both within the theory and within the culture we insist on the ethic of rationality. We justify individual and organizational action in terms of an analysis of means and ends. Impulse, intuition, faith, and tradition are outside that system and viewed as antithetical to it. Faith may be seen as a possible source of values. Intuition may be seen as a possible source of ideas about alternatives. But the analysis and justification of action lie within the context of reason.

These ideas are obviously deeply embedded in the culture. Their roots extend into ideas that have conditioned much of modern western history and interpretations of that history. Their general acceptance is probably highly correlated with the permeation of rationalism and individualism into the style of thinking within the culture. The ideas are even more obviously embedded in modern theories of choice. It is fundamental to those theories that thinking should precede action; that action should serve a purpose; that purpose should be defined in terms of a consistent set of pre-existent goals; and that choice should be based on a consistent theory of the relation between action and its consequences.

Every tool of management decision that is currently a part of management science, operations research, or decision theory assumes the prior existence of a set of consistent goals. Almost the entire structure of microeconomic theory builds on the assumption that there exists a well-defined, stable, and consistent preference-ordering. Most theories of individual or organizational choice behavior accept the idea that goals exist and that (in some sense) an individual or organization acts on those goals, choosing from among some alternatives on the basis of available information. Discussions of educational policy, for example, with the emphasis on goal setting, evaluation, and accountability, are directly in this tradition.

From the perspective of all of man's history, the ideas of purpose, consistency, and rationality are relatively new. Much of the technology currently available to implement them is extremely new. Over the past few centuries, and conspicuously over the past few decades, we have substantially improved man's capability for acting purposively, consistently, and rationally. We have substantially increased his propensity to think of himself as doing so. It is an impressive victory, won – where it has been won – by a happy combination of timing, performance, ideology, and persistence. It is a battle yet to be concluded, or even engaged, in many cultures of the world; but within most of the western world, individuals and organizations see themselves as making choices.

The problem of goals

The tools of intelligence as they are fashioned in modern theories of choice are necessary to any reasonable behavior in contemporary society. It is difficult to see how we could, and inconceivable that we would, fail to continue their development, refinement, and extension. As might be expected, however, a theory and ideology of choice built on the ideas outlined above is deficient in some obvious, elementary ways, most conspicuously in the treatment of human goals.

Goals are thrust upon the intelligent man. We ask that he act in the name of goals. We ask that he keep his goals consistent. We ask that his actions be oriented to his goals. We ask that a social system amalgamate individual goals into a collective goal. But we do not concern ourselves with the origin of goals. Theories of individual organizational and social choice assume actors with pre-existent values.

Since it is obvious that goals change over time and that the character of those changes affects both the richness of personal and social development and the outcome of choice behavior, a theory of choice must somehow justify ignoring the phenomena. Although it is unreasonable to ask a theory of choice to solve all of the problems of man and his development, it is reasonable to ask how something as conspicuous as the fluidity and ambiguity of objectives can plausibly be ignored in a theory that is offered as a guide to human choice behavior.

There are three classic justifications. The first is that goal development and choice are independent processes, conceptually and behaviorally. The second is that the model of choice is never satisfied in fact and that deviations from the model accommodate the problems of introducing change. The third is that the idea of changing goals is so intractable in a normative theory of choice that nothing can be said about it. Since I am unpersuaded of the first and second justifications, my optimism with respect to the third is somewhat greater than most of my fellows'.

The argument that goal development and choice are independent behaviorally seems clearly false. It seems to me perfectly obvious that a description that assumes goals come first and action comes later is frequently radically wrong. Human choice behavior is at least as much a process for discovering goals as for acting on them. Although it is true enough that goals and decisions are 'conceptually' distinct, that is simply a statement of the theory. It is not a defense of it. They are conceptually distinct if we choose to make them so.

The argument that the model is incomplete is more persuasive. There do appear to be some critical 'holes' in the system of intelligence as described by standard theories of choice. There is incomplete information, incomplete goal consistency, and a variety of external processes impinging on goal development – including intuition and tradition. What is somewhat disconcerting about the argument, however, is that it makes the efficacy of the concepts of intelligent choice dependent on their inadequacy. As we become more competent in the techniques of the model, and more committed to it, the 'holes' become smaller. As the model becomes more accepted, our obligation to modify it increases.

The final argument seems to me sensible as a general principle, but misleading here. Why are we more reluctant to ask how human beings might find 'good' goals than we are to ask how they might make 'good' decisions? The second question appears to be a relatively technical problem. The first seems more pretentious. It claims to say something about alternative virtues. The appearance of pretense, however, stems directly from the theory and the ideology associated with it.

In fact, the conscious introduction of goal discovery as a consideration in theories of human choice is not unknown to modern man. For example, we have two kinds of theories of choice behavior in human beings. One is a theory of children. The other is a theory of adults. In the theory of childhood, we emphasize choices as leading to experiences that develop the child's scope, his complexity, his awareness of the world. As parents, or psychologists, we try to lead the child to do things that are inconsistent with his present goals because we know (or believe) that he can only develop into an interesting person by coming to appreciate aspects of experience that he initially rejects.

In the theory of adulthood, we emphasize choices as a consequence of our intentions. As adults, or economists, we try to take actions that (within the limits of scarce resources) come as close as possible to achieving our goals. We try to find improved ways of making decisions consistent with our perceptions of what is valuable in the world.

The asymmetry in these models is conspicuous. Adults have constructed a model world in which adults know what is good for themselves, but children do not. It is hard to react positively to the conceit. The asymmetry has, in fact, stimulated a rather large number of ideologies and reforms designed to allow children the same moral prerogative granted to adults – the right to imagine that they know what they want. The efforts have cut deeply into traditional childrearing, traditional educational policies, traditional politics, and traditional consumer economics.

In my judgment, the asymmetry between models of choice for adults and models of choice for children is awkward; but the solution we have adopted is precisely wrong-headed. Instead of trying to adapt the model of adults to children, we might better adapt the model of children to adults. For many purposes, our model of children is better. Of course, children know what they want. Everyone does. The critical question is whether they are encouraged to develop more interesting 'wants'. Values change. People become more interesting as those values and the interconnections made among them change.

One of the most obvious things in the world turns out to be hard for us to accommodate in our theory of choice: a child of two will almost always have a less interesting set of values (yes, indeed, a *worse* set of values) than a child of twelve. The same is true of adults. Values develop through experience. Although one of the main natural arenas for the modification of human values is the area of choice, our theories of adult and organizational decision making ignore the phenomenon entirely.

Introducing ambiguity and fluidity to the interpretation of individual, organizational, and societal goals obviously has implications for behavioral theories of decision making. The main point here, however, is not to consider how we might describe the behavior of systems that are discovering goals as they act. Rather, it is to examine how we might improve the quality of that behavior, how we might aid the development of interesting goals.

We know how to advise a society, an organization, or an individual if we are first given a consistent set of preferences. Under some conditions, we can suggest how to make decisions if the preferences are only consistent up to the point of specifying a series of independent constraints on the choice. But what about a normative theory of goal-finding behavior? What do we say when our client tells us that he is not sure his present set of values is the set of values in terms of which he wants to act? It is a question familiar to many aspects of ordinary life. It is a question that friends, associates, students, college presidents, business managers, voters, and children ask at least as frequently as they ask how they should act within a set of consistent and stable values.

Within the context of the normative theory of choice as it exists, the answer we give is: first determine the values, then act. The advice is frequently useful. Moreover, we have developed ways in which we can use conventional techniques for decision analysis to help discover value premises and to expose value inconsistencies. These techniques involve testing the decision implications of some successive approximations to a set of preferences. The object is to find a consistent set of preferences with implications that are acceptable to the person or organization making the decisions. Variations on such techniques are used routinely in operations research, as well as in personal counseling and analysis. The utility of such techniques, however, apparently depends on the assumption that a primary problem is the amalgamation or excavation of pre-existent values. The metaphors – 'finding oneself', 'goal clarification', 'self-discovery', 'social-welfare function', 'revealed preference' – are metaphors of search. If our value premises are to be 'constructed' rather than 'discovered', our standard procedures may be useful; but we have no *a priori* reason for assuming they will.

Perhaps we should explore a somewhat different approach to the normative question of how we ought to behave when our value premises are not yet (and never will be) fully determined. Suppose we treat action as a way of creating interesting goals at the same time as we treat goals as a way of justifying action. It is an intuitively plausible and simple idea, but one that is not immediately within the domain of standard normative theories of intelligent choice.

Interesting people and interesting organizations construct complicated theories of themselves. In order to do this, they need to supplement the technology of reason with a technology of foolishness. Individuals and organizations need ways of doing things for which they have no good reason. Not always. Not usually. But sometimes. They need to act before they think.

Sensible foolishness

In order to use the act of intelligent choice as a planned occasion for discovering new goals, we apparently require some idea of sensible foolishness. Which of the many foolish things that we might do now will lead to attractive value consequences? The question is almost inconceivable. Not only does it ask us to predict the value consequences of action, it asks us to evaluate them. In what terms can we talk about 'good' changes in goals?

In effect, we are asked either to specify a set of super-goals in terms of which alternative goals are evaluated, or to choose among alternatives *now* in terms of the unknown set of values we will have at some future time (or the distribution over time of that unknown set of future values). The former alternative moves us back to the original situation of a fixed set of values – now called 'super-goals' – and hardly seems an important step in the direction of inventing procedures for discovering new goals. The latter alternative seems fundamental enough, but it violates severely our sense of temporal order. To say that we make decisions now in terms of goals that will only be knowable later is nonsensical – as long as we accept the basic framework of the theory of choice and its presumptions of pre-existent goals.

I do not know in detail what is required, but I think it will be substantial. As we challenge the dogma of pre-existent goals, we will be forced to re-examine some of our most precious prejudices: the strictures against imitation, coercion, and rationalization. Each of those honorable prohibitions depends on the view of man and human choice imposed on us by conventional theories of choice.

Imitation is not necessarily a sign of moral weakness. It is a prediction. It is a prediction that if we duplicate the behavior or attitudes of someone else, the chances of our discovering attractive new goals for ourselves are relatively high. In order for imitation to be normatively attractive we need a better theory of who should be imitated. Such a theory seems to be eminently feasible. For example, what are the conditions for effectiveness of a rule that you should imitate another person whose values are close to yours? How do the chances of discovering interesting goals through imitation change as the number of other people exhibiting the behavior to be imitated increases?

Coercion is not necessarily an assault on individual autonomy. It can be a device for stimulating individuality. We recognize this when we talk about parents and children (at least sometimes). What has always been difficult with coercion is the possibility for perversion that it involves, not its obvious capability for stimulating change. What we require is a theory of the circumstances under which entry into a coercive system produces behavior that leads to the discovery of interesting goals. We are all familiar with the tactic. We use it in imposing deadlines, entering contracts, making commitments. What are the conditions for its effective use? In particular, what are the conditions for coercion in social systems?

Rationalization is not necessarily a way of evading morality. It can be a test for the feasibility of a goal change. When deciding among alternative actions for which we have no good reason, it may be sensible to develop some definition of how 'near' to intelligence alternative 'unintelligent' actions lie. Effective rationalization permits this kind of incremental approach to changes in values. To use it effectively, however, we require a better idea of the kinds of metrics that might be possible in measuring value distances. At the same time, rationalization is the major procedure for integrating newly discovered goals into an existing structure of values. It provides the organization of complexity without which complexity itself becomes indistinguishable from randomness.

There are dangers in imitation, coercion, and rationalization. The risks are too familiar to elaborate. We should, indeed, be able to develop better techniques. Whatever those techniques may be, however, they will almost certainly undermine the superstructure of biases erected on purpose, consistency, and rationality. They will involve some way of thinking about action now as occurring in terms of a set of unknown future values.

Play and reason

A second requirement for a technology of foolishness is some strategy for suspending rational imperatives toward consistency. Even if we know which of several foolish things we want to do, we still need a mechanism for allowing us to do it. How do we escape the logic of our reason?

Here, I think, we are closer to understanding what we need. It is playfulness. Playfulness is the deliberate, temporary relaxation of rules in order to explore the possibilities of alternative rules. When we are playful, we challenge the necessity of consistency. In effect, we announce – in advance – our rejection of the usual objections to behavior that does not fit the standard model of intelligence. Playfulness allows experimentation. At the same time, it acknowledges reason. It accepts an obligation that at some point either the playful behavior will be stopped or it will be integrated into the structure of intelligence in some way that makes sense. The suspension of the rules is temporary.

The idea of play may suggest three things that are, to my mind, quite erroneous in the present context. First, play may be seen as a kind of Mardi Gras for reason, a release of emotional tensions of virtue. Although it is possible that play performs some such function, that is not the function with which I am concerned. Second, play may be seen as part of some mystical balance of spiritual principles: fire and water, hot and cold, weak and strong. The intention here is much narrower than a general mystique of balance. Third, play may be seen as an antithesis of intelligence, so that the emphasis on the importance of play becomes a support for simple self-indulgence. My present intent is to propose play as an instrument of intelligence, not a substitute.

Playfulness is a natural outgrowth of our standard view of reason. A strict insistence on purpose, consistency, and rationality limits our ability to find new purposes. Play relaxes that insistence to allow us to act 'unintelligently' or 'irrationally', or 'foolishly' to explore alternative ideas of possible purposes and alternative concepts of behavioral consistency. And it does this while maintaining our basic commitment to the necessity of intelligence.

Although play and reason are in this way functional complements, they are often behavioral competitors. They are alternative styles and alternative orientations to the same situation. There is no guarantee that the styles will be equally well-developed. There is no guarantee that all individuals, all organizations, or all societies will be equally adept in both styles. There is no guarantee that all cultures will be equally encouraging to both. Our design problem is either to specify the best mix of styles or, failing that, to assure that most people and most organizations most of the time use an alternation of strategies rather than persevering in either one. It is a difficult problem. The optimization problem looks extremely difficult on the fact of it, and the learning situations that will produce alternation in behavior appear to be somewhat less common than those that produce perseverance.

Consider, for example, the difficulty of sustaining playfulness as a style within contemporary American society. Individuals who are good at consistent rationality are rewarded early and heavily. We define it as intelligence, and the educational rewards of society are associated strongly with it. Social norms press in the same direction, particularly for men. Many of the demands of modern organizational life reinforce the same abilities and style preferences. The result is that many of the most influential, best-educated, and best-placed citizens have experienced a powerful overlearning with respect to rationality. They are exceptionally good at maintaining consistent pictures of themselves, of relating action to purposes. They are exceptionally poor at a playful attitude toward their own beliefs, toward the logic of consistency, or toward the way they see things as being connected in the world. The dictates of manliness, forcefulness, independence, and intelligence are intolerant of playful urges if they arise. The playful urges that arise are weak ones.

The picture is probably overdrawn, but not, I believe, the implications. For societies, for organizations, and for individuals reason and intelligence have had the unnecessary consequence of inhibiting the development of purpose into more complicated forms of consistency. In order to move away from that position, we need to find some ways of helping individuals and organizations to experiment with doing things for which they have no good reason, to be playful with their conception of themselves. It is a facility that requires more careful attention than I can give it, but I would suggest five things as a small beginning:

First, we can treat *goals* as *hypotheses*. Conventional decision theory allows us to entertain doubts about almost everything except the thing about which we frequently have the greatest doubt – our objectives. Suppose we define the decision process as a time for the sequential testing of hypotheses about goals. If we can experiment with alternative goals, we stand some chance of discovering complicated and interesting combinations of good values that none of us previously imagined.

Second, we can treat *intuition* as *real*. I do not know what intuition is, or even if it is any one thing. Perhaps it is simply an excuse for doing something we cannot justify in terms of present values or for refusing to follow the logic of our own beliefs. Perhaps it is an inexplicable way of consulting that part of our intelligence that is not organized in a way anticipated by standard theories of choice. In either case, intuition permits us to see some possible actions that are outside our present scheme for justifying behavior.

Third, we can treat *hypocrisy* as a *transition*. Hypocrisy is an inconsistency between expressed values and behavior. Negative attitudes about hypocrisy stem from two major things. The first is a general onus against inconsistency. The second is a sentiment against combining the pleasures of vice with the appearance of virtue. Apparently, that is an unfair way of allowing evil to escape temporal punishment. Whatever the merits of such a position as ethics, it seems to me distinctly inhibiting towards change. A bad man with good intentions may be a man experimenting with the possibility of becoming good. Somehow it seems to me more sensible to encourage the experimentation than to insult it.

Fourth, we can treat *memory* as an *enemy*. The rules of consistency and rationality require a technology of memory. For most purposes, good memories make good choices. But the ability to forget, or over-look, is also useful. If I do not know what I did yesterday or what other people in the organization are doing today, I can act within the system of reason and still do things that are foolish.

Fifth, we can treat *experience* as a *theory*. Learning can be viewed as a series of conclusions based on concepts of action and consequences that we have invented. Experience can be changed retrospectively. By changing our interpretive concepts now, we modify what we learned earlier. Thus, we expose the possibility of experimenting with alternative histories. The usual strictures against 'self-deception' in experience need occasionally to be tempered with an awareness of the extent to which all experience is an interpretation subject to conscious revision. Personal histories, and national histories, need to be rewritten rather continuously as a base for the retrospective learning of new self-conceptions.

Each of these procedures represents a way in which we temporarily suspend the operation of the system of reasoned intelligence. They are playful. They make greatest sense in situations in which there has been an overlearning of virtues of conventional rationality. They are possibly dangerous applications of powerful devices more familiar to the study of behavioral pathology than to the investigation of human development. But they offer a few techniques for introducing change within current concepts of choice.

The argument extends easily to the problems of social organization. If we knew more about the normative theory of acting before you think, we could say more intelligent things about the functions of management and leadership when organizations or societies do not know what they are doing. Consider, for example, the following general implications.

First, we need to re-examine the functions of management decision. One of the primary ways in which the goals of an organization are developed is by interpreting the decisions it makes, and one feature of good managerial decisions is that they lead to the development of more interesting value premises for the organization. As a result, decisions should not be seen as flowing directly or strictly from a pre-existent set of objectives. Managers who make decisions might well view that function somewhat less as a process of deduction or a process of political negotiation and somewhat more as a process of gently upsetting preconceptions of what the organization is doing.

Second, we need a modified view of planning. Planning in organizations has many virtues, but a plan can often be more effective as an interpretation of past decisions than as a program for future ones. It can be used as a part of the efforts of the organization to develop a new consistent theory of itself that incorporates the mix of recent actions into a moderately comprehensive structure of goals. Procedures for interpreting the meaning of most past events are familiar to the memoirs of retired generals, prime ministers, business leaders, and movie stars. They suffer from the company they keep. In an organization that wants to continue to develop new objectives, a manager needs to be relatively tolerant of the idea that he will discover the meaning of yesterday's action in the experiences and interpretations of today.

Third, we need to reconsider evaluation. As nearly as I can determine, there is nothing in a formal theory of evaluation that requires that the criterion function for evaluation be specified in advance. In particular, the evaluation of social experiments need not be in terms of the degree to which they have fulfilled our *a priori* expectations. Rather, we can examine what they did in terms of what we now believe to be important. The prior specification of criteria and the prior specification of evaluational procedures that depend on such criteria are common presumptions in contemporary social policy making. They are presumptions that inhibit the serendipitous discovery of new criteria. Experience should be used explicitly as an occasion for evaluating our values as well as our actions.

Fourth, we need a reconsideration of social accountability. Individual preferences and social action need to be consistent in some way. But the process of pursuing consistency is one in which both the preferences and the actions change over time. Imagination in social policy formation involves systematically adapting to and influencing preferences. It would be unfortunate if our theories of social action encouraged leaders to ignore their responsibilities for anticipating public preferences through action and for providing social experiences that modify individual expectations.

Fifth, we need to accept playfulness in social organizations. The design of organizations should attend to the problems of maintaining both playfulness and reason as aspects of intelligent choice. Since much of the literature on social design is concerned with strengthening the rationality of decisions, managers are likely to overlook the importance of play. This is partly a matter of making the individuals within an organization more playful by encouraging the attitudes and skills of inconsistency. It is also a matter of making organizational structure and organizational procedure more playful. Organizations can be playful even when the participants in them are not. The managerial devices for maintaining consistency can be varied. We encourage organizational play by permitting (and insisting on) some temporary relief from control, coordination, and communication.

Intelligence and foolishness

Contemporary theories of decision making and the technology of reason have considerably strengthened our capabilities for effective social action. The conversion of the simple ideas of choice into an extensive technology is a major achievement. It is, however, an achievement that has reinforced some biases in the underlying models of choice in individuals and groups. In particular, it has reinforced the uncritical acceptance of a static interpretation of human goals.

There is little magic in the world, and foolishness in people and organizations is one of the many things that fail to produce miracles. Under certain conditions, it is one of several ways in which some of the problems of our current theories of intelligence can be overcome. It may be a good way. It preserves the virtues of consistency while stimulating change. If we had a good technology of foolishness, it might (in combination with the technology of reason) help in a small way to develop the unusual combinations of attitudes and behaviors that describe the interesting people, interesting organizations, and interesting societies of the world.

15   C. E. Lindblom

The Science of 'Muddling Through'

From *Public Administration Review*, 1959, vol. 19, no. 2.

Suppose an administrator is given responsibility for formulating policy
with respect to inflation. He might start by trying to list all related values
in order of importance, e.g. full employment, reasonable business
profit, protection of small savings, prevention of a stock-market crash.
Then all possible policy outcomes could be rated as more or less efficient
in attaining a maximum of these values. This would of course require a
prodigious inquiry into values held by members of society and an equally
prodigious set of calculations on how much of each value is equal to how
much of each other value. He could then proceed to outline all possible
policy alternatives. In a third step, he would undertake systematic
comparison of his multitude of alternatives to determine which attains
the greatest amount of values.

   In comparing policies, he would take advantage of any theory available that generalized about classes of policies. In considering inflation,
for example, he would compare all policies in the light of the theory of
prices. Since no alternatives are beyond his investigation, he would
consider strict central control and the abolition of all prices and markets
on the one hand and elimination of all public controls with reliance
completely on the free market on the other, both in the light of whatever
theoretical generalizations he could find on such hypothetical economies. Finally, he would try to make the choice that would in fact
maximize his values.

   An alternative line of attack would be to set as his principal objective,
either explicitly or without conscious thought, the relatively simple goal
of keeping prices level. This objective might be compromised or complicated by only a few other goals, such as full employment. He would in
fact disregard most other social values as beyond his present interest,
and he would for the moment not even attempt to rank the few values
that he regarded as immediately relevant. Were he pressed, he would
quickly admit that he was ignoring many related values and many
possible important consequences of his policies.

   As a second step, he would outline those relatively few policy alternatives that occurred to him. He would then compare them. In comparing his limited number of alternatives, most of them familiar from past controversies, he would not ordinarily find a body of theory precise enough to carry him through a comparison of their respective consequences. Instead he would rely heavily on the record of past experience with small policy steps to predict the consequences of similar steps extended into the future.

Moreover, he would find that the policy alternatives combined objectives or values in different ways. For example, one policy might offer price-level stability at the cost of some risk of unemployment; another might offer less price stability but also less risk of unemployment. Hence, the next step in his approach – the final selection – would combine into one the choice among values and the choice among instruments for reaching values. It would not, as in the first method of policy making, approximate a more mechanical process of choosing the means that best satisfied goals that were previously clarified and ranked. Because practitioners of the second approach expect to achieve their goals only partially, they would expect to repeat endlessly the sequence just described, as conditions and aspirations changed and as accuracy of prediction improved.

By root or by branch

For complex problems, the first of these two approaches is of course impossible. Although such an approach can be described, it cannot be practiced except for relatively simple problems, and even then only in a somewhat modified form. It assumes intellectual capacities and sources of information that men simply do not possess, and it is even more absurd as an approach to policy when the time and money that can be allocated to a policy problem is limited, as is always the case. Of particular importance to public administrators is the fact that public agencies are in effect usually instructed not to practice the first method. That is to say, their prescribed functions and constraints – the politically or legally possible – restrict their attention to relatively few values and relatively few alternative policies among the countless alternatives that might be imagined. It is the second method that is practiced.

Curiously, however, the literatures of decision making, policy formulation, planning, and public administration formalize the first approach rather than the second, leaving public administrators who handle complex decisions in the position of practicing what few preach. For emphasis I run some risk of overstatement. True enough, the literature is well aware of limits on man's capacities and of the inevitability that policies will be approached in some such style as the second. But attempts to formalize rational policy formulation – to lay out explicitly the necessary steps in the process – usually describe the first approach and not the second.[1]

The common tendency to describe policy formulation even for complex problems as though it followed the first approach has been strengthened by the attention given to, and successes enjoyed by, operations research, statistical decision theory, and systems analysis. The hallmarks of these procedures, typical of the first approach, are clarity of objective, explicitness of evaluation, a high degree of comprehensiveness of overview, and, wherever possible, quantification of values for mathematical analysis. But these advanced procedures remain largely the appropriate techniques of relatively small-scale problem solving where the total number of variables to be considered is small and value problems restricted. Charles Hitch, head of the Economic Division of RAND Corporation, one of the leading centers for application of these techniques, has written:

> I would make the empirical generalization from my experience at RAND and elsewhere that operations research is the art of sub-optimizing, i.e. of solving some lower-level problems, and that difficulties increase and our special competence diminishes by an order of magnitude with every level of decision making we attempt to ascend. The sort of simple explicit model which operations researchers are so proficient in using can certainly reflect most of the significant factors influencing traffic control on the George Washington Bridge, but the proportion of the relevant reality which we can represent by any such model or models in studying, say, a major foreign-policy decision, appears to be almost trivial.[2]

Accordingly, I propose in this paper to clarify and formalize the second method, much neglected in the literature. This might be described as the method of *successive limited comparisons*. I will contrast it with the first approach, which might be called the rational–comprehensive method.[3]

1. James G. March and Herbert A. Simon similarly characterize the literature. They also take some important steps, as have Simon's other recent articles, to describe a less heroic model of policy making. See March and Simon (1958), p. 137.

2. Hitch (1957), p. 718. Hitch's dissent is from particular points made in the article to which his paper is a reply; his claim that operations research is for low-level problems is widely accepted. For examples of the kind of problems to which operations research is applied, see C. W. Churchman, R. L. Ackoff, and E. L. Arnoff (1957) and J. F. McCloskey and J. M. Coppinger (1956).

3. I am assuming that administrators often make policy and advise in the making of policy and am treating decision making and policy making as synonymous for purposes of this paper.

More impressionistically and briefly – and therefore generally used in this article – they could be characterized as the 'branch method' and 'root method', the former continually building out from the current situation, step by step and by small degrees; the latter starting from fundamentals anew each time, building on the past only as experience is embodied in a theory, and always prepared to start completely from the ground up.

Let us put the characteristics of the two methods side by side in simplest terms.

Rational–comprehensive (Root)	Successive limited comparisons (Branch)
1(a) Clarification of values or objectives distinct from and usually prerequisite to empirical analysis of alternative policies.	1(b) Selection of value goals and empirical analysis of the needed action are not distinct from one another but are closely intertwined.
2(a) Policy formulation is therefore approached through means–end analysis: first the ends are isolated, then the means to achieve them are sought.	2(b) Since means and ends are not distinct, means–end analysis is often inappropriate or limited.
3(a) The test of a 'good' policy is that it can be shown to be the most appropriate means to desired ends.	3(b) The test of a 'good' policy is typically that various analysts find themselves directly agreeing on a policy (without their agreeing that it is the most appropriate means to an agreed objective).
4(a) Analysis is comprehensive; every important relevant factor is taken into account.	4(b) Analysis is drastically limited: (i) Important possible outcomes are neglected.

Rational-comprehensive (Root)	Successive limited comparisons (Branch)
	(ii) Important alternative potential policies are neglected.
	(iii) Important affected values are neglected.
5(*a*) Theory is often heavily relied upon.	5(*b*) A succession of comparisons greatly reduces or eliminates reliance on theory.

Assuming that the root method is familiar and understandable, we proceed directly to clarification of its alternative by contrast. In explaining the second, we shall be describing how most administrators do in fact approach complex questions, for the root method, the 'best' way as a blueprint or model, is in fact not workable for complex policy questions, and administrators are forced to use the method of successive limited comparisons.

Intertwining evaluation and empirical analysis: 1(*b*)

The quickest way to understand how values are handled in the method of successive limited comparisons is to see how the root method often breaks down in *its* handling of values or objectives. The idea that values should be clarified, and in advance of the examination of alternative policies, is appealing. But what happens when we attempt it for complex social problems? The first difficulty is that on many critical values or objectives, citizens disagree, congressmen disagree, and public administrators disagree. Even where a fairly specific objective is prescribed for the administrator, there remains considerable room for disagreement on sub-objectives. Consider, for example, the conflict with respect to locating public housing, described in Meyerson and Banfield's study of the Chicago Housing Authority (1955) – disagreement which occurred despite the clear objective of providing a certain number of public housing units in the city. Similarly conflicting are objectives in highway location, traffic control, minimum wage administration, development of tourist facilities in national parks, or insect control.

Administrators cannot escape these conflicts by ascertaining the majority's preference, for preferences have not been registered on most issues; indeed, there often *are* no preferences in the absence of public discussion sufficient to bring an issue to the attention of the electorate. Furthermore, there is a question of whether intensity of feeling should be considered as well as the number of persons preferring each alternative. By the impossibility of doing otherwise, administrators often are reduced to deciding policy without clarifying objectives first.

Even when an administrator resolves to follow his own values as a criterion for decisions, he often will not know how to rank them when they conflict with one another, as they usually do. Suppose, for example, that an administrator must relocate tenants living in tenements scheduled for destruction. One objective is to empty the buildings fairly promptly, another is to find suitable accommodation for persons displaced, another is to avoid friction with residents in other areas in which a large influx would be unwelcome, another is to deal with all concerned through persuasion if possible, and so on.

How does one state even to oneself the relative importance of these partially conflicting values? A simple ranking of them is not enough; one needs ideally to know how much of one value is worth sacrificing for some of another value. The answer is that typically the administrator chooses – and must choose – directly among policies in which these values are combined in different ways. He cannot first clarify his values and then choose among policies.

A more subtle third point underlies both the first two. Social objectives do not always have the same relative values. One objective may be highly prized in one circumstance, another in another circumstance. If, for example, an administrator values highly both the dispatch with which his agency can carry through its projects *and* good public relations, it matters little which of the two possibly conflicting values he favors in some abstract or general sense. Policy questions arise in forms which put to administrators such a question as: given the degree to which we are or are not already achieving the values of dispatch and the values of good public relations, is it worth sacrificing a little speed for a happier clientele, or is it better to risk offending the clientele so that we can get on with our work? The answer to such a question varies with circumstances.

The value problem is, as the example shows, always a problem of adjustments at a margin. But there is no practicable way to state marginal objectives or values except in terms of particular policies. That one value is preferred to another in one decision situation does not mean that it will be preferred in another decision situation in which it can be had only at great sacrifice of another value. Attempts to rank or order values in general and abstract terms so that they do not shift from decision to decision end up by ignoring the relevant marginal preferences. The significance of this third point thus goes very far. Even if all administrators had at hand an agreed set of values, objectives, and constraints, and an agreed ranking of these values, objectives, and constraints, their marginal values in actual choice situations would be impossible to formulate.

Unable consequently to formulate the relevant values first and then choose among policies to achieve them, administrators must choose directly among alternative policies that offer different marginal combinations of values. Somewhat paradoxically, the only practicable way to disclose one's relevant marginal values even to oneself is to describe the policy one chooses to achieve them. Except roughly and vaguely, I know of no way to describe – or even to understand – what my relative evaluations are for, say, freedom and security, speed and accuracy in governmental decisions, or low taxes and better schools than to describe my preferences among specific policy choices that might be made between the alternatives in each of the pairs.

In summary, two aspects of the process by which values are actually handled can be distinguished. The first is clear: evaluation and empirical analysis are intertwined; that is, one chooses among values and among policies at one and the same time. Put a little more elaborately, one simultaneously chooses a policy to attain certain objectives and chooses the objectives themselves. The second aspect is related but distinct: the administrator focuses his attention on marginal or incremental values. Whether he is aware of it or not, he does not find general formulations of objectives very helpful and in fact makes specific marginal or incremental comparisons. Two policies, X and Y, confront him. Both promise the same degree of attainment of objectives a, b, c, d, and e. But X promises him somewhat more of f than does Y, while Y promises him somewhat more of g than does X. In choosing between them, he is in fact offered the alternative of a marginal or incremental amount of f at the expense of a marginal or incremental amount of g. The only values that are relevant to his choice are these increments by which the two policies differ; and, when he finally chooses between the two marginal values, he does so by making a choice between policies.[4]

As to whether the attempt to clarify objectives in advance of policy selection is more or less rational than the close intertwining of marginal evaluation and empirical analysis, the principal difference established is

4. The line of argument is, of course, an extension of the theory of market choice, especially the theory of consumer choice, to public policy choices.

that for complex problems the first is impossible and irrelevant, and the second is both possible and relevant. The second is possible because the administrator need not try to analyse any values except the values by which alternative policies differ and need not be concerned with them except as they differ marginally. His need for information on values or objectives is drastically reduced as compared with the root method; and his capacity for grasping, comprehending, and relating values to one another is not strained beyond the breaking point.

Relations between means and ends: 2(b)

Decision making is ordinarily formalized as a means–ends relationship: means are conceived to be evaluated and chosen in the light of ends finally selected independently of and prior to the choice of means. This is the means–ends relationship of the root method. But it follows from all that has just been said that such a means–ends relationship is possible only to the extent that values are agreed upon, are reconcilable, and are stable at the margin. Typically, therefore, such a means–ends relationship is absent from the branch method, where means and ends are simultaneously chosen.

Yet any departure from the means–ends relationship of the root method will strike some readers as inconceivable. For it will appear to them that only in such a relationship is it possible to determine whether one policy choice is better or worse than another. How can an administrator know whether he has made a wise or foolish decision if he is without prior values or objectives by which to judge his decisions? The answer to this question calls up the third distinctive difference between root and branch methods: how to decide the best policy.

The test of 'good' policy: 3(b)

In the root method, a decision is 'correct', 'good', or 'rational' if it can be shown to attain some specified objective, where the objective can be specified without simply describing the decision itself. Where objectives are defined only through the marginal or incremental approach to values described above, it is still sometimes possible to test whether a policy does in fact attain the desired objectives; but a precise statement of the objectives takes the form of a description of the policy chosen or some alternative to it. To show that a policy is mistaken one cannot offer an abstract argument that important objectives are not achieved; one must instead argue that another policy is more to be preferred.

So far, the departure from customary ways of looking at problem solving is not troublesome, for many administrators will be quick to agree that the most effective discussion of the correctness of policy does take the form of comparison with other policies that might have been chosen. But what of the situation in which administrators cannot agree on values or objectives, either abstractly or in marginal terms? What then is the test of 'good' policy? For the root method, there is no test. Agreement on objectives failing, there is no standard of 'correctness'. For the method of successive limited comparisons, the test is agreement on policy itself, which remains possible even when agreement on values is not.

It has been suggested that continuing agreement in Congress on the desirability of extending old-age insurance stems from liberal desires to strengthen the welfare programs of the federal government and from conservative desires to reduce union demands for private pension plans. If so, this is an excellent demonstration of the ease with which individuals of different ideologies often can agree on concrete policy. Labor mediators report a similar phenomenon: the contestants cannot agree on criteria for settling their disputes but can agree on specific proposals. Similarly, when one administrator's objective turns out to be another's means, they often can agree on policy. Agreement on policy thus becomes the only practicable test of the policy's correctness. And for one administrator to seek to win the other over to agreement on ends as well would accomplish nothing and create quite unnecessary controversy.

If agreement directly on policy as a test for 'best' policy seems a poor substitute for testing the policy against its objectives, it ought to be remembered that objectives themselves have no ultimate validity other than they are agreed upon. Hence agreement is the test of 'best' policy in both methods. But where the root method requires agreement on what elements in the decision constitute objectives and on which of these objectives should be sought, the branch method falls back on agreement wherever it can be found. In an important sense, therefore, it is not irrational for an administrator to defend a policy as good without being able to specify what it is good for.

Non-comprehensive analysis: 4(*b*)

Ideally, rational–comprehensive analysis leaves out nothing important. But it is impossible to take everything important into consideration unless 'important' is so narrowly defined that analysis is in fact quite limited. Limits on human intellectual capacities and on available information set definite limits to man's capacity to be comprehensive. In actual fact, therefore, no one can practice the rational–comprehensive method for really complex problems, and every administrator faced with a sufficiently complex problem must find ways drastically to simplify.

An administrator assisting in the formulation of agricultural economic policy cannot in the first place be competent on all possible policies. He cannot even comprehend one policy entirely. In planning a soil-bank program, he cannot successfully anticipate the impact of higher or lower farm income on, say, urbanization – the possible consequent loosening of family ties, the possible consequent need for revisions in social security and further implications for tax problems arising out of new federal responsibilities for social security and municipal responsibilities for urban services. Nor, to follow another line of repercussions, can he work through the soil-bank program's effects on prices for agricultural products in foreign markets and consequent implications for foreign relations, including those arising out of economic rivalry between the United States and the U.S.S.R.

In the method of successive limited comparisons, simplification is systematically achieved in two principal ways. First, it is achieved through limitation of policy comparisons to those policies that differ in relatively small degree from policies presently in effect. Such a limitation immediately reduces the number of alternatives to be investigated and also drastically simplifies the character of the investigation of each. For it is not necessary to undertake fundamental inquiry into an alternative and its consequences; it is necessary only to study those respects in which the proposed alternative and its consequences differ from the status quo. The empirical comparison of marginal differences among alternative policies that differ only marginally is, of course, a counterpart to the incremental or marginal comparison of values discussed above.[5]

Relevance as well as realism

It is a matter of common observation that in western democracies public administrators and policy analysts in general do largely limit their analyses to incremental or marginal differences in policies that are

5. A more precise definition of incremental policies and a discussion of whether a change that appears 'small' to one observer might be seen differently by another is to be found in C. E. Lindblom (1958), p. 298.

chosen to differ only incrementally. They do not do so, however, solely because they desperately need some way to simplify their problems; they also do so in order to be relevant. Democracies change their policies almost entirely through incremental adjustments. Policy does not move in leaps and bounds.

The incremental character of political change in the United States has often been remarked. The two major political parties agree on fundamentals; they offer alternative policies to the voters only on relatively small points of difference. Both parties favor full employment, but they define it somewhat differently; both favor the development of waterpower resources, but in slightly different ways; and both favor unemployment compensation, but not the same level of benefits. Similarly, shifts of policy within a party take place largely through a series of relatively small changes, as can be seen in their only gradual acceptance of the idea of governmental responsibility for support of the unemployed, a change in party positions beginning in the early thirties and culminating in a sense in the Employment Act of 1946.

Party behavior is in turn rooted in public attitudes, and political theorists cannot conceive of democracy's surviving in the United States in the absence of fundamental agreement on potentially disruptive issues, with consequent limitation of policy debates to relatively small differences in policy.

Since the policies ignored by the administrator are politically impossible and so irrelevant, the simplification of analysis achieved by concentrating on policies that differ only incrementally is not a capricious kind of simplification. In addition, it can be argued that, given the limits on knowledge within which policy makers are confined, simplifying by limiting the focus to small variations from present policy makes the most of available knowledge. Because policies being considered are like present and past policies, the administrator can obtain information and claim some insight. Non-incremental policy proposals are therefore typically not only politically irrelevant but also unpredictable in their consequences.

The second method of simplification of analysis is the practice of ignoring important possible consequences of possible policies, as well as the values attached to the neglected consequences. If this appears to disclose a shocking shortcoming of successive limited comparisons, it can be replied that, even if the exclusions are random, policies may nevertheless be more intelligently formulated than through futile attempts to achieve a comprehensiveness beyond human capacity.

Actually, however, the exclusions, seeming arbitrary or random from one point of view, need be neither.

Achieving a degree of comprehensiveness

Suppose that each value neglected by one policy-making agency were a major concern of at least one other agency. In that case, a helpful division of labor would be achieved, and no agency need find its task beyond its capacities. The shortcomings of such a system would be that one agency might destroy a value either before another agency could be activated to safeguard it or in spite of another agency's efforts. But the possibility that important values may be lost is present in any form of organization, even where agencies attempt to comprehend in planning more than is humanly possible. The virtue of such a hypothetical division of labor is that every important interest or value has its watchdog. And these watchdogs can protect the interests in their jurisdiction in two quite different ways: first, by redressing damages done by other agencies; and second, by anticipating and heading off injury before it occurs.

In a society like that of the United States in which individuals are free to combine to pursue almost any possible common interest they might have and in which government agencies are sensitive to the pressures of these groups, the system described is approximated. Almost every interest has its watchdog. Without claiming that every interest has a sufficiently powerful watchdog, it can be argued that our system often can assure a more comprehensive regard for the values of the whole society than any attempt at intellectual comprehensiveness.

In the United States, for example, no part of government attempts a comprehensive overview of policy on income distribution. A policy nevertheless evolves, and one responding to a wide variety of interests. A process of mutual adjustment among farm groups, labor unions, municipalities and school boards, tax authorities, and government agencies with responsibilities in the fields of housing, health, highways, national parks, fire, and police accomplishes a distribution of income in which particular income problems neglected at one point in the decision processes become central at another point.

Mutual adjustment is more pervasive than the explicit forms it takes in negotiation between groups; it persists through the mutual impacts of groups upon one another even where they are not in communication. For all the imperfections and latent dangers in this ubiquitous process of mutual adjustment, it will often accomplish an adaptation of policies to a wider range of interests than could be done by one group centrally.

Note, too, how the incremental pattern of policy making fits with the multiple pressure pattern. For when decisions are only incremental – closely related to known policies–it is easier for one group to anticipate the kind of moves another might make and easier too for it to make correction for injury already accomplished.[6]

Even partisanship and narrowness, to use pejorative terms, will sometimes be assets to rational decision making, for they can doubly ensure that what one agency neglects, another will not; they specialize personnel to distinct points of view. The claim is valid that effective rational coordination of the federal administration, if possible to achieve at all, would require an agreed set of values[7] – if 'rational' is defined as the practice of the root method of decision making. But a high degree of administrative coordination occurs as each agency adjusts its policies to the concerns of the other agencies in the process of fragmented decision making I have just described.

For all the apparent shortcomings of the incremental approach to policy alternatives with its arbitrary exclusion coupled with fragmentation, when compared to the root method, the branch method often looks far superior. In the root method, the inevitable exclusion of factors is accidental, unsystematic, and not defensible by any argument so far developed, while in the branch method the exclusions are deliberate, systematic, and defensible. Ideally, of course, the root method does not exclude; in practice it must. Nor does the branch method necessarily neglect long-run considerations and objectives. It is clear that important values must be omitted in considering policy, and sometimes the only way long-run objectives can be given adequate attention is through the neglect of short-run considerations. But the values omitted can be either long-run or short-run.

Succession of comparisons: 5(b)

The final distinctive element in the branch method is that the comparisons, together with the policy choice, proceed in a chronological series. Policy is not made once and for all; it is made and remade endlessly. Policy making is a process of successive approximation to some desired objectives in which what is desired itself continues to change under reconsideration. It is at best a very rough process. Neither social

6. The link between the practice of the method of successive limited comparisons and mutual adjustment of interests in a highly fragmented decision-making process adds a new facet to pluralist theories of government and administration.

7. See Herbert Simon, Donald W. Smithburg, and Victor A. Thompson (1950), p. 434.

scientists nor politicians nor public administrators yet know enough about the social world to avoid repeated error in predicting the consequences of policy moves. A wise policy maker consequently expects that his policies will achieve only part of what he hopes and at the same time will produce unanticipated consequences he would have preferred to avoid. If he proceeds through a *succession* of incremental changes, he avoids serious lasting mistakes in several ways.

In the first place, past sequences of policy steps have given him knowledge about the probable consequences of further similar steps. Second, he need not attempt big jumps toward his goals that would require predictions beyond his or anyone else's knowledge, because he never expects his policy to be a final resolution of a problem. His decision is only one step, one that if successful can quickly be followed by another. Third, he is in effect able to test his previous predictions as he moves on to each further step. Lastly, he often can remedy a past error fairly quickly – more quickly than if policy proceeded through more distinct steps widely spaced in time.

Compare this comparative analysis of incremental changes with the aspiration to employ theory in the root method. Man cannot think without classifying, without subsuming one experience under a more general category of experiences. The attempt to push categorization as far as possible and to find general propositions which can be applied to specific situations is what I refer to with the word 'theory'. Where root analysis often leans heavily on theory in this sense, the branch method does not.

The assumption of root analysts is that theory is the most systematic and economical way to bring relevant knowledge to bear on a specific problem. Granting the assumption, an unhappy fact is that we do not have adequate theory to apply to problems in any policy area, although theory is more adequate in some areas – monetary policy, for example – than in others. Comparative analysis, as in the branch method, is sometimes a systematic alternative to theory.

Suppose an administrator must choose among a small group of policies that differ only incrementally from each other and from present policy. He might aspire to 'understand' each of the alternatives – for example, to know all the consequences of each aspect of each policy. If so, he would indeed require theory. In fact, however, he would usually decide that, *for policy-making purposes*, he need know, as explained above, only the consequences of each of those aspects of the policies in which they differed from one another. For this much more modest aspiration, he requires no theory (although it might be helpful, if available), for he can proceed to isolate probable differences by examining the differences in consequences associated with past differences in policies, a feasible program because he can take his observations from a long sequence of incremental changes.

For example, without a more comprehensive social theory about juvenile delinquency than scholars have yet produced, one cannot possibly understand the ways in which a variety of public policies – say on education, housing, recreation, employment, race relations, and policing – might encourage or discourage delinquency. And one needs such an understanding if one undertakes the comprehensive overview of the problem prescribed in the models of the root method. If, however, one merely wants to mobilize knowledge sufficient to assist in a choice among a small group of similar policies – alternative policies on juvenile court procedures, for example – one can do so by comparative analysis of the results of similar past policy moves.

Theorists and practitioners

This difference explains – in some cases at least – why the administrator often feels that the outside expert or academic problem solver is sometimes not helpful and why they in turn often urge more theory on him. And it explains why an administrator often feels more confident when 'flying by the seat of his pants' than when following the advice of theorists. Theorists often ask the administrator to go the long way round to the solution of his problems, in effect ask him to follow the best canons of the scientific method, when the administrator knows that the best available theory will work less well than more modest incremental comparisons. Theorists do not realize that the administrator is often in fact practicing a systematic method. It would be foolish to push this explanation too far, for sometimes practical decision makers are pursuing neither a theoretical approach nor successive comparisons, nor any other systematic method.

It may be worth emphasizing that theory is sometimes of extremely limited helpfulness in policy making for at least two rather different reasons. It is greedy for facts; it can be constructed only through a great collection of observations. And it is typically insufficiently precise for application to a policy process that moves through small changes. In contrast the comparative method both economizes on the need for facts and directs the analyst's attention to just those facts that are relevent to the fine choices faced by the decision maker.

With respect to precision of theory, economic theory serves as an example. It predicts that an economy without money or prices would in certain specified ways misallocate resources, but this finding pertains to an alternative far removed from the kind of policies on which administrators need help. Yet it is not precise enough to predict the consequences of policies restricting business mergers, and this is the kind of issue on which the administrators need help. Only in relatively restricted areas does economic theory achieve sufficient precision to go far in resolving policy questions; its helpfulness in policy making is always so limited that it requires supplementation through comparative analysis.

Successive comparison as a system

Successive limited comparison is, then, indeed a method or system; it is not a failure of method for which administrators ought to apologize. Nonetheless, its imperfections, which have not been explored in this paper, are many. For example, the method is without a built-in safeguard for all relevant values, and it also may lead the decision maker to overlook excellent policies for no other reason than that they are not suggested by the chain of successive policy steps leading up to the present. Hence, it ought to be said that under this method, as well as under some of the most sophisticated variants of the root method – operations research, for example – policies will continue to be as foolish as they are wise.

Why then bother to describe the method in all the above detail? Because it is in fact a common method of policy formulation, and is, for complex problems, the principal reliance of administrators as well as of other policy analysts.[8] And because it will be superior to any other decision-making method available for complex problems in many

8. Elsewhere I have explored this same method of policy formation as practiced by academic analysts of policy (C. E. Lindblom, 1958). Although it has been here presented as a method for public administrators, it is no less necessary to analysts more removed from immediate policy questions, despite their tendencies to describe their own analytical efforts as though they were in the rational–comprehensive method with an especially heavy use of theory. Similarly, this same method is inevitably resorted to in personal problem solving, where means and ends are sometimes impossible to separate, where aspirations or objectives undergo constant development, and where drastic simplification of the complexity of the real world is urgent if problems are to be solved in the time that can be given to them. To an economist accustomed to dealing with the marginal or incremental concept in market processes, the central idea in the method is that both evaluation and empirical analysis are incremental. Accordingly I have referred to the method elsewhere as 'the incremental method'.

circumstances, certainly superior to a futile attempt at superhuman comprehensiveness. The reaction of the public administrator to the exposition of method doubtless will be less a discovery of a new method than a better acquaintance with an old. But by becoming more conscious of their practice of this method, administrators might practice it with more skill and know when to extend or constrict its use. (That they sometimes practice it effectively and sometimes not may explain the extremes of opinion on 'muddling through', which is both praised as a highly sophisticated form of problem solving and denounced as no method at all. For I suspect that in so far as there is a system in what is known as 'muddling through', this method is it.)

One of the noteworthy incidental consequences of clarification of the method is the light it throws on the suspicion an administrator sometimes entertains that a consultant or adviser is not speaking relevantly and responsibly when in fact by all ordinary objective evidence he is. The trouble lies in the fact that most of us approach policy problems within a framework given by our view of a chain of successive policy choices made up to the present. One's thinking about appropriate policies with respect, say, to urban traffic control is greatly influenced by one's knowledge of the incremental steps taken up to the present. An administrator enjoys an intimate knowledge of his past sequences that 'outsiders' do not share, and his thinking and that of the 'outsider' will consequently be different in ways that may puzzle both. Both may appear to be talking intelligently, yet each may find the other unsatisfactory. The relevance of the policy chain of succession is even more clear when an American tries to discuss, say, antitrust policy with a Swiss, for the chains of policy in the two countries are strikingly different and the two individuals consequently have organized their knowledge in quite different ways.

If this phenomenon is a barrier to communication, an understanding of it promises an enrichment of intellectual interaction in policy formulation. Once the source of difference is understood, it will sometimes be stimulating for an administrator to seek out a policy analyst whose recent experience is with a policy chain different from his own.

This raises again a question only briefly discussed above on the merits of like-mindedness among government administrators. While much of organization theory argues the virtues of common values and agreed organizational objectives, for complex problems in which the root method is inapplicable, agencies will want among their own personnel two types of diversification: administrators whose thinking is organized by reference to policy chains other than those familiar to most members of the organization and, even more commonly, administrators whose professional or personal values or interests create diversity of view (perhaps coming from different specialties, social classes, geographical areas) so that, even within a single agency, decision making can be fragmented and parts of the agency can serve as watchdogs for other parts.

References

CHURCHMAN, C. W., ACKOFF, R. L., and ARNOFF, E. L. (1957), *Introduction to Operations Research*, Wiley.

HITCH, C. (1957), 'Operations Research and National Planning: a Dissent', *Operations Research*, 5, October.

LINDBLOM, C. E. (1958), 'Policy Analysis', *American Economic Review*, 48, June.

MARCH, J. G., and SIMON, H. A. (1958), *Organizations*, Wiley.

McCLOSKEY, J. F., and COPPINGER, J. M. (eds.) (1956), *Operations Research for Management*, Johns Hopkins Press, vol. 2.

MEYERSON, M., and BANFIELD, E. C. (1955), *Politics, Planning, and the Public Interest*, Free Press.

SIMON, H. A., SMITHBURG, D. W., and THOMPSON, V. A. (1950), *Public Administration*, Knopf.

16   V. H. Vroom

A Normative Model of Managerial Decision Making

From 'A New Look at Managerial Decision Making',
Organizational Dynamics, 1974, vol. 5, pp. 66–80.

All managers are decision makers. Furthermore, their effectiveness as managers is largely reflected in their track record in making the right decisions. The rightness of these decisions in turn largely depends on whether or not the manager has utilized the right person or persons in the right ways in helping him solve the problem.

Our concern in this article is with decision making as a social process. We view the manager's task as determining how the problem is to be solved, not the solution to be adopted. Within that overall framework, we have attempted to answer two broad sets of questions: what decision-making processes should managers use to deal effectively with the problems they encounter in their jobs? What decision-making processes do they use in dealing with these problems, and what considerations affect their decisions about how much to share their decision-making power with subordinates?

The reader will recognize the former as a normative or prescriptive question. A rational and analytic answer to it would constitute a normative model of decision making as a social process. The second question is descriptive, since it concerns how managers do, rather than should, behave.

Towards a normal model

About four years ago, Philip Yetton, then a graduate student at Carnegie–Mellon University, and I began a major research program in an attempt to answer these normative and descriptive questions.

We began with the normative question. What would be a rational way of deciding on the form and amount of participation in decision making that should be used in different situations? We were tired of debates over the relative merits of Theory X and Theory Y and of the truism that leadership depends upon the situation. We felt that it was time for the behavioral sciences to move beyond such generalities and to attempt to come to grips with the complexities of the phenomena with which they intended to deal.

Our aim was ambitious: to develop a set of ground rules for matching a manager's leadership behavior to the demands of the situation. It was critical that these ground rules be consistent with research evidence concerning the consequences of participation and that the model based on the rules be operational, so that any manager could see it to determine how he should act in any decision-making situation.

Table 1 shows the set of alternative decision processes that we have employed in our research. Each process is represented by a symbol (e.g. AI, CI, GII) that will be used as a convenient method of referring to each process. The first letter in this symbol signifies the basic properties of the process (A stands for autocratic; C for consultative; and G for group). The roman numerals that follow the first letter constitute

Table 1 Types of management decision styles

AI	You solve the problem or make the decision yourself, using information available to you at that time.
AII	You obtain the necessary information from your subordinate(s), then decide on the solution to the problem yourself. You may or may not tell your subordinates what the problem is in getting the information from them. The role played by your subordinates in making the decision is clearly one of providing the necessary information to you, rather than generating or evaluating alternative solutions.
CI	You share the problem with relevant subordinates individually, getting their ideas and suggestions without bringing them together as a group. Then *you* make the decision that may or may not reflect your subordinates' influence.
CII	You share the problem with your subordinates as a group, collectively obtaining their ideas and suggestions. Then *you* make the decision that may or may not reflect your subordinates' influence.
GII	You share a problem with your subordinates as a group. Together you generate and evaluate alternatives and attempt to reach agreement (consensus) on a solution. Your role is much like that of chairman. You do not try to influence the group to adopt 'your' solution and you are willing to accept and implement any solution that has the support of the entire group.

(GI is omitted because it applies only to more comprehensive models outside the scope of the article.)

variants on that process. Thus, AI represents the first variant on an autocratic process, and AII the second variant.

Conceptual and empirical basis of the model

A model designed to regulate, in some rational way, choices among the decision processes shown in Table 1 should be based on sound empirical evidence concerning the likely consequences of the styles. The more complete the empirical base of knowledge, the greater the certainty with which we can develop the model and the greater will be its usefulness. To aid in understanding the conceptual basis of the model, it is important to distinguish among three classes of outcomes that bear on the ultimate effectiveness of decisions. These are:

1. The quality or rationality of the decision.

2. The acceptance or commitment on the part of subordinates to execute the decision effectively.

3. The amount of time required to make the decision.

The effects of participation on each of these outcomes or consequences were summed up by the author in *The Handbook of Social Psychology* as follows:

> The results suggest that allocating problem-solving and decision-making tasks to entire groups requires a greater investment of man hours but produces higher acceptance of decisions and a higher probability that the decision will be executed efficiently. Differences between these two methods in quality of decisions and in elapsed time are inconclusive and probably highly variable . . . It would be naive to think that group decision making is always more 'effective' than autocratic decision making, or vice versa; the relative effectiveness of these two extreme methods depends both on the weights attached to quality, acceptance and time variables and on differences in amounts of these outcomes resulting from these methods, neither of which is invariant from one situation to another. The critics and proponents of participative management would do well to direct their efforts towards identifying the properties of situations in which different decision-making approaches are effective rather than wholesale condemnation or deification of one approach.

We have gone on from there to identify the properties of the situation or problem that will be the basic elements in the model. These problem attributes are of two types: (1) Those that specify the importance for a particular problem of quality and acceptance, and (2) those that, on the basis of available evidence, have a high probability of moderating the effects of participation on each of these outcomes. Table 2 shows the problem attributes used in the present form of the model. For each attribute a question is provided that might be used by a leader in diagnosing a particular problem prior to choosing his leadership style.

In phrasing the questions, we have kept technical language to a minimum. Furthermore, we have phrased the questions in yes–no form, translating the continuous variables defined above into dichotomous variables. For example, instead of attempting to determine how important the decision quality is to the effectiveness of the decision (attribute A), the leader is asked in the first question to judge whether there is any quality component to the problem. Similarly, the difficult task of

Table 2 Problem attributes used in the model

	Problem attributes	Diagnostic questions
A	The importance of the quality of the decision.	Is there a quality requirement such that one solution is likely to be more rational than another?
B	The extent to which the leader possesses sufficient information/ expertise to make a high-quality decision by himself.	Do I have sufficient information to make a high-quality decision?
C	The extent to which the problem is structured.	Is the problem structured?
D	The extent to which acceptance or commitment on the part of subordinates is critical to the effective implementation of the decision.	Is acceptance of decision by subordinates critical to effective implementation?
E	The prior probability that the leader's autocratic decision will receive acceptance by subordinates.	If you were to make the decision by yourself, is it reasonably certain that it would be accepted by your subordinates?
F	The extent to which subordinates are motivated to attain the organizational goals as represented in the objectives explicit in the statement of the problem.	Do subordinates share the organizational goals to be obtained in solving this problem?
G	The extent to which subordinates are likely to be in conflict over preferred solutions.	Is conflict among subordinates likely in preferred solutions?

specifying exactly how much information the leader possesses that is relevant to the decision (attribute B) is reduced to a simple judgment by the leader concerning whether or not he has sufficient information to make a high-quality decision.

We have found that managers can diagnose a situation quickly and accurately by answering this set of seven questions concerning it. But how can such responses generate a prescription concerning the most effective leadership style or decision process? What kind of normative model of participation in decision making can be built from this set of problem attributes?

Figure 1 shows one such model expressed in the form of a decision tree. It is the seventh version of such a model that we have developed over the last three years. The problem attributes, expressed in question form, are arranged along the top of the figure. To use the model for a particular decison-making situation, one starts at the left-hand side and works toward the right, asking oneself the question immediately above any box that is encountered. When a terminal node is reached, a number will be found designating the problem type and one of the decision-making processes appearing in Table 1. AI is prescribed for four problem types (1, 2, 4 and 5); AII is prescribed for two problem types (9 and 10); CI is prescribed for only one problem type (8); CII is prescribed for four problem types (7, 11, 13, and 14); and GII is prescribed for three problem types (3, 6, and 12). The relative frequency with which each of the five decision processes would be prescribed for any manager would, of course, depend on the distribution of problem types encountered in his decision making.

The rationale underlying the model

The decision processes specified for each problem type are not arbitrary. The model's behavior is governed by a set of principles intended to be consistent with existing evidence concerning the consequences of participation in decision making on organizational effectiveness. There are two mechanisms underlying the behavior of the model. The first is a set of seven rules that serve to protect the quality and the acceptance of the decison by eliminating alternatives that risk one or the other of these decision outcomes. Once the rules have been applied, a feasible set of decision processes is generated. The second mechanism is a principle for choosing among alternatives in the feasible set where more than one exists.

Let us examine the rules first, because they do much of the work of the model. As previously indicated, the rules are intended to protect both the quality and acceptance of the decision. In the form of the model shown, there are three rules that protect decision quality and four that protect acceptance.

1. *The information rule*. If the quality of the decision is important and if the leader does not possess enough information or expertise to solve the problem by himself, AI is eliminated from the feasible set. (Its use risks a low-quality decision.)

2. *The goal congruence rule*. If the quality of the decision is important and if the subordinates do not share the organizational goals to be obtained in solving the problem, GII is eliminated from the feasible set. (Alternatives that eliminate the leader's final control over the decision reached may jeopardize the quality of the decision.)

3. *The unstructured problem rule*. In decisions in which the quality of the decision is important, if the leader lacks the necessary information or expertise to solve the problem by himself, and if the problem is unstructured, i.e. he does not know exactly what information is needed and where it is located, the method used must provide not only for him to collect the information but to do so in an efficient and effective manner. Methods that involve interaction among all subordinates with full knowledge of the problem are likely to be both more efficient and more likely to generate a high-quality solution to the problem. Under these conditions, AI, AII, and CI are eliminated from the feasible set. (AI does not provide for him to collect the necessary information, and AII and CI represent more cumbersome, less effective, and less efficient means of bringing the necessary information to bear on the solution of the problem than methods that do permit those with the necessary information to interact.)

4. *The acceptance rule*. If the acceptance of the decision by subordinates is critical to effective implementation, and if it is not certain that an autocratic decision made by the leader would receive that acceptance, AI and AII are eliminated from the feasible set. (Neither provides an opportunity for subordinates to participate in the decision and both risk the necessary acceptance.)

5. *The conflict rule*. If the acceptance of the decision is critical, and an autocratic dcision is not certain to be accepted, and subordinates are likely to be in conflict or disagreement over the appropriate solution, AI, AII, and CI are eliminated from the feasible set. (The method used

in solving the problem should enable those in disagreement to resolve their differences with full knowledge of the problem. Accordingly, under these conditions, AI, AII, and CI, which involve no interaction or only 'one-on-one' relationships and therefore provide no opportunity for those in conflict to resolve their differences, are eliminated from the feasible set. Their use runs the risk of leaving some of the subordinates with less than the necessary commitment to the final decision.)

6. *The fairness rule.* If the quality of decision is unimportant and if acceptance is critical and not certain to result from an autocratic decision, AI, AII, CI, and CII are eliminated from the feasible set. (The method used should maximize the probability of acceptance as this is the only relevant consideration in determining the effectiveness of the decision. Under these circumstances, AI, AII, CI, and CII, which create less acceptance or commitment than GII, are eliminated from the feasible set. To use them is to run the risk of getting less than the needed acceptance of the decision.)

7. *The acceptance priority rule.* If acceptance is critical, not assured by an autocratic decision, and if subordinates can be trusted, AI, AII, CI, and CII are eliminated from the feasible set. (Methods that provide equal partnership in the decision-making process can provide greater acceptance without risking decision quality. Use of any method other than GII results in an unnecessary risk that the decision will not be fully accepted or receive the necessary commitment on the part of subordinates.)

Once all seven rules have been applied to a given problem, we emerge with a feasible set of decision processes. The feasible set for each of the fourteen problem types is shown in Table 3. It can be seen that there are some problem types for which only one method remains in the feasible set, others for which two methods remain feasible, and still others for which five methods remain feasible.

When more than one method remains in the feasible set, there are a number of ways in which one might choose among them. The mechanism we have selected and the principle underlying the choices of the model in Figure 1 utilizes the number of man-hours used in solving the problem as the basis for choice. Given a set of methods with equal likelihood of meeting both quality and acceptance requirements for the decision, it chooses that method which requires the least investment in man-hours. On the basis of the empirical evidence summarized earlier, this is deemed to be the method furthest to the left within the feasible

Table 3   Problem types and the feasible set
of decision processes

Problem type	Acceptable methods
1	AI, AII, CI, CII, GII
2	AI, AII, CI, CII, GII
3	GII
4	AI, AII, CI, CII, GII*
5	AI, AII, CI, CII, GII*
6	GII
7	CII
8	CI, CII
9	AII, CI, CII, GII*
10	AII, CI, CII, GII*
11	CII, GII*
12	GII
13	CII
14	CII, GII*

*Within the feasible set only when the answer
to question F is yes

set. For example, since AI, AII, CI, CII, and GII are all feasible as in problem types 1 and 2, AI would be the method chosen.

To illustrate application of the model in actual administrative situations, we will analyze four cases with the help of the model. While we attempt to describe these cases as completely as is necessary to permit the reader to make the judgments required by the model, there may remain some room for subjectivity. The reader may wish after reading the case to analyze it himself using the model and then to compare his analysis with that of the author.

Case 1. You are a manufacturing manager in a large electronics plant. The company's management has recently installed new machines and put in a new simplified work system, but to the surprise of everyone, yourself included, the expected increase in productivity has not been realized. In fact, production has begun to drop, quality has fallen off, and the number of employee separations has risen.

You do not believe that there is anything wrong with the machines. You have had reports from other companies that are using them and they confirm this opinion. You have also had representatives from the firm that built the machines go over them and they report that they are operating at peak efficiency. You suspect that some parts of the new

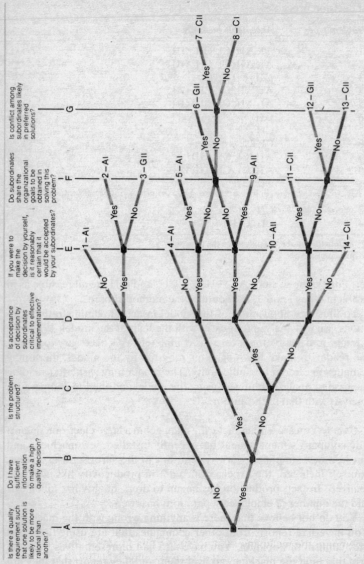

Figure 1 Decision model

work system may be responsible for the change, but this view is not widely shared among your immediate subordinates, who are four first-line supervisors, each in charge of a section, and your supply manager. The drop in production has been variously attributed to poor training of the operators, lack of an adequate system of financial incentives, and poor morale. Clearly, this is an issue about which there is considerable depth of feeling within individuals and potential disagreement among your subordinates.

This morning you received a phone call from your division manager. He had just received your production figures for the last six months and was calling to express his concern. He indicated that the problem was yours to solve in any way that you think best, but that he would like to know within a week what steps you plan to take. You share your division manager's concern with the falling productivity and know that your men are also concerned. The problem is to decide what steps to take to rectify the situation.

Analysis

Questions: A (quality?) = yes
            B (managers information?) = no
            C (structured?) = no
            D (acceptance?) = yes
            E (prior probability of acceptance?) = no
            F (goal congruence?) = yes
            G (conflict?) = yes

Problem type = 12
Feasible set = GII
Minimum man-hours solution (from Figure 1) = GII
Rule violations:

                      AI violates rules 1, 3, 4, 5, 7
                      AII violates rules 3, 4, 5, 7
                      CI violates rules 3, 5, 7
                      CII violates rule 7

Case 2. You are general foreman in charge of a large gang laying an oil pipeline and have to estimate your expected rate of progress in order to schedule material deliveries to the next field site. You know the nature of the terrain you will be traveling and have the historical data needed to compute the mean and variance in the rate of speed over that type of terrain. Given these two variables, it is a simple matter to calculate the earliest and latest times at which materials and support facilities will be needed at the next site. It is important that your estimate be reasonably accurate. Underestimates result in idle foremen and workers, and an overestimate results in tying up materials for a period of time before they are to be used.

Progress has been good and your five foremen and other members of the gang stand to receive substantial bonuses if the project is completed ahead of schedule.

Analysis

Questions: A (quality?) = yes
                    B (manager's information?) = yes
                    D (acceptance?) = no

Problem type = 4
Feasible set = AI, AII, CI, CII, GII
Minimum man-hours solution (from Figure 1) = AI
Rule violations = none

Case 3. You are supervising the work of twelve engineers. Their formal training and work experience are very similar, permitting you to interchange them on projects. Yesterday, your manager informed you that a request had been recei.ed from an overseas affiliate for four engineers to go abroad on extended loan for a period of six to eight months. For a number of reasons, he argued and you agreed that this request should be met from your group.

All your engineers are capable of handling this assignment and, from the standpoint of present and future projects, there is no particular reason why anyone should be retained over any other. The problem is somewhat complicated by the fact that the overseas assignment is in what is generally regarded as an undesirable location.

Analysis

Questions: A (quality?) = no
                    D (acceptance?) = yes
                    E (prior probability of acceptance?) = no
                    G (conflict?) = yes

Problem type = 3
Feasible set = GII
Minimum man-hours solution (from Figure 1) = GII
Rule violations:

                 AI and AII violate rules 4, 5, and 6
                 CI violates rules 5 and 6
                 CII violates rule 6

Case 4. You are on the division manager's staff and work on a wide variety of problems of both an administrative and technical nature. You have been given the assignment of developing a standard method to be used in each of the five plants in the division for manually reading equipment registers, recording the readings, and transmitting the scorings to a centralized information system.

Until now there has been a high error rate in the reading and/or transmission of the data. Some locations have considerably higher error rates than others, and the methods used to record and transmit the data vary among plants. It is probable, therefore, that part of the error variance is a function of specific local conditions rather than anything else, and this will complicate the establishment of any system common to all plants. You have the information on error rates but no information on the local practices that generate these errors or on the local conditions that necessitate the different practices.

Everyone would benefit from an improvement in the quality of the data; it is used in a number of important decisions. Your contacts with the plants are through the quality-control supervisors who are responsible for collecting the data. They are a conscientious group committed to doing their jobs well, but are highly sensitive to interference on the part of higher management in their own operations. Any solution that does not receive the active support of the various plant supervisors is unlikely to reduce the error rate significantly.

Analysis
Questions:

> A (quality?) = yes
> B (manager's information?) = no
> C (structured?) = no
> D (acceptance?) = yes
> E (prior probability of acceptance?) = no
> F (goal congruence?) = yes

Problem type = 12
Feasible set = GII
Minimum man-hours solution (from Figure 1) = GII
Rule violations:

> AI violates rules 1, 3, 4, and 7
> AII violates rules 3, 4, and 7
> CI violates rules 3 and 7
> CII violates rule 7

Short- versus long-term models

The model described above seeks to protect the quality of the decision and to expend the least number of man-hours in the process. Because it focuses on conditions surrounding the making and implementation of a particular decision rather than any long-term considerations, we can term it a short-term model. It seems likely, however, that the leadership methods that may be optimal for short-term results may be different from those that would be optimal over a longer period of time. Consider a leader, for example, who has been uniformly pursuing an autocratic style (AI or AII) and, perhaps as a consequence, has subordinates who might be termed 'yes men' (attribute E) but who also cannot be trusted to pursue organizational goals (attribute F), largely because the leader has never bothered to explain them.

It appears likely, however, that the manager who used more participative methods would, in time, change the status of these problem attributes so as to develop ultimately a more effective problem-solving system. A promising approach to the development of a long-term model is one that places less weight on man-hours as the basis for choice of method within the feasible set. Given a long-term orientation, one would be interested in the possibility of a trade-off between man-hours in problem solving and team development, both of which increase with participation. Viewed in these terms, the time-minimizing model places maximum relative weight on man-hours and no weight on development, and hence chooses the style farthest to the left within the feasible set. A model that places less weight on man-hours and more weight on development would, if these assumptions are correct, choose a style further to the right within the feasible set.

We recognize, of course, that the minimum man-hours solution suggested by the model is not always the best solution to every problem. A manager faced, for example, with the problem of handling any one of the four cases previously examined might well choose more time-consuming alternatives on the grounds that the greater time invested would be justified in developing his subordinates. Similar considerations exist in other decision-making situations. For this reason we have come to emphasize the feasible set of decision methods in our work with managers. Faced with considerations not included in the model, the manager should consider any alternative within the feasible set, not opt automatically for the minimum man-hours solution.

As I am writing this, I have in front of me a 'black box' that constitutes an electronic version of the normative model we have been discussing.

(The author is indebted to Peter Fuss of Bell Telephone Laboratories for his interest in the model and his skill in developing the 'black box'.) The box, which is small enough to fit into the palm of one hand, has a set of seven switches, each appropriately labeled with the questions (A through G) used in Figure 1. A manager faced with a concrete problem or decision can 'diagnose' that problem by setting each switch in either its 'yes' or 'no' position. Once the problem has been described, the manager depresses a button that illuminates at least one or as many as five lights, each of which denotes one of the decision processes (AI, AII, etc.). The lights that are illuminated constitute the feasible set of decision processes for the problem as shown in Table 3. The lights not illuminated correspond to alternatives that violate one or more of the seven rules previously stated.

In this prototype version of the box, the lights are illuminated in decreasing order of brightness from left to right within the feasible set. The brightest light corresponds to the alternative shown in Figure 1. Thus, if both CII and GII were feasible alternatives, CII would be brighter than GII, since it requires fewer man-hours. However, a manager who was not under any undue time pressure and who wished to invest time in the development of his subordinates might select an alternative corresponding to one of the dimmer lights.

Towards a descriptive model of leader behavior

So far we have been concerned with the normative questions defined at the outset. But how do managers really behave? What considerations affect their decisions about how much to share their decision-making power with their subordinates? In what respects is their behavior different from or similar to that of the model? These questions are but a few of those that we attempted to answer in a large-scale research program aimed at gaining a greater understanding of the factors that influence managers in their choice of decision processes to fit the demands of the situation. This research program was financially supported by the McKinsey Foundation, General Electric Foundation, Smith Richardson Foundation, and the Office of Naval Research.

Two different research methods have been utilized in studying these factors. The first investigation utilized a method that we have come to term 'recalled problems'. Over 500 managers from eleven different countries representing a variety of firms were asked to provide a written description of a problem that they had recently had to solve. These varied in length from one paragraph to several pages and covered virtually every facet of managerial decision making. For each case, the manager was asked to indicate which of the decision processes shown in Table 1 they used to solve the problem. Finally, each manager was asked to answer the questions shown in Table 2 corresponding to the problem attributes used in the normative model.

The wealth of data, both qualitative and quantitative, served two purposes. Since each manager had diagnosed a situation that he had encountered in terms that are used in the normative model and had indicated the methods that he had used in dealing with it, it is possible to determine what differences, if any, there were between the model's behavior and his own behavior. Second, the written cases provided the basis for the construction of a standard set of cases used in later research to determine the factors that influence managers to share or retain their decision-making power. Each case depicted a manager faced with a problem to solve or decision to make. The cases spanned a wide range of managerial problems including production scheduling, quality control, portfolio management, personnel allocation, and research and development. In each case, a person could readily assume the role of the manager described and could indicate which of the decision processes he would use if he actually were faced with that situation.

In most of our research, a set of thirty cases has been used and the subjects have been several thousand managers who were participants in management development programs in the United States and abroad. Cases were selected systematically. We desired cases that could not only be coded unambiguously in the terms used in the normative model, but that would also permit the assessment of the effects of each of the problem attributes used in the model on the person's behavior. The solution was to select cases in accordance with an experimental design so that they varied in terms of the seven attributes used in the model and variation in each attribute was independent of each other attribute. Several such standardized sets of cases have been developed, and over a thousand managers have now been studied using this approach.

To summarize everything we learned in the course of this research is well beyond the scope of this paper, but it is possible to discuss some of the highlights. Since the results obtained from the two research methods – recalled and standardized problems – are consistent, we can present the major results independent of the method used.

Perhaps the most striking finding is the weakening of the widespread view that participativeness is a general trait that individual managers exhibit in different amounts. To be sure, there were differences *among* managers in their general tendencies to utilize participative methods as opposed to autocratic ones. On the standardized problems, these differences accounted for about 10 per cent of the total variance in the decision processes observed. These differences in behavior between managers, however, were small in comparison with differences *within* managers. On the standardized problems, no manager has indicated that he would use the same decision process on all problems or decisions, and most use all five methods under some circumstances.

Some of this variance in behavior within managers can be attributed to widely shared tendencies to respond to some situations by sharing power and others by retaining it. It makes more sense to talk about participative and autocratic situations than it does to talk about participative and autocratic managers. In fact, on the standardized problems, the variance in behavior across problems or cases is about three times as large as the variance across managers!

What are the characteristics of an autocratic as opposed to a participative situation? An answer to this question would constitute a partial descriptive model of this aspect of the decision-making process and has been our goal in much of the research that we have conducted. From our observations of behavior on both recalled problems and on standardized problems, it is clear that the decision-making process employed by a typical manager is influenced by a large number of factors, many of which also show up in the normative model. Following are several conclusions substantiated by the results on both recalled and standardized problems: managers use decision processes providing less opportunity for participation (1) when they possess all the necessary information than when they lack some of the needed information, (2) when the problem that they face is well-structured rather than unstructured, (3) when their subordinates' acceptance of the decision is not critical for the effective implementation of the decision or when the prior probability of acceptance of an autocratic decision is high, and (4) when the personal goals of their subordinates are *not* congruent with the goals of the organization as manifested in the problem.

So far we have been talking about relatively common or widely shared ways of dealing with organizational problems. Our results strongly suggest that there are ways of 'tailoring' one's approach to the situation that distinguish managers from one another. Theoretically, these can be thought of as differences among managers in decision rules that they employ about when to encourage participation. Statistically, they are represented as interactions between situational variables and personal characteristics.

Consider, for example, two managers who have identical distributions of the use of the five decision processes shown in Table 1 on a set of thirty cases. In a sense, they are equally participative (or autocratic). However, the situations in which they permit or encourage participation in decision making on the part of their subordinates may be very different. One may restrict the participation of his subordinates to decisions without a quality requirement, whereas the other may restrict their participation to problems with a quality requirement. The former would be more inclined to use participative decision processes (like GII) on such decisions as what color the walls should be painted or when the company picnic should be held. The latter would be more likely to encourage participation in decision making on decisions that have a clear and demonstrable impact on the organization's success in achieving its external goals.

Use of the standardized problem set permits the assessment of such differences in decision rules that govern choices among decision-making processes. Since the cases are selected in accordance with an experimental design, they can indicate differences in the behavior of managers attributable not only to the existence of a quality requirement in the problem but also in the effects of acceptance requirements, conflict, information requirements, and the like. The research using both recalled and standardized problems has also enabled us to examine similarities and differences between the behavior of the normative model and the behavior of a typical manager. Such an analysis reveals, at the very least, what behavioral changes could be expected if managers began using the normative model as the basis for choosing their decision-making processes.

A typical manager says he would (or did) use exactly the same decision process as that shown in Figure 1 in 40 per cent of the situations. In two-thirds of the situations, his behavior is consistent with the feasible set of methods proposed in the model. In other words, in about one-third of the situations his behavior violates at least one of the seven rules underlying the model.

The four rules designed to protect the acceptance or commitment of the decision have substantially higher probabilities of being violated than do the three rules designed to protect the quality or rationality of the decision. One of the acceptance rules, the fairness rule (rule 6) is violated about three-quarters of the time that it could have been violated. On the other hand, one of the quality rules, the information rule (rule 1), is violated in only about 3 per cent of occasions in which it is applicable. If we assume for the moment that these two sets of rules have equal validity, these findings strongly suggest that the decisions made by typical managers are more likely to prove ineffective due to deficiencies of acceptance by subordinates than due to deficiencies in decision quality.

Another striking difference between the behavior of the model and of the typical manager lies in the fact that the former shows far greater variance with the situation. If a typical manager voluntarily used the model as the basis for choosing his methods of making decisions, he would become both more autocratic and more participative. He would employ autocratic methods more frequently in situations in which his subordinates were unaffected by the decision and participative methods more frequently when his subordinates' cooperation and support were critical and/or their information and expertise were required.

It should be noted that the typical manager to whom we have been referring is merely a statistical average of the several thousand who have been studied over the last three or four years. There is a great deal of variance around that average. As evidenced by their behavior on standardized problems, some managers are already behaving in a manner that is highly consistent with the model, while others' behavior is clearly at variance with it.

A new technology for leadership development

The investigations that have been summarized here were conducted for research purposes to shed some light on the causes and consequences of participation in decision making. In the course of the research, we came to realize, partly because of the value attached to it by the managers themselves, that the data-collection procedures, with appropriate additions and modifications, might also serve as a valuable guide to leadership development. From this realization evolved an important by-product of the research activities – a new approach to leadership development based on the concepts in the normative model and the empirical methods of the descriptive research. This approach is based on the assumption stated previously that one of the critical skills required of all leaders is the ability to adapt their behavior to the demands of the situation, and that one component of this skill involves the ability to select the appropriate decision-making process for each problem or decision he confronts.

Managers can derive value from the model by comparing their past or intended behavior in concrete decisions with that prescribed by the model and by seeing what rules, if any, they violate. Used in this way, the model can provide a mechanism for a manager to analyse both the circumstances that he faces and what decisions are feasible under these circumstances. While use of the model without training is possible, we believe that the manager can derive the maximum value from a systematic examination of his leadership style, and its similarities to and dissimilarities from the model, as part of a formal leadership development program.

During the past two years we have developed such a program. It is not intended to 'train' participants in the use of the model, but rather to encourage them to examine their own leadership style and to ask themselves whether the methods they are using are most effective for their own organization. A critical part of the program involves the use of a set of standardized cases, each depicting a leader faced with an administrative problem to solve. Each participant then specifies the decision-making process that he would use if faced with each situation. His responses are processed by computer, which generates a highly detailed analysis of his leadership style. The responses for all participants in the course are typically processed simultaneously, permitting the economical representation of differences between the person and other participants in the same program.

In its present form, a single computer printout for a person consists of three 15 in. × 11 in. pages, each filled with graphs and tables highlighting different features of his behavior. Understanding the results requires a detailed knowledge of the concepts underlying the model, something already developed in one of the previous phases of the training program. The printout is accompanied by a manual that aids in explaining results and provides suggested steps to be followed in extracting full meaning from the printout.

The following are a few of the questions that the printout answers:

1. How autocratic or participative am I in my dealings with subordinates in comparison with other participants in the program?

2. What decision processes do I use more or less frequently than the average?

3. How close does my behavior come to that of the model? How frequently does my behavior agree with the feasible set? What evidence is there that my leadership style reflects the pressure of time as opposed to a concern with the development of my subordinates? How do I compare in these respects with other participants in the class?

4. What rules do I violate most frequently and least frequently? How does this compare with other participants? On what cases did I violate these rules? Does my leadership style reflect more concern with getting

decisions that are high in quality or with getting decisions that are accepted?

5. What circumstances cause me to behave in an autocratic fashion; what circumstances cause me to behave participatively? In what respects is the way in which I attempt to vary my behavior with the demands of the situation similar to that of the model?

When a typical manager receives his printout, he immediately goes to work trying to understand what it tells him about himself. After most of the major results have been understood, he goes back to the set of cases to reread those on which he has violated rules. Typically, managers show an interest in discussing and comparing their results with others in the program. Gatherings of four to six people comparing their results and their interpretation of them, often for several hours at a stretch, were such a common feature that they have recently been institutionalized as part of the procedure.

We should emphasize that the method of providing feedback to managers on their leadership style is just one part of the total training experience, but it is an important part. The program is sufficiently new so that, to date, no long-term evaluative studies have been undertaken. The short-term results, however, appear quite promising.

Conclusion

The efforts reported in this article rest on the conviction that social scientists can be of greater value in solving problems of organizational behavior if their prescriptive statements deal with the complexities involved in the phenomena with which they study. The normative model described in this paper is one step in that direction. Some might argue that it is premature for social scientists to be prescriptive. Our knowledge is too limited and the issues too complex to warrant prescriptions for action, even those that are based on a diagnosis of situational demands. However, organizational problems persist, and managers cannot wait for the behavioral sciences to perfect their disciplines before attempting to cope with them. Is it likely that models that encourage them to deal analytically with the forces impinging upon them would produce less rational choices than those that they now make? We think the reverse is more probable – reflecting on the models will result in decisions that are more rational and more effective. The criterion for social utility is not perfection but improvement over present practice.

Selected bibliography

The interested reader may wish to consult V. H. Vroom and P. W. Yetton, *Leadership and Decision-Making*, University of Pittsburgh Press, 1973, which presents a more complete explication of the model, other models dealing with related aspects of the decision-making process, and their use in leadership development. For another perspective on the normative questions with which this article deals, the reader should consult R. Tannenbaum and W. Schmidt, 'How to Choose a Leadership Pattern', *Harvard Business Review*, September 1958. The descriptive questions are explored by F. Heller in his new book *Managerial Decision-Making*, Tavistock, 1971. Finally, N. R. F. Maier, *Problem-Solving Discussions and Conferences*, McGraw-Hill, 1963, presents the most useful account of the conference leadership techniques and skills required to implement participative approaches to management.

Part Three **Behaviour in Organizations**

Organizations are systems of interdependent human beings. From some points of view the members of an organization may be considered as a resource, but they are a special kind of resource in that they are directly involved in all the functioning processes of the organization and can affect its aims as well as the methods used to accomplish them. The contributors to this section are concerned to analyse the behaviour of people as they affect, and are affected by, organizational processes.

Elton Mayo (Reading 17) was the inspirer of the famous Hawthorne studies and the 'founding father' of the human-relations movement – the first major impact of social science on management thinking. He emphasized that workers must first be understood as people if they are to be understood as organization members. From his work have followed a large number of studies which demonstrate the social processes which inevitably surround the formal management system: the informal organization which is part of every organization's infrastructure.

Likert (Reading 18) maintains that the effective manager is one who can create a situation in which each member of his group feels that his relationships with others are 'supportive', that is, that they satisfy his needs as well as those of others. The work of Likert and his colleagues is often referred to as 'neo human relations'. It is more sophisticated and less sentimental than the original human-relations work, but in terms of influence and achievement Likert may be regarded as the modern inheritor of Elton Mayo's mantle. McGregor (Reading 19) has had most impact in presenting this approach to managers. His formulation of 'Theory X and Theory Y' has applied the neo-human-relations approach throughout the whole organization and has been the vehicle of much work on 'organizational development', particularly when allied to such training methods as 'T-groups'.

Herzberg (Reading 20) challenges existing views on motivation, maintaining that as well as economic needs human beings have psychological needs for autonomy, responsibility and development which have to be satisfied in work. He advocates the 'enrichment' of jobs through additional responsibility and authority in order to promote improved performance and increased mental health. Argyris and Schon (Reading 21) are concerned to analyse the way in which individuals in organizations – and therefore the organizations as such – can learn and develop new behaviours rather than merely continuing to repeat outmoded ones. Fiedler (Reading 22) shows how, to be effective, a leader's style must be appropriate to the situation in which he leads, and suggests how this match can be obtained.

Trist and his colleagues at the Tavistock (Reading 23) have consistently developed a systems approach to organizations in which the task requirements and individuals' needs are interrelated as an interdependent 'socio-technical system'. The present reading, with his colleague Bamforth, was an early and influential demonstration of this approach through the analysis of the behavioural disturbances caused by a major change in methods of coal mining.

Finally, Mintzberg (Reading 24) takes a realistic empirical look at the actual job that a manager has to do and suggests some distinctive characteristics which have not previously been noted.

17 E. Mayo

Hawthorne and the Western Electric Company

From E. Mayo, 'Hawthorne and the Western Electric Company',
The Social Problems of an Industrial Civilization, Routledge, 1949,
chapter 4, pp. 60–76.

A highly competent group of Western Electric engineers refused to accept defeat when experiments to demonstrate the effect of illumination on work seemed to lead nowhere. The conditions of scientific experiment had apparently been fulfilled – experimental room, control room; changes introduced one at a time; all other conditions held steady. And the results were perplexing: Roethlisberger gives two instances – lighting improved in the experimental room, production went up; but it rose also in the control room. The opposite of this: lighting diminished from 10 to 3 foot-candles in the experimental room and production again went up; simultaneously in the control room, with illumination constant, production also rose. [Roethlisberger, n.d.] Many other experiments, and all inconclusive; yet it had seemed so easy to determine the effect of illumination on work.

In matters of mechanics or chemistry the modern engineer knows how to set about the improvement of process or the redress of error. But the determination of optimum working conditions for the human being is left largely to dogma and tradition, guess, or quasi-philosophical argument. In modern large-scale industry the three persistent problems of management are:

1. The application of science and technical skill to some material good or product.
2. The systematic ordering of operations.
3. The organization of teamwork – that is, of sustained cooperation.

The last must take account of the need for continual reorganization of teamwork as operating conditions are changed in an *adaptive* society.

The first of these holds enormous prestige and interest and is the subject of continuous experiment. The second is well developed in practice. The third, by comparison with the other two, is almost wholly neglected. Yet it remains true that if these three are out of balance, the organization as a whole will not be successful. The first two operate to make an industry *effective*, in Chester Barnard's phrase, the third, to make it *efficient*. For the larger and more complex the institution, the more dependent is it upon the wholehearted cooperation of every member of the group.

This was not altogether the attitude of Mr G. A. Pennock and his colleagues when they set up the experimental 'test room'. But the illumination fiasco had made them alert to the need that very careful records should be kept of everything that happened in the room in addition to the obvious engineering and industrial devices.[1] Their observations therefore included not only records of industrial and engineering changes but also records of physiological or medical changes, and, in a sense, of social and anthropological. This last took the form of a 'log' that gave as full an account as possible of the actual events of every day, a record that proved most useful to Whitehead when he was re-measuring the recording tapes and re-calculating the changes in productive output. He was able to relate eccentricities of the output curve to the actual situation at a given time – that is to say, to the events of a specific day or week.

First phase – the test room

The facts are by now well known. Briefly restated, the test room began its inquiry by first attempting to secure the active collaboration of the workers. This took some time but was gradually successful, especially after the retirement of the original first and second workers and after the new worker at the second bench had assumed informal leadership of the group. From this point on, the evidence presented by Whitehead or Roethlisberger and Dickson seems to show that the individual workers became a team, wholeheartedly committed to the project. Second, the conditions of work were changed one at a time: rest periods of different numbers and length, shorter working day, shorter working week, food with soup or coffee in the morning break. And the results seemed satisfactory: slowly at first, but later with increasing certainty, the output record (used as an index of well-being) mounted. Simultaneously the girls claimed that they felt less fatigued, felt that they were not making any special effort. Whether these claims were accurate or no, they at least indicated increased contentment with the general situation in the test room by comparison with the department outside. At every point in the programme, the workers had been consulted with respect to pro-

1. For a full account of the experimental setup, see Roethlisberger and Dickson (1939) and T. North Whitehead, *The Industrial Worker*, vol. 1.

posed changes; they had arrived at the point of free expression of ideas and feelings to management. And it had been arranged thus that the twelfth experimental change should be a return to the original conditions of work – no rest periods, no mid-morning lunch, no shortened day or week. It had also been arranged that, after twelve weeks of this, the group should return to the conditions of period 7, a fifteen-minute mid-morning break with lunch and a ten-minute mid-afternoon rest. The story is now well known: in period 12 the daily and weekly output rose to a point higher than at any other time (the hourly rate adjusted itself downward by a small fraction), and in the whole twelve weeks 'there was no downward trend'. In the following period, the return to the conditions of work as in the seventh experimental change, the output curve soared to even greater heights: this thirteenth period lasted for thirty-one weeks.

These periods, 12 and 13, made it evident that increments of production could not be related point for point to the experimental changes introduced. Some major change was taking place that was chiefly responsible for the index of improved conditions – the steadily increasing output. Period 12 – but for minor qualifications, such as 'personal time out' – ignored the nominal return to original conditions of work and the output curve continued its upward passage. Put in other words, there was no actual return to original conditions. This served to bring another fact to the attention of the observers. Periods 7, 10 and 13 had nominally the same working conditions, as above described – fifteen-minute rest and lunch in mid-morning, ten-minute rest in the afternoon. But the average weekly output for each girl was:

Period   7 – 2500 units
Period 10 – 2800 units
Period 13 – 3000 units.

Periods 3 and 12 resembled each other also in that both required a full day's work without rest periods. But here also the difference of average weekly output for each girl was:

Period   3 – less than 2500 units
Period 12 – more than 2900 units.

Here then was a situation comparable perhaps with the illumination experiment, certainly suggestive of the Philadelphia experience where improved conditions for one team of mule spinners were reflected in improved morale not only in the experimental team but in the two other teams who had received no such benefit.

This interesting, and indeed amusing, result has been so often discussed that I need make no mystery of it now. I have often heard my colleague Roethlisberger declare that the major experimental change was introduced when those in charge sought to hold the situation humanly steady (in the interest of critical changes to be introduced) by getting the cooperation of the workers. What actually happened was that six individuals became a team and the team gave itself wholeheartedly and spontaneously to cooperation in the experiment. The consequence was that they felt themselves to be participating freely and without afterthought, and were happy in the knowledge that they were working without coercion from above or limitation from below. They were themselves astonished at the consequence, for they felt that they were working under less pressure than ever before: and in this, their feelings and performance echoed that of the mule spinners.

Here then are two topics which deserve the closest attention of all those engaged in administrative work – the organization of working teams and the free participation of such teams in the task and purpose of the organization as it directly affects them in their daily round.

Second phase – the interview programme

But such conclusions were not possible at the time: the major change, the question as to the exact difference between conditions of work in the test room and in the plant departments, remained something of a mystery. Officers of the company determined to 'take another look' at departments outside the test room – this, with the idea that something quite important was there to be observed, something to which the experiment should have made them alert. So the interview programme was introduced.

It was speedily discovered that the question-and-answer type of interview was useless in the situation. Workers wished to talk, and to talk freely under the seal of professional confidence (which was never abused) to someone who seemed representative of the company or who seemed, by his very attitude, to carry authority. The experience itself was unusual; there are few people in this world who have had the experience of finding someone intelligent, attentive and eager to listen without interruption to all that he or she has to say. But to arrive at this point it became necessary to train interviewers how to listen, how to avoid interruption or the giving of advice, how generally to avoid anything that might put an end to free expression in an individual instance. Some approximate rules to guide the interviewer in his work were therefore set down. These were, more or less, as follows:[2]

1. Give your whole attention to the person interviewed, and make it evident that you are doing so.

2. Listen – don't talk.

3. Never argue; never give advice.

4. Listen to:
(a) What he wants to say.
(b) What he does not want to say.
(c) What he cannot say without help.

5. As you listen, plot out tentatively and for subsequent correction the pattern (personal) that is being set before you. To test this, from time to time summarize what has been said and present for comment (e.g. 'Is this what you are telling me?'). Always do this with the greatest caution, that is, clarify but do not add or distort.

6. Remember that everything said must be considered a personal confidence and not divulged to anyone. (This does not prevent discussion of a situation between professional colleagues. Nor does it prevent some form of public report when due precaution has been taken.)

It must not be thought that this type of interviewing is easily learned. It is true that some persons, men and women alike, have a natural flair for the work, but, even with them, there tends to be an early period of discouragement, a feeling of futility, through which the experience and coaching of a senior interviewer must carry them. The important rules in the interview (important, that is, for the development of high skill) are two. First, rule 4 that indicates the need to help the individual interviewed to articulate expression of an idea or attitude that he has not before expressed; and, second, rule 5 which indicates the need from time to time to summarize what has been said and to present it for comment. Once equipped to do this effectively, interviewers develop very considerable skill. But, let me say again, this skill is not easily acquired. It demands of the interviewer a real capacity to follow the contours of another person's thinking, to understand the meaning for him of what he says.

2. For a full discussion of this type of interview, see Roethlisberger and Dickson (1939), chapter 13. For a more summary and perhaps less technical discussion, see Homans (1941).

I do not believe that any member of the research group or its associates had anticipated the immediate response that would be forthcoming to the introduction of such an interview programme. Such comments as 'This is the best thing the Company has ever done', or 'The Company should have done this long ago', were frequently heard. It was as if workers had been awaiting an opportunity for expressing freely and without afterthought their feelings on a great variety of modern situations, not by any means limited to the various departments of the plant. To find an intelligent person who was not only eager to listen but also anxious to help to expression ideas and feelings but dimly understood – this, for many thousand persons, was an experience without precedent in the modern world.

In a former statement (Mayo, 1933, p. 114) I named two questions that inevitably presented themselves to the interviewing group in these early stages of the study:

1. Is some experience which might be described as an experience of personal futility a common incident of industrial organization for work?

2. Does life in a modern industrial city, in some unrealized way, predispose workers to obsessive response?

And I said that these two questions 'in some form' continued to preoccupy those in charge of the research until the conclusion of the study.

After twelve years of further study (not yet concluded), there are certain developments that demand attention. For example, I had not fully realized in 1932, when the above was written, how profoundly the social structure of civilization has been shaken by scientific, engineering and industrial development. This radical change – the passage from an *established* to an *adaptive* social order – has brought into being a host of new and unanticipated problems for management and for the individual worker. The management problem appears at its acutest in the work of the supervisor. No longer does the supervisor work with a team of persons that he has known for many years or perhaps a lifetime; he is a leader of a group of individuals that forms and disappears almost as he watches it. Now it is difficult, if not impossible, to relate onself to a working group one by one; it is relatively easy to do so if they are already a fully constituted team. A communication from the supervisor, for example, in the latter instance has to be made to one person only with the appropriate instructions; the individual will pass it on and work it out with the team. In the former instance, it has to be repeated to every individual and may often be misunderstood.

But for the individual worker the problem is really much more serious. He has suffered a profound loss of security and certainty in his actual living and in the background of his thinking. For all of us the feeling of security and certainty derives always from assured membership of a group. If this is lost, no monetary gain, no job guarantee, can be sufficient compensation. Where groups change ceaselessly as jobs and mechanical processes change, the individual inevitably experiences a sense of void, of emptiness, where his fathers knew the joy of comradeship and security. And in such situation, his anxieties – many, no doubt, irrational or ill-founded – increase and he becomes more difficult both to fellow workers and to supervisor. The extreme of this is perhaps rarely encountered as yet, but increasingly we move in this direction as the tempo of industrial change is speeded by scientific and technical discovery.

In the first chapter of this book I have claimed that scientific method has a dual approach – represented in medicine by the clinic and the laboratory. In the clinic one studies the whole situation with two ends in view: first, to develop intimate knowledge of and skill in handling the facts, and, second, on the basis of such a skill to separate those aspects of the situation, that skill has shown to be closely related, for detailed laboratory study. When a study based upon laboratory method fails, or partially fails, because some essential factor has been unknowingly and arbitrarily excluded, the investigator, if he is wise, returns to clinical study of the entire situation to get some hint as to the nature of the excluded determinant. The members of the research division at Hawthorne, after the twelfth experimental period in the test room, were faced by just such a situation and knew it. The so-called interview programme represented for them a return from the laboratory to clinical study. And, as in all clinical study, there was no immediate and welcome revelation of a single discarded determinant: there was rather a slow progress from one observation to another, all of them important – but only gradually building up into a single complex finding. This slow development has been elsewhere described, in *Management and the Worker*; one can however attempt a succinct résumé of the various observations, more or less as they occurred.

Officers of the company had prepared a short statement, a few sentences, to be repeated to the individual interviewed before the conversation began. This statement was designed to assure the worker that nothing he said would be repeated to his supervisors or to any company official outside the interviewing group. In many instances, the worker waved this aside and began to talk freely and at once. What doubts there were seemed to be resident in the interviewers rather than in those interviewed. Many workers, I cannot say the majority for we have no statistics, seemed to have something 'on their minds', in ordinary phrase, about which they wished to talk freely to a competent listener. And these topics were by no means confined to matters affecting the company. This was, I think, the first observation that emerged from the mass of interviews reported daily. The research group began to talk about the need for *emotional release* and the great advantage that accrued to the individual when he had 'talked off' his problem. The topics varied greatly. One worker two years before had been sharply reprimanded by his supervisor for not working as usual: in interview he wished to explain that on the night preceding the day of the incident his wife and child had both died, apparently unexpectedly. At the time he was unable to explain; afterwards he had no opportunity to do so. He told the story dramatically and in great detail; there was no doubt whatever that telling it thus benefited him greatly. But this story naturally was exceptional; more often a worker would speak of his family and domestic situation, of his church, of his relations with other members of the working group – quite usually the topic of which he spoke presented itself to him as a problem difficult for him to resolve. This led to the next successive illumination for the inquiry. It became manifest that, whatever the problem, it was partly, and sometimes wholly, determined by the attitude of the individual worker. And this defect or distortion of attitude was consequent on his past experience or his present situation, or, more usually, on both at once. One woman worker, for example, discovered for herself during an interview that her dislike of a certain supervisor was based upon a fancied resemblance to a detested stepfather. Small wonder that the same supervisor had warned the interviewer that she was 'difficult to handle'. But the discovery by the worker that her dislike was wholly irrational eased the situation considerably (Roethlisberger and Dickson, 1939, pp. 307–10). This type of case led the interviewing group to study carefully each worker's *personal situation* and attitude. These two phrases 'emotional release' and 'personal situation' became convenient titles for the first phases of observation and seemed to resume for the interviewers the effective work that they were doing. It was at this point that a change began to show itself in the study and in the conception of the study.

The original interviewers, in these days, after sixteen years of industrial experience, are emphatic on the point that the first cases singled out for report were special cases – individuals – and not representative either of the working group or of the interviews generally. It is estimated that such cases did not number more than an approximate 2 per cent of the twenty thousand persons originally interviewed. Probably this error of emphasis was inevitable and for two reasons: first, the dramatic changes that occur in such instances seemed good evidence of the efficacy of the method, and, second, this type of interviewing had to be insisted upon as *necessary to the training of a skilled interviewer*. This last still holds good; a skilled interviewer must have passed through the stage of careful and observant listening to what an individual says and to all that he says. This stage of an interviewing programme closely resembles the therapeutic method and its triumphs are apt to be therapeutic. And I do not believe that the study would have been equipped to advance further if it had failed to observe the great benefit of emotional release and the extent to which every individual's problems are conditioned by his personal history and situation. Indeed, even when one has advanced beyond the merely psychotherapeutic study of individuals to study of industrial groups, one has to beware of distortions similar in kind to those named; one has to know how to deal with such problems. The first phase of the interview programme cannot therefore be discarded; it still retains its original importance. But industrial studies must nevertheless move beyond the individual in need of therapy. And this is the more true when the change from established routines to adaptive changes of routine seems generally to carry a consequence of loss of security for many persons.

A change of attitude in the research group came gradually. The close study of individuals continued, but in combination with an equally close study of groups. An early incident did much to set the new pattern for inquiry. One of the earliest questions proposed before the original test-room experiment began was a question as to the fatigue involved in this or that type of work. Later a foreman of high reputation, no doubt with this in mind, came to the research group, now for the most part engaged in interviewing, and asserted that the girls in his department worked hard all day at their machines and must be considerably fatigued by the evening; he wanted an inquiry. Now the interviewers had discovered that this working group claimed a habit of doing most of their work in the morning period and 'taking things easy' during the afternoon. The foreman obviously realized nothing of this, and it was therefore fortunate that the two possibilities could be directly tested. The officer in charge of the research made a quiet arrangement with the engineers to measure during a period the amount of electric current used by the group to operate its machines; this quantity indicated the overall amount of work being done. The results of this test wholly supported the statements made by the girls in interview; far more current was used in the morning period than during the afternoon. And the attention of the research group was, by this and other incidents, thus redirected to a fact already known to them, namely, that the working group as a whole actually determined the output of individual workers by reference to a standard, pre-determined but never clearly stated, that represented the group conception of a fair day's work. This standard was rarely, if ever, in accord with the standards of the efficiency engineers.

The final experiment, reported under the title of the Bank Wiring Observation Room, was set up to extend and confirm these observations (Roethlisberger and Dickson, 1939, part 4, p. 379 ff.). Simultaneously it was realized that these facts did not in any way imply low working morale as suggested by such phrases as 'restriction of output'. On the contrary, the failure of free communication between management and workers in modern large-scale industry leads inevitably to the exercise of caution by the working group until such time as it knows clearly the range and meaning of changes imposed from above. The enthusiasm of the efficiency engineer for the organization of operations is excellent; his attempt to resume problems of cooperation under this heading is not. At the moment, he attempts to solve the many human difficulties involved in whole-hearted cooperation by organizing the organization of organization without any reference whatever to workers themselves. This procedure inevitably blocks communication and defeats his own admirable purpose.[3]

This observation, important as it is, was not however the leading point for the interviewers. The existence and influence of the group – those in active daily relationship with one another – became the important fact. The industrial interviewer must learn to distinguish and specify, as he listens to what a worker says, references to 'personal' or group situations. More often than not, the special case, the individual who talks himself out of a gross distortion, is a solitary – one who has not 'made the team'. The usual interview, on the other hand, though not by any means free from distortion, is speaking as much for the working group as for the person. The influence of the communication in the interview, therefore, is not limited to the individual but extends to the group.

Two girl workers in a large industry were recently offered 'upgrading'; to accept would mean leaving their group and taking a job in another

3. For further evidence on this point, see Mathewson (1969) and also Mayo (1933), pp. 119–21.

department: they refused. Then representatives of the union put some pressure on them, claiming that, if they continued to refuse, the union organizers 'might just as well give up' their efforts. With reluctance the girls reversed their decision and accepted the upgrading. Both girls at once needed the attention of an interviewer: they had liked the former group in which they had earned informal membership. Both felt adjustment to a new group and a novel situation as involving effort and private discontent. From both much was learned of the intimate organization and common practices of their groups, and their adjustments to their new groups were eased, thereby effectively helping to reconstitute the teamwork in those groups.

In another recent interview a girl of eighteen protested to an interviewer that her mother was continually urging her to ask Mr X, her supervisor, for a 'raise'. She had refused, but her loyalty to her mother and the pressure the latter exerted were affecting her work and her relations at work. She talked her situation out with an interviewer, and it became clear to her a 'raise' would mean departure from her daily companions and associates. Although not immediately relevant, it is interesting to note that, after explaining the situation at length to the interviewer, she was able to present her case dispassionately to her mother – without exaggeration or protest. The mother immediately understood and abandoned pressure for advancement, and the girl returned to effective work. This last instance illustrates one way in which the interview clears lines of communication of emotional blockage – within as without the plant. But this is not my immediate topic; my point is rather that the age-old human desire for persistence of human association will seriously complicate the development of an adaptive society if we cannot devise systematic methods of easing individuals from one group of associates into another.

But such an observation was not possible in the earliest inquiry. The important fact brought to the attention of the research division was that the ordinary conception of management–worker relation as existing between company officials, on the one hand, and an unspecified number of individuals, on the other, is utterly mistaken. Management, in any continuously successful plant, is not related to single workers, but always to working groups. In every department that continues to operate, the workers have – whether aware of it or not – formed themselves into a group with appropriate customs, duties, routines, even rituals; and management succeeds (or fails) in proportion as it is accepted without reservation by the group as authority and leader. This, for example, occurred in the relay-assembly test room at Hawthorne.

Management, by consultation with the girl workers, by clear explanation of the proposed experiments and the reasons for them, by accepting the workers' verdict in special instances unwittingly scored a success in two most important human matters – the girls became a self-governing team, and a team that cooperated whole-heartedly with management. The test room was responsible for many important findings – rest periods, hours of work, food, and the like: but the most important finding of all was unquestionably in the general area of teamwork and cooperation.

It was at this time that the research division published, for private circulation within the company, a monograph entitled 'Complaints and Grievances'. Careful description of many varied situations within the interviewers' experience showed that an articulate complaint only rarely, if ever, gave any logical clue to the grievance in which it had origin; this applied at least as strongly to groups as to individuals. Whereas economists and industry generally *tend to concentrate upon the complaint and upon logical inferences from its articulate statement* as an appropriate procedure, the interviewing group had learned almost to ignore, except as symptom, the – sometimes noisy – manifestation of discomfort and to study the situation anew to gain knowledge of its source. Diagnosis rather than argument became the proper method of procedure.

It is possible to quote an illustration from a recently published book, *China Enters the Machine Age* (Shih Kuo-heng, 1944). When industries had to be moved, during this war, from Shanghai and the Chinese coast to Kunming in the interior of China, the actual operation of an industry still depended for the most part on skilled workers who were refugees from Shanghai and elsewhere. These skilled workers knew their importance to the work and gained considerable prestige from it; nevertheless discontent was rife among them. Evidence of this was manifested by the continual, deliberate breaking of crockery in the company mess hall and complaints about the quality of the food provided. Yet this food was much better than could have been obtained outside the plant – especially at the prices charged. And in interview the individual workers admitted freely that the food was good and could not rightly be made the subject of complaint. But the relationship between the skilled workers as a group and the *Chih Yuan* – the executive and supervisory officers – was exceedingly unsatisfactory.

Many of these officers – the *Chih Yuan* – have been trained in the United States – enough at least to set a pattern for the whole group. Now in America we have learned in actual practice to accept the rabble hypothesis with reservations. But the logical Chinese student of engineering or economics, knowing nothing of these practical reservations, returns to his own country convinced that the workman who is not wholly responsive to the 'financial incentive' is a troublemaker and a nuisance. And the Chinese worker lives up to this conviction by breaking plates.[4] Acceptance of the complaint about the food and collective bargaining of a logical type conducted at that level would surely have been useless.

Yet this is what industry, not only in China, does every day, with the high sanction of State authority and the alleged aid of lawyers and economists. In their behaviour and their statements, economists indicate that they accept the rabble hypothesis and its dismal corollary of financial incentive as the only effective human motive. They substitute a logical hypothesis of small practical value for the actual facts.

The insight gained by the interviewing group, on the other hand, cannot be described as substituting irrational for rational motive, emotion for logic. On the contrary, it implies a need for competent study of complaints and the grievances that provoke them, a need for knowledge of the actual facts rather than acceptance of an outdated theory. It is amusing that certain industrialists, rigidly disciplined in economic theory, attempt to shrug off the Hawthorne studies as 'theoretic'. Actually the shoe is on the other foot; Hawthorne has restudied the facts without prejudice, whereas the critics have unquestioningly accepted that theory of man which had its vogue in the nineteenth century and has already outlived its usefulness.

The Hawthorne interview programme has moved far since its beginning in 1929. Originally designed to study the comfort of workers in their work as a mass of individuals, it has come to clear specification of the relation of working groups to management as one of the fundamental problems of large-scale industry. It was indeed this study that first enabled us to assert that the third major preoccupation of management must be that of organizing teamwork, that is to say, of developing and sustaining cooperation.

References

BARNARD, C. (1938), 'The executive functions', *The Functions of the Executive*, Harvard University Press, chapter 15, pp. 215–34.
HOMANS, G. C. (1941), *Fatigue of Workers*, Reinhold.

4. Shih Kuo-heng (1944), chapter 8, pp. 111–27; also chapter 10, pp. 151–3.

MATHEWSON, S. B. (1931), *Restriction of Output among Unorganized Workers*, Viking.

MAYO, E. (1933), *The Human Problems of an Industrial Civilization*, Macmillan Co.

ROETHLISBERGER, F. J. (n.d.), *Management and Morale*, Harvard University Press, pp. 9–10.

ROETHLISBERGER, F. J., and DICKSON, W. J. (1939), *Management and the Worker*, Harvard University Press, pp. 379–510.

SHIH KUO-HENG (1944), *China Enters the Machine Age*, Harvard University Press.

18 R. Likert

The Principle of Supportive Relationships

From R. Likert, 'An integrating principle and an overview',
New Patterns of Management, McGraw-Hill, 1961, chapter 8, pp. 97–118.

The managers whose performance is impressive appear to be fashioning a better system of management. Two generalizations can be stated based on the available research findings:

1. The supervisors and managers in American industry and government who are achieving the highest productivity, lowest costs, least turnover and absence, and the highest levels of employee motivation and satisfaction display, on the average, a different pattern of leadership from those managers who are achieving less impressive results. The principles and practices of these high-producing managers are deviating in important ways from those called for by present-day management theories.

2. The high-producing managers whose deviations from existing theory and practice are creating improved procedures have not yet integrated their deviant principles into a theory of management. Individually, they are often clearly aware of how a particular practice of theirs differs from generally accepted methods, but the magnitude, importance, and systematic nature of the differences when the total pattern is examined do not appear to be recognized.

Based upon the principles and practices of the managers who are achieving the best results, a newer theory of organization and management can be stated. An attempt will be made in this chapter to present briefly some of the overall characteristics of such a theory and to formulate a general integrating principle which can be useful in attempts to apply it.

There is no doubt that further research and experimental testing of the theory in pilot operations will yield evidence pointing to modifications of many aspects of the newer theory suggested in this volume. Consequently, in reading this and subsequent chapters it will be well not to quarrel with the specific aspects of the newer theory as presented. These specifics are intended as stimulants for discussion and as encouragement for experimental field tests of the theory. It will be more profitable to seek to understand the newer theory's general basic character and, whenever a specific aspect or derivation appears to be in error, to formulate more valid derivations and propositions.

Research findings indicate that the general pattern of operations of the highest-producing managers tends to differ from that of the managers of mediocre and low-producing units by more often showing the following characteristics:

1. A preponderance of favorable attitudes on the part of each member of the organization toward all the other members, toward superiors, toward the work, toward the organization – toward all aspects of the job. These favorable attitudes toward others reflect a high level of mutual confidence and trust throughout the organization. The favourable attitudes toward the organization and the work are not those of easy complacency, but are the attitudes of identification with the organization and its objectives and a high sense of involvement in achieving them. As a consequence, the performance goals are high and dissatisfaction may occur whenever achievement falls short of the goals set.

2. This highly motivated, cooperative orientation toward the organization and its objectives is achieved by harnessing effectively all the major motivational forces which can exercise significant influence in an organizational setting and which, potentially, can be accompanied by cooperative and favorable attitudes. Reliance is not placed solely or fundamentally on the economic motive of buying a man's time and using control and authority as the organizing and coordinating principle of the organization. On the contrary, the following motives are all used fully and in such a way that they function in a cumulative and reinforcing manner and yield favorable attitudes:
(a) The ego motives. These are referred to throughout this volume as the desire to achieve and maintain a sense of personal worth and importance. This desire manifests itself in many forms, depending upon the norms and values of the persons and groups involved. Thus, it is responsible for such motivational forces as the desire for growth and significant achievement in terms of one's own values and goals, i.e. self-fulfillment, as well as the desire for status, recognition, approval, acceptance and power and the desire to undertake significant and important tasks.
(b) The security motives.
(c) Curiosity, creativity, and the desire for new experiences.
(d) The economic motives.

By tapping all the motives which yield favorable and cooperative attitudes, maximum motivation oriented toward realizing the organization's goals as well as the needs of each member of the organization is achieved. The substantial decrements in motivational forces which occur when powerful motives are pulling in opposite directions are thereby avoided. These conflicting forces exist, of course, when hostile and resentful attitudes are present.

3. The organization consists of a tightly knit, effectively functioning social system. This social system is made up of interlocking work groups with a high degree of group loyalty among the members and favorable attitudes and trust between superiors and subordinates. Sensitivity to others and relatively high levels of skill in personal interaction and the functioning of groups are also present. These skills permit effective participation in decisions on common problems. Participation is used, for example, to establish organizational objectives which are a satisfactory integration of the needs and desires of all members of the organization and of persons functionally related to it. High levels of reciprocal influence occur, and high levels of total coordinated influence are achieved in the organization. Communication is efficient and effective. There is a flow from one part of the organization to another of all the relevant information important for each decision and action. The leadership in the organization has developed what might well be called a highly effective social system for interaction and mutual influence.

4. Measurements of organizational performance are used primarily for self-guidance rather than for superimposed control. To tap the motives which bring cooperative and favorable rather than hostile attitudes, participation and involvement in decisions is a habitual part of the leadership processes. This kind of decision making, of course, calls for the full sharing of available measurements and information. Moreover, as it becomes evident in the decision-making process that additional information or measurements are needed, steps are taken to obtain them.

In achieving operations which are more often characterized by the above pattern of highly cooperative, well-coordinated activity, the highest-producing managers use all the technical resources of the classical theories of management, such as time-and-motion study, budgeting and financial controls. They use these resources at least as completely as do the low-producing managers, but in quite different ways. This difference in use arises from the differences in the motives which the high-producing, in contrast to the low-producing, managers believe are important in influencing human behavior.

The low-producing managers, in keeping with traditional practice, feel that the way to motivate and direct behavior is to exercise control through authority. Jobs are organized, methods are prescribed, standards are set, performance goals and budgets are established. Compliance with them is sought through the use of hierarchical and economic pressures.

The highest-producing managers feel, generally, that this manner of functioning does not produce the best results, that the resentment created by direct exercise of authority tends to limit its effectiveness. They have learned that better results can be achieved when a different motivational process is employed. As suggested above, they strive to use all those major motives which have the potentiality of yielding favorable and cooperative attitudes in such a way that favorable attitudes are, in fact, elicited and the motivational forces are mutually reinforcing. Motivational forces stemming from the economic motive are not then blunted by such other motivations as group goals which restrict the quantity or quality of output. The full strength of all economic, ego and other motives is generated and put to use.

Widespread use of participation is one of the more important approaches employed by the high-producing managers in their efforts to get full benefit from the technical resources of the classical theories of management coupled with high levels of reinforcing motivation. This use of participation applies to all aspects of the job and work, as, for example, in setting work goals and budgets, controlling costs, organizing the work, etc.

In these and comparable ways, the high-producing managers make full use of the technical resources of the classical theories of management. They use these resources in such a manner, however, that favorable and cooperative attitudes are created and all members of the organization endeavor to pull concertedly toward commonly accepted goals which they have helped to establish.

This brief description of the pattern of management which is more often characteristic of the high-producing than of the low-producing managers points to what appears to be a critical difference. The high-producing managers have developed their organizations into highly coordinated, highly motivated, cooperative social systems. Under their leadership, the different motivational forces in each member of the organization have coalesced into a strong force aimed at accomplishing the mutually established objectives of the organization. This general pattern of highly motivated, cooperative members seems to be a central characteristic of the newer management system being developed by the highest-producing managers.

How do these high-producing managers build organizations which display this central characteristic? Is there any general approach or underlying principle which they rely upon in building highly motivated organizations? There seems to be: the research findings show, for example, that those supervisors and managers whose pattern of leadership yields consistently favorable attitudes more often think of employees as 'human beings rather than just as persons to get the work done'. Consistently, in study after study, the data show that treating people as 'human beings' rather than as 'cogs in a machine' is a variable highly related to the attitudes and motivation of the subordinate at every level in the organization.

The superiors who have the most favorable and cooperative attitudes in their work groups display the following characteristics.

1. The attitude and behavior of the superior toward the subordinate as a person, *as perceived by the subordinate*, is as follows:
(*a*) He is supportive, friendly and helpful rather than hostile. He is kind but firm, never threatening, genuinely interested in the well-being of subordinates and endeavors to treat people in a sensitive, considerate way. He is just, if not generous. He endeavors to serve the best interests of his employees as well as of the company.
(*b*) He shows confidence in the integrity, ability and motivations of subordinates rather than suspicion and distrust.
(*c*) His confidence in subordinates leads him to have high expectations as to their level of performance. With confidence that he will not be disappointed, he expects much, not little. (This, again, is fundamentally a supportive rather than a critical or hostile relationship.)
(*d*) He sees that each subordinate is well trained for his particular job. He endeavors also to help subordinates be promoted by training them for jobs at the next level. This involves giving them relevant experience and coaching whenever the opportunity offers.
(*e*) He coaches and assists employees whose performance is below standard. In the case of a subordinate who is clearly misplaced and unable to do his job satisfactorily, he endeavors to find a position well suited to that employee's abilities and arranges to have the employee transferred to it.

2. The behavior of the superior in directing the work is characterized by such activity as:

(a) Planning and scheduling the work to be done, training subordinates, supplying them with material and tools, initiating work activity, etc.

(b) Providing adequate technical competence, particularly in those situations where the work has not been highly standardized.

3. The leader develops his subordinates into a working team with high group loyalty by using participation and the other kinds of group-leadership practices.

The integrating principle

These results and similar data from other studies (Argyris, 1957; March and Simon, 1958; Viteles, 1953) show that subordinates react favorably to experiences which they feel are supportive and contribute to their sense of importance and personal worth. Similarly, persons react unfavorably to experiences which are threatening and decrease or minimize their sense of dignity and personal worth. These findings are supported also by substantial research on personality development (Argyris, 1957; Rog rs, 1942) and group behavior (Cartwright and Zander, 1960). Each of us wants appreciation, recognition, influence, a feeling of accomplishment, and a feeling that people who are important to us believe in us and respect us. We want to feel that we have a place in the world.

This pattern of reaction appears to be universal and seems to be the basis for the general principle used by the high-producing managers in developing their highly motivated, cooperative organizations. These managers have discovered that the motivational forces acting in each member of an organization are most likely to be cumulative and reinforcing when the interactions between each individual and the others in the organization are of such a character that they convey to the individual a feeling of support and recognition for his importance and worth as a person. These managers, therefore, strive to have the interactions between the members of their organizations of such a character that each member of the organization feels confident in his potentialities and believes that his abilities are being well used.

A second factor, however, is also important. An individual's reaction to any situation is always a function not of the absolute character of the interaction, but of his perception of it. It is how he sees things that counts, not objective reality. Consequently, an individual member of an organization will always interpret an interaction between himself and the organization in terms of his background and culture, his experience and expectations. The pattern of supervision and the language used that might be effective with a railroad's maintenance-of-way crew, for example, would not be suitable in an office full of young women. A subordinate tends also to expect his superior to behave in ways consistent with the personality of the superior. All this means that each of us, as a subordinate or as a peer or as a superior, reacts in terms of his own particular background, experience, and expectations. In order, therefore, to have an interaction viewed as supportive, it is essential that it be of such a character that the individual himself, in the light of his experience and expectations, sees it as supportive. This provides the basis for stating the general principle which the high-producing managers seem to be using and which will be referred to as the *principle of supportive relationships*. This principle, which provides an invaluable guide in any attempt to apply the newer theory of management in a specific plant or organization, can be briefly stated: *The leadership and other processes of the organization must be such as to ensure a maximum probability that in all interactions and all relationships with the organization each member will, in the light of his background, values and expectations, view the experience as supportive and one which builds and maintains his sense of personal worth and importance.*

The principle of supportive relationships as an organizing concept

This general principle provides a fundamental formula for obtaining the full potential of every major motive which can be constructively harnessed in a working situation. There is impressive evidence, for example, that economic motivations will be tapped more effectively when the conditions specified by the principle of supportive relationships are met (Katz and Kahn, 1951; Krulee, 1955). In addition, as motives are used in the ways called for by this general principle, the attitudes accompanying the motives will be favorable and the different motivational forces will be cumulative and reinforcing. Under these circumstances, the full power from each of the available motives will be added to that from the others to yield a maximum of coordinated, enthusiastic effort.

The principle of supportive relationships points to a dimension essential for the success of every organization, namely, that the mission of the organization be seen by its members as genuinely important. To be highly motivated, each member of the organization must feel that the organization's objectives are of significance and that his own particular task contributes in an indispensable manner to the organization's achievement of its objectives. He should see his role as difficult, important and meaningful. This is necessary if the individual is to achieve and maintain a sense of personal worth and importance. When jobs do not meet this specification they should be reorganized so that they do. This is likely to require the participation of those involved in the work in a manner suggested in subsequent chapters.

The term 'supportive' is used frequently in subsequent chapters and also is a key word in the principle of supportive relationships. Experiences, relationships, etc., are considered to be supportive when the individual involved sees the experience (in terms of his values, goals, expectations and aspirations) as contributing to or maintaining his sense of personal worth and importance.

The principle of supportive relationships contains within it an important clue to its effective use. To apply this general principle, a superior must take into consideration the experience and expectations of each of his subordinates. In determining what these expectations are, he cannot rely solely on his observations and impressions. It helps the superior to try to put himself in his subordinate's shoes and endeavor to see things as the subordinate sees them, but this is not enough. Too often, the superior's estimates are wrong. He needs direct evidence if he is to know how the subordinate views things and to estimate the kinds of behavior and interaction which will be seen by the subordinate as supportive. The superior needs accurate information as to how his behavior is actually seen by the subordinate. Does the subordinate, in fact, perceive the superior's behavior as supportive?

There are two major ways to obtain this evidence. In a complex organization it can be found by the use of measurements of the intervening variables. It can also be obtained by the development of work-group relationships, which not only facilitate but actually require, as part of the group building and maintenance functions, candid expressions by group members of their perceptions and reactions to the behavior of others.

The central role of the work group

An important theoretical derivation can be made from the principle of supportive relationships. This derivation is based directly on the desire to achieve and maintain a sense of personal worth, which is a central concept of the principle. The most important source of satisfaction for this desire is the response we get from the people we are close to, in whom we are interested, and whose approval and support we are eager to have. The face-to-face groups with whom we spend the bulk of our time are, consequently, the most important to us. Our work group is one in which we spend much of our time and one in which we are particularly eager to achieve and maintain a sense of personal worth. As a consequence, most persons are highly motivated to behave in ways consistent with the goals and values of their work group in order to obtain recognition, support, security, and favorable reactions from this group. It can be concluded, therefore, that *management will make full use of the potential capacities of its human resources only when each person in an organization is a member of one or more effectively functioning work groups that have a high degree of group loyalty, effective skills of interaction and high-performance goals*.

The full significance of this derivation becomes more evident when we examine the research findings that show how groups function when they are well knit and have effective interaction skills. Research shows, for example, that the greater the attraction and loyalty to the group, the more the individual is motivated (1) to accept the goals and decisions of the group; (2) to seek to influence the goals and decisions of the group so that they are consistent with his own experience and his own goals; (3) to communicate fully to the members of the group; (4) to welcome communication and influence attempts from the other members; (5) to behave so as to help implement the goals and decisions that are seen as most important to the group; and (6) to behave in ways calculated to receive support and favorable recognition from members of the group and especially from those who the individual feels are the more powerful and higher-status members (Cartwright and Zander, 1960). Groups which display a high level of member attraction to the group and high levels of the above characteristics will be referred to in this volume as *highly effective groups*.

As our theoretical derivation has indicated, an organization will function best when its personnel function not as individuals but as members of highly effective work groups with high-performance goals. Consequently, management should deliberately endeavor to build these effective groups, linking them into an overall organization by means of people who hold overlapping group membership (Figure 1). The superior in one group is a subordinate in the next group, and so on through the organization. If the work groups at each hierarchical level are well knit and effective, the linking process will be accomplished

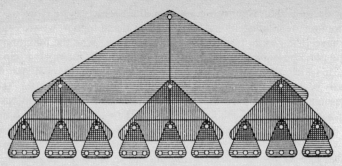

Figure 1 The overlapping group form of organization. Work groups vary in size as circumstances require although shown here as consisting of four persons

well. Staff as well as line should be characterized by this pattern of operation.

The dark lines in Figure 1 are intended to show that interaction occurs between individuals as well as in groups. The dark lines are omitted at the lowest level in the chart in order to avoid complexity. Interaction between individuals occurs there, of course, just as it does at higher levels in the organization.

In most organizations, there are also various continuing and *ad hoc* committees, committees related to staff functions, etc., which should also become highly effective groups and thereby help further to tie the many parts of the organization together. These links are in addition to the linking provided by the overlapping members in the line organization. Throughout the organization, the supervisory process should develop and strengthen group functioning. This theoretically ideal organizational structure provides the framework for the management system called for by the newer theory.

The traditional company organization

Let us examine the way an organization would function were it to apply this one derivation and establish highly effective groups with high performance goals, instead of adhering to the traditional man-to-man pattern. First, let us look briefly at how the traditional man-to-man pattern usually functions. Figure 2 shows the top of an ordinary organization chart. Such an organization ordinarily functions on a man-to-man basis as shown in Figure 3a. In Figure 3a, the president, vice-presidents, and others reporting to the president are represented by 0s.

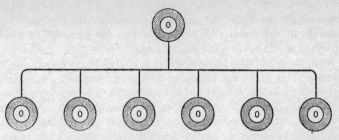

Figure 2   Typical organization chart

The solid lines in Figure 3*a* indicate the boundaries of well-defined areas of responsibility.

The president of such a man-to-man organization has said to us, 'I have been made president of this company by the board of directors because they believe I am more intelligent or better trained or have more relevant experience than my fellow managers. Therefore, it is my

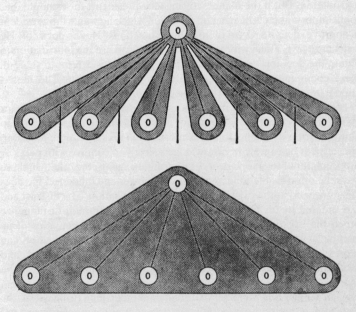

Figure 3   Man-to-man and group patterns of organization:
(*a*) man-to-man pattern of organization, (*b*) group pattern of organization

responsibility to make the top-level decisions.' He regularly holds meetings of the people who report to him for purposes of sharing information, but *not* for decision making.

What happens? The vice-president in charge of manufacturing, for example, may go to the president with a problem and a recommendation. Because it involves a model change, the vice-president in charge of sales is called in. On the basis of the discussion with the two vice-presidents and the recommendations they make, the president arrives at a decision. However, in any organization larger than a few hundred employees, that decision usually will affect other vice-presidents and subordinates whose interests were not represented in it. Under the circumstances, they are not likely to accept this decision wholeheartedly nor strive hard to implement it. Instead, they usually begin to plan how they can get decisions from the president which are going to be beneficial to them but not necessarily to sales and manufacturing.

And what happens to the communication process? This president, it will be recalled, holds meetings for the primary purpose of sharing information. But if the manufacturing vice-president, for example, has some important facts bearing on an action which he wants the president to approve, does he reveal them at these meetings? No, he does not. He waits until he is alone with the president and can use the information to obtain the decision he seeks. Each vice-president is careful to share in these communication meetings only trivial information. The motivational pressures are against sharing anything of importance.

The man-to-man pattern of operation enables a vice-president or manager to benefit by keeping as much information as possible to himself. Not only can he obtain decisions from his superior beneficial to himself, but he can use his knowledge secretly to connive with peers or subordinates or to pit one peer or subordinate against the other. In these ways, he often is able to increase his own power and influence. He does this, however, at the expense of the total organization. The distrust and fear created by his behavior adversely affect the amount of influence which the organization can exert in coordinating the activities of its members. Measures of the amount of influence an organization can exert on its members show that distrust of superiors, colleagues, and subordinates adversely affects the amount of influence that can be exercised.

Another serious weakness of the communication process in the man-to-man method of operating is that communications upward are highly filtered and correspondingly inaccurate. Orders and instructions flow down through the organization, at times with some distortion. But when management asks for information on the execution of orders and on difficulties encountered, incomplete and partially inaccurate information is often forthcoming. With these items and with other kinds of communication as well, those below the boss study him carefully to discover what he is interested in, what he approves and disapproves of, and what he wants to hear and does not want to hear. They then tend to feed him the material he wants. It is difficult and often hazardous for an individual subordinate in man-to-man discussion to tell the boss something which he needs to know but which runs counter to the boss's desires, convictions, or prejudices. A subordinate's future in an organization often is influenced appreciably by how well he senses and communicates to his boss material which fits the latter's orientation.

Another characteristic of the man-to-man pattern concerns the point of view from which problems are solved. When a problem is brought to the president, each vice-president usually states and discusses the problem from a departmental orientation, despite efforts by the president to deal with it from a company-wide point of view. This operates to the disadvantage of the entire organization. Problems tend to be solved in terms of what is best for a department, not what is best for the company as a whole.

Effect of competition between functions

In the man-to-man situation it is clear that sharply defined lines of responsibility are necessary (Figure 3a) because of the nature of the promotion process and because the men involved are able people who want promotion.

Now, what are the chances of having one's competence so visible that one moves up in such an organization or receives offers elsewhere? Two factors are important: the magnitude of one's responsibility and the definition of one's functions so as to assure successful performance. For example, if you are head of sales and can get the president to order the manufacturing department to make a product or to price it in such a way that it is highly competitive, that will be to your advantage, even though it imposes excessive difficulties and cost problems on the manufacturing operation.

Each man, in short, is trying to enlarge his area of responsibility, thereby encroaching on the other's territory. He is also trying to get decisions from the president which set easily attained goals for him and enable him to achieve excellent performance. Thus, the sales vice-president may get prices set which make his job easy but which put undue pressure on the manufacturing vice-president to cut production costs.

One consequence of this struggle for power is that each department or operation has to be staffed for peak loads, and job responsibilities and boundaries have to be precisely defined. No one dares let anybody else take over any part of his activity temporarily for fear that the line of responsibility will be moved over permanently.

The tighter the hierarchical control in an organization, in the sense that decisions are made at the top and orders flow down, the greater tends to be the hostility among subordinates. In autocratic organizations, subordinates bow down to superiors and fight among themselves for power and status. Consequently, the greater the extent to which the president makes the decisions, the greater is the probability that competition, hostility, and conflict will exist between his vice-presidents and staff members.

The group system of operation

Figure 3b represents a company patterned on the group system of organization. One of the presidents we interviewed follows this pattern. He will not permit an organization chart to be drawn because he does not want people to think in terms of man-to-man hierarchy. He wants to build working groups. He holds meetings of his top staff regularly to solve problems and make decisions. Any member of his staff can propose problems for consideration, but each problem is viewed from a company-wide point of view. It is virtually impossible for one department to force a decision beneficial to it but detrimental to other departments if the group, as a whole, makes the decisions.

An effectively functioning group pressing for solutions in the best interest of *all* the members and refusing to accept solutions which unduly favor a particular member or segment of the group is an important characteristic of the group pattern of organization. It also provides the president, or the superior at any level in an organization, with a powerful managerial tool for dealing with special requests or favors from subordinates. Often the subordinate may feel that the request is legitimate even though it may not be in the best interest of the organization. In the man-to-man operation (Figure 3a), the chief sometimes finds it difficult to turn down such requests. With the group pattern of operation, however, the superior can suggest that the subordinate submit his proposal to the group at their next staff meeting. If the request is legitimate and in the best interest of the organization, the group will grant the request. If the request is unreasonable, an effectively functioning group can skillfully turn it down by analyzing it in relation to what is best for the entire organization. Subordinates in this situation soon find they cannot get special favors or preferred treatment from the chief. This leads to a tradition that one does not ask for any treatment or decision which is recognized as unfair to one's colleagues.

The capacity of effective groups to press for decisions and action in the best interest of all members can be applied in other ways. An example is provided by the president of a subsidiary of a large corporation. He was younger (age forty-two) than most of his staff and much younger than two of his vice-presidents (ages sixty-one and sixty-two). The subsidiary had done quite well under its previous president, but the young president was eager to have it do still better. In his first two years as president, his company showed substantial improvement. He found, however, that the two older vice-presidents were not effectively handling their responsibilities. Better results were needed from them if the company was to achieve the record performance which the president and the other vice-presidents sought.

The president met the situation by using his regular staff meetings to analyze the company's present position, evaluate its potential, and decide on goals and on the action required to reach them. The president had no need to put pressure on his coasting vice-presidents. The other vice-presidents did it for him. One vice-president, in particular, slightly younger but with more years of experience than the two who were dragging their feet, gently but effectively pushed them to commit themselves to higher performance goals. In the regular staff meetings, progress toward objectives was watched and new short-term goals were set as needed. Using this group process, steady progress was made. The two oldest vice-presidents became as much involved and worked as enthusiastically as did the rest of the staff.

Group decision making

With the model of organization shown in Figure 3b, persons reporting to the president, such as vice-presidents for sales, research and manufacturing, contribute their technical knowledge in the decision-making process. They also make other contributions. One member of the group, for example, may be an imaginative person who comes up rapidly with many stimulating and original ideas. Others, such as the general counsel or the head of research, may make the group do a rigorous job of sifting ideas. In this way, the different contributions required for a competent job of thinking and decision making are introduced.

In addition, these people become experienced in effective group functioning. They know what leadership involves. If the president grows absorbed in some detail and fails to keep the group focused on the topic for discussion, the members will help by performing appropriate leadership functions, such as asking, 'Where are we? What have we decided so far? Why don't we summarize?'

There are other advantages to this sort of group action. The motivation is high to communicate accurately all relevant and important information. If any one of these men holds back important facts affecting the company so that he can take it to the president later, the president is likely to ask him why he withheld the information and request him to report it to the group at the next session. The group also is apt to be hard on any member who withholds important information from them. Moreover, the group can get ideas across to the boss that no subordinate dares tell him. As a consequence, there is better communication, which brings a better awareness of problems, and better decision making than with the man-to-man system.

Another important advantage of effective group action is the high degree of motivation on the part of each member to do his best to implement decisions and to achieve the group goals. Since the goals of the group are arrived at through group decisions, each individual group member tends to have a high level of ego identification with the goals because of his involvement in the decisions.

Finally, there are indications that an organization operating in this way can be staffed for less than peak loads at each point. When one man is overburdened, some of his colleagues can pick up part of the load temporarily. This is possible with group methods of supervision because the struggle for power and status is less. Everybody recognizes his broad area of responsibility and is not alarmed by occasional shifts in one direction or the other. Moreover, he knows that his chances for promotion depend not upon the width of his responsibility, but upon his total performance, of which his work in the group is an important part. The group, including the president, comes to know the strengths and weaknesses of each member well as a result of working closely with him.

A few years ago a department of fifteen people in a medium-sized company shifted from a man-to-man pattern of supervision to the group pattern. Each operation under the man-to-man system was staffed to carry adequately the peak loads encountered, but these peaks virtually never occurred for all jobs at the same time. In shifting to group supervision, the department studied how the work was being done. They concluded that seven persons instead of fifteen could carry the load except in emergencies. Gradually, over several months, the persons not needed transferred to other departments and the income of those doing the work was increased 50 per cent. The work is being done well, peak loads are handled, those doing it have more favorable attitudes, and there is less absence and turnover than under the man-to-man system.

Responsibility and situational requirements

In every organization there are many basic facts of life which cannot be ignored if the organization is to achieve its objectives. For example, there are often deadlines or minimum financial conditions as to earnings and reserves to be met. These hard, objective realities are the *situational requirements* which impose limitations on the decision-making processes.

The supervisor of every work group must be fully aware of the situational requirements which apply to the operation of his group. In making decisions, he and his group should never lose sight of them. If the group is so divided in opinion that there is not time to reach decisions by consensus which adequately meet these requirements, the superior has the responsibility of making a decision which does meet them. In this event, the superior may be wise to accept the solution preferred by the individuals in the group who will have the major responsibility for implementing the decision, provided, of course, the superior himself feels that the solution is reasonably sound.

Sometimes the differences of opinion exist not between members of the work group, but between the superior and his subordinates. In this event, the superior should participate fully in the discussion and present clearly the evidence which makes him hold another point of view. If, after further discussion, the group still prefers a course of action different from that which the chief favors, the superior faces a tough decision. He can overrule the group and take the action he favors. This is likely to affect adversely group loyalties and the capacity of his work group to function well as a group. Or he can go along with the group and accept the decision they prefer. If he overrules the group, the superior usually reduces the amount of work-group loyalty which he has 'in the bank'. If the costs of a mistake are not too great, he may prefer to accept the group's decision in order to strengthen the group as a group and to provide an opportunity for his group to learn from its mistakes. If the costs of a mistake are likely to be excessive, the superior may feel that he has no choice but to do what his own experience indicates is best. But whatever course of action is taken, *he is responsible and must accept full responsibility for what occurs*.

The 'linking pin' function

Figure 3 and the preceding discussion have been concerned with the group pattern of organization at the very top of a company. Our theoretical derivation indicates, however, that this pattern is equally applicable at all levels of an organization. If an organization is to apply this system effectively at all organizational levels, an important linking function must be performed.

The concept of the 'linking pin' is shown by the arrows in Figure 4. The study by Pelz (1951, 1952) showed that there was only a slight relationship between some fifty different measures of supervisory practices and points of view, as reported by the supervisors, and the attitudes and morale of the subordinates. Pelz found that an important variable was responsible for the absence of more marked relationships. This variable proved to be the amount of influence which a supervisor felt he had with his own superior. To function effectively, a supervisor must have sufficient influence with his own superior to be able to affect the superior's decisions. Subordinates expect their supervisors to be able to exercise an influence upward in dealing with problems on the job and in handling problems which affect them and their well-being. As Pelz's analysis shows, when a supervisor cannot exert sufficient influence upward in the hierarchy to handle these problems constructively, an

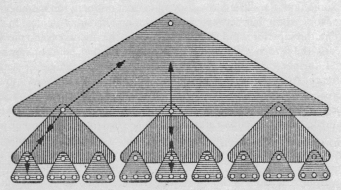

Figure 4   The linking pin

unfavorable reaction to the supervisor and to the organization is likely to occur.

Other research confirms the importance of Pelz's findings and also indicates that the ability to exert an influence upward affects not only morale and motivation but also productivity and performance variables (Katz *et al.*, 1951; Likert and Willits, 1940). Ronken and Lawrence (1952) summarize their findings on this matter as follows:

An additional complication for the foreman was the necessity of learning how to work with new supervisors and a new group of subordinates. When the foreman experienced difficulty in communicating with his superior, he was not able to understand his subordinates' problems or to gain their spontaneous cooperation, and the work suffered. When he felt more confident of his relations upward, he administered his own group with greater skill. During such periods his operators showed considerable initiative in their work, contributed more useful suggestions, and raced with themselves and each other to increase output.

These results demonstrate that *the capacity to exert influence upward is essential if a supervisor (or manager) is to perform his supervisory functions successfully*. To be effective in leading his own work group, a superior must be able to influence his own boss; that is, he needs to be skilled both as a supervisor and as a subordinate. In terms of group functioning, he must be skilled in both leadership and membership functions and roles.

Effective groups with high group loyalty are characterized by efficient and full communication and by the fact that their members respect each other, welcome attempts by the other members to influence them, and are influenced in their thinking and behavior when they believe that the evidence submitted by the other members warrants it. The linking-pin function will consequently be performed well in an organization when each work group at all the different hierarchical levels above the nonsupervisory level is functioning effectively as a group and when every member of each group is performing his functions and roles well. Whenever an individual member of one of these groups fails in his leadership and membership roles, the group or groups under him will not be linked into the organization effectively and will fail in the performance of their tasks. When an entire work group ceases to function effectively as a group, the activities and performance of all the work groups below such a group will be correspondingly adversely affected.

The linking-pin function requires effective group processes and points to the following:

1. An organization will not derive the full benefit from its highly effective groups unless they are linked to the total organization by means of equally effective overlapping groups such as those illustrated in Figures 1 and 4. The use of highly effective groups in only one part or in scattered portions of an organization will fail, therefore, to achieve the full potential value of such groups.

2. The potential power of the overlapping group form of organization will not be approached until all the groups in the organization are functioning reasonably well. The failure of any group will adversely affect the performance of the total organization.

3. The higher an ineffective group is in the hierarchy, the greater is the adverse effect of its failure on the performance of the organization. The linking process is more important at high levels in an organization than at low because the policies and problems dealt with are more important to the total organization and affect more people.

4. To help maintain an effective organization, it is desirable for superiors not only to hold group meetings of their own subordinates, but also to have occasional meetings over two hierarchical levels. This enables the superior to observe any breakdown in the linking-pin process as performed by the subordinates reporting to him. If in such meetings the subordinates under one of his subordinates are reluctant to talk, never question any procedure or policy, or give other evidence of fear, the superior can conclude that he has a coaching job to do with his own subordinate, who is failing both as a leader and in his performance of the linking-pin function. This subordinate needs help in learning how to build his own subordinates into a work group with high group loyalty and with confidence and trust in their supervisor.

5. An organization takes a serious risk when it relies on a single linking pin or single linking process to tie the organization together. As will be discussed further in subsequent chapters, an organization is strengthened by having staff groups and *ad hoc* committees provide multiple overlapping groups through which linking functions are performed and the organization bound together.

Organizational objectives and goals of units

The ability of a superior to behave in a supportive manner is circumscribed by the degree of compatibility between the objectives of the organization and the needs of the individuals comprising it. If the objectives of the organization are in basic conflict with the needs and desires of the individual members, it is virtually impossible for the superior to be supportive to subordinates and at the same time serve the objectives of the organization. The principle of supportive relationships, consequently, points to the necessity for an adequate degree of harmony between organizational objectives and the needs and desires of its individual members.

This conclusion is applicable to every kind of organization: industrial, governmental, or voluntary. A business organization, if it is to function well, needs to have objectives which represent a satisfactory integration of the needs and desires of all the major segments involved: its share owners, its suppliers, its consumers, its employees (including all levels of supervisory and nonsupervisory personnel) and its union(s). If governmental agencies are to function effectively, their objectives similarly must be a satisfactory integration of the needs and desires of all the different segments involved in their activities: employees, citizens and legislators.

Neither the needs and desires of individuals nor the objectives of organizations are stable and unchanging. The desires of individuals grow and change as people interact with other people. Similarly, the objectives of organizations must change continuously to meet the requirements of changed technologies, changed conditions, and the changes in needs and desires of those involved in the organization or served by it. The interaction process of the organization must be capable of dealing effectively with these requirements for continuous change.

In every healthy organization there is, consequently, an unending process of examining and modifying individual goals and organizational objectives as well as consideration of the methods for achieving them. The newer theory specifies that:

1. The objectives of the entire organization and of its component parts must be in satisfactory harmony with the relevant needs and desires of the great majority, if not all, of the members of the organization and of the persons served by it.

2. The goals and assignments of each member of the organization must be established in such a way that he is highly motivated to achieve them. The methods and procedures used by the organization and its subunits to achieve the agreed-upon objectives must be developed and adopted in such a way that the members are highly motivated to use these methods to their maximum potentiality.

3. The members of the organization and the persons related to it must feel that the reward system of the organization – salaries, wages, bonuses, dividends, interest payments – yields them equitable compensation for their efforts and contributions.

The overlapping group form of organization offers a structure which, in conjunction with a high level of group interactional skills, is particularly effective in performing the processes necessary to meet these requirements.

Constructive use of conflict

An organization operating under the newer theory is not free from conflict. Conflict and differences of opinion always exist in a healthy, virile organization, for it is usually from such differences that new and better objectives and methods emerge. Differences are essential to progress, but bitter, unresolved differences can immobilize an organization. The central problem, consequently, becomes not how to reduce or eliminate conflict, but how to deal constructively with it. Effective organizations have extraordinary capacity to handle conflict. Their success is due to three very important characteristics:

1. They possess the machinery to deal constructively with conflict. They have an organizational structure which facilitates constructive interaction between individuals and between work groups.

2. The personnel of the organization is skilled in the processes of effective interaction and mutual influence.

3. There is high confidence and trust among the members of the organization in each other, high loyalty to the work group and to the organization, and high motivation to achieve the organization's objectives. Confidence, loyalty and cooperative motivation produce earnest, sincere and determined efforts to find solutions to conflict. There is greater motivation to find a constructive solution than to maintain an irreconcilable conflict. The solutions reached are often highly creative and represent a far better solution than any initially proposed by the conflicting interests (Metcalf and Urwick, 1940).

The discussion in this chapter has deliberately focused on and emphasized the group aspects of organization and management. This has been done to make clear some of the major differences between the classical and the newer theories of management. It should also sharpen the awareness of the kind of changes needed to start applying the newer theory.

Any organization which bases its operation on this theory will necessarily make use of individual counseling and coaching by superiors of subordinates. There is need in every situation for a balanced use of both procedures, individual and group. Here, as with other aspects of supervision, the balance which will be most appropriate and work best will depend upon the experience, expectations and skills of the people involved.

Tests of the newer theory

The validity of the newer theory of management and of its derivations can be tested in two ways. Tests can be applied experimentally in pilot plants to see whether the newer system significantly improves all aspects of performance: productivity, quality, costs, employee satisfaction, etc. Although it will take several years to know the results, this kind of test is now under way.

The second kind of test is an examination of the extent to which the methods and procedures called for by the theory, or by the derivations based on the theory, are associated with above-average performance in the current operations of companies. The results of this kind of test do not require waiting for the outcome of an experimental application of the theory, but can be examined now. Several tests of this latter kind have recently been made. These were based on data which have been collected during the past few years. The results indicate that the newer theory, skilfully used, will produce an organization with impressive performance characteristics.

References

ARGYRIS, C. (1957), *Personality and Organisation*, Harper & Row.
CARTWRIGHT, D., and ZANDER, A. (eds.) (1960), *Group Dynamics: research and theory*, 2nd edn., Ron Peterson.
KATZ, D., and KAHN, R. L. (1951), 'Human organization and worker motivation', in L. Reed Tripp (ed.), *Industrial Productivity*, Industrial Relations Research Association, pp. 146–71.
KATZ, D., et al. (1951), *Productivity, Supervision and Morale in an Office Situation*, Institute for Social Research.
KRULEE, G. K. (1955), 'The Scanlon plan: co-operation through participation', *Journal of Business*, no. 28 (2), pp. 100–113.

LIKERT, R., and WILLITS, J. M. (1940), *Morale and Agency Management*, Life Insurance Agency Management Association.

MARCH, J. G., and SIMON, H. A. (1958), *Organizations*, Wiley.

METCALF, H. C., and URWICK, L. (eds.) (1940), *Dynamic Administration: the collected works of Mary Parker Follett*, Harper & Row.

PELZ, D. C. (1951), *The Influence of the Supervisor Within his Department as a Conditioner of the Way Supervisory Practices Affect Employee Attitudes*, unpublished doctoral dissertation, University of Michigan.

PELZ, D. C. (1952), 'Influence: a key to effective leadership in the first-line supervisor', *Personnel*, November, pp. 3–11.

ROGERS, C. R. (1942), *Counseling and Psychotherapy*, Houghton Mifflin.

RONKEN, H. O., and LAWRENCE, P. R. (1952), *Administering Changes*, Harvard Graduate School of Business Administration.

VITELES, M. S. (1953), *Motivation and Morale in Industry*, Norton.

19 D. McGregor

Theory X and Theory Y

From D. McGregor, 'Theory X: the traditional view of direction and control' and 'Theory Y: the integration of individual and organizational goals', *The Human Side of Enterprise*, McGraw-Hill, 1960, chapters 3 and 4, pp. 33–57.

Theory X: the traditional view of direction and control

Behind every managerial decision or action are assumptions about human nature and human behavior. A few of these are remarkably pervasive. They are implicit in most of the literature of organization and in much current managerial policy and practice.

1. *The average human being has an inherent dislike of work and will avoid it if he can.* This assumption has deep roots. The punishment of Adam and Eve for eating the fruit of the Tree of Knowledge was to be banished from Eden into a world where they had to work for a living. The stress that management places on productivity, on the concept of 'a fair day's work', on the evils of featherbedding and restriction of output, on rewards for performance – while it has a logic in terms of the objectives of enterprise – reflects an underlying belief that management must counteract an inherent human tendency to avoid work. The evidence for the correctness of this assumption would seem to most managers to be incontrovertible.

2. *Because of this human characteristic of dislike of work, most people must be coerced, controlled, directed, threatened with punishment to get them to put forth adequate effort toward the achievement of organizational objectives.* The dislike of work is so strong that even the promise of rewards is not generally enough to overcome it. People will accept the rewards and demand continually higher ones, but these alone will not produce the necessary effort. Only the threat of punishment will do the trick.

The current wave of criticism of 'human relations', the derogatory comments about 'permissiveness' and 'democracy' in industry, the trends in some companies toward recentralization after the postwar wave of decentralization – all these are assertions of the underlying assumption that people will only work under external coercion and control. The recession of 1957–8 ended a decade of experimentation with the 'soft' managerial approach, and this assumption (which never really was abandoned) is being openly espoused once more.

3. *The average human being prefers to be directed, wishes to avoid responsibility, has relatively little ambition, wants security above all*. This assumption of the 'mediocrity of the masses' is rarely expressed so bluntly. In fact, a good deal of lip service is given to the ideal of the worth of the average human being. Our political and social values demand such public expressions. Nevertheless, a great many managers will give private support to this assumption, and it is easy to see it reflected in policy and practice. Paternalism has become a nasty word, but it is by no means a defunct managerial philosophy.

I have suggested elsewhere the name Theory X for this set of assumptions. In later chapters of this book I will attempt to show that Theory X is not a straw man for purposes of demolition, but is in fact a theory which materially influences managerial strategy in a wide sector of American industry today. Moreover, the principles of organization which comprise the bulk of the literature of management *could only have been derived from assumptions such as those of Theory X*. Other beliefs about human nature would have led inevitably to quite different organizational principles.

Theory X provides an explanation of some human behavior in industry. These assumptions would not have persisted if there were not a considerable body of evidence to support them. Nevertheless, there are many readily observable phenomena in industry and elsewhere which are not consistent with this view of human nature.

Such a state of affairs is not uncommon. The history of science provides many examples of theoretical explanations which persist over long periods despite the fact that they are only partially adequate. Newton's laws of motion are a case in point. It was not until development of the theory of relativity during the present century that important inconsistencies and inadequacies in Newtonian theory could be understood and corrected.

The growth of knowledge in the social sciences during the past quarter century has made it possible to reformulate some assumptions about human nature and human behavior in the organizational setting which resolve certain of the inconsistencies inherent in Theory X. While this reformulation is, of course, tentative, it provides an improved basis for prediction and control of human behavior in industry.

Some assumptions about motivation

At the core of any theory of the management of human resources are assumptions about human motivation. This has been a confusing subject because there have been so many conflicting points of view even among social scientists. In recent years, however, there has been a convergence of research findings and a growing acceptance of a few rather basic ideas about motivation. These ideas appear to have considerable power. They help to explain the inadequacies of Theory X as well as the limited sense in which it is correct. In addition, they provide the basis for an entirely different theory of management.

The following generalizations about motivation are somewhat over-simplified. If all of the qualifications which would be required by a truly adequate treatment were introduced, the gross essentials which are particularly significant for management would be obscured. These generalizations do not misrepresent the facts, but they do ignore some complexities of human behavior which are relatively unimportant for our purposes.

Man is a wanting animal – as soon as one of his needs is satisfied, another appears in its place. This process is unending. It continues from birth to death. Man continuously puts forth effort – works, if you please – to satisfy his needs.

Human needs are organized in a series of levels – a hierarchy of importance. At the lowest level, but pre-eminent in importance when they are thwarted, are the physiological needs. Man lives by bread alone, when there is no bread. Unless the circumstances are unusual, his needs for love, for status, for recognition are inoperative when his stomach has been empty for a while. But when he eats regularly and adequately, hunger ceases to be an important need. The sated man has hunger only in the sense that a full bottle has emptiness. The same is true of the other physiological needs of man – for rest, exercise, shelter, protection from the elements.

A satisfied need is not a motivator of behavior! This is a fact of profound significance. It is a fact which is unrecognized in Theory X and is, therefore, ignored in the conventional approach to the management of people. I shall return to it later. For the moment, an example will make the point. Consider your own need for air. Except as you are deprived of it, it has no appreciable motivating effect upon your behavior.

When the physiological needs are reasonably satisfied, needs at the next higher level begin to dominate man's behavior – to motivate him.

These are the safety needs, for protection against danger, threat, deprivation. Some people mistakenly refer to these as needs for security. However, unless man is in a dependent relationship where he fears arbitrary deprivation, he does not demand security. The need is for the 'fairest possible break'. When he is confident of this, he is more than willing to take risks. But when he feels threatened or dependent, his greatest need is for protection, for security.

The fact needs little emphasis that since every industrial employee is in at least a partially dependent relationship, safety needs may assume considerable importance. Arbitrary management actions, behavior which reflects favoritism or discrimination, unpredictable administration of policy – these can be powerful motivators of the safety needs in the employment relationship at every level from worker to vice-president. In addition, the safety needs of managers are often aroused by their dependence downward or laterally. This is a major reason for emphasis on management prerogatives and clear assignments of authority.

When man's physiological needs are satisfied and he is no longer fearful about his physical welfare, his social needs become important motivators of his behavior. These are such needs as those for belonging, for association, for acceptance by one's fellows, for giving and receiving friendship and love.

Management knows today of the existence of these needs, but it is often assumed quite wrongly that they represent a threat to the organization. Many studies have demonstrated that the tightly knit, cohesive work group may, under proper conditions, be far more effective than an equal number of separate individuals in achieving organizational goals. Yet management, fearing group hostility to its own objectives, often goes to considerable lengths to control and direct human efforts in ways that are inimical to the natural 'groupiness' of human beings. When man's social needs – and perhaps his safety needs, too – are thus thwarted, he behaves in ways which tend to defeat organizational objectives. He becomes resistant, antagonistic, uncooperative. But this behavior is a consequence, not a cause.

Above the social needs – in the sense that they do not usually become motivators until lower needs are reasonably satisfied – are the needs of greatest significance to management and to man himself. They are the egoistic needs, and they are of two kinds:

1. Those that relate to one's self-esteem: needs for self-respect and self-confidence, for autonomy, for achievement, for competence, for knowledge.

2. Those that relate to one's reputation: needs for status, for recognition, for appreciation, for the deserved respect of one's fellows.

Unlike the lower needs, these are rarely satisfied; man seeks indefinitely for more satisfaction of these needs once they have become important to him. However, they do not usually appear in any significant way until physiological, safety and social needs are reasonably satisfied. Exceptions to this generalization are to be observed, particularly under circumstances where, in addition to severe deprivation of physiological needs, human dignity is trampled upon. Political revolutions often grow out of thwarted social and ego, as well as physiological, needs.

The typical industrial organization offers only limited opportunities for the satisfaction of egoistic needs to people at lower levels in the hierarchy. The conventional methods of organizing work, particularly in mass production industries, give little heed to these aspects of human motivation. If the practices of 'scientific management' were deliberately calculated to thwart these needs – which, of course, they are not – they could hardly accomplish this purpose better than they do.

Finally – a capstone, as it were, on the hierarchy – there are the needs for self-fulfillment. These are the needs for realizing one's own potentialities, for continued self-development, for being creative in the broadest sense of that term.

The conditions of modern industrial life give only limited opportunity for these relatively dormant human needs to find expression. The deprivation most people experience with respect to other lower-level needs diverts their energies into the struggle to satisfy *those* needs, and the needs for self-fulfillment remain below the level of consciousness. Now, briefly, a few general comments about motivation.

We recognize readily enough that a man suffering from a severe dietary deficiency is sick. The deprivation of physiological needs has behavioral consequences. The same is true, although less well recognized, of the deprivation of higher-level needs. The man whose needs for safety, association, independence, or status are thwarted is sick, just as surely as is he who has rickets. And his sickness will have behavioral consequences. We will be mistaken if we attribute his resultant passivity, or his hostility, or his refusal to accept responsibility to his inherent 'human nature'. These forms of behavior are *symptoms* of illness – of deprivation of his social and egoistic needs.

The man whose lower-level needs are satisfied is not motivated to satisfy *those* needs. For practical purposes they exist no longer. (Remember my point about your need for air.) Management often asks,

'Why aren't people more productive? We pay good wages, provide good working conditions, have excellent fringe benefits and steady employment. Yet people do not seem to be willing to put forth more than minimum effort.' It is unnecessary to look far for the reasons.

Consideration of the rewards typically provided the worker for satisfying his needs through his employment leads to the interesting conclusion that most of these rewards can be used for satisfying his needs *only when he leaves the job*. Wages, for example, cannot be spent at work. The only contribution they can make to his satisfaction on the job is in terms of status differences resulting from wage differentials. (This, incidentally, is one of the reasons why small and apparently unimportant differences in wage rates can be the subject of so much heated dispute. The issue is not the pennies involved, but the fact that the status differences which they reflect are one of the few ways in which wages can result in need satisfaction in the job situation itself.)

Most fringe benefits – overtime pay, shift differentials, vacations, health and medical benefits, annuities and the proceeds from stock purchase plans or profit-sharing plans – yield needed satisfaction only when the individual leaves the job. Yet these, along with wages, are among the major rewards provided by management for effort. It is not surprising, therefore, that for many wage earners *work is perceived as a form of punishment* which is the price to be paid for various kinds of satisfaction away from the job. To the extent that this is their perception, we would hardly expect them to undergo more of this punishment than is necessary.

Under today's conditions management has provided relatively well for the satisfaction of physiological and safety needs. The standard of living in our country is high; people do not suffer major deprivation of their physiological needs except during periods of severe unemployment. Even then, the social legislation developed since the thirties cushions the shock.

But the fact that management has provided for these physiological and safety needs has shifted the motivational emphasis to the social and the egoistic needs. Unless there are opportunities *at work* to satisfy these higher-level needs, people will be deprived; and their behavior will reflect this deprivation. Under such conditions, if management continues to focus its attention on physiological needs, the mere provision of rewards is bound to be ineffective, and reliance on the threat of punishment will be inevitable. Thus one of the assumptions of Theory X will appear to be validated, but only because we have mistaken effects for causes.

People *will* make insistent demands for more money under these conditions. It becomes more important than ever to buy the material goods and services which can provide limited satisfaction of the thwarted needs. Although money has only limited value in satisfying many higher-level needs, it can become the focus of interest if it is the only means available.

The 'carrot and stick' theory of motivation which goes along with Theory X works reasonably well under certain circumstances. The *means* for satisfying man's physiological and (within limits) safety needs can be provided or withheld by management. Employment itself is such a means, and so are wages, working conditions, and benefits. By these means the individual can be controlled so long as he is struggling for subsistence. Man tends to live for bread alone when there is little bread.

But the 'carrot and stick' theory does not work at all once man has reached an adequate subsistence level and is motivated primarily by higher needs. Management cannot provide a man with self-respect, or with the respect of his fellows, or with the satisfaction of needs for self-fulfillment. We can create conditions such that he is encouraged and enabled to seek such satisfactions for himself, or we can thwart him by failing to create those conditions.

But this creation of conditions is not 'control' in the usual sense; it does not seem to be a particularly good device for directing behavior. And so management finds itself in an odd position. The high standard of living created by our modern technological know-how provides quite adequately for the satisfaction of physiological and safety needs. The only significant exception is where management practices have not created confidence in a 'fair break' – and thus where safety needs are thwarted. But by making possible the satisfaction of lower-level needs, management has deprived itself of the ability to use the control devices on which the conventional assumptions of Theory X has taught it to rely: rewards, promises, incentives or threats and other coercive devices.

The philosophy of management by direction and control – *regardless of whether it is hard or soft* – is inadequate to motivate because the human needs on which this approach relies are relatively unimportant motivators of behavior in our society today. Direction and control are of limited value in motivating people whose important needs are social and egoistic.

People, deprived of opportunities to satisfy at work the needs which are now important to them, behave exactly as we might predict – with indolence, passivity, unwillingness to accept responsibility, resistance to change, willingness to follow the demagogue, unreasonable demands for economic benefits. It would seem that we may be caught in a web of our own weaving.

Theory X explains the *consequences* of a particular managerial strategy; it neither explains nor describes human nature although it purports to. Because its assumptions are so unnecessarily limiting, it prevents our seeing the possibilities inherent in other managerial strategies. What sometimes appear to be new strategies – decentralization, management by objectives, consultative supervision, 'democratic' leadership – are usually but old wine in new bottles because the procedures developed to implement them are derived from the same inadequate assumptions about human nature. Management is constantly becoming disillusioned with widely touted and expertly merchandised 'new approaches' to the human side of enterprise. The real difficulty is that these new approaches are no more than different tactics – programs, procedures, gadgets – within an unchanged strategy based on Theory X.

In child rearing, it is recognized that parental strategies of control must be progressively modified to adapt to the changed capabilities and characteristics of the human individual as he develops from infancy to adulthood. To some extent industrial management recognizes that the human *adult* possesses capabilities for continued learning and growth. Witness the many current activities in the fields of training and management development. In its *basic* conceptions of managing human resources, however, management appears to have concluded that the average human being is permanently arrested in his development in early adolescence. Theory X is built on the least common human denominator: the factory 'hand' of the past. As Chris Argyris has shown dramatically in his *Personality and Organization*, conventional managerial strategies for the organization, direction, and control of the human resources of enterprise are admirably suited to the capacities and characteristics of the child rather than the adult.

In one limited area – that of research administration – there has been some recent recognition of the need for selective adaptation in managerial strategy. This, however, has been perceived as a unique problem, and its broader implications have not been recognized. As pointed out in this and the previous chapter, changes in the population at large – in educational level, attitudes and values, motivation, degree of dependence – have created both the opportunity and the need for other forms of selective adaptation. However, so long as the assumptions of Theory

X continue to influence managerial strategy, we will fail to discover, let alone utilize, the potentialities of the average human being.

Theory Y: the integration of individual and organizational goals

To some, the preceding analysis will appear harsh. Have we not made major modifications in the management of the human resources of industry during the past quarter century? Have we not recognized the importance of people and made vitally significant changes in managerial strategy as a consequence? Do the developments since the twenties in personnel administration and labor relations add up to nothing?

There is no question that important progress has been made in the past two or three decades. During this period the human side of enterprise has become a major preoccupation of management. A tremendous number of policies, programs and practices which were virtually unknown thirty years ago have become commonplace. The lot of the industrial employee – be he worker, professional, or executive – has improved to a degree which could hardly have been imagined by his counterpart of the nineteen twenties. Management has adopted generally a far more humanitarian set of values; it has successfully striven to give more equitable and more generous treatment to its employees. It has significantly reduced economic hardships, eliminated the more extreme forms of industrial warfare, provided a generally safe and pleasant working environment, *but it has done all these things without changing its fundamental theory of management*. There are exceptions here and there, and they are important; nevertheless, the assumptions of Theory X remain predominant throughout our economy.

Management was subjected to severe pressures during the Great Depression of the thirties. The wave of public antagonism, the open warfare accompanying the unionization of the mass production industries, the general reaction against authoritarianism, the legislation of the New Deal, produced a wide 'pendulum swing'. However, the changes in policy and practice which took place during that and the next decade were primarily adjustments to the increased power of organized labor and to the pressures of public opinion.

Some of the movement was away from 'hard' and toward 'soft' management but it was short-lived, and for good reasons. It has become clear that many of the initial strategic interpretations accompanying the 'human relations approach' were as naïve as those which characterized the early stages of progressive education. We have now discovered that there is no answer in the simple removal of control – that abdication is not a workable alternative to authoritarianism. We have learned that there is no direct correlation between employee satisfaction and productivity. We recognize that 'industrial democracy' cannot consist in permitting everyone to decide everything, that industrial health does not flow automatically from the elimination of dissatisfaction, disagreement, or even open conflict. Peace is not synonymous with organizational health; socially responsible management is not co-extensive with permissive management.

Now that management has regained its earlier prestige and power, it has become obvious that the trend towards 'soft' management was a temporary and relatively superficial reaction rather than a general modification of fundamental assumptions or basic strategy. Moreover, while the progress we have made in the past quarter century is substantial, it has reached the point of diminishing returns. The tactical possibilities within conventional managerial strategies have been pretty completely exploited, and significant new developments will be unlikely without major modifications in theory.

The assumptions of Theory Y

There have been few dramatic break-throughs in social science theory like those which have occurred in the physical sciences during the past half century. Nevertheless, the accumulation of knowledge about human behavior in many specialized fields has made possible the formulation of a number of generalizations which provide a modest beginning for new theory with respect to the management of human resources. Some of these assumptions, which will hereafter be referred to as Theory Y, are as follows:

1. *The expenditure of physical and mental effort in work is as natural as play or rest.* The average human being does not inherently dislike work. Depending upon controllable conditions, work may be a source of satisfaction (and will be voluntarily performed) or a source of punishment (and will be avoided if possible).

2. *External control and the threat of punishment are not the only means for bringing about effort toward organizational objectives. Man will exercise self-direction and self-control in the service of objectives to which he is committed.*

3. *Commitment to objectives is a function of the rewards associated with their achievement.* The most significant of such rewards, e.g. the satisfac-

tion of ego and self-actualization needs, can be direct products of effort directed toward organizational objectives.

4. *The average human being learns, under proper conditions, not only to accept but to seek responsibility.* Avoidance of responsibility, lack of ambition and emphasis on security are generally consequences of experience, not inherent human characteristics.

5. *The capacity to exercise a relatively high degree of imagination, ingenuity and creativity in the solution of organizational problems is widely, not narrowly, distributed in the population.*

6. *Under the conditions of modern industrial life, the intellectual potentialities of the average human being are only partially utilized.*

These assumptions involve sharply different implications for managerial strategy than do those of Theory X. They are dynamic rather than static: they indicate the possibility of human growth, and development; they stress the necessity for selective adaptation rather than for a single absolute form of control. They are not framed in terms of the least common denominator of the factory hand, but in terms of a resource which has substantial potentialities.

Above all, the assumptions of Theory Y point up the fact that the limits on human collaboration in the organizational setting are not limits of human nature but of management's ingenuity in discovering how to realize the potential represented by its human resources. Theory X offers management an easy rationalization for ineffective organizational performance: it is due to the nature of the human resources with which we must work. Theory Y, on the other hand, places the problems squarely in the lap of management. If employees are lazy, indifferent, unwilling to take responsibility, intransigent, uncreative, uncooperative, Theory Y implies that the causes lie in management's methods of organization and control.

The assumptions of Theory Y are not finally validated. Nevertheless, they are far more consistent with existing knowledge in the social sciences than are the assumptions of Theory X. They will undoubtedly be refined, elaborated, modified as further research accumulates, but they are unlikely to be completely contradicted.

On the surface, these assumptions may not seem particularly difficult to accept. Carrying their implications into practice, however, is not easy. They challenge a number of deeply ingrained managerial habits of thought and action.

The principle of integration

The central principle of organization which derives from Theory X is that of direction and control through the exercise of authority – what has been called 'the scalar principle'. The central principle which derives from Theory Y is that of integration: the creation of conditions such that the members of the organization can achieve their own goals *best* by directing their efforts toward the success of the enterprise. These two principles have profoundly different implications with respect to the task of managing human resources, but the scalar principle is so firmly built into managerial attitudes that the implications of the principle of integration are not easy to perceive.

Someone once said that fish discover water last. The 'psychological environment' of industrial management – like water for fish – is so much a part of organizational life that we are unaware of it. Certain characteristics of our society, and of organizational life within it, are so completely established, so pervasive, that we cannot conceive of their being otherwise. As a result, a great many policies and practices and decisions and relationships could only be – it seems – what they are.

Among these pervasive characteristics of organizational life in the United States today is a managerial attitude (stemming from Theory X) toward membership in the industrial organization. It is assumed almost without question that organizational requirements take precedence over the needs of individual members. Basically, the employment agreement is that in return for the rewards which are offered, the individual will accept external direction and control. The very idea of integration and self-control is foreign to our way of thinking about the employment relationship. The tendency, therefore, is either to reject it out of hand (as socialistic, or anarchistic, or inconsistent with human nature) or to twist it unconsciously until it fits existing conceptions.

The concept of integration and self-control carries the implication that the organization will be more effective in achieving its economic objectives if adjustments are made, in significant ways, to the needs and goals of its members.

A district manager in a large, geographically decentralized company is notified that he is being promoted to a policy-level position at headquarters. It is a big promotion with a large salary increase. His role in the organization will be a much more powerful one, and he will be associated with the major executives of the firm.

The headquarters group who selected him for this position have carefully considered a number of possible candidates. This man stands out among them in a way which makes him the natural choice. His performance has been under observation for some time, and there is little question that he possesses the necessary qualifications, not only for this opening but for an even higher position. There is genuine satisfaction that such an outstanding candidate is available.

The man is appalled. He doesn't want the job. His goal, as he expresses it, is to be the 'best damned district manager in the company'. He enjoys his direct associations with operating people in the field, and he doesn't want a policy-l vel job. He and his wife enjoy the kind of life they have created in a small city, and they dislike actively both the living conditions and the social obligations of the headquarters city.

He expresses his feelings as strongly as he can, but his objections are brushed aside. The organization's needs are such that his refusal to accept the promotion would be unthinkable. His superiors say to themselves that of course when he has settled into the new job, he will recognize that it was the right thing. And so he makes the move.

Two years later he is in an even higher position in the company's headquarters organization, and there is talk that he will probably be the executive vice-president before long. Privately he expresses considerable unhappiness and dissatisfaction. He (and his wife) would 'give anything' to be back in the situation he left two years ago.

Within the context of the pervasive assumptions of Theory X, promotions and transfers in large numbers are made by unilateral decision. The requirements of the organization are given priority automatically and almost without question. If the individual's personal goals are considered at all, it is assumed that the rewards of salary and position will satisfy him. Should an individual actually refuse such a move without reason, such as health or a severe family crisis, he would be considered to have jeopardized his future because of this 'selfish' attitude. It is rare indeed for management to give the individual the opportunity to be a genuine and active partner in such a decision, even though it may affect his most important personal goals. Yet the implications following from Theory Y are that the organization is likely to suffer if it ignores these personal needs and goals. In making unilateral decisions with respect to promotion, management is failing to utilize its human resources in the most effective way.

The principle of integration demands that both the organization's and the individual's needs be recognized. Of course, when there is a sincere joint effort to find it, an integrative solution which meets the needs of the individual *and* the organization is a frequent outcome. But not always – and this is the point at which Theory Y begins to appear unrealistic. It collides head on with pervasive attitudes associated with management by direction and control.

The assumptions of Theory Y imply that unless integration is achieved *the organization will suffer*. The objectives of the organization are *not* achieved best by the unilateral administration of promotions, because this form of management by direction and control will not create the commitment which would make available the full resources of those affected. The lesser motivation, the lesser resulting degree of self-direction and self-control are costs which, when added up for many instances over time, will more than offset the gains obtained by unilateral decisions 'for the good of the organization'.

One other example will perhaps clarify further the sharply different implications of Theory X and Theory Y.

It could be argued that management is already giving a great deal of attention to the principle of integration through its efforts in the field of economic education. Many millions of dollars and much ingenuity have been expended in attempts to persuade employees that their welfare is intimately connected with the success of the free enterprise system and of their own companies. The idea that they can achieve their own goals best by directing their effort toward the objectives of the organization has been explored and developed and communicated in every possible way. Is this not evidence that management is already committed to the principle of integration?

The answer is a definite no. These managerial efforts, with rare exceptions, reflect clearly the influence of the assumptions of Theory X. The central message is an exhortation to the industrial employee to work hard and follow orders in order to protect his job and his standard of living. Much has been achieved, it says, by our established way of running industry, and much more could be achieved if employees would adapt themselves *to management's definition* of what is required. Behind these exhortations lies the expectation that of course the requirements of the organization and its economic success must have priority over the needs of the individual.

Naturally, integration means working together for the success of the enterprise so we all may share in the resulting rewards. But management's implicit assumption is that working together means adjusting to the requirements of the organization *as management perceives them*. In terms of existing views, it seems inconceivable that individuals, seeking their own goals, would further the ends of the enterprise. On the contrary, this would lead to anarchy, chaos, irreconcilable conflicts of self-interest, lack of responsibility, inability to make decisions and failure to carry out those that were made.

All these consequences, and other worse ones, *would* be inevitable unless conditions could be created such that the members of the organization perceived that they could achieve their own goals *best* by directing their efforts toward the success of the enterprise. If the assumptions of Theory Y are valid, the practical question is whether, and to what extent, such conditions can be created. To that question the balance of this volume is addressed.

The application of Theory Y

In the physical sciences there are many theoretical phenomena which cannot be achieved in practice. Absolute zero and a perfect vacuum are examples. Others, such as nuclear power, jet aircraft and human space flight, are recognized theoretically to be possible long before they become feasible. This fact does not make theory less useful. If it were not for our theoretical convictions, we would not even be attempting to develop the means for human flight into space today. In fact, were it not for the development of physical science theory during the past century and a half, we would still be depending upon the horse and buggy and the sailing vessel for transportation. Virtually all significant technological developments wait on the formulation of relevant theory.

Similarly, in the management of the human resources of industry, the assumptions and theories about human nature at any given time limit innovation. Possibilities are not recognized, innovating efforts are not undertaken, until theoretical conceptions lay a groundwork for them. Assumptions like those of Theory X permit us to conceive of certain possible ways of organizing and directing human effort, *but not others*. Assumptions like those of Theory Y open up a range of possibilities for new managerial policies and practices. As in the case of the development of new physical science theory, some of these possibilities are not immediately feasible, and others may forever remain unattainable. They may be too costly, or it may be that we simply cannot discover how to create the necessary 'hardware'.

There is substantial evidence for the statement that the potentialities of the average human being are far above those which we typically realize in industry today. If our assumptions are like those of Theory X, we will not even recognize the existence of these potentialities and there will be no reason to devote time, effort, or money to discovering how to realize them. If, however, we accept assumptions like those of Theory Y, we will be challenged to innovate, to discover new ways of organizing and directing human effort, even though we recognize that the perfect organization, like the perfect vacuum, is practically out of reach.

We need not be overwhelmed by the dimensions of the managerial task implied by Theory Y. To be sure, a large mass-production operation in which the workers have been organized by a militant and hostile union faces management with problems which appear at present to be insurmountable with respect to the application of the principle of integration. It may be decades before sufficient knowledge will have accumulated to make such an application feasible. Applications of Theory Y will have to be tested initially in more limited ways and under more favorable circumstances. However, a number of applications of Theory Y *in managing managers and professional people* are possible today. Within the managerial hierarchy, the assumptions can be tested and refined, techniques can be invented and skill acquired in their use. As knowledge accumulates, some of the problems of application at the worker level in large organizations may appear less baffling than they do at present.

Perfect integration of organizational requirements and individual goals and needs is, of course, not a realistic objective. In adopting this principle, we seek that degree of integration in which the individual can achieve his goals *best* by directing his efforts toward the success of the organization. 'Best' means that this alternative will be more attractive than the many others available to him: indifference, irresponsibility, minimal compliance, hostility, sabotage. It means that he will continuously be encouraged to develop and utilize voluntarily his capacities, his knowledge, his skill, his ingenuity in ways which contribute to the success of the enterprise.[1]

Acceptance of Theory Y does not imply abdication, or 'soft' management, or 'permissiveness'. As was indicated above, such notions stem from the acceptance of authority as the *single* means of managerial control, and from attempts to minimize its negative consequences. Theory Y assumes that people will exercise self-direction and self-control in the achievement of organizational objectives *to the degree that they are committed to those objectives*. If that commitment is small, only a slight degree of self-direction and self-control will be likely, and a

1. A recent, highly significant study of the sources of job satisfaction and dissatisfaction among managerial and professional people suggests that these opportunities for 'self-actualization' are the essential requirements of both job satisfaction and high performance. The researchers find that 'the wants of employees divide into two groups. One group revolves around the need to develop in one's occupation as a source of personal growth. The second group operates as an essential base to the first and is associated with fair treatment in compensation, supervision, working conditions, and administrative practices. *The fulfillment of the needs of the second group does not motivate the individual to high levels of job satisfaction and . . . to extra performance on the job.* All we can expect from satisfying [this second group of needs] is the prevention of dissatisfaction and poor job performance.' Herzberg, Mausner and Snyderman (1959), pp. 114–15. (Italics mine.)

substantial amount of external influence will be necessary. If it is large, many conventional external controls will be relatively superfluous, and to some extent self-defeating. Managerial policies and practices materially affect this degree of commitment.

Authority is an inappropriate means for obtaining commitment to objectives. Other forms of influence – help in achieving integration, for example – are required for this purpose. Theory Y points to the possibility of lessening the emphasis on external forms of control to the degree that commitment to organizational objectives can be achieved. Its underlying assumptions emphasize the capacity of human beings for self-control, and the consequent possibility of greater managerial reliance on other means of influence. Nevertheless, it is clear that authority *is* an appropriate means for control under certain circumstances – particularly where genuine commitment to objectives cannot be achieved. The assumptions of Theory Y do not deny the appropriateness of authority, but they do deny that it is appropriate for all purposes and under all circumstances.

Many statements have been made to the effect that we have acquired today the know-how to cope with virtually any technological problems which may arise, and that the major industrial advances of the next half century will occur on the human side of enterprise. Such advances, however, are improbable so long as management continues to organize and direct and control its human resources on the basis of assumptions – tacit or explicit – like those of Theory X. Genuine innovation, in contrast to a refurbishing and patching of present managerial strategies, requires first the acceptance of less limiting assumptions about the nature of the human resources we seek to control, and second the readiness to adapt selectivity to the implications contained in those new assumptions. Theory Y is an invitation to innovation.

Reference

HERZBERG, F., MAUSNER, B., and SNYDERMAN, B. B. (1959), *The Motivation to Work*, Wiley.

20 F. Herzberg

The Motivation–Hygiene Theory

From F. Herzberg. 'The motivation–hygiene theory', *Work and the Nature of Man*, World Publishing Co., 1966, chapter 6, pp. 71–91.

With the duality of man's nature in mind, it is well to return to the significance of these essays to industry by reviewing the motivation–hygiene concept of job attitudes as it was reported in Herzberg, Mausner and Snyderman (1959). This study was designed to test the concept that man has two sets of needs: his need as an animal to avoid pain and his need as a human to grow psychologically.

For those who have not read *The Motivation to Work* (Herzberg, Mausner and Snyderman, 1959), I will summarize the highlights of that study. Two hundred engineers and accountants, who represented a cross-section of Pittsburgh industry, were interviewed. They were asked about events they had experienced at work which either had resulted in a marked improvement in their job satisfaction or had led to a marked reduction in job satisfaction.

The interviewers began by asking the engineers and accountants to recall a time when they had felt exceptionally good about their jobs. Keeping in mind the time that had brought about the good feelings, the interviewers proceeded to probe for the reasons why the engineers and accountants felt as they did. The workers were asked also if the feelings of satisfaction in regard to their work had affected their performance, their personal relationships and their well-being.

Finally, the nature of the sequence of events that served to return the workers' attitudes to 'normal' was elicited. Following the narration of a sequence of events, the interview was repeated, but this time the subjects were asked to describe a sequence of events that resulted in negative feelings about their jobs. As many sequences as the respondents were able to give were recorded within the criteria of an acceptable sequence. These were the criteria.

First, the sequence must revolve around an event or series of events; that is, there must be some objective happening. The report cannot be concerned entirely with the respondent's psychological reactions or feelings.

Second, the sequence of events must be bound by time; it should have a beginning that can be identified, a middle and, unless the events are still in process, some sort of identifiable ending (although the cessation of events does not have to be dramatic or abrupt).

Third, the sequence of events must have taken place during a period in which feelings about the job were either exceptionally good or exceptionally bad.

Fourth, the story must be centered on a period in the respondent's life when he held a position that fell within the limits of our sample. However, there were a few exceptions. Stories involving aspirations to professional work or transitions from subprofessional to professional levels were included.

Fifth, the story must be about a situation in which the respondent's feelings about his job were directly affected, not about a sequence of events unrelated to the job that caused high or low spirits.

Figure 1, reproduced from *The Motivation to Work*, shows the major findings of this study. The factors listed are a kind of shorthand for summarizing the 'objective' events that each respondent described. The length of each box represents the frequency with which the factor appeared in the events presented. The width of the box indicates the period in which the good or bad job attitude lasted, in terms of a classification of short duration and long duration. A short duration of attitude change did not last longer than two weeks, while a long duration of attitude change may have lasted for years.

Five factors stand out as strong determiners of job satisfaction – *achievement*, *recognition*, *work itself*, *responsibility* and *advancement* – the last three being of greater importance for lasting change of attitudes. These five factors appeared very infrequently when the respondents described events that paralleled job dissatisfaction feelings. A further word on *recognition*: when it appeared in a 'high' sequence of events, it referred to recognition for achievement rather than to recognition as a human-relations tool divorced from any accomplishment. The latter type of recognition does not serve as a 'satisfier'.

When the factors involved in the job dissatisfaction events were coded, an entirely different set of factors evolved. These factors were similar to the satisfiers in their unidimensional effect. This time, however, they served only to bring about job dissatisfaction and were rarely involved in events that led to positive job attitudes. Also, unlike the 'satisfiers', the 'dissatisfiers' consistently produced short-term changes in job attitudes. The major dissatisfiers were *company policy and administration*, *supervision*, *salary*, *interpersonal relations* and *working conditions*.

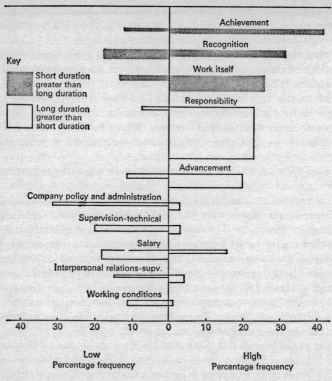

Figure 1 Comparison of satisfiers and dissatisfiers (reproduced from Herzberg, Mausner and Snyderman, *The Motivation to Work*, Wiley, 1959, by permission of the publishers)

What is the explanation of such results? Do the two sets of factors have two separate themes? It appears so, for the factors on the right of Figure 1 all seem to describe man's relationship to what he does: his job content, achievement on a task, recognition for task achievement, the nature of the task, responsibility for a task and professional advancement or growth in task capability.

What is the central theme for the dissatisfiers? Restating the factors as the kind of administration and supervision received in doing the job, the nature of interpersonal relationships and working conditions that surround the job and the effect of salary suggest the distinction from the 'satisfier' factors. Rather than describe man's relationship to what he does, the 'dissatisfier' factors describe his relationship to the context or environment in which he does his job. One cluster of factors relates to what the person does and the other to the situation in which he does it.

Since the dissatisfier factors essentially describe the environment and serve primarily to prevent job dissatisfaction, while having little effect on positive job attitudes, they have been named the *hygiene* factors. This is an analogy to the medical use of the term meaning 'preventative and environmental'. Another term for these factors in current use is *maintenance* factors. I am indebted to Dr Robert Ford of the American Telephone and Telegraph Company for this excellent synonym. The 'satisfier' factors were named the *motivators*, since other findings of the study suggest that they are effective in motivating the individual to superior performance and effort.

So far, I have described that part of the interview that was restricted to determining the actual objective events as reported by the respondents (first level of analysis). They were also asked to interpret the events, to tell why the particular event led to a change in their feelings about their jobs (second level of analysis). The principal result of the analysis of this data was to suggest that the hygiene or maintenance events led to job dissatisfaction because of a need to *avoid* unpleasantness; the motivator events led to job satisfaction because of a need for growth or self-actualization. At the psychological level, the two dimensions of job attitudes reflected a two-dimensional need structure: one need system for the avoidance of unpleasantness and a parallel need system for personal growth.

The discussion so far has paved the way for the explanation of the duality of job-attitude results. Why do the hygiene factors serve as dissatisfiers? They represent the environment to which man the animal is constantly trying to adjust, for the environment is the source of Adam's suffering. The hygiene factors listed are the major environmental aspects of work.

Why do the motivators affect motivation in the positive direction? An analogy drawn from a familiar example of psychological growth in children may be useful. When a child learns to ride a bicycle, he is becoming more competent, increasing the repertory of his behavior, expanding his skills – psychologically growing. In the process of the child's learning to master a bicycle, the parents can love him with all the zeal and compassion of the most devoted mother and father. They can safeguard the child from injury by providing the safest and most hygienic area in which to practice; they can offer all kinds of incentives and rewards, and they can provide the most expert instructions. But the child will never, never learn to ride the bicycle – unless he is given a bicycle! The hygiene factors are not a valid contributor to psychological growth. The substance of a task is required to achieve growth goals. Similarly, you cannot love an engineer into creativity, although by this approach you can avoid his dissatisfactions with the way you treat him. Creativity will require a potentially creative task to do.

In summary, two essential findings were derived from this study. First, the factors involved in producing job satisfaction were *separate* and *distinct* from the factors that led to job dissatisfaction. Since separate factors needed to be considered, depending on whether job satisfaction or job dissatisfaction was involved, it followed that these two feelings were not the obverse of each other. Thus, the opposite of job satisfaction would not be job dissatisfaction, but rather *no* job satisfaction; similarly, the opposite of job dissatisfaction is *no* job dissatisfaction, not satisfaction with one's job. The fact that job satisfaction is made up of two unipolar traits is not unique, but it remains a difficult concept to grasp.

Perhaps another analogy will help explain this new way of thinking about job attitudes. Let us characterize job satisfaction as vision and job dissatisfaction as hearing. It is readily seen that we are talking about two separate dimensions, since the stimulus for vision is light, and increasing and decreasing light will have no effect on man's hearing. The stimulus for audition is sound, and, in a similar fashion, increasing or decreasing loudness will have no effect on vision.

Man's basic needs can be diagrammed as two parallel arrows pointing in opposite directions. One arrow depicts his Animal–Adam nature, which is concerned with avoidance of pain stemming from the environment, and for man the psychological environment is the major source of this pain. The other arrow represents man's Human–Abraham nature, which is concerned with approaching self-fulfillment or psychological growth through the accomplishment of tasks.

Animal-Adam: avoidance of pain from environment

←─────────────────────────────────────

Human-Abraham: seeking growth from tasks

─────────────────────────────────────→

The problem of establishing a zero point in psychology, with the procedural necessity of using instead a bench mark (e.g. the mean of a population) from which to start our measurement, has led to the conception that psychological traits are bipolar. Recent empirical investigations, however, have cast some shadows on the assumptions of bipolarity for many psychological attributes, in addition to job attitudes, as shown in *The Motivation to Work*.

Thus, the hypothesis with which the study of motivation began appears to be verified. The factors on the right of Figure 1 that led to satisfaction (*achievement*, *recognition*, *work itself*, *responsibility* and *advancement*) are mainly unipolar; that is, they contribute very little to job dissatisfaction. Conversely, the dissatisfiers (*company policy and administration*, *supervision*, *interpersonal relations*, *working conditions* and *salary*) contribute very little to job satisfaction.

Sixteen separate job–attitude factors were investigated in the original study dealing with accountants and engineers. Only those motivators and hygiene factors that were found to differentiate statistically between positive and negative job attitudes were presented. However, the other factors have similarly been shown to fall into one category or the other in the follow-up studies to be described in subsequent chapters. These factors are *possibility of growth*, a task-centered motivator, and the hygiene factors, *salary*, *status*, *job security* and *effect on personal life*.

If we are to be able to define a human being, the following sections represent an attempt to organize man's needs in order to reach such a definition. Since man is capable of such a variety of behavior and still can survive, it is little wonder that so many ways of acting can be declared normal, dependent on their cultural acceptance. In this sense, a prominent difference between cultures lies in the kinds of pathology that are declared normal. At this point, the theory of job motivation will be expanded to a general concept of mental health, and this in turn will allow for a culture-free definition of mental illness.

Just as there are two sets of needs at work – hygiene needs and motivator needs – and two continua to represent them, so we may speak of two continua in mental health: a mental-illness continuum and a mental-health continuum. We have seen that a conceptual shift in viewpoint regarding job attitudes has been made in order to incorporate the two-dimensional motivation–hygiene theory. Essentially the same shift might well lead to an equally important change in theory and research on mental health.

The argument for this generalization has been presented in two papers by Dr Roy Hamlin of the Veterans Administration and myself. The implications for mental health are best introduced by recalling the subjective reactions of the employees as to why the various factors affected them as they did. For the job-dissatisfied situation the subjects reported that they were made unhappy mostly because they felt they were being treated unfairly or that they found the situation unpleasant or painful. On the other hand, the common denominator for the reasons for positive job attitudes seemed to be variations on the theme of feelings of psychological growth, the fulfillment of self-actualizing needs. There was an approach-avoidance dichotomy with respect to job adjustment. A need to avoid unpleasant job environments led to job dissatisfaction; the need for self-realization led to job satisfaction when the opportunity for self-realization was afforded.

A 'hygienic' environment prevents discontent with a job, but such an environment cannot lead the individual beyond a minimal adjustment consisting of the absence of dissatisfaction. A positive 'happiness' seems to require some attainment of psychological growth.

It is clear why the hygiene factors fail to provide for positive satisfactions: they do not possess the characteristics necessary for giving an individual a sense of growth. To feel that one has grown depends on achievement in tasks that have meaning to the individual, and since the hygiene factors do not relate to the task, they are powerless to give such meaning to the individual. Growth is dependent on some achievements, but achievement requires a task. The motivators are task factors and thus are necessary for growth; they provide the psychological stimulation by which the individual can be activated toward his self-realization needs.

To generalize from job attitudes to mental attitudes, we can think of two types of adjustment for mental equilibrium. First, an adjustment to the environment, which is mainly an avoidance adjustment; second, an adjustment to oneself, which is dependent on the successful striving for psychological growth, self-actualization, self-realization or, most simply, being psychologically more than one has been in the past.

Traditionally, mental health has been regarded as the obverse of mental illness. Mental health, in this sense, is the mere *absence* of mental illness. At one time, the psychiatrist anticipated that mental health would be automatically *released* when the conflicts of mental illness were resolved. And, currently, the biochemist hopes that mental health will bloom once neuroenzymes are properly balanced and optimally distributed in the brain.

In essence, this traditional view ignores *mental health*. In general, the focus has been on mental illness – on anxiety, anxiety-reducing mechanisms, past frustrations, childhood trauma, distressing interpersonal relations, disturbing ideas and worries, current patterns of inefficiency and stressful present environment. Except for sporadic lip service, positive attitudes and experiences have been considered chiefly in an atmosphere of alleviating distress and dependency.

The factors that determine mental illness are *not the obverse* of the mental health factors. Rather, the mental illness factors belong to the category of hygiene factors, which describe the environment of man and serve to cause illness when they are deficient but effect little positive increase in mental health. They are factors that cause avoidance behavior; yet, as will be explained, only in the 'sick' individual is there an attempt to activate approach behavior. The implications of the conceptual shift for job satisfaction have been discussed. Traditional research on job attitudes has focused almost exclusively on only one set of factors, on the hygiene or job-context factors. The motivating factors, the positive or self-actualizing factors, have been largely neglected. The thesis holds that a very similar neglect has characterized traditional research on mental health.

Specifically, the resolution of conflicts, the correction of biochemical imbalance and the modification of psychic defenses might all be assigned to the attempts to modify the hygiene or avoidance needs of the individual. The positive motivating factors – self-actualization and personal growth – have received treatment of two sorts. Either they have been neglected or dismissed as irrelevant, or they have been regarded as so individually sacred and vague as to defy research analysis. At best, the mental health factors have been looked upon as important *forces* that might be released by the removal of mental illness factors.

The motivation–hygiene concept stresses three points regarding mental adjustment. The first is the proposition that mental illness and mental health are not of the same dimension. Contrary to classical psychiatric belief, there are degrees of sickness and there are degrees of health. The degree of sickness reflects an individual's reaction to the hygiene factors, while the degree of mental health represents his reaction to the motivator factors.

Second, the motivator–mental-health aspect of personal adjustment has been sadly neglected in theory, in research and in application. The positive side of personal adjustment has been considered to be a dividend or consequence of successful attention to the 'negative maladjustment' side.

The third point is a new definition or idea of mental illness. The new definition derives from the first proposition that mental illness is not the opposite of mental health, as is suggested by some of the data on job satisfaction.

While the incidents in which job satisfaction were reported almost always contained the factors that related to the job task – the motivators – there were some individuals who reported receiving job satisfaction solely from hygiene factors, that is, from some aspect of the job environment. Commenting on this reversal, the authors of *The Motivation to Work* suggest that 'there may be individuals who because of their training and because of the things that have happened to them have learned to react positively to the factors associated with the *context* of their jobs'. The hygiene seekers are primarily attracted to things that usually serve only to prevent dissatisfaction, not to be a source of positive feelings. The hygiene seekers have not reached a stage of personality development at which self-actualizing needs are active. From this point of view, they are fixated at a less mature level of personal adjustment.

Implied in *The Motivation to Work* is the admonition to industry that the lack of 'motivators' in jobs will increase the sensitivity of employees to real or imagined bad job hygiene, and consequently the amount and quality of hygiene given to employees must be constantly improved. There is also the reported finding that the relief from job dissatisfaction by hygiene factors has only a temporary effect and therefore adds to the necessity for more frequent attention to the job environment. The graphs shown in Figure 1 indicate that the hygiene factors stem from short-range events, as contrasted with the longer range of motivator events. Animal or hygiene drives, being cyclical, are only temporarily satisfied. The cyclical nature of these drives is necessary in order to sustain life. The hygiene factors on the job partake of the quality of briefly acting analgesics for meaningless work; the individual becomes unhappy without them, but is relieved only temporarily with them, for their effects soon wear off and the hygiene seeker is left chronically dissatisfied.

A hygiene seeker is not merely a victim of circumstances, but is *motivated* in the direction of temporary satisfaction. It is not that his job offers little opportunity for self-actualization; rather, it is that his needs lie predominantly in another direction, that of satisfying avoidance needs. He is seeking positive happiness via the route of avoidance behavior, and thus his resultant chronic dissatisfaction is an illness of motivation. Chronic unhappiness, a motivation pattern that ensures continual dissatisfaction, a failure to grow or to want to grow – these characteristics add up to a neurotic personality.

So it appears that the neurotic is an individual with a lifetime pattern of hygiene seeking and that the definition of a neurotic, in terms of defenses against anxiety arising from early psychological conflicts, represents at best the *origin* of his hygiene seeking. The motivation–hygiene view of a neurotic adjustment is free of substantial ties with any theory of etiology, and therefore the thesis is independent of conceptualizations regarding the traditional dynamics of personality development and adjustment. The neurotic motivation pattern of hygiene-seeking is mostly a learned process that arises from the value systems endemic in society.

Since total adaptation depends on the gratification of two separate types of needs, a rough operational categorization of adjustment can be made by examining the sources of a person's satisfactions.

A first category is characterized by positive mental health. Persons in this category show a preponderance of lifetime contentment stemming from situations in which the motivator factors are paramount. These factors are necessary in providing them with a sense of personal growth. They can be identified as directly involving the individual in some task, project or activity in which achievement or the consequences of achievement are possible. Those factors found meaningful for industrial job satisfaction may not be complete or may not be sufficiently descriptive to encompass the total life picture of an individual.

Other factors may be necessary to describe the motivators in this larger sense. Whatever they may be, the criteria for their selection must include activity on the part of the individual – some task, episode, adventure or activity in which the individual achieves a growth experience and without which the individual *will not* feel unhappy, dissatisfied or uncomfortable. In addition, to belong to this positive category the individual must have frequent opportunity for the gratification of these motivator needs. How frequent and how challenging the growth opportunities must be will depend on the level of ability (both genetic and learned) of the individual and, secondly, on his tolerance for delayed success. This tolerance, too, may be constitutional, learned or governed by dynamic conflicts; the source does not really matter to the argument.

The motivation–hygiene concept may seem to involve certain paradoxes. For example, is all achievement work and no play? Is the individual of limited ability doomed to be a nonachiever, and therefore a hygiene seeker?

In regard to work and play, achievements include all personal growth experience. While it is true that *The Motivation to Work* focuses on industrial production, as demanded by society or company policy, the satisfying sequences reported are rich in examples of creativity and individual initiative. Artistic and scholarly interests, receptive openness to new insights, true relaxation and regrouping of growth potentials (as contrasted with plain laziness) are all achievement or elements in achievement. Nowhere is the balanced work–play growth element in achievement more apparent than in the mentally healthy individual.

In regard to limitations resulting from meager ability, the motivating history of achievement depends to an important degree on a realistic attitude. The individual who concerns himself largely with vague aspirations, completely unrelated to his abilities and to the actual situation, is simply one kind of hygiene seeker. He does not seek satisfaction in the job itself, but rather in those surrounding conditions that include such cultural noises as 'any American boy can be president' or 'every young man should have a college degree'. The quotation by Carl Jung bears repetition: 'The supreme goal of man is to fulfil himself as a creative, *unique* individual according to his own *innate potentialities* and within the *limits of reality*.' (Italics supplied.)

A final condition for membership in this mentally healthy group would be a good life environment or the successful avoidance of poor hygiene factors. Again, those conditions mentioned previously for the work situation may not suffice for all the environments of the individual.

Three conditions, then, will serve to define a mentally healthy individual: seeking life satisfaction through personal growth experiences (experiences defined as containing the motivator factors); sufficient success, commensurate with ability and tolerance for delay, to give direct evidence of growth, and, finally, successful avoidance of discomfort from poor hygiene.

If the hygiene is poor, the mental health is not affected, but obviously the individual becomes unhappy. This second category of adjustment – self-fulfillment, accompanied by dissatisfaction with the rewards of life – perhaps characterizes that large segment of the population that continues to do a good job despite reason for complaint. There is research evidence to support the idea that a motivator seeker who is effective in his performance will be listed among the gripers in a company. This is not surprising, for he feels justified in his criticisms because he earns his right to complain and is perhaps bright enough to see reasons for his ill temper.

A third category consists of individuals characterized by symptom-free adjustment. Individuals grouped in this category would also have sought and obtained their satisfactions primarily from the motivator factors. However, their growth needs will be much less reinforced during their life because of lack of opportunity. Such individuals will not have achieved a complete sense of accomplishment because of circumstances extrinsic to their motivation. Routine jobs and routine life-experiences attenuate the growth of these individuals, not their motivation. Because their motivation is healthy, we do not place these persons on the sick continuum. In addition, those in this category must have sufficient satisfactions of their hygiene needs.

It is not unusual, though it is infrequent, to find that a respondent in the job-attitude investigations will stress one or more of the motivator factors as contributing to his job dissatisfaction. In other words, a satisfier acts as a dissatisfier. This occurrence most frequently includes the factors of failure of advancement, lack of recognition, lack of responsibility and uninteresting work. Closer inspection of these incidents reveals that many are insincere protestations covering a more latent hygiene desire. For example, the respondent who declares that his unhappiest time on the job occurred when his boss did not recognize his work is often saying that he misses the comfort and security of an accepting supervisor. His hygiene needs are simply wrapped in motivator clothing.

However, there are some highly growth-oriented persons who so desire the motivators and seek so very much a positive aspect for their lives that deprivation in this area may be interpreted by them as pain. In this case, their inversion of a motivator for a dissatisfaction episode is legitimate, but it represents a misinterpretation of their feelings. Their lack of happiness is felt as unhappiness, although it is qualitatively quite different from the unhappiness they experience because of the lack of the 'hygiene' factors. Often these people summarize their job-attitude feelings by saying, 'I really can't complain, but I sure don't like what I am doing' or 'As a job goes, this isn't bad, but I'm not getting anywhere.'

The fourth category of essentially health-oriented people includes those who, paradoxically, are miserable. These are the motivator seekers who are denied any psychological growth opportunities and, in addition, find themselves with their hygiene needs simultaneously deprived. However miserable they might be, they are differentiated from the next three categories by their reluctance to adopt neurotic or psychotic defense mechanisms to allay their dual pain.

The next category represents a qualitative jump from the mental health dimension to the mental illness dimension. This category may be called the *maladjusted*. The basic characteristic of persons in this group is that they have sought positive satisfaction from the hygiene factors. There is an inversion of motivation away from the approach behavior of growth to the avoidance behavior of comfortable environments. Members of this group are the hygiene seekers, whose maladjustment is defined by the direction of their motivation and is evidenced by the environmental source of their satisfactions.

Many in this category will have had a significant number of personal achievements that result in no growth experience. It has been noted that hygiene satisfactions are short-lived and partake of the characteristics of opiates. The environmental satisfactions for persons whom we call maladjusted must be rather frequent and of substantial quality. It is the satisfactions of their hygiene needs that differentiate the maladjusted from the next category in our system – the mentally ill.

The mentally ill are lifetime hygiene seekers with poor hygiene satisfactions (as perceived by the individual). This poor hygiene may be realistic or it may reflect mostly the accentuated sensitivity to hygiene deprivation because of the inversion of motivation.

One of the extremes to which the 'hygiene or maintenance' seeker resorts is to deny his hygiene needs altogether. This is termed the 'monastic' defense. Seemingly, this line of reasoning asserts that the denial of man's animal nature will reward the individual with happiness, because the proponents of the 'monastic' view of man's nature have discovered that no amount of hygiene rewards lead to human happiness. This sometime revered approach to the human dilemma now emerges as the blatant non sequitur that it is. How can psychological growth be achieved by denying hygiene realities? The illness is at two levels. The primary sickness is the denial of man's animal nature. Second, psychological growth and happiness depend on two separate factors, and no denial of irrelevant factors will serve man in his pursuit of happiness.

The motivation–hygiene concept holds that mental health depends on the individual's history or past experience. The history of the healthy individual shows success in growth achievements. In contrast, mental illness depends on a different pattern of past experience. The unhealthy individual has concerned himself with surrounding conditions. His search for satisfaction has focused on the limitations imposed by objective reality and by other individuals, including society and culture.

In the usual job situation these limitations consist of company policy, supervision, interpersonal relations and the like. In broader life adjustments the surrounding conditions include cultural taboos, social demands for material production and limited native ability. The hygiene seeker devotes his energies to concern with the surrounding limitations, to 'defenses' in the Freudian sense. He seeks satisfaction, or mental health, in a policy of 'defense'. No personal growth occurs and his search for health is fruitless, for it leads to ever more intricate maneuvers of defense or hygiene seeking. Mental illness is an inversion – the attempt to accentuate or deny one set of needs in the hope of obtaining the other set.

To reiterate, mankind has two sets of needs. Think about man twice: once about events that cause him pain and, secondly, about events that make him happy. Those who seek only to gratify the needs of their animal natures are doomed to live in dreadful anticipation of pain and suffering. This is the fate of those human beings who want to satisfy only their biological needs. But some men have become aware of the advantage humans have over their animal brothers. In addition to the compulsion to avoid pain, the human being has been blessed with the potentiality to achieve happiness. And, as I hope I have demonstrated, man can be happy only by seeking to satisfy both his animal need to avoid pain and his human need to grow psychologically.

The seven classifications of adjustment continua are shown in Figure 2, using the motivation–hygiene theory frame of reference of parallel and diverging arrows. Within each category, the top arrow depicts the mental-illness continuum and the bottom arrow the mental-health continuum. The triangle signifies the scale on which the individual is operating and the degree of his gratification with the factors of that scale.

Category I: The healthy motivator seeker is shown to be on both the mental-illness and the mental-health continua, and he is successful in achieving the motivator (mental health) needs and in avoiding the pain of the hygiene (mental illness) needs.

Category II: The unhappy motivator seeker is depicted as obtaining human significance from his job but receiving little amelioration of his animal-avoidance pains.

Category III: This shows the motivator seeker searching for gratification of both sets of needs but being successful only in avoiding hygiene deprivation.

Category IV: The miserable motivator seeker is illustrated as basically healthy but, unfortunately, with neither need system being serviced.

Category V: The hygiene seeker who is motivated only by his hygiene needs is indicated here. He is successful at avoiding mental illness but debarred from achieving mental health.

Category VI: These people are the true mentally ill. They are the hygiene seekers who fail in their hygiene gratification.

Category VII: Finally, there is that interesting form of hygiene seeker, the 'monastic', who also is living by only one need system and is fulfilling

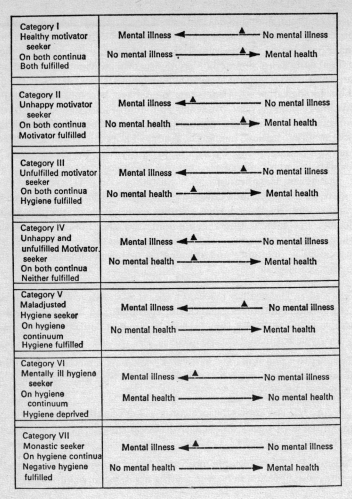

Figure 2

his hygiene requirements by denying them. Familiar examples are the no-talent beatnik, the sacrificing mother, the severe disciplinarian in the military world and, less often today, his counterpart in industry.

These types are summarized in Table 1.

Can we identify the people on jobs who are the healthy individuals,

Table 1   Types of adjustments

Classification	Orientation	Motivator satisfaction	Hygiene satisfaction
Mental Health	Motivator	Yes	Yes
Unhappy	Motivator	Yes	No
Unfulfilled	Motivator	No	Yes
Unhappy and unfulfilled	Motivator	No	No
Maladjusted	Hygiene	Not pertinent	Yes
Mental illness	Hygiene	Not pertinent	No
Monastic	Hygiene	Not pertinent	Denied

that is, who are the motivator seekers, as distinguished from the hygiene seekers? What are the consequences to companies that select and reinforce hygiene seekers? These questions will be examined in the final chapter, but at this point a brief description of hygiene seekers and of the consequences to the company hiring them will be useful.

The hygiene seeker, as opposed to the motivator seeker, is motivated by the nature of the environment of his job rather than by his tasks. He suffers from a chronic and heightened dissatisfaction with his job hygiene. Why? Because he lives by it. He has an overreaction to improvement in hygiene factors. You give him a salary raise and you become the most wonderful boss in the world; he is in the most wonderful company in the world – he protests too much. In other words, you have given him a shot in the arm. But the satisfactions of hygiene factors are of short duration – and the short action applies as well to the motivator seeker, because this is the nature of the beast.

The hygiene seeker realizes little satisfaction from accomplishments and consequently shows little interest in the kind and quality of the work he does. Why? Since he is basically an avoidance-oriented organism, how can he have a positive outlook on life? He does not profit professionally from experience. The only profit he desires is a more comfortable environment. 'What did you learn?' 'Nothing, it was a complete waste of time.' Obviously, there was no definite reward. In other words, even though you can stimulate him for a temporary action, he does not have his own generator. And I think, also, that many companies feel they have to keep doing his stimulating.

The hygiene seeker is ultraliberal or ultraconservative. He parrots management's philosophy. As a means of reducing ambiguity he acts more like top management than top management does. The question arises whether he may be successful on the job because of talent. The

Table 2   Characteristics of hygiene and motivation seekers

Hygiene seeker	Motivation seeker
1. Motivated by nature of the environment	Motivated by nature of the task
2. Chronic and heightened dissatisfaction with various aspects of his job context, e.g. salary, supervision, working conditions, status, job security, company policy and administration, fellow employees	Higher tolerance for poor hygiene factors
3. Overreaction with satisfaction to improvement in hygiene factors	Less reaction to improvement in hygiene factors
4. Short duration of satisfaction when the hygiene factors are improved	Similar
5. Overreaction with dissatisfaction when hygiene factors are not improved	Milder discontent when hygiene factors need improvement
6. Realizes little satisfaction from accomplishments	Realizes great satisfaction from accomplishments
7. Shows little interest in the kind and quality of the work he does	Shows capacity to enjoy the kind of work he does
8. Cynicism regarding positive virtues of work and life in general	Has positive feelings toward work and life in general
9. Does not profit professionally from experience	Profits professionally from experience
10. Prone to cultural noises (a) Ultraliberal, ultraconservative (b) Parrots management philosophy (c) Acts more like top management than top management does	Belief systems sincere and considered
11. May be successful on the job because of talent	May be an overachiever

question is then legitimately asked: If a man does well on the job because of hygiene satisfactions, what difference does it make?

The answer is twofold. I believe that hygiene seekers will let the company down when their talents are most needed. They are motivated only for short times and only when there is an external reward to be obtained. It is just when an emergency situation arises, and when the organization cannot be bothered with hygiene, that these key men may fail to do their jobs. In the army they are known as 'barracks soldiers'.

The second answer I suggest, and one that I believe to be of more serious import, is that hygiene seekers offer their own motivational characteristics as the pattern to be instilled in their subordinates. They become the template from which the new recruit to industry learns his motivational pattern. Hygiene seekers in key positions set the extrinsic reward atmosphere for the units of the company that they control. Because of the talent they possess, their influence on conditioning the atmosphere is generally out of proportion to their long-term effectiveness to the company.

If we accept the notion that one of the most important functions of a manager is the development of future managers, the teaching of hygiene motivations becomes a serious defect to the company. This, I believe, is one of the major implications that the motivation–hygiene theory has for modern personnel practices. Previous research knowledge has strongly indicated that the effectiveness of management development is attuned to its congruence with the company atmosphere, as it is manifested in the superior's beliefs and behavior. The superior who is a hygiene seeker cannot but have an adverse effect on management development, which is aimed at the personal growth and actualization of subordinates.

Reference

HERZBERG, F., MAUSNER, B., and SNYDERMAN, B. B. (1959), *The Motivation to Work*, Wiley.

21   C. Argyris and D. A. Schon

Organizational Learning

From C. Argyris and D. A. Schon, *Organizational Learning: A Theory of Action Perspective*, Addison-Wesley, 1978, chapter 1, pp. 8–29.

The question

There has probably never been a time in our history when members, managers, and students of organizations were so united on the importance of organizational learning. Costs of health care, sanitation, police, housing, education, and welfare have risen precipitously, and we urge agencies concerned with these services to learn to increase their productivity and efficiency. Governments are torn by the conflicting demands of full employment, free collective bargaining, social welfare, and the control of inflation; we conclude that governments must learn to understand and accommodate these demands. Corporations have found themselves constrained by a web of increasingly stringent regulations for environmental protection and consumer safety, at the same time that we are most sensitive to the need for jobs and for economic growth. Government and business must learn, we say, to work together to solve these problems.

Sometimes our demands for learning turn back on our history, as when politicians and planners ask, 'What have we learned from the last twenty years of housing policy?' 'What have we learned from the Great Depression?' 'What have we learned from Vietnam?' In a bicentennial article on 'The American Experiment', Daniel Moynihan begins by asking, 'What have we learned?' (Glazer and Kristol, 1976).

It is not only that we are poignantly aware of our dilemmas and of the need for learning. We are also beginning to notice that there is nothing more problematic than solutions. Some of our most agonizing problems have been triggered by our solutions to slum eradication and urban renewal, by the success of the Labor Movement in achieving income security for workers, by rising expectations consequent to our economic growth, by the unwanted consequences of technological innovations. We begin to suspect that there is no stable state awaiting us over the horizon. On the contrary, our very power to solve problems seems to multiply problems. As a result, our organizations live in economic, political, and technological environments which are predictably unstable. The requirement for organizational learning is not an occasional, sporadic phenomenon, but is continuous and endemic to our society.

Nevertheless, it is not all clear what it means for an organization to learn. Nor is it clear how we can enhance the capacity of organizations to learn.

The difficulty has first to do with the notion of learning itself. When we call for learning or change, we seem to be calling for something good. But there are kinds of change which are not good, such as deterioration, regression and stagnation. And there are kinds of learning, such as government's learning to deceive and manipulate society, which are no better. So we need to spell out both the kinds of change we have in mind when we speak of learning, and the kinds of learning we have in mind when we call for more of it.

Further, it is clear that organizational learning is not the same thing as individual learning, even when the individuals who learn are members of the organization. There are too many cases in which organizations know *less* than their members. There are even cases in which the organization cannot seem to learn what every member knows. Nor does it help to think of organizational learning as the prerogative of a man at the top who learns *for* the organization; in large and complex organizations bosses succeed one another while the organization remains very much itself, and learns or fails to learn in ways that often have little to do with the boss.

There is something paradoxical here. Organizations are not merely collections of individuals, yet there is no organization without such collections. Similarly, organizational learning is not merely individual learning, yet organizations learn only through the experience and actions of individuals.

What, then, are we to make of organizational learning? What is an organization that it may learn?

Theory of action

In our earlier book, *Theory in Practice* (Argyris and Schon, 1974), we set out to understand how practitioners of management, consultation, and intervention might learn to become more competent and effective. Our concern was especially directed to learning about interpersonal interaction. In that context, we found it useful to look at professional practice as informed by *theories of action*:

All human beings – not only professional practitioners – need to become competent in taking action and simultaneously reflecting on this action to learn from it. The following pages provide a conceptual framework for this task by analyzing theories of action that determine all deliberate human behavior, how these theories are formed, how they come to change, and in what senses they may be considered adequate or inadequate (p. 4).

When we attributed theories of action to human beings, we argued that all deliberate action had a cognitive basis, that it reflected norms, strategies, and assumptions or models of the world which had claims to general validity. As a consequence human learning, we said, need not be understood in terms of the 'reinforcement' or 'extinction' of patterns of behavior but as the construction, testing, and restructuring of a certain kind of knowledge. Human action and human learning could be placed in the larger context of knowing.

We found it necessary to connect theories of action to other kinds of theory:

whatever else a theory of action may be, it is first a theory. Its most general properties are properties that all theories share, and the most general criteria that apply to it – such as generality, centrality, and simplicity – are criteria that apply to all theories (p. 4).

And we also found it necessary to differentiate theories of action from theories of explanation, prediction, and control:

A full schema for a theory of action, then, would be as follows: in situation S, if you want to achieve consequence C, under assumptions $a \ldots n$, do A . . . A theory of action is a theory of deliberate human behavior which is for the agent a theory of control but which, when attributed to the agent, also serves to explain or predict his behavior (p. 6).

Because we wished to do empirical research into human learning in situations of interpersonal interaction, we distinguished espoused theory from theory-in-use:

When someone is asked how he would behave under certain circumstances, the answer he usually gives is his espoused theory of action for that situation. This is the theory of action to which he gives allegiance and which, upon request, he communicates to others. However, the theory that actually governs his actions is his theory-in-use, which may or may not be compatible with his espoused theory; furthermore, the individual may or may not be aware of the incompatibility of the two theories (p. 7).

From the directly observable data of behavior, we could then ground our construction of the models of action theories which guided interpersonal behavior. And we could relate these models to the capacity for types of learning in professional practice.

It is tempting to apply this line of thought to the problem of understanding organizational learning. Perhaps organizations also have theories of action which inform their actions, espoused theories which they announce to the world and theories-in-use which may be inferred from their directly observable behavior. If so, then organizational learning might be understood as the testing and restructuring of organizational theories of action and, in the organizational context as in the individual one, we might examine the impact of models of action theories upon the capacity for kinds of learning.

But this path is full of obstacles. It is true that we do apply to organizations many of the terms we also apply to individuals. We speak of organizational action and organizational behavior. We speak also of organizational intelligence and memory. We say that organizations learn, or fail to learn. Nevertheless, a closer examination of these ways of speaking suggests that such terms are metaphors. Organizations do not literally remember, think, or learn. At least, it is not initially clear how we might go about testing whether or not they do so.

It is even puzzling to consider what it means for an organization to act or behave – notions which are essential to the construction of organizational theories of action. Does an organization act whenever one of its members acts? If so, there would appear to be little difference between an organization and a collection of individuals. Yet it is clear that some collections of people are organizations and others are not. Furthermore, even when a collection of people is clearly an organization, individual members of the organization do many things (such as breathe, sleep, gossip with their friends) which do not seem, in some important sense, to be examples of organizational action.

If we are to speak of organizational theories of action, we must dispel some of the confusion surrounding terms like organizational intelligence, memory, and action. We must say what it means for an organization to act, and we must show how organizational action is both different from and conceptually connected to individual action. We must say what it means for an organization to know something, and we must spell out the metaphors of organizational memory, intelligence, and learning.

Perspectives on organization

Let us begin by exploring several different ways of looking at an organization. An organization is:

1. A government, or *polis*.
2. An agency.
3. A task system.

Each of these perspectives will illuminate the sense in which an organization may be said to act. Further, an organization is:

4. A theory of action.
5. A cognitive enterprise undertaken by individual members.
6. A cognitive artifact made up of individual images and public maps.

Each of these descriptions will reveal the sense in which an organization may be said to know something, and to learn.

Consider a mob of students protesting against their university's policy. At what point do they cease to be a mob and begin to be an organization?

The mob is a collectivity. It is a collection of people who may run, shout, and mill about together. But it is a collectivity which cannot make a decision or take an action in its own name, and its boundaries are vague and diffuse.

As the mob begins to meet three sorts of conditions, it becomes more nearly an organization. Members must devise procedures for (1) making decisions in the name of the collectivity, (2) delegating to individuals the authority to act for the collectivity, and (3) setting boundaries between the collectivity and the rest of the world. As these conditions are met, members of the collectivity begin to be able to say 'we' about themselves; they can say, 'We have decided', 'We have made our position clear', 'We have limited our membership.' There is now an organizational 'we' that can decide and act.

When the members of the mob become an identifiable vehicle for collective decision and action, they become, in the ancient Greek sense of the term, a *polis*, a political entity. Before an organization can be anything else, it must be in this sense political, because it is as a political entity that the collectivity can take organizational action. It is individuals who decide and act, but they do these things *for* the collectivity by virtue of the rules for decision, delegation, and membership. When the members of the collectivity have created such rules, they have organized.

Rule making need not be a conscious, formal process. What is important is that members' behavior be rule-governed in the crucial respects. The rules themselves may remain tacit, unless for some reason they are called into question. So long as there is continuity in the rules which govern the behavior of individuals, the organization will persist, even though members come and go. And what is most important for our purposes, it now becomes possible to set up criteria of relevance for constructing organizational theory-in-use. Organizational theory-in-use is to be inferred from observation of organizational behavior – that is, from organizational decisions and actions. The decisions and actions carried out by individuals are organizational insofar as they are governed by collective rules for decision and delegation. These alone are the decisions and actions taken in the name of the organization.

Through such a process, a mob becomes an organization. But if we are interested in organizational theory of action, we must ask what *kind* of an organization it becomes.

If a collection of people begins to decide and to act on a continuing basis, it becomes an instrument for continuing collective action, an *agency*. In this sense, the collections of workers involved in the labor movement organized from time to time to form unions, and collections of individual investors organized to form limited liability corporations. Such agencies have functions to fulfill, work to do. Their theories-in-use may be inferred from the ways in which they go about doing their work.

Generally speaking, an agency's work is a complex task, continually performed. The agency – an industrial corporation, a labor union, a government bureau, or even a household – embodies a strategy for decomposing that complex task into simpler components which are regularly delegated to individuals. Organizational roles – president, lathe operator, shop steward – are the names given to the clusters of component tasks which the agency has decided to delegate to individual members. The organization's *task system*, its pattern of interconnected roles, is at once a design for work and a division of labor.

An agency is thus the solution to a problem. It is a strategy for performing a complex task which might have been carried out in other ways. This is true not only for the design of the task system, the division of labor, but also for the selection of strategies for performing component tasks.

We can view a sugar-refining company, for example, as an answer to questions such as these: What is the best way to grow and harvest cane? How should it be refined? How is it best distributed and marketed? For each sub-question the organization is an answer. The company's way of growing cane reflects certain strategies (for the cultivation of land, for harvesting and fertilizing), certain norms (for productivity and quality, for the use of labor), and certain assumptions (about the yields to be expected from various patterns of cultivation). The norms, strategies, and assumptions embedded in the company's cane-growing practices constitute its *theory of action* for cane-growing. There are comparable theories of action implicit in the company's ways of distributing and marketing its products. Taken together, these component theories of action represent a theory of action for achieving corporate objectives. This global theory of action we call 'instrumental'. It includes norms for corporate performance (for example, norms for margin of profit and for return on investment), strategies for achieving norms (for example, strategies for plant location and for process technology), and assumptions which bind strategies and norms together (for example, the assumption that maintenance of a high rate of return on investment depends on the continual introduction of new technologies).

The company's instrumental theory of action is a complex system of norms, strategies, and assumptions. It includes in its scope the organization's patterns of communication and control, its ways of allocating resources to goals, and its provisions for self-maintenance – that is, for rewarding and punishing individual performance, for constructing career ladders and regulating the rate at which individuals climb them, and for recruiting new members and instructing them in the ways of the organization.

Like the rules for collective decision and action, organizational theories of action need not be explicit. Indeed, formal corporate documents such as organization charts, policy statements, and job descriptions often reflect a theory of action (the *espoused theory*) which conflicts with the organization's *theory-in-use* (the theory of action constructed from observation of actual behavior) – and the theory-in-use is often tacit. Organizational theory-in-use may remain tacit, as we will see later on, because its incongruity with espoused theory is *undiscussable*. Or it may remain tacit because individual members of the organization know more than they can say – because the theory-in-use is *inaccessible* to them. Whatever the reason for tacitness, the largely tacit theory-in-use accounts for organizational identity and continuity.

Consider a large, enduring organization such as the U.S. Army. Over fifty years or so, its personnel may turn over completely, yet we still speak of it as 'the Army'. It is no longer the same collection of people, so in what sense is it still the same? Suppose we wanted to discover whether it was in fact the same organization. How would we proceed? We might examine uniforms and weapons, but in fifty years these might have changed entirely. We might then study the fifty-year evolution of military practices – that is, the norms for military behavior, the strategies for military action, the assumptions about military functioning. We would then be studying the evolution of the Army's theory-in-use. And we might learn that certain features of it – for example, the pattern of command, the methods of training, the division into regiments and platoons – had remained essentially unchanged, while other features of it – battle strategies, norms for performance – had evolved continuously from earlier forms. We might conclude that we were dealing with a single organization, self-identical, whose theory-in-use had evolved considerably over time.

It is this theory-in-use, an apparently abstract thing, which is most distinctively real about the Army. It is what old soldiers know and new ones learn through a continuing process of socialization. And it is the history of change in theory-in-use which we would need to consult in order to inquire into the Army's organizational learning.

In order to discover an organization's theory-in-use, we must examine its practice, that is, the continuing performance of its task system as exhibited in the rule-governed behavior of its members. This is, however, an outside view. When members carry out the practices appropriate to their organization, they are also manifesting a kind of knowledge. And this knowledge represents the organization's theory-in-use as seen from the inside.

Images and maps

Each member of the organization constructs his or her own representation, or image, of the theory-in-use of the whole. That picture is always incomplete. The organization members strive continually to complete it, and to understand themselves in the context of the organization. They try to describe themselves and their own performance insofar as they interact with others. As conditions change, they test and modify that description. Moreover, others are continually engaged in similar inquiry. It is this continual, concerted meshing of individual images of self and others, of one's own activity in the context of collective interaction, which constitutes an organization's knowledge of its theory-in-use.

An organization is like an organism each of whose cells contains a particular, partial, changing image of itself in relation to the whole. And like such an organism, the organization's practice stems from those very images. Organization is an artifact of individual ways of representing organization.

Hence, our inquiry into organizational learning must concern itself not with static entities called organizations, but with an active process of organizing which is, at root, a cognitive enterprise. Individual members are continually engaged in attempting to know the organization, and to know themselves in the context of the organization. At the same time, their continuing efforts to know and to test their knowledge represent the object of their inquiry. Organizing is reflexive inquiry.

From this perspective, organizational continuity is a considerable achievement. But we could not account for organizational continuity if the cognitive enterprise of organizing were limited to the private inquiry of individuals. Even when individuals are in face-to-face contact, private images of organization erode and diverge from one another. When the task system is large and complex, most members are unable to use face-to-face contact in order to compare and adjust their several images of organizational theory-in-use. They require external references. There must be public representations of organizational theory-in-use to which individuals can refer.

This is the function of organizational maps. These are the shared descriptions of organization which individuals jointly construct and use to guide their own inquiry. They include, for example, diagrams of work flow, compensation charts, statements of procedure, even the schematic drawings of office space. A building itself may function as a kind of map, revealing patterns of communication and control. Whatever their form, maps have a dual function. They describe actual patterns of activity, and they are guides to future action. As musicians perform their scores, members of an organization perform their maps.

Organizational theory-in-use, continually constructed through individual inquiry, is encoded in private images and in public maps. These are the media of organizational learning.

Organizational learning

As individual members continually modify their maps and images of the organization, they also bring about changes in organizational theory-in-use.

Not all of these changes qualify as learning. Members may lose enthusiasm, become sloppy in task performance, or lose touch with one another. They may leave the organization, carrying with them important information which becomes lost to the organization. Or changes in the organization's environment (a slackening of demand for product, for example) may trigger new patterns of response which undermine organizational norms. These are kinds of deterioration, sometimes called organizational entropy.

But individual members frequently serve as agents of changes in organizational theory-in-use which run counter to organizational entropy. They act on their images and on their shared maps with expectations of patterned outcomes, which their subsequent experience confirms or disconfirms. When there is a mismatch of outcome to expectation (error), members may respond by modifying their images, maps, and activities so as to bring expectations and outcomes back into line. They detect an error in organizational theory-in-use and they correct it. This fundamental learning loop is one in which individuals act from organizational theory-in-use, which leads to match or mismatch of expectations with outcome, and thence to confirmation or disconfirmation of organizational theory-in-use..

Quality control inspectors detect a defect in product, for example; they feed that information back to production engineers, who then change production specifications to correct that defect. Marketing managers observe that monthly sales have fallen below expectations; they inquire into the shortfall, seeking an interpretation which they can use to devise new marketing strategies which will bring the sales curve back on target. When organizational turnover of personnel increases to the point where it threatens the steady performance of the task system, managers may respond by investigating the sources of worker dissatisfaction; they look for factors they can influence – salary levels, fringe benefits, job design – so as to re-establish the stability of their work force.

Single-loop learning

In these examples, *members of the organization respond to changes in the internal and external environments of the organization by detecting errors which they then correct so as to maintain the central features of organizational theory-in-use.* These are learning episodes which function to preserve a certain kind of constancy. As Gregory Bateson has pointed out (Bateson, 1972), the organization's ability to remain stable in a changing context denotes a kind of learning. Following his usage, we call this learning 'single-loop'. There is a single feedback loop which connects detected outcomes of action to organizational strategies and assumptions which are modified so as to keep organizational performance within the range set by organizational norms. The norms themselves – for product quality, sales, or task performance – remain unchanged.

These examples also help to make clear the relationship between individual and organizational learning. The key to this distinction is the notion of *agency*. *Just as individuals are the agents of organizational action, so they are the agents for organizational learning.* Organizational learning occurs when individuals, acting from their images and maps, detect a match or mismatch of outcome to expectation which confirms or disconfirms organizational theory-in-use. In the case of disconfirmation, individuals move from error detection to error correction. Error correction takes the form of inquiry. The learning agents must discover the sources of error – that is, they must attribute error to strategies and assumptions in existing theory-in-use. They must invent new strategies, based on new assumptions, in order to correct error. They must produce those strategies. And they must evaluate and generalize the results of that new action. 'Error correction' is shorthand for a complex learning cycle.

But in order for *organizational* learning to occur, learning agents' discoveries, inventions, and evaluations must be embedded in organizational memory. They must be encoded in the individual images and the shared maps of organizational theory-in-use from which individual members will subsequently act. If this encoding does not occur, individuals will have learned but the organization will not have done so.

Suppose, for example, that the quality-control inspectors find a product defect which they then decide to keep to themselves, perhaps because they are afraid to make the information public. Or suppose that they try to communicate this information to the production engineers, but the production engineers do not wish to listen to them. Or suppose that the interpretation of error requires collaborative inquiry on the part of several different members of the organization who are unwilling or unable to carry out such a collaboration. (Indeed, because organizations are strategies for decomposing complex tasks into task/role systems, error correction normally requires collaborative inquiry.) In all of these instances, individual learning may or may not have occurred, but individuals do not function as agents of organizational learning. What individuals may have learned remains as an unrealized potential for organizational learning.

From this it follows both that there is no organizational learning without individual learning, and that individual learning is a necessary but insufficient condition for organizational learning. We can think of organizational learning as a process mediated by the collaborative inquiry of individual members. In their capacity as agents of organizational learning, individuals restructure the continually changing artifact called organizational theory-in-use. Their work as learning agents is unfinished until the results of their inquiry – their discoveries, inventions, and evaluations – are recorded in the media of organizational memory, the images and maps which encode organizational theory-in-use.

If we should wish to test whether organizational learning has occurred, we must ask questions such as the following. Did individuals detect an outcome which matched or mismatched the expectations derived from their images and maps of organizational theory-in-use? Did they carry out an inquiry which yielded discoveries, inventions, and evaluations pertaining to organizational strategies and assumptions? Did these results become embodied in the images and maps employed for purposes such as control, decision, and instruction? Did members subsequently act from these images and maps so as to carry out new organizational practices? Were these changes in images, maps, and organizational practices regularized so that they were unaffected by some individual's departure? Do new members learn these new features of organizational theory of action as part of their socialization to the organization?

Each of these questions points to a possible source of failure in organizational learning, as well as to the sources of organizational learning capacity. So far, however, we have limited ourselves to the kind of learning called 'single-loop'. Let us now consider learning of another kind.

Double-loop learning

Organizations are continually engaged in transactions with their internal and external environments. Industrial corporations, for example, continually respond to the changing pattern of external competition, regulation and demand, and to the changing internal environment of workers' attitudes and aspirations. These responses take the form of error detection and error correction. Single-loop learning is sufficient where error correction can proceed by changing organizational strategies and assumptions within a constant framework of norms for performance. It is concerned primarily with effectiveness – that is, with how best to achieve existing goals and objectives and how best to keep organizational performance within the range specified by existing norms. In some cases, however, error correction requires an organizational learning cycle in which organizational norms themselves are modified.

Consider an industrial firm which has set up a research and development division charged with the discovery and development of new technologies. This has been a response to the perceived imperative for growth in sales and earnings and the belief that these are to be generated through internally managed technological innovation. But the new division generates technologies which do not fit the corporation's familiar pattern of operations. In order to exploit some of these technologies, for example, the corporation may have to turn from the production of intermediate materials with which it is familiar to the manufacture and distribution of consumer products with which it is unfamiliar. But this, in turn, requires that members of the corporation adopt new approaches to marketing, managing, and advertising; that they become accustomed to a much shorter product life-cycle and to a more rapid cycle of changes in their pattern of activities; that they, in fact, change the very image of the business they are in. And these requirements for change come into conflict with another sort of corporate norm, one that requires predictability in the management of corporate affairs.

Hence, the corporate managers find themselves confronted with conflicting requirements. If they conform to the imperative for growth, they must give up on the imperative for predictability. If they decide to keep their patterns of operations constant, they must give up on the imperative for growth, at least insofar as that imperative is to be realized through internally generated technology. A process of change initiated with an eye to effectiveness under existing norms turns out to yield a conflict in the norms themselves.

If corporate managers are to engage this conflict, they must undertake a process of inquiry which is significantly different from the inquiry characteristic of single-loop learning. They must, to begin with, recognize the conflict itself. They have set up a new division which has yielded unexpected outcomes; this is an error, in the sense earlier described. They must reflect upon this error to the point where they become aware that they cannot correct it by doing better what they already know how to do. They must become aware, for example, that they cannot correct the error by getting the new division to perform more effectively under existing norms; indeed, the more effective the new division is, the more its results will plunge the managers into conflict. The managers must discover that it is the norm for predictable management which they hold, perhaps tacitly, that conflicts with their wish to achieve corporate growth through technological innovation.

Then the managers must undertake an inquiry which resolves the conflicting requirements. The results of their inquiry will take the form of a restructuring of organizational norms, and very likely a restructuring of strategies and assumptions associated with those norms, which must then be embedded in the images and maps which encode organizational theory-in-use.

We call this sort of learning *double-loop*. There is in this sort of episode a double feedback loop with connects the detection of error not only to strategies and assumptions for effective performance but to the very norms which define effective performance.

Single-loop learning, as we have defined it, consists not only of a change in organizational strategies and assumptions but of the particular sort of change appropriately described as learning. In single-loop learning, members of the organization carry out a collaborative inquiry through which they discover sources of error, invent new strategies designed to correct error, produce those strategies, and evaluate and generalize the results. Similarly, double-loop learning consists not only of a change in organizational norms but of the particular sort of inquiry into norms which is appropriately described as learning.

In organizational double-loop learning, incompatible requirements in organizational theory-in-use are characteristically expressed through a conflict among members and groups within the organization. In the industrial organization, for example, some managers may become partisans of growth through research and of a new image of the business based upon research, while others may become opponents of research through their allegiance to familiar and predictable patterns of corporate operation. Double-loop learning, if it occurs, will consist of the process of inquiry by which these groups of managers confront and resolve their conflict.

In this sense, the organization is a medium for translating incompatible requirements into interpersonal and intergroup conflict.

Members of the organization may respond to such a conflict in several ways, not all of which meet the criteria for organizational double-loop learning. First, the members may treat the conflict as a fight in which choices are to be made among competing requirements, and weightings and priorities are to be set on the basis of prevailing power. The 'R. & D. faction', for example, may include the chief executive who wins out over the 'old guard' through being more powerful. Or the two factions may fight it out to a draw, settling their differences in the end by a compromise which reflects nothing more than the inability of either faction to prevail over the other.

In both of these cases, the conflict is settled for the time being, but not by a process that could be appropriately described as learning. The conflict is settled not by inquiry but by fighting it out. Neither side emerges from the settlement with a new sense of the nature of the conflict, of its causes and consequences, or of its meaning for organizational theory-in-use.

On the other hand, parties to the conflict may engage the conflict through inquiry of the following kinds:

1. They may invent new strategies of performance which circumvent the perceived incompatibility of requirements. They may, for example, succeed in defining a kind of research and development addressed solely to the existing pattern of business, which offers the likelihood of achieving existing norms for growth. They will then have succeeded in finding a single-loop solution to what at first appeared as a double-loop problem.

2. They may carry out a 'trade-off analysis' which enables them to conclude jointly that so many units of achievement of one norm are balanced by so many units of achievement of another. On this basis, they may decide that the prospects for R. & D. pay-off are so slim that the R. & D. option should be abandoned, and with that abandonment there should be a lowering of corporate expectations for growth. Or they may decide to limit R. & D. targets so that the disruptions of patterns of business operation generated by R. & D. are limited to particular segments of the corporation.

Here there is a compromise among competing requirements, but it is achieved through inquiry into the probabilities and values associated with the options for action.

3. In the context of the conflict, the incompatible requirements may not lend themselves to trade-off analysis. They may be perceived as incommensurable. In such a case, the conflict may still be resolved through inquiry which looks beyond the members' starting perceptions of the incompatible requirements. Participants must then ask why they hold the positions they do, and what they mean by them. They may ask what factors have led them to adopt these particular standards for growth in sales and earnings, what their rationale is, and what are likely to be the consequences of attempting to achieve them through any means whatever. Similarly, they may ask what kinds of predictability in operations are of greatest importance, to whom they are most important, and what conditions make them important.

Such inquiry may lead to a significant restructuring of the configuration of corporate norms. Or it may lead to the invention of new patterns of incentives, budgeting, and control which take greater account of requirements for both growth and predictability.

We will give the name 'double-loop learning' to those sorts of organizational inquiry which resolve incompatible organizational norms by setting new priorities and weightings of norms, or by restructuring the norms themselves together with associated strategies and assumptions.

In these cases, individual members resolve the interpersonal and intergroup conflicts which express incompatible requirements by creating new understandings of the conflicting requirements, their sources, conditions, and consequences – understandings which then become embedded in the images and maps of organization. By doing so, they make the new, more nearly compatible requirements susceptible to effective realization. There are three observations we wish to make about distinction between single- and double-loop organizational learning.

First, it is often impossible, in the real-world context of organizational life, to find inquiry clearly separated from the uses of power. Inquiry and power-play are often combined. Given such a mixture, we will want to differentiate the two kinds of processes so that we may speak of those aspects of interpersonal and intergroup conflict which involve organizational learning and those which do not.

Second, while we have described the *kinds* of inquiry which are essential to single- and double-loop learning, we have not yet dwelt on the *quality* of inquiry. Two different examples of double-loop learning, both of which exhibit detection of error and correction of error through the restructuring of organizational norms, may be of unequal quality. The same is true of single-loop learning. Organizations may learn more or less well, yet their inquiries may still qualify as learning of the single- or double-loop kind.

Finally, we must point out that the distinction between single- and double-loop learning is less a binary one than might first appear. Organizational theories-in-use are systemic structures composed of many interconnected parts. We can examine these structures from the point of view of a particular, local theory of action, such as the industrial firm's theory of action for quality control, or we can attend to more global aspects of the structure, such as the firm's theory of action for achieving targeted return on investment. Furthermore, certain elements are more fundamental to the structure and others are more peripheral. For example, the industrial firm's norms for growth and for predictability of management are fundamental to its theory of action – in the sense that if they were changed, a great deal of the rest of the theory of action would also have to change – and it is their fundamental status which gives a special poignancy to their conflict. On the other hand, a particular norm for product quality may be quite peripheral to the organization's theory of action; it could change without affecting much of the rest of the theory of action.

Now, an inquiry into a *strategy* fundamental to the firm's theory of action, such as the strategy of measuring divisional performance by monthly profit-and-loss statements, will be likely to involve much of the rest of the organization's theory of action, including its norms. But an inquiry into a *norm* peripheral to the organization's theory of action may involve very little of the rest of its theory of action. From this, two conclusions may be drawn. First, in judging whether learning is single- or double-loop, it is important to notice where inquiry goes as well as where it begins. Second, it is possible to speak of organizational learning as *more or less* double-loop. In place of the binary distinction we have a more continuous concept of depth of learning.

It is possible, we think, to make clear distinctions between relatively deep and relatively peripheral examples of organizational learning. We will continue to call the former 'double-' and the latter 'single-loop' learning. Our examples of double-loop learning will involve norms fundamental to organizational theories of action, for these are the examples we believe to be of greatest importance. The reader should keep in mind, however, that we speak of these categories as discrete when they are actually parts of a continuum. With these *caveats*, we can return to our main line of argument.

Deutero-learning

Since the Second World War it has gradually become apparent not only to business firms but to all sorts of organizations that the requirements of organizational learning, especially for double-loop learning, are not one-shot but continuing. There has been a sequence of ideas in good currency – such as 'creativity', 'innovation', 'the management of change' – which reflect this awareness.

In our earlier example, to take one instance, managers of the industrial firm might conclude that their organization needs to learn how to restructure itself, at regular intervals, so as to exploit the new technologies generated by research and development. That is, the organization needs to learn how to carry out single- and double-loop learning.

This sort of learning to learn Gregory Bateson has called *deutero-learning* (that is, second-order learning). Bateson illustrates the idea through the following story:

A female porpoise . . . is trained to accept the sound of the trainer's whistle as a 'secondary reinforcement'. The whistle is expectably followed by food, and if she later repeats what she was doing when the whistle blew, she will expect again to hear the whistle and receive food.

The porpoise is now used by the trainers to demonstrate 'operant conditioning' to the public. When she enters the exhibition tank, she raises her head above the surface, hears the whistle and is fed . . .

But this pattern is (suitable) only for a single episode in the exhibition tank. She must break that pattern to deal with the *class* of such episodes. There is a larger context of contexts which will put her in the wrong . . .

When the porpoise comes on stage, she again raises her head. But she gets no whistle. The trainer waits for the next piece of conspicuous behavior, likely a tail flip, which is a common expression of annoyance. This behavior is then reinforced and repeated (by giving her food).

But the tail flip was, of course, not rewarded in the third performance.

Finally the porpoise learned to deal with the context of contexts – by offering a different or new piece of conspicuous behavior whenever she came on stage.

Each time the porpose learns to deal with a larger class of episodes, she learns *about* the previous contexts for learning. Her creativity reflects deutero-learning.

When an organization engages in deutero-learning, its members learn, too, about previous contexts for learning. They reflect on and inquire into previous contexts for learning. They reflect on and inquire into previous episodes of organizational learning, or failure to learn. They discover what they did that facilitated or inhibited learning, they invent new strategies for learning, they produce these strategies, and they evaluate and generalize what they have produced. The results become encoded in individual images and maps and are reflected in organizational learning practice.

The deutero-learning cycle is relatively familiar in the context of organizational learning curves. Aircraft manufacturers, for example, project the rate at which their organizations will learn to manufacture a new aircraft and base cost estimates on their projections of the rate of organizational learning. In the late 1950s, the Systems Development Corporation undertook the 'Cogwheel' experiment, in which members of an aircraft-spotting team were invited to inquire into their own organizational learning and then to produce conditions which would enable them more effectively to learn to improve their performance (Chapman and Kennedy, 1956).

In these examples, however, deutero-learning concentrates on single-loop learning; emphasis is on learning for effectiveness rather than on learning to resolve conflicting norms for performance. But the concept of deutero-learning is also relevant to double-loop learning. How, indeed, can organizations learn to become better at double-loop learning? How can members of an organization learn to carry out the kinds of inquiry essential to double-loop learning? What are the conditions which enable members to meet the tests of organizational learning? And how can they learn to produce those conditions?

Organizations are not only theories of action. They are also small societies composed of persons who occupy roles in the task system. What we have called the internal environment of an organization is the society of persons who make up the organization at any given time. These societies have their own characteristic behavioral worlds. These enable us to recognise a person as 'an army man', 'a government man', 'a General Electric man'. Within these societies, members tend to share characteristic languages, styles, and models of *individual* theory-in-use for interaction with others. In the light of these behavioral worlds, we can and do describe organizations as more or less 'open', 'experimental', 'confronting', 'demanding', or 'defensive'. These behavioral worlds, with their characteristic models of individual theory-in-use, may be more or less conducive to the kinds of collaborative inquiry required for organizational learning.

Hence, if we wish to learn more about the conditions that facilitate or inhibit organizational learning, we must explore the ways in which the behavioral worlds of organizations affect the capacity for inquiry into organizational theory-in-use.

Summary

Organizational learning is a metaphor whose spelling out requires us to re-examine the very idea of organization. A collection of individuals organizes when its members develop rules for collective decision delegation and membership. In their rule-governed behavior, they act for the collectivity in ways that reflect a task system. Just as individual theories of action may be inferred from individual behavior, so organizational theories of action may be inferred from patterns of organizational action. As individuals have espoused theories which may be incongruent with their (often tacit) theories-in-use, so with organizations.

Organizational learning occurs when members of the organization act as learning agents for the organization, responding to changes in the internal and external environments of the organization by detecting and correcting errors in organizational theory-in-use, and embedding the results of their inquiry in private images and shared maps of organization.

In organizational single-loop learning, the criterion for success is effectiveness. Individuals respond to error by modifying strategies and assumptions within constant organizational norms. In double-loop learning, response to detected error takes the form of joint inquiry into organizational norms themselves, so as to resolve their inconsistency and make the new norms more effectively realizable. In both cases, organizational learning consists of restructuring organizational theory of action.

When an organization engages in deutero-learning, its members learn about organizational learning and encode their results in images and maps. The quest for organizational learning capacity must take the form of deutero-learning; most particularly about the interactions between the organization's behavioral world and its ability to learn.

References

ARGYRIS, C., and SCHON, D. (1974), *Theory in Practice*, Fossey-Bass.

BATESON, G. (1972), *Steps to an Ecology of Mind*, Ballantine.

CHAPMAN, R. L., and KENNEDY, J. L. (1956), *Background and Implications of Systems Research Laboratory Studies*, Rand Corporation Report.

GLAZER, N., and KRISTOL, I. (eds.) (1976), 'The American Experiment', *The American Commonwealth – 1976*, Basic Books.

22 F. E. Fiedler

Situational Control and a Dynamic Theory of Leadership[1]

From B. King *et al.* (eds.), *Managerial Control and Organizational Democracy*, Wiley, 1978, pp. 107–31.

Although empirical studies of leadership behavior and performance became a serious concern of social scientists some fifty years ago, we are only now beginning to understand the structure of the leader–situation interaction and the dynamics of the leadership process. By dynamics, we mean here how the leader and organization interact, and how group performance is affected by a change in the leader's personality or experience or by the changes in the organization which occur almost continuously in the course of time. An insight into these interactions is essential if we are more fully to understand and improve organizational performance. This study presents an integration of some key concepts which may enable us to develop a dynamic theory of leadership that takes into account the ever changing leader–organization interaction.

Traditionally, the main business of leadership research has been the relationship between personality attributes of the leader and the performance of his or her group or organization. At first, this search focused on finding the magic personality trait which might predict leadership performance. This enterprise finally received the coup de grâce from Stogdill's (1948) and Mann's (1959) now classic reviews of the literature.

The emphasis then shifted to the identification of specific types of leader behavior which would determine the effectiveness of a group. While this effort did not succeed, it did result in the monumental factor-analytic research by the Ohio State group under Carroll Shartle and his associates (Stogdill and Coons, 1957) which identified the consideration and structuring dimensions as the two major types of leadership behavior which are seen by subordinates. Others, e.g. Cattell (1951), Likert (1961), and Bales (1951), identified similar types of behavior on which leaders differed in their interactions with groups. The hope that these or similar behaviors would be directly related to

1. Keynote address, N.A.T.O. International Conference on Coordination and Control of Group and Organizational Performance, 17 July 1976.

leadership performance has not been realized, although a number of investigators still deal with this problem.

In particular, a number of leadership training programs have been devoted to teaching managers how to be more considerate or more structuring. The well-known Fleishman, Harris, and Burt (1955) study showed that training of this type would not give lasting results unless the entire organization were to be changed. However, other types of training, working with the entire organization, have not been able to report much success in improving organizational performance. This applies to the orthodox approaches as well as such avant-garde programs as T-group and sensitivity training. Stogdill (1974), in his authoritative and comprehensive *Handbook of Leadership*, summarizes this type of research by censuring its 'failure to employ legitimate criteria of the effects of training' (p. 199). And he goes on to say:

> It is necessary to demonstrate that change in leader behavior is related to change in group productivity, cohesiveness, esprit, or satisfaction in order to claim that leadership is improved or worsened by training. Only a few of the studies examined for this report satisfy the above requirements. The results of this small body of research suggest that group cohesiveness and esprit increase after sensitivity training of the leader but productivity declines.

The acid test of leadership must obviously be its ability to improve organizational performance. For this reason, the ability to change and control and especially to train leaders is a very powerful test of our understanding of the process and theory. Our previous difficulties in this area may well derive from our inadequate understanding of the complex interaction which is inherent in leadership and even the way in which training itself affects the dynamics of the process. The simple notion that a particular type of behavior, or a particular behavior pattern, will result in effective leadership performance is no more viable than the earlier notion of a leadership trait. Leadership exists in the context of an organizational environment which determines, in large part, the specific kind of leadership behavior which the situation requires.

Since the publication of the contingency model (Fiedler, 1964, 1967), leadership theory has increasingly turned to formulations which consider not only the leader's personality or behavior, but also critical situational factors. Such situational effects or contingencies also have been explicitly recognized by theorists like House (1971), Vroom and Yetton (1973), and others. It seems fair to say that we are now beginning to predict the relationship between certain leader attributes and organizational performance at a given point in time with a reasonable degree of accuracy.

However, most of our predictions in this field tend to be cross-sectional. We cannot predict well for organizations which are undergoing change and we do not understand fully what factors are critical to leadership performance in this change process. Our major challenge in the area of leadership is to develop a theory which takes account of the changing organizational environment as well as the changes which occur in the leader.

The key concept, which is here proposed as a basis for developing a dynamic theory of leadership, is the leader's situational control. This is essentially the 'situational favorableness' dimension of the contingency model. I hope to show that this concept gives us considerable understanding of the leadership process and also enables us to control the process, that is, to develop an effective leadership training program which meets Stogdill's requirement that it affect organizational performance.

The contingency model

Although the contingency model has been fully described in numerous publications, a brief summary provides the basis for the remainder of this study. This theory holds that the effectiveness of a group or an organization depends upon two interacting factors: (1) the personality of the leader (leadership style) and (2) the degree to which the situation gives the leader control and influence, or, in somewhat different terms, the degree to which the situation is free of uncertainty for the leader.

The leader's personality, and more specifically, his or her motivational structure, is identified by a measure which reflects the individual's primary goals in the leadership situation. One type of person, whom we call 'relationship-motivated', obtains self-esteem from good interpersonal relationships with group members and accomplishes the task through these good relations. These basic goals are most apparent in uncertain and anxiety-provoking situations in which we try to assure that our most important needs are secured. Under these conditions, relationship-motivated individuals will seek the support of those who are most closely associated with them. In a leadership situation, we hypothesize that these are, of course, their immediate subordinates and co-workers. Once the support of co-workers and subordinates is assured and this basic goal is no longer in doubt, relationship-motivated leaders will seek support and esteem from others who are important. In a leadership situation in which esteem and approbation are given for good task performance, these individuals will devote themselves to the task in order to obtain the approval of their superiors, even if this means correspondingly less concern with the well-being and approval of subordinates. Thus, when relationship-motivated leaders enjoy a high degree of situational control, they tend to show task-relevant behavior which is most likely to impress superiors.

The other major personality type is the 'task-motivated' leader who obtains satisfaction and self-esteem from the more tangible evidence of his or her competence. In a leadership situation which is uncertain and anxiety-provoking, this individual will focus primarily on the completion of the task. However, when task-accomplishment is assured, as would be the case whenever the leader enjoys a high degree of situational control, the leader will relax and devote more time to cementing the relationship with his or her subordinates. Thus, 'business before pleasure', but business with pleasure whenever this is possible.

These two motivational systems are measured by the Least Preferred Co-worker (or L.P.C.) score, which is obtained by asking the individual to think of all those with whom he or she has ever worked, and then to describe the one person with whom he or she has been able to work least well. This description is made on a short bipolar scale of the semantic differential format, shown below. We have used 16 or 18 eight-point scale items, e.g.

$$\text{friendly:} \underline{} : \underline{} : \underline{} : \underline{} : \underline{} : \underline{} : \underline{} : \underline{} : \text{unfriendly}$$
$$\phantom{\text{friendly:}} \;\; 8 \;\; 7 \;\; 6 \;\; 5 \;\; 4 \;\; 3 \;\; 2 \;\; 1$$

$$\text{cooperative:} \underline{} : \underline{} : \underline{} : \underline{} : \underline{} : \underline{} : \underline{} : \underline{} : \text{uncooperative}$$
$$\phantom{\text{cooperative:}} \;\; 8 \;\; 7 \;\; 6 \;\; 5 \;\; 4 \;\; 3 \;\; 2 \;\; 1$$

The L.P.C. score is simply the sum of the item scores. A task-motivated person describes the least-preferred co-worker in very negative and rejecting terms. This person says, in effect, that the task is so important it is impossible to differentiate between others as co-workers and as individuals apart from the work relationship. That is, an individual who does not perform well must also have a very objectionable personality, i.e. unfriendly, uncooperative, unpleasant, etc.

The relationship-motivated person is less dependent on esteem from task accomplishment and is, therefore, quite capable of seeing another as a poor co-worker but as otherwise quite pleasant, friendly, or helpful. Since this leader's emotional involvement in the task is comparatively less intense, a person who is difficult to work with is seen in a more positive manner.

Although the L.P.C. score is normally distributed, there is a relatively small segment in the middle of the distribution which cannot be clearly identified as task- or relationship-motivated persons. We shall be concerned primarily with the high- and the low-L.P.C. leaders who are much better understood.

A recent review of the literature by Rice (1977) shows that the L.P.C. score reflects a relatively stable personality attribute. Rice located twenty-three test–retest correlations which ranged 'from 0.01 to 0.92 with a median of 0.67 and a mean (using Fisher's Z transformation) of 0.64 (standard deviation $= 0.36$, $n = 23$)'. He goes on to say: 'Somewhat surprisingly the test–retest reliability data . . . show only a moderate negative correlation between length of the test–retest interval and the magnitude of the stability coefficient ($r = -0.30$, $n = 23$, ns). This analysis suggests that the variance in stability coefficients is primarily due to factors other than the simple passing of time.' Exactly what other factors might affect the stability of the score is still not clear.

It is also of interest to note that the median retest reliability of L.P.C. is well within the range of several other widely used personality measures. For example, Sax (1974) lists the stability of the M.M.P.I. for a period of only one week as 0.60, and the median stability coefficient of the Hartshorne and May honesty scales of a six-month interval as 0.50. Mehrens and Lehmann (1968) report the stability of the California Psychological Inventory for 13,000 subjects over a one-year period as 0.65 for males and 0.68 for females. While the retest correlations for such measures of cognitive abilities as intelligence are generally higher, relatively few stability coefficients of personality-test scores fall above 0.70 for intervals of several months.

The leadership situation. The other major variable of the contingency model is the leader's situational control or 'situational favorableness'. The method for operationally defining this concept is based on three subscales which indicate the degree to which (1) the leader is or feels accepted and supported by group members (leader–member relations); (2) the task is clear-cut, structured, and identifies the goals, procedures, and progress of the work (task structure); and (3) the leader has the ability to reward and punish, and thus to obtain compliance through organizational sanctions (position power).

Groups can be categorized as being high or low on each of these three dimensions by dividing them at the median or on the basis of normative scores. This leads to an eight-cell classification from high situational control (octant 1) to low control (octant 8) (shown in Figure 1). Leaders

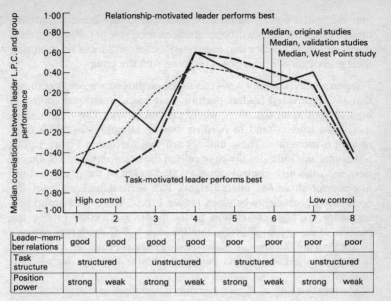

Figure 1 Median correlations between leader L.P.C. and group performance for studies conducted to test the contingency model

will have high control if they enjoy the support of the group, have a clearly structured task, and high position power. They will have low control if the group does not support them, the task is vague and unstructured, and position power is weak. When measuring situational control, leader–member relations are given a weight of 4, task structure a weight of 2, and position power a weight of 1. This weighting system has been supported by several empirical studies (Beach, Mitchell, and Beach, 1975; Nebeker, 1975).

Having high control implies that leaders will be assured that their particular goals and needs will be attained. Under these conditions, relationship-motivated leaders will worry less about interpersonal relations with the group and more about earning esteem from their boss or other important people in the organization. They accomplish this by showing concern for the job and exhibiting task-directive behavior. Task-motivated leaders in a high control situation are assured that the job will be accomplished and will devote themselves to improving and cementing relations with group members.

Low situational control will result in uncertainty and greater anxiety that the leader's goals will not be attained. Under these conditions, task-motivated leaders will concentrate on their goal of task accomplishment, while the relationship-motivated leaders will focus on achieving their goal of good interpersonal relations with the group.

The personality-situation interaction. The contingency model has shown that task-motivated leaders perform best when situational control is high as well as in situations where control is low. The relationship-motivated leaders tend to perform best in situations in which their control is moderate. These findings are summarized in Figure 1. The horizontal axis indicates the eight cells of the situational-control dimension, with the high-control situations on the left of the graph and the low-control situations on the right. The vertical axis indicates the correlation coefficients between leader L.P.C. scores and group performance. A high correlation in the positive direction (above the midline of the graph) indicates that the high-L.P.C. leaders performed better than did the low-L.P.C. leaders. A negative correlation indicates that the low-L.P.C. leaders performed better than the high-L.P.C. leaders.

The broken line in Figure 1 connects the median correlation coefficients of studies conducted prior to 1963; the solid line connects the median correlations obtained in validation studies since 1964. The dotted line shows the results of a major validation experiment conducted by Chemers and Skrzypek (1972) and provides the most convincing support of the contingency model.

In this study, L.P.C. scores as well as sociometric ratings to determine leader–member relations were obtained six weeks prior to the study. Eight groups were then experimentally assembled for each of the octants so that half the groups had high-L.P.C. leaders and half had low-L.P.C. leaders. Half of the groups consisted of men who had chosen each other sociometrically as preferred work companions while the other half had indicated a dislike for working with others who were placed on the same team. Half the groups, moreover, were given leaders with high-position power, and half the groups had leaders with low-position power.

As can be seen, the results of the Chemers and Skrzypek study almost exactly replicated the findings of the original studies. The correlation points of the original studies and the West Point study correlated 0·86 ($p < 0·01$) and a subsequent reanalysis by Shiflett (1973) showed that the West Point study accounted for 28 per cent of the variance in group performance.

As Figure 1 clearly indicates, the effectiveness of the group or organization depends on leader personality (leadership style) as well as situational control. For this reason, we cannot really talk about a 'good' leader or a 'poor' leader. Rather, leaders may be good in situations which match their leadership style and poor in situations in which leadership style and situational control are mismatched.

Situational control and the dynamics of the leadership process

Let us now extend the contingency model to encompass the dynamic interactions in the leadership process. The integrating concept which allows us to do this is the leader's situational control and influence. Situational control will change partly in response to environmental and organizational events and in part as the leader's abilities to cope with the organizational environment change. Thus, leaders may be given different assignments, greater or lesser authority, more compliant or more 'difficult' subordinates, or a more or a less supportive boss. Leaders may also learn through experience or training how to cope more effectively with the situation which confronts them, giving increased situational control or, in some cases, less control over their leadership situation.

As the contingency model has shown, leadership effectiveness depends on the proper match between situational control and leadership style as measured by the L.P.C. score. A major change in the organization or in the leader will necessarily change this match and thus increase or decrease leadership performance. The nature of this relationship is schematically shown in Figure 2. The horizontal axis indicates the degree to which the situation gives the leader control. The vertical axis indicates leadership performance. The solid line shows the performance of relationship-motivated (high-L.P.C.) leaders, and the dotted line the performance of task-motivated (low-L.P.C.) leaders. Again, of course, task-motivated leaders are shown as performing best in high- and low-control situations; relationship-motivated leaders are shown as performing best in moderate-control situations. Some of the major factors which would cause changes in the match to occur are presented below.

Experience. The most obvious and inevitable change which generally takes place in the leader's control is the result of time on the job and the concomitant increase in experience. The first days and months on a new job are almost invariably bewildering to the point where it is difficult to cope with the many problems which arise. This feeling of being out of

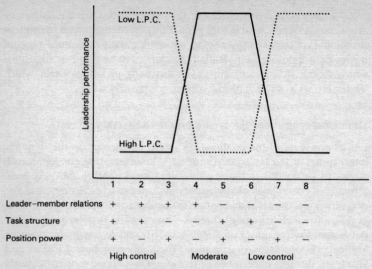

Figure 2 Schematic representation of the contingency model

control and in need of help gradually gives way, over time, to increasing confidence that we know what is going on. This process of feeling in control may take no longer than a few days for simple jobs, or several years for the complex and difficult assignments. Indeed, there are some jobs in which a leader may never really feel in control, no matter how long he or she has been in the position.

What does experience do for us? First of all, we learn the routines of the job. We know where things are, how we can get certain things done, and what the exact standards and requirements of the job are. In other words, the task, in our eyes, becomes more structured. Leaders also will become more familiar with subordinates. They learn what the group's idiosyncrasies are and how to handle them, and relations with them tend to become easier, more cordial, and mutually more supportive. Moreover, leaders will get to know their boss, what the superior's standards and expectations are, how to manage a relationship with him or her. Finally, with greater support from the boss and a better grasp of the informal and formal rules of the organization, leaders will know exactly how much power their position has, and how to use it.

By and large, then, we expect that the typical experience which comes with time on the job will correspondingly increase the leader's control over the leadership situation. This means that inexperienced leaders who come into low-control situations will perform well if they are task-motivated, but will gradually decrease in performance as the gain in experience makes the situation one of moderate control. Under the same conditions, relationship-motivated leaders will perform poorly, initially, and gradually become better as experience increases.

Similarly, if we take a situation in which the leader has moderate control upon beginning the job, we should find that the relationship-motivated person performs well at first, but decreases in effectiveness as he or she gains in experience and the situation becomes high in control. The opposite will be true of task-motivated leaders.

A study by Fielder, Bons, and Hastings (1975), using squad leaders of an infantry division, supports this hypothesis. These are first level supervisors who command a squad of between eight and twelve soldiers. The squad leaders were evaluated by two superiors shortly after the squads were formed, that is, while the division was still in a rather unsettled state; the leaders did not yet know their subordinates well, nor did they know their superiors well. A second performance evaluation was obtained from the same raters about five months later, after the unit had gone through training and completed their combat readiness tests.

An assessment of the leadership situation was obtained from outside judges and indicated that the situational control was moderate for the leaders at the time the division was established, but high after the leaders had gained experience and the division had shaken down. Figure 3 shows the results when we compare the performance ratings of the same leaders by the same raters at the first and second time of evaluation. Similar results have been reported elsewhere (Fielder and Chemers, 1974).

Training. We would expect, of course, that the effect of training will be quite similar to that of experience, provided that the training is relevant and reflects the experience of others who have been successful in the position. However, a considerable amount of leadership training has been devoted to participative and non-directive approaches which would, by and large, reduce the leader's control since the leader must share information and decision making functions with group members. It is, therefore, not always clear what effects training will have on leadership control. On the other hand, task training almost certainly will increase the perceived structure of the assignment and the leader's situational control.

A well-designed leadership training experiment conducted by Chemers, Rice, Sundstrom, and Butler (1975) demonstrates the effects of this

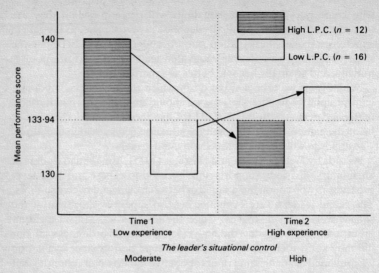

Figure 3 Change in performance of high- and low-L.P.C. leaders as a function of increased experience over five months (interaction significant)

intervention. A sample of twenty R.O.T.C. cadets with high and twenty with low L.P.C. scores were selected as leaders, while those with intermediate L.P.C. scores along with students from a psychology class served as group members in this experiment. The three-man groups were further divided at random into those who received task training and those who were given no training. The assignment consisted of deciphering a series of coded messages. The training consisted of teaching the leaders some simple rules of decoding, e.g. that the most frequent letter in the English alphabet is 'e', that the most frequent three-letter word with 'e' at the end is 'the', that the only one-letter words are 'I' and 'a', etc.

The group climate scores were quite low, and the position power of the leaders was also low. Untrained leaders, who had an unstructured task, had low control, while trained leaders had a moderate degree of situational control. This means that the untrained low-L.P.C. leaders should perform better than the untrained high-L.P.C. leaders, while the trained high-L.P.C. leaders should outperform the trained low-L.P.C. leaders. The interaction between L.P.C. and training is statistically highly significant (Figure 4). The finding is especially startling since the trained low-L.P.C. leaders not only performed less well than high-

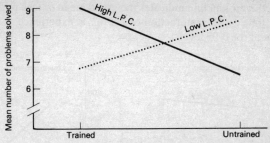

Figure 4   The effect of training and L.P.C. on group productivity

L.P.C. leaders, but they also performed less well than did the untrained low-L.P.C. leaders.

Organizational turbulence. Changes in the organizational structure and function also affect the leader's situational control. These changes require the leader to adapt to new conditions and to learn how to cope with situations which are unfamiliar and which have less certain and less predictable outcomes. This is particularly true when the leader is given a new job which typically also means that the boss is new as are the leader's subordinates.

A study by Bons and Fiedler (1976) of squad leaders illustrates the effects of these changes on leader performance and behavior. One additional point needed to be considered in this study. Some of the squad leaders were newly appointed to this first-level command position while others had been squad leaders for several years – in fact, some for as many as ten years. For the latter, the situation obviously presented fewer new elements than it did for the newer, younger soldiers. For this reason, data for experienced and inexperienced squad leaders were analyzed separately, with the expectation that the situation would provide more control for the experienced than for the inexperienced leaders. Performance was assessed on the basis of ratings by two superiors.

In the sample of experienced leaders there was no evidence that task performance had been affected substantially by organizational turbulence. In the group of inexperienced leaders, however, a change in job was associated with a markedly lower task performance on the part of high-L.P.C. leaders at time 2. Since we had made variance adjustments for time 1 performance scores, these data imply that task performance of relationship-motivated leaders had decreased as a result of change in job, while that of task-motivated leaders had slightly increased. (See

Figure 5; the broken line indicates the grand mean of task performance scores at time 1. The interaction of L.P.C. × experience × change is significant at the 0·05 level.)

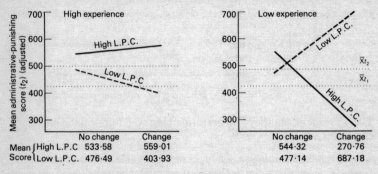

Figure 5   Task-performance behavior as a function of L.P.C. and change in job for given levels of leader experience

Leadership selection and placement

Current theory and practice in leadership selection best typifies the non-dynamic nature of present thinking in this area. We try to select managers and leaders with the well-worn notion that round pegs belong in round holes and square pegs in square holes. This is fine as long as the pegs and holes do not change their shape. As we have seen, however, changes in leaders' ability and job knowledge affect their situational control, and thus the match between leadership style and situational control.

This match may be excellent as the leader enters on a new job and he or she tends to perform well at first. However, leadership performance is likely to change as the leader gains greater control over the situation through experience and training. Thus, if the situation provides low control for the new leader, we would expect that the task-motivated individual will perform well and the relationship-motivated person will perform poorly. As experience and training increase situational control to 'moderate', the performance of the task-motivated leader will decrease and that of the relationship-motivated leader will increase. The opposite will be the case if the situational control is moderate in the beginning and high later on. Then, the relationship-motivated leader will perform well at first and poorly later on.

If selection and placement procedures are to be effective, they must take account of these dynamic changes. We must explicitly decide on the strategy which the organization should follow. As a rule, of course, selecting leaders to perform well when they are experienced will be best if the leadership job can be learned within a few weeks or months, even though the chosen leader may perform poorly at first.

A long-run strategy also will be more appropriate in very stable organizations in which the turnover of managerial personnel is very slow. However, in many organizations and especially in the military, it is rather unusual for a person to remain in the same job for more than one, two, or three years. This is also true in large organizations which have a policy of rotation as part of a managerial development program. Rapid change in the leadership structure may also be the result of various economic and environmental forces which impinge on the organization. Examples are found in large manufacturing and research-and-development organizations which utilize matrix or program management in order to accomplish special tasks or to develop specific product lines which are expected to discontinue after a given period of time.

Under these latter conditions, the requirements of the organization call for immediate top performance and a short-run strategy is clearly indicated. The organization must then be prepared to accept the possibility that a particular leader, who has been assigned to the same job for an extended period of time, is likely to become less effective and must again be moved to a more challenging job.

The amount of time which will elapse before a leadership situation will change from low control to moderate control, or from moderate to high control, will depend on the degree of structure and complexity of the task, and the intellectual abilities of the personnel who are available for these positions. For such tasks as infantry squad leader, the time at which this occurs may be four or five months; for school principals, it appears to be between two and three years; and for community college presidents, between five and six years. Some management jobs may require even longer before the leader gains maximum control.

The important point is, of course, that a rational selection and placement strategy cannot assume that the match between leader and job will remain a good fit forever. Rather, we must consider the effects which increased or decreased situational control will have on the selection process.

Situational control and leader behavior

Having shown that a change in situational control results in a change of leadership performance, we must now ask why a situational change should have this effect. Since we must eventually look to leader behavior as the mainspring for leadership performance, we need to determine how situational control affects the behaviors of relationship- and task-motivated leaders.

As mentioned earlier, the behavior of task- and relationship-motivated leaders differs in relaxed, high-control situations and in stressful, anxiety-arousing, low-control situations (Fiedler, 1972). A study by Meuwese and Fiedler (cited in Fiedler, 1967) will serve as an illustration. In this laboratory experiment, we compared the behavior of task- and relationship-motivated leaders of Reserve Officer Training Corps teams which were engaged in creative tasks. In one condition, the cadets worked under low stress, assured that their performance would have no bearing on their future military career. In another condition, the cadets were asked to appear in uniform and were continuously evaluated by a high-ranking officer who was seated directly across the table from the team. This latter condition was rated as quite stressful.

The comments made by leaders were categorized as relevant to developing good interpersonal relationships in the team, specifically involving group participation and democratic leadership behavior, and as task-relevant (proposing new ideas and integrating ideas of others). The results are shown in Figure 6 and support the interpretation that high- and low-L.P.C. scores reflect different goal- or motivational structures. That is, the behavior of the leader in the stressful condition

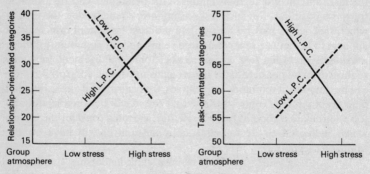

Figure 6   Effect of stress on behavior of relationship-motivated (high-L.P.C.) and task-motivated (low-L.P.C.) leaders

appears directed towards achieving the more basic goals, namely task achievement for the low-L.P.C., and good interpersonal relations for the high-L.P.C. leader. In the non-stressful condition in which the leader's control is high and he can feel sure of achieving his basic goals, the leader's behavior appears directed toward the attainment of secondary goals. These are a pleasant relationship for the low-L.P.C. leader and gaining the approval of others by task-relevant behavior on the part of the high-L.P.C. leader.

It is also possible to ask whether the leader's behavior will change as a result of a deliberate change in the leadership situation or one caused by organizational turbulence. According to the contingency model, an increase in the leader's control should make task-motivated individuals behave in a more considerate, social–emotional manner, while it should lessen the relationship-motivated leader's concern for group members. Lowering the leader's situational control should increase the relationship-motivated leader's concern for the group but decrease that of the task-motivated leader. Chemers (1969) tested this hypothesis using a culture-training program which was designed to improve the American leader's ability to deal with Iranian co-workers in a more effective and more secure manner.

Chemer's experiment used three-person groups which were to make recommendations on two controversial issues in Iran at the time: (1) employment of women and (2) appropriate training for low-status supervisors. At the end of the task sessions, the two Iranian group members described the leader's consideration behavior, the group climate, and their evaluation of the leader.

Half the leaders in the experiment were high- and the other half low-L.P.C. persons. These were randomly assigned either to the culture-training condition or to a condition involving control training: that is, training in the physical geography of Iran. The culture training was, of course, expected to increase the leader's control, enabling more effective interaction with group members.

As can be seen from Figure 7, the task-motivated leaders with culture training were seen as more considerate. They also were more esteemed and developed better group climate. The relationship-motivated leaders, on the other hand, were seen as less considerate and as having developed a poorer group climate. (The interaction between L.P.C. and training is significant.)

Let us now consider the effects which a stable leadership situation and an unstable, turbulent leadership environment will have on leader behavior. A stable environment should increase the leader's control and

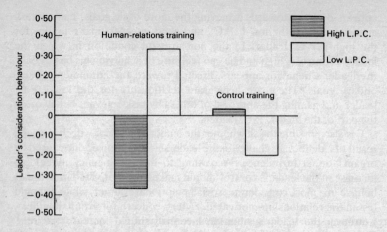

Figure 7 Effects of human-relations training on considerate behavior of high- and low-L.P.C. leaders

thus cause the relationship-motivated leader to become less concerned with group member relations, while the task-motivated leader should become more concerned with interpersonal relations in the group. However, a leadership environment characterized by change and turbulence should cause anxiety and insecurity. Under these conditions the relationship-motivated leader will seek the support of group members, while the task-motivated leader will become more dominant in order to assure that the job gets done. We assume, then, that a tendency to reward will improve interpersonal relations, while a tendency to be punitive implies the desire for stronger control and concern for task accomplishment.

The study of infantry squad leaders, discussed earlier, provides data which support this hypothesis. Figure 8 shows time 2 mean scores on rewarding behavior as rated by subordinates and adjusted for time 1 scores. The broken line indicates the grand mean for time 1. As can be seen, there is little difference in rewarding behavior for the group leaders who experienced no job change in the six to eight months which intervened between the first and second testing sessions. However, in the group which experienced a turbulent environment, the differences in time 2 rewarding behavior are substantial and the L.P.C. × change interaction is significant. We may thus infer that the high-L.P.C. leaders became more rewarding while the low-L.P.C. leaders became less

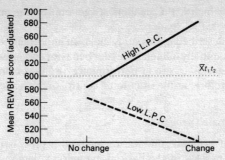

Figure 8 Rewarding behavior (REWBH) as a function of L.P.C. and change in job

rewarding as a consequence of the lower situational control resulting from being assigned to a new job.

The opposite trend emerged from the analysis of administrative punishment behaviors (e.g. threatened or actual reduction or demotion or placement in the stockade). Figure 9 indicates the effects on administrative punishment behavior when both of the leader's superiors (platoon sergeant and platoon leader) are replaced in the time period $t_1 - t_2$. The L.P.C. × experience × change interaction is significant. For the inexperienced leaders the turbulent condition (new superiors) is associated with more punitive behavior on the part of low-L.P.C. leaders but less punitive behavior on the part of high-L.P.C. leaders. Among leaders with high experience who have considerable control over their

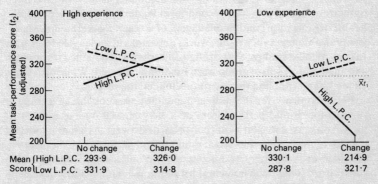

Figure 9 Administrative punishing behavior as a function of L.P.C. and change in boss for leaders with high and low experience

situation, the high-L.P.C. leaders are generally more punitive at time 2 than are low-L.P.C. leaders.

The data described in this study make an important point. Situational control substantially influences leader behavior and, presumably, leader behavior determines group performance. Behavior and performance change, therefore, as the situational control of the leader changes.

The leader match program

One type of evidence that we understand a process is the ability to change the process in the desired manner. A demonstration that we know how to improve leadership performance, therefore, gives some hope that we are beginning to understand the dynamics of organizational leadership.

We recently developed a self-paced programmed instruction manual entitled *Leader Match* (Fiedler, Chemers, & Mahar, 1976), which incorporates the principles of the contingency model. Specifically, leaders are instructed to take the L.P.C. scale and to interpret their score. They are given detailed instructions on how to measure leader–member relations, task structure, and position power, using various scales and appropriate exercises and feedback. Finally, the manual provides guidance on how to modify the leadership situation so that it will provide the appropriate degree of situational control.

As of this date, eight successive validation studies have yielded significant results which indicate that leaders who are trained with this program tend to perform significantly more effectively than do those not so trained. Four of these studies were conducted in various civilian organizations and involved second-level leaders of a volunteer public-health organization, middle managers of a county government, supervisors and managers of a public works department, and police sergeants. In each of these studies, a list of eligible leaders was obtained from which a trained and a control group were randomly selected. While all studies yielded significant findings, attrition clouded the results.

Better control over the subject population was possible in a study of junior officers and petty officers of a navy air station and a study of junior officers and petty officers on a destroyer. Again trained and control subjects were selected at random, and performance ratings were obtained at the time of training and six months later from the same supervisors. There was no voluntary attrition in either study. As can be seen from Table 1, the trained group significantly improved in performance when compared to the control group.

Table 1 Comparison of mean change scores for trained and control group leaders

Change score for	Group	N	$\bar{X}$	S.D.	t	p*	ω^2
Overall performance	Trained	27	0·5741	0·786	3.58	<0·001	0·174
	Control	29	−0·4595	1·257			
Task performance	Trained	27	0·5872	0·696	3·89	<0·001	0·202
	Control	29	−0·5158	1·283			
Personnel performance	Trained	27	0·5213	0·921	2·93	<0·002	0·120
	Control	29	−0·3659	1·246			

*Probability is one-tailed

Two other studies were conducted by Csoka and Bons (personal communication). The first used officer trainees who were scheduled to become acting platoon leaders in operational units. One-third of 154 men were randomly selected for training while the others were used as controls. At the end of the test period, the unit officers' evaluations showed the *Leader-Match*-trained leaders to be performing better than untrained men within the same unit.

A second study involved training one randomly selected platoon leader in three from each of twenty-seven training companies. At the end of a four-month period, evaluation of all platoon leaders showed that the trained leaders were significantly more often chosen as the best of the three in their company.

Although the investigations are not yet complete, preliminary data show that the training with the *Leader Match* program did enable leaders to modify their leadership so as to maintain the appropriate balance between their leadership style and situational control. Thus using situational control as the key concept in a dynamic interpretation of the leadership process appears to be a highly promising and cost-effective approach.

Conclusion

This study presents a dynamic interpretation of the contingency model in which the leader's situational control emerges as the critical variable for interpreting the complex processes of leadership performance in changing organizational environments. This interpretation accounts for the disappointing results which previous leadership-training programs have yielded and the low correlations between years of leadership experience and leadership performance. Training and experience typically provide the leader with greater control while organizational turbulence, shake-ups in management, and similar events cause uncertainty and lessen the leader's control over the situation.

Recent research shows that we can improve organizational performance by teaching the leader how to diagnose and modify situational control in order to maintain an optimal match between leadership style and situation in a continuously changing organizational environment. These findings provide further important evidence that we are beginning to understand the dynamics of the leadership process.

References

BALES, R. F. (1951), *Interaction Process Analysis*, Addison-Wesley.

BEACH, B. H., MITCHELL, T. R., and BEACH, L. R. (1975), *Components of Situational Favorableness and Probability of Success*, Organizational Research Technical Report 75–66, University of Washington, Seattle.

BONS, P. M., and FIEDLER, F. E. (1976), 'The effect of changes in command on the behavior of subordinate leaders in military units', *Administrative Science Quarterly*, 21, pp. 433–72.

CATTELL, R. B. (1951), 'New concepts for measuring leadership in terms of group syntality', *Human Relations*, 4, pp. 161–84.

CHEMERS, M. M. (1969), 'Cross-cultural training as a means for improving situational favorableness', *Human Relations*, 22, pp. 531–46.

CHEMERS, M. M., RICE, R. W., SUNDSTROM, E., and BUTLER, W. (1975), 'Leader esteem for the least preferred coworker score, training, and effectiveness: An experimental examination', *Journal of Personality and Social Psychology*, 31, pp. 401–9.

CHEMERS, M. M., and SKRZYPEK, G. J. (1972), 'An experimental test of the Contingency Model of leadership effectiveness', *Journal of Personality and Social Psychology*, 24, pp. 172–7.

FIELDER, F. E. (1964), 'A contingency model of leadership effectiveness', *Advances in experimental social psychology*, L. Berkowitz (ed.), vol. 1, Academic Press.

FIEDLER, F. E. (1967), *A theory of leadership effectiveness*, McGraw-Hill.

FIEDLER, F. E. (1972), 'Personality, motivational systems, and behavior of high and low L.P.C. persons', *Human Relations*, 25, pp. 391–412.

FIEDLER, F. E., BONS, P. M., and Hastings, L. L. (1975), 'The utilization of leadership resources', *Measurement of human resources*, W. T. Singleton and P. Spurgeon (eds.), Taylor and Francis.

FIEDLER, F. E., and CHEMERS, M. M. (1974), *Leadership and effective management*, Scott Foresman.

FIEDLER, F. E., CHEMERS, M. M., and MAHAR, L. (1976), *Improving leadership effectiveness: The leader match concept*, Wiley.

FLEISHMAN, E. A., HARRIS, E. F., and BURT, H. E. (1955), *Leadership and supervision in industry*, Ohio State University.

HOUSE, R. J. (1971), 'A path goal theory of leader effectiveness', *Administrative Science Quarterly*, 16, pp. 321–38.

LIKERT, R. (1961), *New patterns of management*, McGraw-Hill.

MANN, R. D. (1959), 'A review of the relationships between personality and performance in small groups', *Psychological Bulletin*, 56, pp. 241–70.

MEHRENS, W. A., and LEHMANN, I. J. (1973), *Standardized tests in education*. Macmillan.

NEBEKER, D. M. (1975), 'Situational favorability and environmental uncertainty: An integrative study', *Administrative Science Quarterly*, 20, pp. 281–94.

RICE, R. W. (1977), 'Psychometric properties of the esteem for least preferred coworker (L.P.C) scale', *Academy of Management Review*, in press.

SAX, G. (1974), *Principles of education measurement and evaluation*, Wadsworth.

SHIFLETT, S. C. (1973), 'The contingency model of leadership effectiveness: Some implications of its statistical and methodological properties', *Behavioral Science*, 18, pp. 429–40.

STOGDILL, R. (1948), 'Personal factors associated with leadership: A survey of the literature', *Journal of Psychology*, 25, pp. 35–71.

STOGDILL, R. (1974), *Handbook of leadership*. The Free Press.

STOGDILL, R. M., and COONS, A. E. (1957), *Leader behavior: Its description and measurement*, Ohio State University Monograph 88.

VROOM, V. H., and YETTON, P. W. (1973), *Leadership and decision making*, University of Pittsburgh Press.

23 E. A. Trist and K. W. Bamforth

Some Social and Psychological Consequences of the Longwall Method of Coal-getting

From E. L. Trist and K. W. Bamforth, 'Some social and psychological consequences of the longwall method of coal-getting', *Human Relations*, 1951, vol. 4, no. 1, pp. 6–24 and 37–8.

The character of the pre-mechanized equilibrium and the nature of its disturbance

Hand-got systems and the responsible autonomy of the pair-based work group

The outstanding feature of the social pattern with which the pre-mechanized equilibrium was associated is its emphasis on small group organization at the coal-face. The groups themselves were interdependent working pairs to whom one or two extra individuals might be attached. It was common practice for two colliers – a hewer and his mate – to make their own contract with the colliery management and to work their own small face with the assistance of a boy 'trammer'. This working unit could function equally well in a variety of engineering layouts both of the advance and retreat type, whether step-wise or direct. Sometimes it extended its numbers to seven or eight, when three or four colliers, and their attendant trammers, would work togther.[1]

A primary work-organization of this type had the advantage of placing responsibility for the complete coal-getting task squarely on the shoulders of a single, small, face-to-face group which experiences the entire cycle of operations within the compass of its membership. For each participant the task has total significance and dynamic closure. Though the contract may have been in the name of the hewer, it was regarded as a joint undertaking. Leadership and 'supervision' were internal to the group, which had a quality of *responsible autonomy*. The capacity of these groups for self-regulation was a function of the wholeness of their work task, this connection being represented in their contractual status. A whole has power as an independent detachment, but a part requires external control.

1. Hand-got methods contained a number of variants, but discussion of these is beyond present scope.

Within these pair-based units was contained the full range of coal-face skills; each collier being an all-round workman, usually able to substitute for his mate. Though his equipment was simple, his tasks were multiple. The 'underground skill' on which their efficient and safe execution depended was almost entirely person-carried. He had craft pride and artisan independence. These qualities obviated status difficulties and contributed to responsible autonomy.

Choice of workmates posed a crucial question. These choices were made by the men themselves, sociometrically, under full pressure of the reality situation and with long-standing knowledge of each other. Stable relationships tended to result, which frequently endured over many years. In circumstances where a man was injured or killed, it was not uncommon for his mate to care for his family. These work relationships were often reinforced by kinship ties, the contract system and the small group autonomy allowing a close but spontaneous connection to be maintained between family and occupation, which avoided tying the one to the other. In segregated mining communities the link between kinship and occupation can be oppressive as well as supportive; against this danger, 'exogamous' choice was a safeguard. But against too emotional a relationship, more likely to develop between non-kin associates, kinship barriers were in turn a safeguard.

The wholeness of the work task, the multiplicity of the skills of the individual, and the self-selection of the group were congruent attributes of a pattern of responsible autonomy that characterized the pair-based face teams of hand-got mining.

The adaptability of the small group to the underground situation

Being able to work their own short faces continuously, these pair, or near pair, groups could stop at whatever point may have been reached by the end of a shift. The flexibility in work pace so allowed had special advantages in the underground situation; for when bad conditions were encountered, the extraction process in a series of stalls could proceed unevenly in correspondence with the uneven distribution of these bad conditions, which tend to occur now in one and now in another section along a seam. Even under good conditions, groups of this kind were free to set their own targets, so that aspirations levels with respect to production could be adjusted to the age and stamina of the individuals concerned.

In the underground situation external dangers must be faced in darkness. Darkness also awakens internal dangers. The need to share with others anxieties aroused by this double threat may be taken as self-evident. In view of the restricted range of effective communication, these others have to be immediately present. Their number therefore is limited. These conditions point to the strong need in the underground worker for a role in a small primary group.

A second characteristic of the underground situation is the wide dispersal of particular activities, in view of the large area over which operations generally are extended. The small groups of the hand-got systems tended to become isolated from each other even when working in the same series of stalls; the isolation of the group, as of the individual, being intensified by the darkness. Under these conditions there is no possibility of continuous supervision, in the factory sense, from any individual external to the primary work group.

The small group, capable of responsible autonomy, and able to vary its work pace in correspondence with changing conditions, would appear to be the type of social structure ideally adapted to the underground situation. It is instructive that the traditional work systems, evolved from the experience of successive generations, should have been founded on a group with these attributes.

But to earn a living under hand-got conditions often entailed physical effort of a formidable order, and possession of exceptional skill was required to extract a bare existence from a hard seam with a bad roof. To tram tubs was 'horse-work'. Trammers were commonly identified by scabs, called 'buttons', on the bone joints of their backs, caused by catching the roof while pushing and holding tubs on and off 'the gates'. Hand-got conditions still obtain, for by no means all faces are serviced by conveyors and coal-cutters. In some circumstances this equipment is unsuitable. But hardness of work is a separate consideration from the quality of the group.

The counter balance of the large undifferentiated collectivity

The psychological disadvantages of a work system, the small group organization of which is based on pair relationships, raised issues of a far-reaching kind only recently submitted to study in group dynamics (Bion, 1949). It would appear that the self-enclosed character of the relationship makes it difficult for groups of this kind to combine effectively in differentiated structures of a somewhat larger social magnitude, though this inability does not seem to hold in respect of much larger collectivities of a simpler mass character. But in pre-mechanized mining there was no technological necessity for intermediate structures, equivalent to factory departments, to make their appearance between the small pair-based primary units and the larger collectivities called into action by situations of crisis and common danger. To meet situations requiring the mobilization of the large mass group, mining communities have developed traditions generally recognized as above the norm commonly attained by occupational groups in our society. This supra-normative quality was present also in the traditions of the small pair-based organizations. But between these extremes there was little experience.

Sociologically, this situation is not atypical of industries which, though large-scale, have experienced delay in undergoing mechaniz-ation. The pair-based face teams corresponded to the technological simplicity of the hand-got methods, with their short faces, auton-omously worked and loosely coordinated on a district basis. The mass collectivities reflected the large-scale size of the pit as an overall indus-trial unit. Absent were structures at the level of the factory depart-ment, whose process-linked, fractionated role-systems, dependent on external supervision, were antithetical alike to the pattern of small group autonomy and to the artisan outlook of the collier.

In the pre-mechanized pattern, the pair-based primaries and the large relatively undifferentiated collectivities composed a dynamically inter-related system that permitted an enduring social balance. The intense reciprocities of the former, with their personal and family significance, and the diffuse identifications of the latter, with their community and class connectedness, were mutually supportive. The face teams could bear the responsibility of their autonomy through the security of their dependence on the united collectivity of the pit.

Difficulties arose largely from rivalries and conflicts between the various pairs and small teams. A common form of 'graft' was to bribe the deputy in order to secure a good 'benk', i.e. a 'length' with a 'rack roof', under which the coal was notoriously soft and easy to work. Trammers were encouraged to resort to sharp practices to obtain adequate supplies of tubs. As supplies were often short, the amount of coal a working pair could send up depended not a little on the prowess of their trammer. Going early to work, he would turn two or three tubs on their sides in his 'gate', maintaining he had taken only one. Ensuing disputes caused frequent fights both underground and in the community. In the common saying, it was he who could lie, cheat, or bully the most who made the best trammer. All this was accepted as part of the system.

Inter-team conflict provided a channel for aggression that preserved intact the loyalties on which the small group depended. In the large group aggression received structured expression in trade-union resistance. If the struggle was harsh, it was at least direct and understandable. It was not the insidious kind that knocked the bottom out of life, leaving those concerned without a sense of a scheme in things – the 'anomic' described by Halliday (1949) after the transition to the longwall. The system as a whole contained its bad in a way that did not destroy its good. The balance persisted, albeit that work was of the hardest, rewards often meagre, and the social climate rough at times and even violent.

Mechanization and the problem of intermediate organization

With the advent of coal-cutters and mechanical conveyors, the degree of technological complexity of the coal-getting task was raised to a different level. Mechanization made possible the working of a single long face in place of a series of short faces. In thin seams short faces increase costs, since a large number of 'gates' (see Figure 1) have to be 'ripped' up several feet above the height of the seam to create haulage and travelling facilities. In British coal, seams less than 4 ft in thickness are common, so that there was a tendency to make full use of the possibility of working optimally long rather than optimally short faces. For this reason, and for others also, discussion of which is beyond present scope, the longwall method came into being. Applicable to thick as well as to thin seams, it became the general method of coal-getting in the British industry, enabling the average type of pit, which may contain three or four seams of different thickness, to work its entire coal economically, and to develop its layout and organize its production in terms of a single, self-consistent plan. In America, where thick seams are the rule, mechanization has developed in terms of shorter faces and room-and-pillar techniques.

The associated characteristics of mechanized complexity, and of largeness as regards the scale of the primary production unit, created a situation in which it was impossible for the method to develop as a technological system without bringing into existence a work relationship structure radically different from that associated with hand-got procedures. The artisan type of pair, composed of the skilled man and his mate, assisted by one or more labourers, was out of keeping as a model for the type of work group required. Need arose for a unit more of the size and differentiated complexity of a small factory department. A structure of intermediate social magnitude began therefore to emerge. The basic pattern round which the work relationships of the longwall production unit were organized became the cycle group of 40–50 men, their shot-firer and shift 'deputies', who were responsible to the pit management for the working as a whole. Only in relation to this total cycle group could various smaller sub-groups secure function and acquire social form.

This centring of the new system on a differentiated structure of intermediate social magnitude disturbed the simple balance that had existed between the very small and very large traditional groups, and impaired the quality of responsible autonomy. The psychological and sociological problems posed by the technological needs of the longwall system were those with respect to which experience in the industry was least, and towards which its traditions were antithetical. The consequences of this conflict between the demands of the new situation and the resources available from past experience will be taken up in the light of the detailed account, which will now be presented, of the longwall system itself.

The lack of recognition of the nature of the difficulties

No new equilibrium came into being. As was mentioned in the introduction, disturbances associated with industrial struggle and economic depression have tended to mask those associated with the coal-getting method. Though perception of these latter has begun to clarify since nationalization, shortcomings such as those in the haulage system, more readily appreciated in engineering terms, continue to attract the wider attention. It is only since the morale changes accompanying recent face-work innovations have begun actually to be experienced in working groups that the nature of longwall troubles is becoming manifest. That they require understanding in social and psychological terms is something that still remains largely unrecognized. Accounts so far appearing have presented recent changes almost exclusively in engineering terms.

Anyone who has listened to the talk of older miners who have experienced in their own work-lives the change-over to the longwall cannot fail to be impressed by the confused mourning for the past that still goes on in them together with a dismay over the present coloured by despair and indignation. To the clinical worker the quality of these talks has at times a ring that is familiar. Those with rehabilitation experience will recognize it as similar to the quality of feeling expressed by rehabilitees when ventilating the aftermath in themselves of an impairment accepted as irreversible.

Expectation was widespread that something magical would happen as a result of nationalization. But as one filler put it: 'My coals don't wear any new look since Investment Day. They give me a look as black as before.' When some of these same men take on a new lease of life, perhaps exaggeratedly, after experiencing one of the new group methods and refuse to return to a conventional working having found a new spirit in themselves and their work-mates, strong clues are already to hand regarding the character of longwall deficiencies. But what has been intuitively grasped has still to become articulate. So close is the relationship between the various aspects that the social and the psychological can be understood only in terms of the detailed engineering facts and of the way the technological system as a whole behaves in the environment of the underground situation. These points will be taken up in the next two Sections.

Features and difficulties of the longwall production unit as a whole[2]

The scale and spatio-temporal structure of the three-shift cycle

In the longwall method, a direct advance is made into the coal on a continuous front; faces of 180–200 yds being typical, though longer faces are not uncommon. The work is broken down into a standard series of component operations that follow each other in rigid succession over three shifts of seven and a half hours each, so that a total coal-getting cycle may be completed once in each twenty-four hours of the working week. The shift spread of the forty workmen on an average face is: ten

2. The procedure followed both in the text and in Figures 1 and 2 and Table 1 has been to build up a model of the system in terms of the experience of a group of faces similarly run and well known at first hand. What follows is therefore an account of one version of the system, though the version is a common one. Faces exist that are twice as long as that given. In thick seams these may require 40–50 fillers alone (even more), apart altogether from other personnel. In thin seams with high gates more than twice the number of rippers given may be employed, eight or more on the main gate and some 6–4 on the side gates respectively. On shorter faces there may be only one borer and at least one gummer. Under some conditions packing and drawing-off are separated from belt-work, and loading-point personnel are included as face workers. There are differences in nomenclature in different areas, e.g. 'dinters' for 'rippers'. Variations arise partly from differences in natural conditions (thickness of seam, hardness of coal, type of roof and floor, etc.), partly from preferences in the matter of lay-out, and partly from the amount and character of the equipment available or judged necessary. Though conveyor serviced, quite a long face may be hand-got if the coal is soft; alternatively, two cutting units may be employed if it is hard and the face exceptionally long. Belts are of several varieties ('floor', 'plate', 'top', etc.). Where the seam is thick enough to eliminate ripping an approximation may be made to a two-shift system. Productivity varies widely in accordance with these differences, as does smoothness of functioning and the degree of stress experienced. Nevertheless, all are versions of one method. The basic pattern is the same.

each to the first ('cutting') and second ('ripping') shifts; twenty to the third ('filling') shift. The amount of coal scheduled for extraction varies under different conditions but is commonly in the neighbourhood of 200 tons per cycle. A medium-size pit with three seams would have 12–15 longwall faces in operation simultaneously.

These faces are laid out in districts as shown in Figure 1. Since the longwall method is specially applicable to thin seams, Figure 1 has been set up in terms of a 3-ft working. The face, extending 90 yds on either side of the main gate, is within average limits for a seam of this thickness. The height of the face area – that of the 3-ft seam itself – may be contrasted with the 9 ft and 7 ft to which the main and side gates have been ripped and built up as permanent structures with cambers and

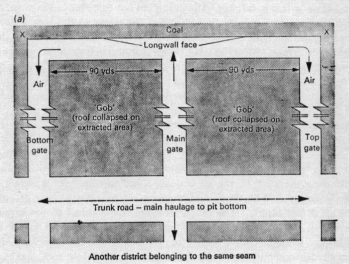

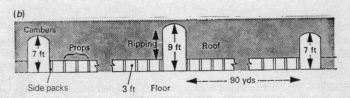

Figure 1   Layout of a district, longwall method: (a) horizontal section, (b) vertical section (at point X in (a))

side-packs. By regulation, props must be placed every 3 ft, and the line of props shown in Figure 1(b) is that placed immediately against a coal-face waiting to be filled off. The area marked 'Gob' (to use a term common in mining vernacular) indicates the expanse from which the coal has already been extracted. On this area the roof is left to collapse. Only the tunnels made by the main and side gates, which are used for ventilation and for haulage and travelling, are kept open. These tunnels may sometimes extend for distances of two miles, and even more, before the coal face itself is reached from the trunk road leading from the pit bottom.

In each coal-getting cycle the advance made into the coal is equal to the depth of the undercut. A cut of 6 ft represents typical practice in a thin seam with a good roof. All equipment has to be moved forward as each cycle contributes to the advance. The detail in the face area is represented in Figure 2, where the coal is shown cut and waiting for the shot-firer, whose task is the last to be performed before the fillers come on. The combined width of the lanes marked 'New Creeping Track' and 'New Conveyor Track' equal the depth of 6 ft, from which the coal has been removed by the fillers on the last shift of the previous cycle. As part of the preparation work of the current cycle (before the fillers can come on again), the conveyor has to be moved from its previous position in the 'Old Conveyor Track' to its present position, shown in Figure 2, in the 'new Conveyor Track', against the face. At the same time the two lines of props on either side of the 'Old Creeping Track' are withdrawn (allowing the roof to sag or collapse) and thrown over beside the conveyor for the fillers to use in propping up their roof as they get into the next 6 ft of coal. The term 'creeping track' refers to the single, propped, 3-ft lane, adjacent to that occupied by the conveyor but on the side away from the coal. It allows free passage up and down the face, and is called a creeping track since in thin seams the low roof makes it necessary for all locomotion to take the form of 'creeping', i.e. crawling on the hands and knees.

The mass-production character of the longwall operation necessitates a large-scale, mobile layout of the type described. But the spatio-temporal structure imposed by the long face and the shift sequence makes a difficult habitat when considered as a theatre in which effective communication and good working relationships must be maintained between forty men, their shot-firer and shift deputies. On the one hand, the group is spread over 200 yds in a tunnel 2 yds wide and 1 yd high, cross-cut only by the main and side gates; on the other, it is spread over twenty-four hours and divided up in three successive shifts. The produc-

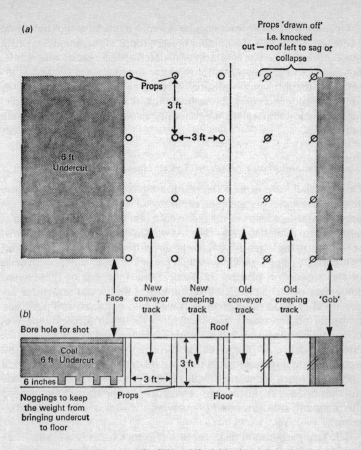

(a)

Props 'drawn off' i.e. knocked out — roof left to sag or collapse

Props

3 ft

← 3 ft →

6 ft Undercut

Face   New conveyor track   New creeping track   Old conveyor track   Old creeping track   'Gob'

(b)

Bore hole for shot   Roof

Coal 6 ft Undercut

3 ft

6 inches   ← 3 ft →

Noggings to keep the weight from bringing undercut to floor   Props   Floor

Figure 2   Coal face as set for filling shift: (a) horizontal section, (b) vertical section – side elevation

tion engineer might write a simple equation: 200 tons equals forty men over 200 yds over twenty-four hours. But there are no solutions of equivalent simplicity to the psychological and social difficulties raised. For psychological and social difficulties of a new order appear when the scale of a task transcends the limits of simple spatio-temporal structure. By this is meant conditions under which those concerned can complete a job in one place at one time, i.e. the situation of the face-to-face or singular group.

Once a job is too big for a singular group, a multiple group comes into existence, composed of a number of sub-groups of the singular type. In these differentiated organizations of intermediate social magnitude, problems of inter-group relationships are superimposed on, and interact with, the intra-group tensions of the primary components. In the longwall production unit, the scale of the task introduces the contradiction of spatio-temporal disintegration as a condition of multiple group integration.

The differentiation and interdependence of tasks

Occupational roles express the relationship between a production process and the social organization of the group. In one direction, they are related to tasks, which are related to each other; in the other, to people, who are also related to each other. At workman level, there are seven of these roles in the longwall system – borer, cutter, gummer, belt-breaker, belt-builder, ripper and filler – which are linked to the component tasks of the product on process. In Table 1 the functions of these seven categories in the interrelated technological and social structures are described in detail in a comprehensive table. For analytical purposes, however, it is necessary to treat separately these two different aspects of occupational roles; and, in this section, consideration will be given to the interdependence of component tasks in the production process, and to occupational roles so far as they are related to this. These tasks fall into four groups, concerned with (1) the preparation of the coalface for shot-firing, (2) shifting the conveyor, (3) ripping and building up the main and side gates and (4) moving the shot coal on to the conveyor.

The face preparation tasks are all performed on the first shift. They include boring holes for the shot-firer, with pneumatic or electrically operated drills, near the roof of the seam through to the depth of the undercut, at short distances (within each filler's 'length') along the entire expanse of face; driving the coal-cutter so that the blade or 'jib' makes an even undercut into the coal some six inches from the floor to whatever depth has been assigned, again along the entire expanse of face; taking out the six inches of coal (called the 'gummings') left in the undercut, so that the main weight of coal can drop and break freely when the shots are fired; placing supporting 'noggings' underneath it so that this weight does not cause it to sag down to the floor while the 'cut' is standing during the next shift. These tasks are performed in the order given. Three of the seven work roles are associated with their execution, two men being fully occupied boring the holes, a further two in managing the coal-cutter, and four in clearing out the undercut.

The success of the shots fired at the end of the second shift to make the coal finally ready for the filler depends on the efficiency with which each of these interdependent preparation tasks has been carried out. Bad execution of any one of them diminishes, and may even cancel out, the effect of the shots, with consequent havoc in the lengths of the particular fillers where such breakdowns have occurred. Holes bored too low leave a quantity of coal, difficult to extract, clinging to the roof after the shots have been fired. If the roof is sticky, this gives rise to 'sticky tops'. Holes not bored through to the full depth of the undercut create the condition of 'hard backs', the shots having no effect on this part of the coal. The coal-cutter only too frequently has a tendency to leave the floor and 'get up into the coal', producing an uneven cut. This means less working height for the filler, and also less wages, since his tonnage is reduced. When the 'gummings' are left in, the shot is wasted; the coal has nowhere to drop and the powder blows out of the hole (usually up the 'cutting break' in the roof) so that the mass to be extracted is left solid. Failure to insert noggings, which leads to the cut sagging down, also renders useless the services of the shot-firer.

The group of operations concerned with the conveyor involves – since forward movement is blocked by props which must be left standing – breaking up the sections of belt in the old conveyor track and building them up in the new. Each of these tasks requires two men: the belt-breakers and belt-builders. The dismantling part is done on the first shift in the wake of the cutting operation. The reasons include the necessity of shifting belt-engines and tension-ends out of the gate areas (where they are positioned when the conveyor is working) in order to allow the ripping operation to proceed. The reassembly of the conveyor is the only task performed in the face area during the second shift. Unless the conveyor is properly jointed, set close to the new face, and accurately sighted in a straight line, a further crop of difficulties arise, and frequent stoppages may interfere with filling. The most modern types of belt, e.g. floor belts, avoid the labour of breaking up and re-assembling plates. Belt-engines and tension-ends are cumbersome equipment, but they must nevertheless be shifted every day. Similarly, the last two lines of props have to be taken down and thrown forward.

The third group of tasks comprises those that entail ripping up the roof of the main and side gates to the depth of the undercut, and building them up with a stable roof and firmly packed sides so that haulage- and air-ways can advance with the face. Unless this work is expertly done, the danger of roof falls is acute, with the likelihood of both men and equipment being blocked in the face. This work is carried out by a team of 7–8 rippers.

Only when all these operations have been completed can the shots be fired and the fillers come on. For the filling operation, the entire face is divided up into equal lengths – except that the corner positions are somewhat shorter in view of difficulties created by the proximity of belt-engines and tension-ends. In a 3-ft seam, lengths would be 8–10 yds, and some twenty fillers would be required, ten in each half-face of 90–100 yds. Each filler is required to extract the entire coal from his length, going back to the depth of the 6 ft undercut. When he has thrown his last load on to the conveyor he has 'filled off', i.e. finished his 'length' or 'stint'. As he progresses into his coal, he has the additional task of propping up his roof every 3 ft. As well as a handpick and shovel, his tool kit includes an air pick, used for dealing with some of the difficulties created by bad preparation, or in any case when his coal is hard.

At a later point there will be a discussion of the differential distribution of bad conditions among the lengths of a face. Here it may be noted that the face is not 'filled off' until each and every length has been cleared, and that until this has been done, the new cycle cannot begin. Disorganization on the filling shift disorganizes the subsequent shifts, and its own disorganization is often produced by the bad preparation left by these teams. Every time the cycle is stopped, some two hundred tons of coal are lost.

So close is the task interdependence that the system becomes vulnerable from its need for one hundred per cent performance at each step. The most sensitive interaction is between the face-preparation activities and filling, but it is in relation to this that social organization is weakest. This point will be taken up in later sections.

The segmented quality of the social organization

With respect to the way in which the work roles have been institutionalized as regards the persons and groups concerned, a basic segregation of the various categories of workers from each other follows from the fact that it has been the traditional practice for a face-worker to be trained in only one of the seven roles, and to spend all or most of his underground life in this one occupation. This basic segregation of roles is intensified by the five different methods of payment described in Table 1, and by the exaggeration of status differences, despite the common background of 'underground skill' and the equivalence of earnings (apart from the rather lower rate received by the gummers).

It is still further reinforced by the segregation of shifts. As will be seen from the shift time-tables, the three shifts never meet. Moreover, the two preparation groups alternate on the so-called 'back shifts' while the fillers alternate on 'days' and 'afternoons', so that a far-reaching community, as well as work, split is effected between the fillers and the others. The 'back shift' men are either going to or coming from work in the evening, so that they are cut off from normal community activities during the week. Even at weekends they are down the pit either on Saturday afternoon or Sunday evening.

As regards the primary work groups in which those performing the various roles participate, there are four radically different patterns: the series of interdependent pairs – borers, belt-builders and belt-breakers; the extended pair organization of the cutters and gummers; the self-sufficient group of eight rippers; and the aggregate of twenty fillers spread out over the 200-yd face. This unevenness, taken together with the role and shift segregation, works against the social integration of the cycle group as a whole. Yet, in view of the close interdependence of tasks, the social integration of the total work group is a first essential of the system.

It is submitted that the non-existence of the cycle group as a social whole in face of the interdependence of the component tasks is one of the major contradictions present in the longwall method. The social organization is a simple reflection of the 'job breakdown'. Because this latter is integrated into a technological whole by the task sequence it does not follow that the differentiated role-groups concerned are also and thereby reintegrated into a social whole. Differentiation gives rise to the need for social as well as technological integration. No attempt seems to have been made in the longwall method to achieve any living social integration of the primary and shift groups into which the cycle aggregate has been differentiated. This, of course, is a common omission in mass-production systems.

The stress of mass production in the underground situation

The interaction of bad conditions and bad work

Differentiated, rigidly sequenced work systems, organized on mass-production lines to deal with large quantities of material on a multi-shift cycle, are a basic feature of the factory pattern. Even in the factory

Table 1 Occupational structure in the longwall system

Shift sequence	Occupational roles	No. of men	Methods of payment	Group organization	Tasks	Skills	Status differences and ranking
First (usually called 'cutting' shift). Either night, 8 p.m.– 3.30 a.m. or afternoon, 12 noon–7.30 p.m. (borers start an hour earlier). Though alternating between night and afternoon, personnel on the cutting shift are never on days.	Borer	2	Per hole	Inter-dependent pair on same note.	Boring holes for shot-firer in each stint to depth of undercut.	Management of electric or pneumatic drills, placing of holes, judgement of roof, hardness of coal, etc.	4–5, equal in pair.
	Cutter	2	Per yard	Inter-dependent pair on same note, front man and back man.	Operating coal-cutter to achieve even cut at assigned depth the entire length of the face; knocking out (front man), re-setting (back man) props as cutter passes. Back man inserts noggings.	Requires rather more 'engineering' skill than other coal-face tasks. Mining skills in keeping cut even under changing conditions, watching roof control.	1, front man senior and responsible for cut; back man assists; cutting is the key preparation task.
	Gummer	4	Day wage	Loose group attached to cutters, though front man without supervisory authority.	Cleaning out undercut, so that clear space for coal to drop and level floor for filler. The coal between undercut and floor is called 'the gummings'.	Unskilled, heavy manual task, which unless conscientiously done creates difficulties for filler, for when gummings left in, the shot simply blows out and coal is left solid.	7, equal in group; some chance of promotion to cutter eventually.
	Belt-breaker	2	Per yard	Inter-dependent pair on same note.	Shifting belt-engine and tension-end face clear of rippers; breaking up conveyor in old track, placing plates, etc., ready in new track, drawing off props in old creeping track; some packing as required.	Belt-breaking is a relatively simple engineering task; engine shifting is awkward and heavy; drawing off and packing involve responsibility for roof control and require solid underground experience.	4–5, equal in pair.
Second (usually called the 'ripping' shift).	Belt-builder	2	Per yard	Inter-dependent pair on	Reassembling conveyor in new track; positioning belt-	As with breaking, the level of engineering skill is relatively simple;	4–5, equal in pair.

Shift	Role	No.	Measure	Group	Task	Work conditions	Status
or *afternoon* alternating with cutting shift. Rippers may start rather later than builders. None of these personnel go on *day* shift proper.	Ripper	8	Cubic measure	Cohesive functionally inter-related group on same note.	To 'rip' 'dirt' out of main and side gates to assigned heights; place cambers and build up roof into a solid, safe and durable structure; pack-up the sides. The ripping team carries out all operations necessary to their task, doing their own boring. The task is a complete job in itself, seen through by the group within the compass of one shift.	This work requires the highest degree of building skill among coal-face tasks. Some very heavy labour is entailed. Since the work is relatively permanent there is much pride of craft. On the ripper depends the safety of all gates and main ways.	2, the status of the 'main ripper' is next to that of the front man on the cutter, but he is not separately paid. The group usually contains all degrees of experience and is egalitarian.
Third (usually called 'filling' shift). Either *day*, 6 a.m.–1.30 p.m., or *afternoon*, 2 p.m.–9.30 p.m. Never *night*.	Filler	20	Weight-tonnage on conveyors	Aggregate of individuals with equal 'stints'; all on same note; fractionated relationships and much isolation.	The length of the 'stint' is determined by the depth of the cut and the thickness of the seam. Using hand or air pick and shovel, the filler 'throws' the 'shot' coal on to the conveyor until he has cleared his length, i.e. 'filled off'. He props up every 2 ft 6 in as he works in.	The filler remains in one work place while conditions change. Considerable underground experience is required to cope with bad conditions. Each man is responsible for his own section of roof. Bad work on other shifts makes the task harder. It is heavy in any case and varies in different parts of the wall.	4–5, equal throughout the group; 'corner' men are envied, reputation of being good or bad workman is important
3 shifts	7 roles	40 men	5 methods	4 types	The common background of 'underground' skill is more important than the task differences.		Differences in status and weekly earnings are small, apart from the case of the gummers.

Fragments from the row continued from the previous page:

in line with this; testing running of reassembled conveyor; placing chocks; packing as required.

to fillers it belt out of position. The roof control responsibilities demand solid underground experience.

situation, their maintenance at a level which allows full and continuous realization of their technological potentialities creates a difficult problem of industrial management. In the underground situation these difficulties are of a higher order, it being virtually impossible to establish the kind of constant background to the task that is taken for granted in the factory. A very large variety of unfavourable and changing environmental conditions is encountered at the coal-face, many of which are impossible to predict. Others, though predictable, are impossible to alter.

The factory and underground situations are different with respect to the 'figure-ground' relationship of the production process to its environmental background. In the factory a comparatively high degree of control can be exercised over the complex and moving 'figure' of a production sequence, since it is possible to maintain the 'ground' in a comparatively passive and constant state. But at the coal-face, there is always present the threat of some untoward activity in the 'ground'. The internal organization of the task 'figure' is therefore much more liable to disorganization. The instability of the 'ground' limits the applicability in the underground situation of methods derived from the factory.

Unfavourable natural conditions, as distinct from 'bad work' – which is the result of human shortcomings – are referred to as 'bad conditions'. Some of the most dreaded, such as wet, heat, or dust, are permanent features of the working environment of certain faces. But others, less known outside the industry, may also make the production tasks of the face-worker both difficult and dangerous, even though the seam in which he is working is well ventilated, cool, and dry without being dusty. Rolls or faults may appear in the seam. Control may be lost over the roof for considerable periods. Especially in the middle of a long face, certain types of roof are apt to sag down. Changes may occur in the floor; the condition known as 'rising floor' being not uncommon. Since some of these conditions reduce working height, their appearance is particularly troublesome in thin seams. If the difference between working in 5 ft 6 in and 5 ft may be of small account, that between working in 3 ft and 2 ft 6 in may often produce intolerable conditions. Loss of roof-control is serious, whatever the working height. In general, bad conditions mean not only additional danger but additional labour. The need to insert packs to support a loose roof is a common example.

Special tasks of any kind, over and above the specific production operation for which a given category of face-worker receives his basic pay, are known as 'bye-work'. Though many bye-work tasks have gained the status of specially remunerated activities, the rates are such that the overall wage received at the end of a week during which a good deal of bye-work has been necessary is less than that which would have been received had the whole of the five shifts been available for production work. From the face-worker's point of view, bad conditions mean not only more danger and harder work but less pay; and they may also compel overtime. To stay behind an hour or sometimes three hours longer under bad conditions may involve a degree of hardship beyond the capacity of many face-workers to endure, especially if they are older, and if overtime demands are repeated in close succession.

'Bad conditions' tend to instigate 'bad work'. When they occur, the smooth sequence of tasks in the production cycle is more likely to be disturbed by faulty performance. Bad work can, and does, arise when conditions are good, from personal shortcomings and social tensions, in themselves independent of bad conditions; but difficulties arising from human failings are more readily – and conveniently – expressed when the additional difficulty, and excuse, of bad conditions is also present. The result is a tendency for circular causal processes of a disruptive character to be touched off. Unless rapidly checked by special measures, often of an emergency character, these, once started, threaten to culminate in the fillers not filling off, and the cycle being stopped. The system is therefore always to some extent working against the threat of its own breakdown, so that tension and anxiety are created.

The magnification of local disturbances

Under these conditions, the closeness of the functional inter-dependence of tasks tends to rebound on itself. Mistakes and difficulties made or encountered at one stage are carried forward, producing yet other difficulties in the next. The inflexible character of the succession gives no scope for proceeding with later tasks when hold-ups have occurred earlier, and the temporal extension of the cycle increases the likelihood of interference from unpredictable events, which are provided with twenty-four hours in which to occur. The aspects of mass-production engineering methods (rigid sequence, functional inter-dependence and spatio-temporal extension), which create vulnerability in the underground situation, all stem from the large-scale character of the longwall cycle. For it is the magnitude of the cycle, produced by the long expanse of face scheduled for clearance, that leads to the segregated treatment of the component tasks – in view of the large amount of work required on each – and thence to their fixed, extended succession. In an organization of this scale, local disturbances at specific points –

resulting from the interaction of bad conditions and bad work – resonate through a relatively large social space, becoming magnified for this reason.

Stricter field-theory formulation may assist the more dynamic description of this situation. The size of the bounded region in which the system exists as a whole, together with the high degree of differentiation in its unidirectional internal connectedness, first increases the number of points at which small disturbances may occur, and thereafter enlarges the scope of their effects to a scale proportional to the magnitude of the whole. Since these effects must be contained within a closed system, single events are, as the result of induction which takes place from the power field of the whole, endowed with the potentiality of disrupting the cycle. No matter that this potentiality is realized only in the extreme case; disturbance is always experienced to some extent under pressure of this potentiality. Stress arising from this pressure itself produces fresh disturbances. Measures necessary to prevent these from still further spreading absorb a correspondingly greater amount of the available concern and energy.

Variations in the level of functioning

It has been mentioned that a characteristic of bad conditions and bad work is their uneven distribution – not only between different faces, but also over different sections and among different tasks within the same face. The consequence is an uneven level of functional efficiency, more generally lowered also by the magnified resonances and induced pressures described above. The atmosphere of uncertainty thus created arouses the expectation in the individual that bad work done by someone else will increase his own difficulties, or that some untoward event will occur to keep him down at the end of his shift. The resulting attitudes and suspicions are ingrained in the culture of the longwall work group and adversely affect the entire pattern of relationships at the coal-face.

No systematic survey of the incidence of cycle stoppages was possible within the limits of the present study. But on one of the best faces known at first hand by the writers it was a matter of self-congratulation that the fillers had failed to fill off only three times during the past year. Experienced informants gave once in two months, or five or six times during the course of a year, as a more usual frequency, with instances of many more stoppages in 'bad faces' in 'bad pits'. If one week's work is commonly lost in this way during a year, the overall loss in production would amount to some 2 per cent. This relatively low figure expresses the extent of the efforts made to check disturbances short of the point where the cycle is stopped.

The strain of cycle control

The main burden of keeping down the number of cycle stoppages falls on the deputy, who is the only person in the face area with cycle, as distinct from task, responsibility. Discussion with groups of deputies readily yields evidence of the strain involved. A common and reality-based complaint is that the authority of the deputy is incommensurate with responsibility of this order. The background to this complaint is the fact, noted in the discussion of the hand-got systems, that, in view of the darkness and the spread out character of the work, there is no possibility of close supervision. Responsibility for seeing to it that bad work is not done, however bad the conditions, rests with the face-workers themselves. But the responsible autonomy of some, especially, of the occupational sub-groups has been impaired in the longwall method. This problem will be taken up in succeeding sections.

As a result, management complain of lack of support from the men, who are accused of being concerned only with their own fractional tasks and unwilling to take broader cycle responsibility. The parallel complaint of the workers is of being driven and tricked by management, who are resented as outsiders – intermittent visitors and 'stick' men, who interfere without sharing the hard, physical work and in-group life of the face. On occasions, for example, the deputy is reduced to bargaining with the men as to whether they will agree to carry out essential bye-work. The complaint of the men is that deputies' promises are rarely kept, and that they have gone unpaid too often to be again easily persuaded. The deputy's answer is that the under-manager or manager has refused to uphold his case. Whether he presented it, how he presented it, or what reasons may have dictated the managerial view are a type of issue on which effective communication back to the men breaks down. The deputy has equally little chance of increasing the insight of the workmen into their own tendency to drive sharp bargains.

The strain of cycle control tends to produce a group 'culture' of angry and suspicious bargaining over which both management and men are in collusion. There is displacement both upwards and downwards of the tensions generated. The 'hell' that breaks loose in the under-manager's office when news comes in that the fillers are unlikely to fill off in one or more faces resounds through the pit.

The norm of low productivity

In all work at the coal-face two distinct tasks are simultaneously present; those that belong to the production cycle being always to some extent carried out on the background of a second activity arising from the need to contend with interferences, actual or threatened, emanating from the underground situation. The activity of the 'ground' has always to be dealt with, and ability to contend with this second or background task comprises the common fund of underground skill shared alike by all experienced face-workers. This common skill is of a higher order than that required simply to carry out, as such, any of the operations belonging to the production cycle. For these, initial training is short, and may be measured in months; it is longest for those, such as cutting, where the engineering component is largest. But the specifically mining skill of contending with underground conditions, and of maintaining a high level of performance when difficulties arise, is developed only as the result of several years of experience at the face. A work-system basically appropriate to the underground situation requires to have built into its organization the findings of this experience. Unless this has been done, it will not only fail to engage the face-worker to the limit of his capabilities, but will restrict him to a level of performance below his potentiality.

The evidence suggests that the longwall method acts in this way. The crises of cycle stoppages and the stress of the deputy's role are but symptoms of a wider situation characterized by the establishment of a norm of low productivity, as the only adaptive method of handling, in the contingencies of the underground situation, a complicated, rigid, and large-scale work system, borrowed with too little modification from an engineering culture appropriate to the radically different situation of the factory. At the time the longwall method developed, there were no precedents for the adaptive underground application of a machine technology. In the absence of relevant experience in the mining tradition itself it was almost inevitable that heavy culture-borrowing of this kind should have taken place. There was no psychological or sociological knowledge in existence at that time which might have assisted in lessening the difficulties.[. . .]

Conclusions

The fact that the desperate economic incentives of the between-war period no longer operate means a greater intolerance of unsatisfying or difficult working conditions, or systems of organization, among miners, even though they may not always be clear as to the exact nature of the resentment or hostility which they often appear to feel. The persistence of socially ineffective structures at the coal-face is likely to be a major factor in preventing a rise of morale, in discouraging recruitment, and in increasing labour turnover.

The innovations in social organization of face-work groups, which have begun to appear, and the success of some of these developments, suggest that the organizational changes brought about by nationalization provide a not inappropriate opportunity for the experimental working through of problems of the types which have been indicated. It can certainly be said with some confidence that within the industry there exist the necessary resources and creativity to allow widespread constructive developments to take place.

As regards the longwall system, the first need is for systematic study and evaluation of the changes so far tried.[3] It seems to the present writers, however, that a qualitative change will have to be effected in the general character of the method, so that a social as well as a technological whole can come into existence. Only if this is achieved can the relationships of the cycle work-group be successfully integrated and a new social balance be created.

The immediate problems are to develop formal small-group organization on the filling shift and to work out an acceptable solution to the authority questions in the cutting team. But it is difficult to see how these problems can be solved effectively without restoring responsible autonomy to primary groups throughout the system and ensuring that each of these groups has a satsifying sub-whole as its work task, and some scope for flexibility in work-pace. Only if this is done will the stress of the deputy's role be reduced and his task of maintaining the cycle receive spontaneous support from the primary work groups.

It is likely that any attempts in this direction would require to take advantage of the recent trend of training face-workers for more than one role, so that interchangeability of tasks would be possible within work teams. Moreover, the problem of shift segregation will not be overcome until the situation is altered in which one large group is permanently organized round the day shift and the others round the back shifts. Some interchange between roles in preparation and filling tasks would seem worth consideration. Once preparation workers and fillers could experi-

3. One of the most interesting of these is W. V. Sheppard, 'An Experiment in Continuous Longwall Mining at Bolsover Colliery', *The Institution of Mining Engineers*, January 1951.

ence each other's situations, mutual understanding and tolerance would be likely to increase.

It is to be borne in mind that developments in room-and-pillar methods appear to be stressing the value of the strongly-knit primary work-group and that the most recent advances in mechanization, such as power loaders or strippers, both require work teams of this kind.

References

BION, W. R. (1949), 'Experiences in groups, III', *Human Relations*, vol. 2, no. 1, pp. 13–22.
HALLIDAY, J. L. (1949), *Psychosocial Medicine: A Study of the Sick Society*, Heinemann.

24 H. Mintzberg

The Manager's Job: Folklore and Fact

From *Harvard Business Review*, July–August 1975, pp. 49–61.

If you ask a manager what he does, he will most likely tell you that he plans, organizes, coordinates, and controls. Then watch what he does. Don't be surprised if you can't relate what you see to these four words.

When he is rung up and told that one of his factories has just burned down, and he advises the caller to see whether temporary arrangements can be made to supply customers through a foreign subsidiary, is he planning, organizing, coordinating, or controlling? What about when he presents a gold watch to a retiring employee? Or when he attends a conference to meet people in the trade? Or, on returning from that conference, when he tells one of his employees about an interesting product idea he picked up there? The fact is that these four words, which have dominated management vocabulary since the French industrialist Henri Fayol first introduced them in 1916, tell us little about what managers actually do. At best, they indicate some vague objectives managers have when they work.

The field of management, so devoted to progress and change, has for more than half a century not seriously addressed the basic question, 'What do managers do?' Without a proper answer, how can we teach management? How can we design planning or information systems for managers? How can we improve the practice of management at all?

Our ignorance of the nature of managerial work shows up in various ways in the modern organization – in the boast by the successful manager that he has never spent a single day in a management-training program; in the turnover of corporate planners who have never quite understood what it is the manager wants; in the computer consoles gathering dust in the back room because the managers never use the fancy on-line M.I.S. some analyst thought they needed. Perhaps most importantly, our ignorance shows up in the inability of our large public organizations to come to grips with some of their most serious policy problems.

Somehow, in the rush to automate production, to use management science in the functional areas of marketing and finance, and to apply the skills of the behavioral scientist to the problem of worker motivation, the manager – that person in charge of the organization or one of its sub-units – has been forgotten.

My intention in this article is simple: to break the reader away from Fayol's words and to introduce him to a more supportable, and what I believe to be a more useful, description of managerial work. This description derives from my review and synthesis of the available research on how various managers have spent their time.

In some studies, managers were observed intensively ('shadowed' is the word some of them used); in a number of others, they kept detailed diaries of their activities; in a few studies, their records were analyzed. All kinds of managers were studied – foremen, factory supervisors, staff managers, field sales managers, hospital administrators, presidents of companies and nations, and even street gang leaders. These 'managers' worked in the United States, Canada, Sweden and Great Britain. At the end of this article I have given a brief review of the major studies that I found most useful in developing this description, including my own study of five American chief-executive officers.

A synthesis of these findings paints an interesting picture, one as different from Fayol's classical view as a cubist abstract is from a Renaissance painting. In a sense this picture will be obvious to anyone who has ever spent a day in a manager's office, whether in front of the desk or behind it. Yet at the same time this picture may turn out to be revolutionary, in that it throws doubt upon so much of the folklore that we have accepted about the manager's work.

I will first discuss some of this folklore and contrast it with some of the discoveries of systematic research – the hard facts about how managers spend their time. I will then synthesize these research findings in a description of ten roles that seem to describe the essential content of all managers' jobs. In a concluding section, I will discuss a number of implications of this synthesis for those trying to achieve more effective management, both in classrooms and in the business world.

Some folklore and facts about managerial work

There are four myths about the manager's job that do not withstand careful scrutiny of the facts.

1. *Folklore: 'The manager is a reflective, systematic planner.'* The evidence on this issue is overwhelming, but not a shred of it supports this statement.

Fact: study after study has shown that managers work at an unrelenting pace, that their activities are characterized by brevity, variety and discontinuity, and that they are strongly orientated towards action and dislike reflective activities. Consider the following evidence.

Half the activities engaged in by the five chief executives of my study lasted less than nine minutes and only 10 per cent exceeded one hour (all the data from my study can be found in Mintzberg, 1973). A study of fifty-six U.S. foremen found that they averaged 583 activities per eight-hour shift, an average of one every 48 seconds (R. H. Guest, 1956). The work pace for both chief executives and foremen was unrelenting. The chief executives met a steady stream of callers and mail from the moment they arrived in the morning until they left in the evening. Coffee breaks and lunches were inevitably work-related, and ever-present subordinates seemed to usurp any free moment. A diary study of 160 British middle and top managers found that they worked for half an hour or more without interruption about once every two days (R. Stewart, 1967; see also S. Carlson, 1951, the first of the diary studies).

Of the verbal contacts of the chief executives in my study, 93 per cent were arranged on an *ad hoc* basis. Only 1 per cent of the executives' time was spent in open-ended observational tours. Only one out of 368 verbal contacts was unrelated to a specific issue and could be called general planning. Another researcher finds that '*in not one single case* did a manager report the obtaining of important external information from a general conversation or other undirected personal communication' (F. J. Aguilar, 1967, p. 102). No study has found important patterns in the way managers schedule their time. They seem to jump from issue to issue, continually responding to the needs of the moment.

Is this the planner that the classical view describes? Hardly. How, then, can we explain this behavior? The manager is simply responding to the pressures of his job. I found that my chief executives terminated many of their own activities, often leaving meetings before the end, and interrupted their desk work to call in subordinates. One president not only placed his desk so that he could look down a long hallway but also left his door open when he was alone – an invitation for subordinates to come in and interrupt him.

Clearly, these managers wanted to encourage the flow of current information. But more significantly, they seemed to be conditioned by their own work loads. They appreciated the opportunity cost of their own time, and they were continually aware of their ever-present obligations: mail to be answered, callers to attend to, and so on. It seems that no matter what he is doing, the manager is plagued by both what he might do and what he must do.

When the manager must plan, he seems to do so implicitly in the context of daily actions, not in some abstract process reserved for two weeks in the organization's mountain retreat. The plans of the chief executives I studied seemed to exist only in their heads – as flexible, but often specific, intentions. The traditional literature notwithstanding, the job of managing does not breed reflective planners; the manager responds to stimuli as an individual who is conditioned by his job to prefer live to delayed action.

2. *Folklore: 'The effective manager has no regular duties to perform.'*
Managers are constantly being told to spend more time planning and delegating, and less time seeing customers and engaging in negotiations. These are not, after all, the true tasks of the manager. To use the popular analogy, the good manager, like the good conductor, carefully orchestrates everything in advance, then sits back to enjoy the fruits of his labor, responding occasionally to an unforeseeable exception. But here again the pleasant abstraction just does not seem to hold. We had better take a closer look at those activities in which managers feel compelled to engage before we arbitrarily define them away.

Fact: in addition to handling exceptions, managerial work involves performing a number of regular duties, including ritual and ceremony, negotiations, and processing soft information that links the organization with its environment. Consider some evidence from the research studies.

A study of the work of the presidents of small companies found that they engaged in routine activities because their companies could not afford staff specialists and were so thin on operating personnel that a single absence often required the president to substitute.[1] One study of field sales managers and another of chief executives suggest that it is a natural part of both jobs to see important customers, assuming the managers wish to keep those customers (R. T. Davis, 1957, and G. H. Copeman, 1963).

Someone once described the manager only half in jest as that person who sees visitors so that everyone else can get his work done. In my study, I found that certain ceremonial duties – meeting visiting dignitaries, giving out gold watches, presiding at Christmas dinners – were an intrinsic part of the chief executive's job.

Studies of managers' information-flow suggest that managers play a

1. Unpublished study by Irving Choran, reported in Mintzberg (1973).

key role in securing 'soft' external information (much of it available only to them because of their status) and passing it along to their subordinates.

3. *Folklore:* '*The senior manager needs aggregated information, which a formal management-information system best provides.*' Not too long ago, the words *total-information system* were everywhere in the management literature. In keeping with the classical view of the manager as that individual perched at the apex of a regulated, hierarchical system, the literature's manager was to receive all his important information from a giant, comprehensive M.I.S.

Lately, however, as it has become increasingly evident that these giant M.I.S. systems are not working – that managers are simply not using them – the enthusiasm has waned. A look at how managers actually process information makes the reason quite clear. Managers have five media at their command – documents, telephone calls, scheduled and unscheduled meetings, and observational tours.

Fact: 'Managers strongly favor the verbal media – namely, telephone calls and meetings. The evidence comes from every single study of managerial work. Consider the following.

In two British studies, managers spent an average of 66 per cent and 80 per cent of their time in verbal (oral) communication (R. Stewart, 1967, and T. Burns, 1954). In my study of five American chief executives, the figure was 78 per cent. These five chief executives treated mail processing as a burden to be dispensed with. One came in on Saturday morning to process 142 pieces of mail in just over three hours, to 'get rid of all the stuff'. This same manager looked at the first piece of 'hard' mail he had received all week, a standard cost report, and put it aside with the comment, 'I never look at this.'

These same five chief executives responded immediately to two of the forty routine reports they received during the five weeks of my study and to four items in the 104 periodicals. They skimmed most of these periodicals in seconds, almost ritualistically. In all, these chief executives of sizeable organizations initiated on their own – that is, not in response to something else – a grand total of twenty-five pieces of mail during the twenty-five days I observed them.

An analysis of the mail the executives received reveals an interesting picture – only 13 per cent was of specific and immediate use. So now we have another piece in the puzzle: not much of the mail provides live, current information – the action of a competitor, the mood of a government legislator, or the rating of last night's television show. Yet this is the information that drove the managers, interrupting their meetings and rescheduling their workdays.

Consider another interesting finding. Managers seem to cherish 'soft' information, especially gossip, hearsay, and speculation. Why? The reason is its timeliness: today's gossip may be tomorrow's fact. The manager who is not accessible for the telephone call informing him that his biggest customer was seen golfing with his main competitor may read about a dramatic drop in sales in the next quarterly report. But by then it's too late.

To assess the value of historical, aggregated, 'hard' M.I.S. information, consider two of the manager's prime uses for his information: to identify problems and opportunities and to build his own mental models of the things around him (e.g. how his organization's budget system works, how his customers buy his product, how changes in the economy affect his organization, and so on).[2] Every bit of evidence suggests that the manager identifies decision situations and builds models not with the aggregated abstractions an M.I.S. provides, but with specific tidbits of data.

Consider the words of Richard Neustadt, who studied the information-collecting habits of Presidents Roosevelt, Truman, and Eisenhower:

> It is not information of a general sort that helps a President see personal stakes; not summaries, not surveys, not the *bland amalgams*. Rather . . . it is the odds and ends of *tangible detail* that pieced together in his mind illuminate the underside of issues put before him. To help himself he must reach out as widely as he can for every scrap of fact, opinion, gossip, bearing on his interests and relationships as President. He must become his own director of his own central intelligence.[3]

The manager's emphasis on verbal media raises two important points.

First, verbal information is stored in people's brains. Only when people write this information down can it be stored in the files of the organization – whether in metal cabinets or on magnetic tape – and managers apparently do not write down much of what they hear. Thus the strategic data-bank of the organization is not in the memory of its computers but in the minds of its managers.

2. See H. E. Wrapp, 1967. Wrapp refers to this as spotting opportunities and relationships in the stream of operating problems and decisions; Wrapp raises a number of excellent points related to this analysis in his article.

3. R. E. Neustadt, 1960, pp. 153–4.

Second, the manager's extensive use of verbal media helps to explain why he is reluctant to delegate tasks. When we note that most of the manager's important information comes in verbal form and is stored in his head, we can well appreciate his reluctance. It is not as if he can hand a dossier over to someone; he must take the time to 'dump memory' – to tell someone all he knows about the subject. But this could take so long that the manager may find it easier to do the task himself. Thus the manager is damned by his own information system to a 'dilemma of delegation' – to do too much himself or to delegate to his subordinates with inadequate briefing.

4. *Folklore: 'Management is, or at least is quickly becoming, a science and a profession.'* By almost any definitions of *science* and *profession*, this statement is false. Brief observation of any manager will quickly lay to rest the notion that managers practise a science. A science involves the enaction of systematic, analytically determined procedures or programs. If we do not even know what procedures managers use, how can we prescribe them by scientific analysis? And how can we call management a profession if we cannot specify what managers are to learn? For, after all, a profession involves 'knowledge of some department of learning of science' (*Random House Dictionary*).[4]

Fact: the managers' programmes – to schedule time, process information, make decisions, and so on – remain locked deep inside their brains. Thus, to describe these programmes, we rely on words like *judgment* and *intuition*, seldom stopping to realize that they are merely labels for our ignorance.

I was struck during my study by the fact that the executives I was observing – all very competent by any standard – were fundamentally indistinguishable from their counterparts of a hundred years ago (or a thousand years ago, for that matter). The information they need differs, but they seek it in the same way: by word of mouth. Their decisions concern modern technology, but the procedures they use are the same as the procedures of the nineteenth-century manager. Even the computer, so important for the specialized work of the organization, has apparently had no influence on the work procedures of general managers. In fact, the manager is in a kind of loop, with increasingly heavy work pressures but no aid forthcoming from management science.

Considering the facts about managerial work, we can see that the

4. For a more thorough, though rather different, discussion of this issue, see K. R. Andrews (1969).

manager's job is enormously complicated and difficult. The manager is overburdened with obligations; yet he cannot easily delegate his tasks. As a result, he is driven to overwork and is forced to do many tasks superficially. Brevity, fragmentation, and verbal communication characterize his work. Yet these are the very characteristics of managerial work that have impeded scientific attempts to improve it. As a result, the management scientist has concentrated his efforts on the specialized functions of the organization, where he could more easily analyze the procedures and quantify the relevant information.[5]

But the pressures of the manager's job are becoming worse. Where before he needed only to respond to owners and directors, now he finds that his subordinates with democratic norms continually reduce his freedom to issue unexplained orders, and a growing number of outside influences (consumer groups, government agencies, and so on) expect his attention. And the manager has nowhere to turn for help. The first step in providing the manager with some help is to find out what his job really is.

Back to a basic description of managerial work

Now let us try to put some of the pieces of this puzzle together. Earlier I defined the manager as that person in charge of an organization or one of its sub-units. Besides chief executive officers, this definition would include vice-presidents, bishops, foremen, hockey coaches, and prime ministers. Can all of these people have anything in common? Indeed they can. To begin with, all are vested with formal authority over an organizational unit. From formal authority comes status, which leads to various interpersonal relations, and from these comes access to information. Information, in turn, enables the manager to make decisions and construct strategies for his unit.

The manager's job can be described in terms of various 'roles', or organized sets of behaviors identified with a position. My description, shown in Figure 1, comprises ten roles. As we shall see, formal authority gives rise to the three interpersonal roles, which in turn give rise to the three informational roles; these two sets of roles enable the manager to play the four decisional roles.

5. C. J. Grayson, Jr (1973) explains in similar terms why, as chairman of the Price Commission, he did not use those very techniques that he himself promoted in his earlier career as a management scientist.

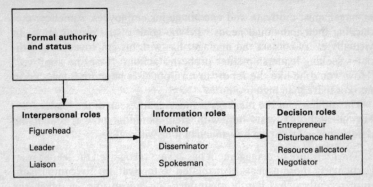

Figure 1   The manager's roles

Interpersonal roles

Three of the manager's roles arise directly from his formal authority and involve basic interpersonal relationships.

1. The first is the *figurehead* role. By virtue of his position as head of an organizational unit, every manager must perform some duties of a ceremonial nature. The president greets the touring dignitaries, the foreman attends the wedding of a lathe operator, and the sales manager takes an important customer to lunch.

The chief executives of my study spent 12 per cent of their contact time on ceremonial duties; 17 per cent of their incoming mail dealt with acknowledgements and requests related to their status. For example, a letter to a company president requested free merchandise for a crippled schoolchild; diplomas were put on the desk of the school superintendent for his signature.

Duties that involve interpersonal roles may sometimes be routine, involving little serious communication and no important decision making. Nevertheless, they are important to the smooth functioning of an organization and cannot be ignored by the manager.

2. Because he is in charge of an organizational unit, the manager is responsible for the work of the people of that unit. His actions in this regard constitute the *leader* role. Some of these actions involve leadership directly – for example, in most organizations the manager is normally responsible for hiring and training his own staff.

In addition, there is the indirect exercise of the leader role. Every manager must motivate and encourage his employees, somehow reconciling their individual needs with the goals of the organization. In virtually every contact the manager has with his employees, subordinates seeking leadership clues probe his actions: 'Does he approve?' 'How would he like the report to turn out?' 'Is he more interested in market share than high profits?'

The influence of the manager is most clearly seen in the leader role. Formal authority vests him with great potential power; leadership determines in large part how much of it he will realize.

3. The literature of management has always recognized the leader role, particularly those aspects of it related to motivation. By comparison, until recently it has hardly mentioned the *liaison* role, in which the manager makes contacts outside his vertical chain of command. This is remarkable in the light of the finding of virtually every study of managerial work that managers spend as much time with peers and other people outside their units as they do with their own subordinates, and surprisingly little time with their own superiors.

In Rosemary Stewart's diary study (R. Stewart, 1967), the 160 British middle and top managers spent 47 per cent of their time with peers, 41 per cent of their time with people outside their unit, and only 12 per cent of their time with their superiors. For Robert H. Guest's study of U.S. foremen (I . H. Guest, 1956), the figures were 44 per cent, 46 per cent, and 10 per cent. The chief executives of my study averaged 44 per cent of their contact time with people outside their organization, 48 per cent with subordinates, and 7 per cent with directors and trustees.

The contacts the five C.E.O.s made were with an incredibly wide range of people: subordinates; clients; business associates and suppliers; and peers (managers of similar organizations, government- and trade-organization officials, fellow directors on outside boards, and independents with no relevant organizational affiliations). The chief executives' time with and mail from these groups is shown in Figure 2. Guest's study of foremen shows, likewise, that their contacts were numerous and wide ranging, seldom involving fewer than twenty-five individuals, and often more than fifty.

As we shall see shortly, the manager cultivates such contacts largely to find information. In effect, the liaison role is devoted to building up the manager's own external information system – informal, private, verbal, but nevertheless effective.

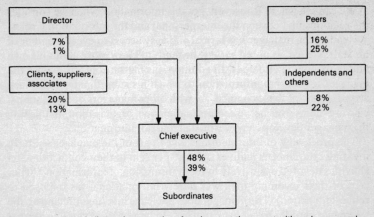

Note: the top figure indicates the proportion of total contact time spent with each group and the bottom figure, the proportion of mail from each group.

Figure 2   The chief executives' contacts

Informational roles

By virtue of his interpersonal contacts, both with his subordinates and with his network of contacts, the manager emerges as the nerve center of his organizational unit. He may not know everything, but he typically knows more than any member of his staff.

Studies have shown this relationship to hold for all managers, from street gang leaders to U.S. presidents. In *The Human Group*, George C. Homans explains how, because they were at the center of the information flow of their own gangs and were also in close touch with other gang leaders, street gang leaders were better informed than any of their followers (G. C. Homans, 1950, based on W. F. Whyte, 1955). And Richard Neustadt gives the following account from his study of Franklin D. Roosevelt:

> The essence of Roosevelt's technique for information-gathering was competition. 'He would call you in,' one of his aides once told me, 'and he'd ask you to get the story on some complicated business, and you'd come back after a couple of days of hard labor and present the juicy morsel you'd uncovered under a stone somewhere, and *then* you'd find out he knew all about it, along with something else you didn't know. Where he got this information from he wouldn't mention, usually, but after he had done this to you once or twice you got damn careful about your information.'[6]

6. R. Neustadt, 1960, p. 157.

We can see where Roosevelt 'got this information' when we consider the relationship between the interpersonal and the informational roles. As leader, the manager has formal and easy access to every member of his staff. Hence, as noted earlier, he tends to know more about his own unit than anyone else does. In addition, his liaison contacts expose the manager to external information to which his subordinates often lack access. Many of these contacts are with other managers of equal status, who are themselves nerve centers in their own organization. In this way the manager develops a powerful data base of information.

The processing of information is a key part of the manager's job. In my study, the chief executives spent 40 per cent of their contact time on activities devoted exclusively to the transmission of information; 70 per cent of their incoming mail was purely informational (as opposed to request for action). The manager does not leave meetings or hang up the telephone in order to get back to work. In large part, communication *is* his work. Three roles describe these informational aspects of managerial work.

1. As *monitor*, the manager perpetually scans his environment for information, interrogates his liaison contacts and his subordinates, and receives unsolicited information, much of it as a result of the network of personal contacts he has developed. Remember that a good part of the information the manager collects in his monitor role arrives in verbal form, often as gossip, hearsay, and speculation. By virtue of his contacts, the manager has a natural advantage in collecting this soft information for his organization.

2. He must share and distribute much of this information. Information he gleans from outside personal contacts may be needed within his organization. In his *disseminator* role, the manager passes some of his privileged information directly to his subordinates, who would otherwise have no access to it. When his subordinates lack easy contact with one another, the manager will sometimes pass information from one to another.

3. In his *spokesman* role, the manager sends some of his information to people outside his unit – a president makes a speech to a lobby for an organization cause, or a foreman suggests a product modification to a supplier. In addition, as part of his role as spokesman, every manager must inform and satisfy the influential people who control his organizational unit. For the foreman, this may simply involve keeping the plant manager informed about the flow of work through the shop.

The president of a large corporation, however, may spend a great deal of his time dealing with a host of influences. Directors and shareholders must be advised about financial performance; consumer groups must be assured that the organization is fulfilling its social responsibilities; and government officials must be satisfied that the organization is abiding by the law.

Decisional roles

Information is not, of course, an end in itself; it is the basic input to decision making. One thing is clear in this study of managerial work: the manager plays the major role in his unit's decision-making system. As its formal authority, only he can commit the unit to important new courses of action; and as its nerve center, only he has full and current information to make the set of decisions that determine the unit's strategy. Four roles describe the manager as decision maker.

1. As *entrepreneur*, the manager seeks to improve his unit and to adapt it to changing conditions in the environment. In his monitor role, the president is constantly on the lookout for new ideas. When a good one appears, he initiates a development project that he may supervise himself or delegate to an employee (perhaps with the stipulation that he must approve the final proposal).

There are two interesting features about these development projects at the chief-executive level. First, these projects do not involve single decisions or even unified clusters of decisions. Rather, they emerge as a series of small decisions and actions sequenced over time. Apparently, the chief executive prolongs each project so that he can fit it bit by bit into his busy, disjointed schedule and so that he can gradually come to comprehend the issue, if it is a complex one.

Second, the chief executives I studied supervised as many as fifty of these projects at the same time. Some projects entailed new products or processes; others involved public-relations campaigns, improvement of the cash position, reorganization of a weak department, resolution of a morale problem in a foreign division, integration of computer operations, various acquisitions at different stages of development, and so on.

The chief executive appears to maintain a kind of inventory of the development projects that he himself supervises – projects that are at various stages of development, some active and some in limbo. Like a juggler, he keeps a number of projects in the air: periodically one comes down, is given a new burst of energy, and is sent back into orbit. At various intervals, he puts new projects on-stream and discards old ones.

2. While the entrepreneurial role describes the manager as the voluntary initiator of change, the *disturbance handler* role depicts the manager involuntarily responding to pressures. Here change is beyond the manager's control. He must act because the pressures of the situation are too severe to be ignored: a strike looms, a major customer has gone bankrupt, or a supplier reneges on his contract.

It has been fashionable, I noted earlier, to compare the manager to an orchestra conductor, just as Peter F. Drucker wrote in *The Practice of Management*:

> The manager has the task of creating a true whole that is larger than the sum of its parts, a productive entity that turns out more than the sum of the resources put into it. One analogy is the conductor of a symphony orchestra, through whose effort, vision and leadership individual instrumental parts that are so much noise by themselves become the living whole of music. But the conductor has the composer's score; he is only interpreter. The manager is both composer and conductor.[7]

Now consider the words of Leonard R. Sayles, who has carried out systematic research on the manager's job:

> (The manager) is like a symphony orchestra conductor, endeavouring to maintain a melodious performance in which the contributions of the various instruments are coordinated and sequenced, patterned and paced, while the orchestra members are having various personal difficulties, stage hands are moving music stands, alternating excessive heat and cold are creating audience and instrument problems, and the sponsor of the concert is insisting on irrational changes in the program.[8]

In effect, every manager must spend a good part of his time responding to high-pressure disturbances. No organization can be so well run, so standardized, that it has considered in advance every contingency in the uncertain environment. Disturbances arise not only because poor managers ignore situations until they reach crisis proportions, but also because good managers cannot possibly anticipate all the consequences of the actions they take.

3. The third decisional role is that of *resource allocator*. To the manager falls the responsibility of deciding who will receive what in his organizational unit. Perhaps the most important resource the manager allocates

7. P. F. Drucker, 1954, pp. 341–2.
8. L. R. Sayles, 1964, p. 162.

is his own time. Access to the manager constitutes exposure to the unit's nerve center and decision maker. The manager is also charged with designing his unit's structure, that pattern of formal relationships that determines how work is to be divided and coordinated.

Also in his role as resource allocator the manager authorizes the important decisions of his unit before they are implemented. By retaining this power, the manager can ensure that decisions are interrelated; all must pass through a single brain. To fragment this power is to encourage discontinuous decision making and disjointed strategy.

There are a number of interesting features about the manager's authorizing others' decisions. First, despite the widespread use of capital-budgeting procedures – a means of authorizing various capital expenditures at one time – executives in my study made a great many authorization decisions on an *ad hoc* basis. Apparently, many projects cannot wait or simply do not have the quantifiable costs and benefits that capital budgeting requires.

Second, I found that the chief executives faced incredibly complex choices. They had to consider the impact of each decision on other decisions and on the organization's strategy. They had to ensure that the decision would be acceptable to those who influence the organization as well as ensuring that resources would not be overextended. They had to understand the various costs and benefits as well as the feasibility of the proposal. They also had to consider questions of timing. All this was necessary for the simple approval of someone else's proposal. At the same time, however, delay could cost time, while quick approval could be ill considered and quick rejection might discourage the subordinate who had spent months developing a pet project.

One common solution to approving projects is to pick the man instead of the proposal. That is, the manager authorizes those projects presented to him by people whose judgment he trusts. But he cannot always use this simple dodge.

4. The final decisional role is that of *negotiator*. Studies of managerial work at all levels indicate that managers spend considerable time in negotiations: the president of the football team is called in to work out a contract with the holdout superstar; the corporation president leads his company's contingent to negotiate a new strike issue; the foreman argues a grievance problem to its conclusion with the shop steward. As Leonard Sayles puts it, negotiations are a 'way of life' for the sophisticated manager.

These negotiations are duties of the manager's job; perhaps routine, they are not to be shirked. They are an integral part of his job, for only he has the authority to commit organizational resources in 'real time', and only he has the nerve-center information that important negotiations require.

The integrated job

It should be clear by now that the ten roles I have been describing are not easily separable. In the terminology of the psychologist, they form a gestalt, an integrated whole. No role can be pulled out of the framework leaving the job intact. For example, a manager without liaison contact lacks external information. As a result, he can neither disseminate the information his employees need nor make decisions that adequately reflect external conditions. (In fact, this is a problem for the new person in a managerial position, since he cannot make effective decisions until he has built up his network of contacts.)

Here lies a clue to the problems of team management.[9] Two or three people cannot share a single managerial position unless they can act as one entity. This means they cannot divide up the ten roles unless they can very carefully reintegrate them. The real difficulty lies with the informational roles. Unless there can be a full sharing of managerial information – and, as I pointed out earlier, it is primarily verbal – team management breaks down. A single managerial job cannot be arbitrarily split, for example, into internal and external roles, for information from both sources must be brought to bear on the same decisions.

To say that the ten roles form a gestalt is not to say that all managers give equal attention to each role. In fact, I found in my review of the various research studies that:

1. Sales managers seem to spend relatively more of their time in the interpersonal roles, presumably a reflection of the extrovert nature of the marketing activity.

2. Production managers give relatively more attention to the decisional roles, presumably a reflection of their concern with efficient work flow.

3. Staff managers spend the most time in the informational roles, since they are experts who manage departments that advise other parts of the organization.

Nevertheless, in all cases the interpersonal, informational and decisional roles remain inseparable.

9. See R. C. Hodgson, D. J. Levinson, and A. Zaleznik, 1965, for a discussion of the sharing of roles.

Towards more effective management

What are the messages for management in this description? I believe, first and foremost, that this description of managerial work should prove more important to managers than any prescription they might derive from it. That is to say, *the manager's effectiveness is significantly influenced by his insight into his own work.* His performance depends on how well he understands and responds to the pressures and dilemmas of the job. Thus managers who can be introspective about their work are likely to be effective at their jobs. Table 1 offers fourteen groups of self-study questions for managers. Some may sound rhetorical; none is meant to be. Even though the questions cannot be answered simply, the manager should address himself to them.

Let us take a look at three specific areas of concern. For the most part, the managerial log-jams – the dilemmas of delegation, the data base centralized in one brain, the problems of working with the management scientist – revolve around the verbal nature of the manager's information. There are great dangers in centralizing the organization's data bank in the minds of its managers. When they leave they take their memory with them. And when subordinates are out of convenient verbal reach of the manager, they are at an informational disadvantage.

1. *The manager is challenged to find systematic ways to share his privileged information.* A regular debriefing session with key subordinates, a weekly memory dump on the dictating machine, the maintaining of a diary of important information for limited circulation, or other similar methods may ease the log-jam of work considerably. Time spent disseminating this information will be more than regained when decisions must be made. Of course, some will raise the question of confidentiality. But managers would do well to weigh the risks of exposing privileged information against having subordinates who can make effective decisions.

If there is a single theme that runs through this article, it is that the pressures of his job drive the manager to be superficial in his actions – to overload himself with work, encourage interruption, respond quickly to every stimulus, seek the tangible and avoid the abstract, make decisions in small increments, and do everything abruptly.

2. *Here again the manager is challenged to deal consciously with the pressures of superficiality by giving serious attention to the issues that require it, by stepping back from his tangible bits of information in order to see a broad picture, and by making use of analytical inputs.* Although

Table 1 Self-study questions for managers

1. Where do I get my information, and how? Can I make greater use of my contacts to get information? Can other people do some of my scanning for me? In what area is my knowledge weakest, and how can I get others to provide me with the information I need? Do I have powerful enough mental models of those things I must understand within the organization and in its environment?

2. What information do I disseminate in my organization? How important is it that my subordinates get my information? Do I keep too much information to myself because dissemination of it is time consuming or inconvenient? How can I get more information to others so they can make better decisions?

3. Do I balance information collecting with action taking? Do I tend to act before information is in? Or do I wait so long for all the information that opportunities pass me by and I become a bottleneck in my organization?

4. What pace of change am I asking my organization to tolerate? Is this change balanced so that our operations are neither excessively static nor overly disrupted? Have we sufficiently analyzed the impact of this change on the future of our organization?

5. Am I sufficiently well informed to pass judgement on the proposals that my subordinates make? Is it possible to leave final authorization for more of the proposals with subordinates? Do we have problems of coordination because subordinates in fact now make too many of these decisions independently?

6. What is my vision of direction for this organization? Are these plans primarily in my own mind in loose form? Should I make them explicit in order to guide the decisions of others in the organization better? Or do I need flexibility to change them at will?

7. How do my subordinates react to my managerial style? Am I sufficiently sensitive to the powerful influence my actions have on them? Do I fully understand their reactions to my actions? Do I find an appropriate balance between encouragement and pressure? Do I stifle their initiative?

8. What kind of external relationships do I maintain, and how? Do I spend too much of my time maintaining these relationships? Are there certain types of people whom I should get to know better?

9. Is there any system to my scheduling, or am I just reacting to the pressures of the moment? Do I find the appropriate mix of activities, or do I tend to concentrate on one particular function or one type of problem just because I find it interesting? Am I more efficient with particular kinds of work at special times of the day or week? Does my schedule reflect this? Can someone else (in addition to my secretary) take responsibility for much of my scheduling and do it more systematically?

Table 1 – *cont.*

10. Do I overwork? What effect does my work load have on my efficiency? Should I force myself to take breaks or to reduce the pace of my activity?

11. Am I too superficial in what I do? Can I really shift moods as quickly and frequently as my work patterns require? Should I attempt to decrease the amount of fragmentation and interruption in my work?

12. Do I orientate myself too much towards current, tangible activities? Am I slave to the action and excitement of my work, so that I am no longer able to concentrate on issues? Do key problems receive the attention they deserve? Should I spend more time reading and probing into certain issues? Could I be more reflective? Should I be?

13. Do I use the different media appropriately? Do I know how to make the most of written communication? Do I rely excessively on face-to-face communication, thereby putting all but a few of my subordinates at an informational disadvantage? Do I schedule enough of my meetings on a regular basis? Do I spend enough time touring my organization to observe activity first hand? Am I too detached from the heart of my organization's activities, seeing things only in an abstract way?

14. How do I blend my personal rights and duties? Do my obligations consume all my time? How can I free myself sufficiently from obligations to ensure that I am taking this organization where I want it to go? How can I turn my obligations to my advantage?

---

effective managers do have to be adept at responding quickly to numerous and varying problems, the danger in managerial work is that they will respond to every issue equally (and that means abruptly) and that they will never work the tangible bits and pieces of informational input into a comprehensive picture of their world.

As I noted earlier, the manager uses these bits of information to build models of his world. But the manager can also avail himself of the models of the specialists. Economists describe the functioning of markets, operations researchers stimulate financial flow processes, and behavioral scientists explain the needs and goals of people. The best of these models can be sought out and learned.

In dealing with complex issues, the senior manager has much to gain from a close relationship with the management scientists of his own organization. They have something important that he lacks: time to probe complex issues. An effective working relationship hinges on the resolution of what a colleague and I have called 'the planning dilemma'.[10] Managers have the information and the authority, analysts have the time and the technology. A successful working relationship between the two will be effected when the manager learns to share his information and the analyst learns to adapt to the manager's needs. For the analyst, adaptation means worrying less about the elegance of the method and more about its speed and flexibility.

It seems to me that analysts can especially help the top manager to schedule his time, feed in analytical information, monitor projects under his supervision, develop models to aid in making choices, design contingency plans for disturbances that can be anticipated, and conduct 'quick-and-dirty' analysis for those that cannot. But there can be no cooperation if the analysts are out of the mainstream of the manager's information flow.

3. *The manager is challenged to gain control of his own time by turning obligations to his advantage and by turning those things he wishes to do into obligations*. The chief executives of my study initiated only 32 per cent of their own contacts (and another 5 per cent by mutual agreement). And yet to a considerable extent they seemed to control their time. There were two key factors that enabled them to do so.

First, the manager has to spend so much time discharging obligations that if he were to view them as just that, he would leave no mark on his organization. The unsuccessful manager blames failure on the obligations; the effective manager turns his obligations to his own advantage. A speech is a chance to lobby for a cause; a meeting is a chance to reorganize a weak department; a visit to an important customer is a chance to extract trade information.

Second, the manager frees some of his time to do those things that he (and perhaps no one else) thinks important by turning them into obligations. Free time is made, not found, in the manager's job; it is forced into the schedule. Hoping to leave some time open for contemplation or general planning is tantamount to hoping that the pressures of the job will go away. The manager who wants to innovate initiates a project and obligates others to report back to him; the manager who needs certain environmental information establishes channels that will automatically keep him informed; the manager who has to tour facilities commits himself publicly.

10. J. S. Hekimian and H. Mintzberg, 1968, p. 4.

The educator's job

Finally, a word about the training of managers. Our management schools have done an admirable job of training the organization's specialists – management scientists, marketing researchers, accountants, and organizational development specialists. But for the most part they have not trained managers.[11]

Management schools will begin the serious training of managers when skill training takes a serious place next to cognitive learning. Cognitive learning is detached and informational, like reading a book or listening to a lecture. No doubt much more important cognitive material must be assimilated by the manager-to-be. But cognitive learning no more makes a manager than it does a swimmer. The latter will drown the first time he jumps into the water if his coach never takes him out of the lecture hall, gets him wet, and gives him feedback on his performance.

In other words, we are taught a skill through practice plus feedback, whether in a real or a simulated situation. Our management schools need to identify the skills managers use, select students who show potential in these skills, put the students into situations where these skills can be practiced, and then give them a systematic feedback on their performance.

My description of managerial work suggests a number of important managerial skills – developing peer relationships, carrying out negotiations, motivating subordinates, resolving conflicts, establishing information networks and subsequently disseminating information, making decisions in conditions of extreme ambiguity, and allocating resources. Above all, the manager needs to be introspective about his work so that he may continue to learn on the job. Many of the manager's skills can, in fact, be practiced using techniques that range from role playing to videotaping real meetings. And our management schools can enhance the entrepreneurial skills by designing programs that encourage sensible risk taking and innovation.

No job is more vital to our society than that of the manager. It is the manager who determines whether our social institutions serve us well or whether they squander our talents and resources. It is time to strip away the folklore about managerial work, and time to study it realistically so that we can begin the difficult task of making significant improvements in its performance.

11. See Livingston, 1971, p. 79.

Research on managerial work

Considering its central importance to every aspect of management, there has been surprisingly little research on the manager's work, and virtually no systematic building up of knowledge from one group of studies to another. In seeking to describe managerial work, I conducted my own research and also scanned the literature widely to integrate the findings of studies from many diverse sources with my own. These studies focused on two very different aspects of managerial work. Some were concerned with the characteristics of the work – how long managers work, where, at what pace and with what interruptions, with whom they work and through what media they communicate. Other studies were more concerned with the essential content of the work – what activities the managers actually carry out and why. Thus, after a meeting, one researcher might note that the manager spent forty-five minutes with three government officials in their Washington office, while another might record that he presented his company's stand on some proposed legislation in order to change a regulation.

A few of the studies of managerial work are widely known, but most have remained buried as single journal articles or isolated books. Among the more important ones I cite are the following.

Sune Carlson developed the diary method to study the work characteristics of nine Swedish managing directors. Each kept a detailed log of his activities. Carlson's results are reported in his book *Executive Behavior*. A number of British researchers, notably Rosemary Stewart, have subsequently used Carlson's method. In *Managers and Their Jobs* she describes the study of 160 top and middle managers of British companies during four weeks, with particular attention to the differences in their work.

Leonard Sayles's book *Managerial Behavior* is another important source of reference. Using a method he refers to as 'anthropological', Sayles studied the work content of middle- and lower-level managers in a large U.S. corporation. Sayles moved freely in the company, collecting whatever information struck him as important.

Perhaps the best-known source is *Presidential Power*, in which Richard Neustadt analyzes the power and managerial behavior of Presidents Roosevelt, Truman and Eisenhower. Neustadt used secondary sources – documents and interviews with other parties – to generate his data.

Robert H. Guest, in *Personnel*, reports on a study of the foreman's working day. Fifty-six U.S. foremen were observed and each of their activities recorded during one eight-hour shift.

Richard C. Hodgson, Daniel J. Levinson, and Abraham Zaleznik studied a team of three top executives of a U.S. hospital. From that study they wrote *The Executive Role Constellation*. These researchers addressed in particular the way in which work and socio-emotional roles were divided among the three managers.

William F. Whyte, from his study of a street gang during the Depression, wrote *Street Corner Society*. His findings about the gang's leadership, which George C. Homans analyzed in *The Human Group*, suggest some interesting similarities of job content between street gang leaders and corporate managers.

My own study involved five American C.E.O.s of middle- to large-sized organizations – a consulting firm, a technology company, a hospital, a consumer-goods company, and a school system. Using a method called 'structural observation', during one intensive week of observation for each executive I recorded various aspects of every piece of mail and every verbal contact. My method was designed to capture data on both work characteristics and job content. In all, I analyzed 890 pieces of incoming and outgoing mail and 368 verbal contacts.

References

AGUILAR, F. J. (1967), *Scanning the Business Environment*, Macmillan.

ANDREWS, K. R. (1969), 'Towards Professionalism in Business Management', *Harvard Business Review*, March–April.

BURNS, T. (1954), 'The Directions of Activity and Communication in a Departmental Executive Group', *Human Relations*, 7, no. 1.

CARLSON, S. (1951), *Executive Behaviour*, Strombergs.

COPEMAN, G. H. (1963), *The Role of the Managing Director*, Business Publications.

DAVIS, R. T. (1957), *Performance and Development of Field Sales Managers*, Boston Division of Research, Harvard Business School.

DRUCKER, P. F. (1954), *The Practice of Management*, Harper & Row.

GRAYSON, Jr, C. J. (1973), 'Management Science and Business Practice', *Harvard Business Review*, July–August.

GUEST, R. H. (1956), 'Of Time and the Foreman', *Personnel*, May.

HEKIMIAN, J. S., and MINTZBERG, H. (1968) 'The Planning Dilemma', *The Management Review*, May.

HODGSON, R. C., LEVINSON, D. J., and ZALEZNIK, A. (1965), *The Executive Role Constellation*, Boston Division of Research, Harvard Business School.

HOMANS, G. C. (1950), *The Human Group*, Harcourt, Brace & World.

LIVINGSTON, J. S. (1971), 'Myth of the Well-Educated Manager', *Harvard Business Review*, January–February.

MINTZBERG, H. (1973), *The Nature of Managerial Work*, Harper & Row.

NEUSTADT, R. E. (1960), *Presidential Power*, Wiley.

SAYLES, L. R. (1964), *Managerial Behavior*, McGraw-Hill.

STEWART, R. (1967), *Managers and their Jobs*, Macmillan.

WHYTE, W. F. (1955), *Street Corner Society*, rev. ed., University of Chicago Press.

WRAPP, H. E. (1967), 'Good Managers Don't Make Policy Decisions', *Harvard Business Review*, September–October.

Acknowledgements

Permission to reprint the readings in this volume is acknowledged to the following sources:

1 Free Press
2 John Wiley & Sons, Inc.
3 Tom Burns
4 Her Majesty's Stationery Office
5 Organizational Dynamics
6 Harvard University Press
7 Van Gorcum
8 Heinemann
9 Pitman & Sons, Ltd
10 Harper & Row Publishers, Inc.
11 Doubleday & Co., Inc., and Sidgwick & Jackson, Ltd
12 Management Today
13 Harper & Row Publishers, Inc.
14 Universitetsforlaget
15 Public Administration Review
16 Organizational Dynamics
17 Routledge & Kegan Paul Ltd and Division of Research, Harvard University Graduate School of Business Administration
18 McGraw-Hill Book Co.
19 McGraw-Hill Book Co.
20 World Publishing Co. and MacGibbon & Kee Ltd
21 Addison-Wesley
22 V. H. Winston & Sons
23 Plenum Publishing Co.
24 The President and Fellows of Harvard College

Author Index

Subject Index